CONTENTS

PSYCHOLOGY
IN A COMPLEX WORLD

JENNIFER
BONDS-RAACKE
Fort Hays State University

Kendall Hunt
publishing company

Cover image © 2014 Shutterstock, Inc.

Kendall Hunt
publishing company
www.kendallhunt.com
Send all inquiries to:
4050 Westmark Drive
Dubuque, IA 52004-1840

Copyright © 2014 by Kendall Hunt Publishing Company

ISBN 978-1-4652-5824-3

Printed in the United States of America

CONTRIBUTORS

Chapter 1: Dr. Bonds-Raacke and Dr. Raacke

Dr. Jennifer Bonds-Raacke is currently the Chair and Associate Professor of Psychology at Fort Hays State University (FHSU). Her primary research interests are the psychology of mass communication, decision making, and the psychology of teaching. Prior to joining the faculty at FHSU, Dr. Bonds-Raacke served as the Associate Dean of the Maynor Honors College and as a Faculty Teaching Fellow for the Teaching and Learning Center at the University of North Carolina at Pembroke. She has also been an Assistant Professor and Faculty Advisor of the Honors Program at Briar Cliff University. Dr. Bonds-Raacke obtained her PhD and MS from Kansas State University in Experimental Psychology and her BA from Christian Brothers University. She has been happily married to Dr. John Raacke for over 15 years and they have two daughters, Callie and Brooke.

Photo courtesy of Mitch Weber.

Dr. Bonds-Raacke

Dr. John Raacke is currently Chair and Associate Professor in the Department of Justice Studies at Fort Hays State University (FHSU). His primary research interests are juror/jury decision making, team decision making, and studying the impact of social networking sites. Prior to joining the faculty at FHSU, Dr. Raacke served as the Associate Dean of the College of Arts and Sciences, an Academic Affairs Administrative Fellow, and Chair of the Internal Review Board (IRB) at the University of North Carolina at Pembroke. Dr. Raacke obtained his PhD and MS from Kansas State University in Experimental Psychology and his BA from Christian Brothers University. Dr. Raacke is originally from southern Louisiana and enjoys cooking Cajun food for his family.

Photo courtesy of Mitch Weber.

Dr. Raacke

Chapter 2: Mr. Arndt

I have been deeply interested in psychology since 2007: the year I completed my first psychology class. Generally speaking, my primary research interests in psychology involve drugs of abuse and how they affect behavior. I find it interesting how minute chemical substances can either beneficially or detrimentally impact people's lives. In the laboratory, I help investigate how environmental enrichment-induced alterations in the glutamate system can influence rates of amphetamine self-administration. Outside of the laboratory, I enjoy running, biking, bowling, cheering on Chicago sports teams, grilling, and watching Netflix. The thing I love most about teaching psychology is sharing interesting and applicable phenomena to my students that they can then share with their family and friends outside the classroom.

Mr. Arndt

Chapter 3: Dr. Park and Dr. Hill

Photo courtesy of Mitch Weber.

Dr. Park

I joined Fort Hays State University in August 2011 after receiving my PhD in cognitive psychology from Kansas State University. I teach classes closely related to my field of expertise such as cognitive psychology, experimental design, statistics for behavioral sciences, perception, and general psychology.

I also conduct research projects with students. I have been studying consumer decision-making strategies and understand the causes and remedies for post-purchase regret. For example, results from my lab suggest that you have to make sure that the amount of effort that you put forth is justifiable to you. If you are satisfied with the amount of effort you've invested, then you are less likely to experience regret!

Friends and family are a very important part of my life and I truly enjoy spending time and traveling with them. Though not a very talented cook, I enjoy cooking as well.

I look forward to working with students taking psychology classes! If you have any questions please send me an email at j_park7@fhsu.edu.

Photo courtesy of Mitch Weber.

Dr. Hill

I am an experimental cognitive psychologist who specializes in studying risky decision making from an evolutionary perspective. I received my degrees from Oklahoma State University (B.S.), the University of Louisiana at Monroe (M.S.), and Kansas State University (Ph.D.). Above all else, I decided to become a psychologist because of my fascination with science and its potential application to the seemingly random nature of human behavior. When I'm not listening to science podcasts, or watching college wrestling, I enjoy distance running and spending time with my family.

Chapter 5: Dr. Park, Dr. Hill, and Dr. Engler

Photo courtesy of Mitch Weber.

Dr. Engler

Dr. Joseph Engler currently serves as an Assistant Professor of School Psychology at Minot State University. Prior to this appointment, Dr. Engler was the Director of School Psychology at Fort Hays State University. Dr. Engler received his PhD from The University of South Dakota and BA from Minot State University. Dr. Engler practiced for 3 years as a school psychologist for the Tooele County School District in Tooele, UT. His research interests and publications include cognitive assessment, academic interventions, motivation, and increasing parental involvement.

Chapter 6: Dr. Engler

Chapter 7: Dr. Naylor-Tincknell

Dr. Naylor-Tincknell is a developmental psychologist. She received her PhD from the University of Oklahoma. She currently serves as the Director of the Experimental Graduate Program. She teaches a variety of classes including developmental psychology, statistics, and graduate level research courses.

Dr. Naylor-Tincknell

Chapter 8: Mrs. Mann

Brooke Mann received both her BS in Psychology and MS in Clinical Psychology from Fort Hays State University. She is currently working on her PhD in Educational Psychology from Texas A&M University-Commerce. Brooke remembers wondering about differences in personality, behaviors, and attitudes of individuals at a young age, fostering a longtime interest in psychology. Her favorite thing about FHSU, both from a student's and instructor's views, is the smaller class sizes. It provides for more opportunities to get to know students and work closely with them. Her favorite food is chocolate—chocolate anything. For fun she enjoys reading, watching the Kansas City Chiefs, and spending time with her family.

Mrs. Mann

Chapter 9: Dr. Herrman and Mrs. Smith

Ms. Gina Smith obtained a Master of Science degree in Clinical Psychology in 1992 and has been practicing as a mental health provider for 22 years. Throughout her employment history, she has worked in outpatient mental health, in foster care reintegration services, and in a private practice setting. Gina has been teaching at Fort Hays State University (FHSU) for 13 years and definitely enjoys both teaching and providing mental health services. Being an advisor is also rewarding for Gina as she thoroughly enjoys interacting with students and aiding in the process of career development. In addition to teaching in the Psychology Department, Gina provides therapy services at the on-campus counseling center at FHSU, the Kelly Center. Her research interests include clinical psychology topics, factors that impact teaching evaluations, successful transitions for veterans to begin or return to college, and concussion in football athletes. Gina is married and has a 15-year-old son, who keeps her very busy with all of his school activities and sporting events.

Mrs. Smith

I am currently the director of Fort Hays State University's Clinical Psychology Program. My interests and expertise lie in the forensic area of clinical psychology. I came to education after an extensive career as a clinical psychologist working in community mental health centers, children and families services, juvenile justice agencies, substance abuse treatment programs, and inpatient psychiatric facilities.

Dr. Herrman

Chapter 10: Mr. Challacombe

Darin Challacombe is a graduate of and adjunct instructor for Fort Hays State University's Psychology Department. He has taught at Fort Hays for 8years, and is currently pursuing a doctorate in psychology. His broad research interests center around social, forensic, and cognitive psychology. Darin enjoys traveling—he has been to over 50 countries, and lived and worked abroad twice. He considers understanding social psychological aspects to be paramount to effective cross-cultural communication.

Mr. Challacombe

CHAPTER ONE

THE SCIENCE OF PSYCHOLOGY

Dr. Jenn Bonds-Raacke and Dr. John Raacke
Fort Hays State University

LEARNING OBJECTIVES

- Define psychology
- Identify major perspectives within the field
- State types of degrees in psychology and common places of employment
- Explain the roles of philosophy and physiology in the founding of psychology
- Recall the founding schools of thought
- Explain psychoanalysis and behaviorism
- Identify key contributors to the founding of psychology
- Describe the steps of the scientific method
- Differentiate between experimental and nonexperimental research methodologies
- List examples of nonexperimental research methodologies
- Explain key terms for experimental research methodologies
- Assess reliability and validity in research designs
- Analyze limitations of various research methodologies
- Recognize the need for ethical behavior

Introduction to Psychology

Are you familiar with Penn and Teller? These entertainers are magicians and comedians. They have a show in Las Vegas and a television show called *Penn & Teller: Bullshit!*. The show focuses on debunking myths people commonly believe to be true. You might be surprised to learn that psychologists are very similar to Penn and Teller. Like Penn and Teller, psychologists use the scientific method to test statements people believe to be true. Sometimes our results confirm what people thought all along. However, many times psychologists find that folk wisdom (or an everyday saying) is actually not supported when tested empirically. For example, did you know it is not true that opposites attract?

1

Lilienfeld, Lynn, Ruscio, and Beyerstein (2010) recently published a book examining myths in popular psychology. Take a look at some of the chapter titles below:

- "Most People Use Only 10% of Their Brain Power"
- "Extrasensory Perception Is a Well-Established Scientific Phenomenon"
- "Subliminal Messages Can Persuade People to Purchase Products"
- "Playing Mozart's Music to Infants Boosts Their Intelligence"
- "Most People Experience a Midlife Crisis in Their 40s or Early 50s"
- "Intelligence Tests Are Biased Against Certain Groups of People"
- "The Defining Feature of Dyslexia Is Reversing Letters"
- "Researchers Have Demonstrated That Dreams Possess Symbolic Meaning"
- "Opposites Attract: We Are Romantically Attracted to People Who Differ From Us"
- "People's Responses to Inkblots Tell Us a Great Deal About Their Personalities"
- "People With Schizophrenia Have Multiple Personalities"
- "Most Mentally Ill People Are Violent"

You might wonder how these myths developed or where they came from. Although no one place is solely responsible, the media does provide some inaccurate information on psychological topics. We can't help but think of how media portrayals have helped to reinforce the popular myths shared in the preceding. For example, *Ghost Busters* (1984) was about "parapsychology" professors and included scenes with the professors testing extrasensory perception of participants. This could have contributed to the myth stating that extrasensory perception is a well-established phenomenon. In the movie *Me, Myself, and Irene* (2000), the plot confuses multiple personalities with schizophrenia. In the more recent movie *Lucy* (2014), the plot centers around a drug that allows a woman to utilize the full capacity of her brain, thus further perpetuating the myth that people use only 10% of their brain power. However, no matter the source of the misinformation, psychologists help society to test everyday notions and better understand human thought and behavior, just like Penn and Teller.

American Psychological Association Goals

The American Psychological Association has set five goals for students taking psychology courses. As you go through this chapter and subsequent ones, you will want to keep in mind how the material relates to the following goals:

- **Goal 1. Knowledge Base in Psychology**
  You will demonstrate fundamental knowledge and comprehension of the major concepts, theoretical perspectives, historical trends, and empirical findings to discuss how psychological principles apply to behavioral problems.

- **Goal 2. Scientific Inquiry and Critical Thinking**
  You will demonstrate scientific reasoning and problem solving, including effective research methods.

Goal 3: Ethical and Social Responsibility in a Diverse World

You will apply ethical standards to evaluate psychological science and practice and you will develop ethically and socially responsible behaviors for professional and personal settings in a landscape that involves increasing diversity.

Goal 4: Communication

You will demonstrate competence in writing and in oral and interpersonal communication skills.

Goal 5. Professional Development

You will apply psychological content and skills to career goals and develop meaningful professional direction for life after graduation.

Psychology Defined

Psychology is the systematic investigation of human behavior and thought. This means psychologists study what people do and think and they study this in an organized and consistent manner. In the next section, we discuss the origins of psychology and how the field has evolved over time. For example, even the definition of psychology has grown and it is important to note psychologists now recognize the importance of studying behavior and thought (commonly referred to as cognition) and not just overt actions. In addition, psychologists are not limited to studying humans. Frequently, psychologists study animals, too.

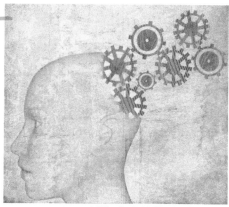

© Ellerslie, 2014. Used under license from Shutterstock, Inc.

Psychology: Systematic investigation of human behavior and thought

The field of psychology has two main national organizations. These organizations are the American Psychological Association (APA) and the Association for Psychological Science (APS). Both APA and APS allow students taking psychology courses to join their organizations as student affiliates. Even if you are not interested in joining as student affiliates, much information is available for free from these associations, including summaries of news releases and resources for students. If you are interested in learning more about the organizations or joining, visit the respective websites at the following addresses: www.apa.org and www.psychologicalscience.org.

Majors Perspectives, Types of Degrees, and Common Employment

Psychology is a diverse field. Although most of us might think of a psychologist as someone who provides therapy to individuals, this is not an accurate depiction of the breadth of the field. Experts in the field approach the study of human behavior and cognition from a variety of perspectives. APA highlights the perspectives listed in Table 1.1, where you will find brief definitions. For additional information and examples of each, visit: www.apa.org/careers/resources/guides/careers.aspx#

© iQoncept, 2014. Used under license from Shutterstock, Inc.

TABLE 1.1

Clinical psychologists	Work with individuals who have psychology disorders
Cognitive and perceptual psychologists	Study human memory, thinking, and perception
Community psychologists	Work to improve the lives of individuals within a community and assist individuals in locating needed community resources
Counseling psychologists	Work with individuals to help with everyday life stressors
Developmental psychologists	Study human development throughout the life span, from birth to death
Educational psychologists	Study how people learn and ways to make teaching practices more effective for learners
Engineering psychologists	Study how people work with machines, commonly referred to as human factors
Environmental psychologists	Study the interaction of the person and the environment (including the physical and social settings)
Evolutionary psychologists	Focus on how evolution impacts thoughts, feelings, and behavior
Experimental psychologists	Use experimental methods to study a wide range of topics
Forensic psychologists	Apply psychological theories and research findings to the legal setting
Health psychologists	Study factors that impact an individual's health and wellness
Industrial/organizational psychologists	Apply psychological theories, methodology, and findings to workplace settings and issues
Neuropsychologists (and behavioral neuropsychologists)	Study the brain and its relation to behavior
Quantitative and measurement psychologists	Focus on designing experiments and analyzing data for a wide range of topics
Rehabilitation psychologists	Work with individuals with disabilities to address rehabilitation needs
School psychologists	Deliver a variety of psychological services to those in the school setting
Social psychologists	Study how behaviors and thoughts are influenced by others
Sport psychologists	Work with athletes, especially on motivational issues to improve performance

As you can see from this list, psychology is a very broad field and you can do almost anything! There are three main types of degrees in the field. The most basic degree is a bachelor's degree. The bachelor's degree is normally attained in 4 years, requiring over 30 hours in the field. This provides a general overview of the disciplines and graduates have strong communication and research skills. The next degree is the master's degree. At this level, students begin to specialize in the perspectives we discussed in Table 1.1. The master's degree typically requires an additional 2 years of course work beyond the bachelor's degree and for many specialty areas, a practicum or internship is required. Finally, indi-

© michaeljung, 2014. Used under license from Shutterstock, Inc.

viduals can obtain a doctorate degree in psychology. This can take an additional 2 or more years beyond the master's degree. It is important to know what the job outlook is like for a discipline before you consider a career in that area. To learn more about the job outlook for psychologists, you can visit the Bureau of Labor Statistics at www.bls.gov/home.htm

Due to the diverse interests of psychologists, the workplace setting varies across the field. The following chart provides information on employment settings for individuals with doctorates. As you can see, there is not one predominant setting. Rather, psychologists are employed in many places.

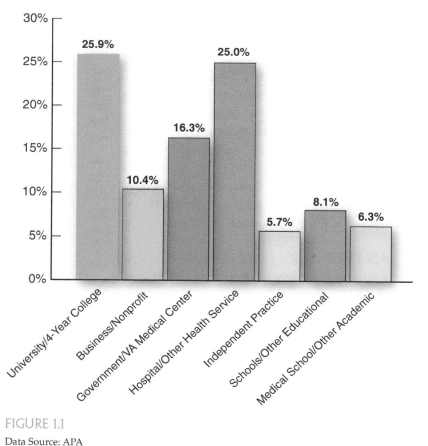

FIGURE 1.1

Data Source: APA

Beginnings of Psychology

Psychology as a discipline is a paradox in that the field is both old and new. Although the formalization of the discipline did not occur until the latter part of the 19th century, the subject matter of psychology has been studied by many people for thousands of years. Historically, the origins of psychology have been grounded in two separate fields: philosophy and physiology. Philosophy is the field from which psychology gains much of the subject matter we study today, while physiology provides researchers in psychology the tools to study the subject matter.

PHILOSOPHY. Plato, Aristotle, and other philosophers contemplated questions about human nature and behavior some 2,500 years ago, confronting issues still raised in contemporary psychology. Plato spent much of his life discussing the need to ignore sensory information by looking inward to understand the true nature of the soul. Only by using the rational powers of the mind could one truly gain understanding of the world. As a student of Plato, Aristotle took a different approach and was known to contemplate many issues in regard to human behavior that were externally influenced. For example, Aristotle studied the topics of human memory, motivation, perception, sleep, and dreams (Hergenhahn & Henley, 2014). Over the next several thousand years, the teachings of Plato and Aristotle would impact society as topics for exploration.

In the early 17th century, a French philosopher, Rene Descartes, changed the way people thought about the mind. Specifically, his work on the mind–body problem became, arguably, one of the most important early contributions to the field of psychology. Descartes reshaped people's thinking that the mind–body was unidirectional; that is, in which the mind controlled the body. Rather, Descartes concluded that not only do they interact, but that the body (physical) has more influence on the mind (mental) than was previously thought. In discussing the nature of the body, he described the theory of reflex action, in which an external object can bring about an involuntary response (Hergenhahn & Henley, 2014). For example, when someone scares you, you react to the external stimuli without having to think, "I should be scared and react this way." Rather, you react without the use of mental processes. Like Descartes's mind–body problem, those in contemporary psychology still investigate many of the same topics that Plato and Aristotle both viewed as important to understanding mental processes.

PHYSIOLOGY. Much of the early work on psychological principles was based in thought about philosophical constructs, as mentioned previously. During the latter part of the 18th century and the early part of the 19th century, a new breed of medical doctors, physiologists, and researchers became interested in psychological principles. Specifically, this new breed began to use their training in physiology to research psychological principles that previously had only been thought about in philosophy. These psychological principles included things such as memory, sensation, perceptions, and the influence of mental processes on behavior. However, although the subject matter being studied was not unique, it was the use of the scientific method (which we discuss later in this chapter) to systematically test these psychological principles that was the hallmark of this new breed of researchers. Whereas early philosophers built theories based on their own thoughts and observations, the use of the scientific method in physiology allowed these new researchers to empirically evaluate many of the historical topics in psychology. Research showing the impact of brain damage on behavior, as well as the discovery of basic brain physiology, began to shed light on the link between the brain and behavior. Thus, a new age in psychological discovery was underway.

Wilhelm Wundt and Early Schools of Thought

Wilhelm Wundt (1832–1920) was one of the early aforementioned physiologists to study psychological principles. Following graduation from medical school in 1855, Wundt worked as an assistant in many early psychophysics and physiology research laboratories in Western Europe. It was during this time that Wundt began to develop his ideas for a new scientific discipline, psychology. Although others helped to contribute along the way, Wundt is considered the founder of modern psychology due to his publication of the first psychology book, *Principles of Physiological Psychology,* in 1874. Thus, much of modern psychology can trace its academic lineage back to Wundt. Five years later, Wundt established the world's first psychological laboratory at the University of Leipzig in 1879, which remained active until 1910. It was from this laboratory that Wundt trained the first generation of psychologists who would go out into the world and make psychology the discipline it is today (Benjamin, Jr., 2008).

Wilhelm Wundt.
© Nicku, 2014. Used under license from Shutterstock, Inc.

In addition to establishing the field of psychology, Wundt also made several contributions that led to the separation of psychology from philosophy. In order to make this separation complete, Wundt stressed the scientific exploration of conscious experience through the use of empirical methods. To do this, Wundt developed an empirical method he called **introspection**. Introspection is the examination of one's own mind to inspect and report on personal thoughts or feelings about conscious experiences. In order to properly use this technique, Wundt would rigorously train individuals over months and sometimes years. During the introspective process, individuals were presented with a physical stimulus and were to report on the size, intensity, and duration of their conscious experience. Wundt used the results of each experiment to draw inferences about the elements and processes of conscious experience.

Introspection: The examination of one's own mind to inspect and report on personal thoughts or feelings about conscious experiences

Can you see any problems with this technique? Unfortunately, much of the criticism of Wundt's early work centered on his use of introspection. Many researchers disapproved of the introspective method. Specifically, researchers argued there were problems with a method in which results could vary by different observers for the same stimulus. This led people to wonder which introspection was correct. Furthermore, since introspection is a private, personal method of study, how can the results be replicated? Despite these issues, Wundt is still considered to be the most important figure in the history of psychology, primarily as a result of founding psychology as a science, rejecting nonscientific thinking, publishing extensively on the topic, and training the first generation of psychologists.

Structuralism: The study of breaking down conscious experience into its fundamental elements: sensations, feelings, and images

STRUCTURALISM. Edward Titchener (1867–1927) established the first brand of psychology (or school of thought) known as **structuralism**. Titchener developed structuralism at Cornell University in New York shortly after receiving his PhD from Wundt in 1892. Titchener believed psychology was to be used to study the structure of the mind. Structuralism is the breaking down of conscious experience into its fundamental elements: sensations, feelings, and images. As did Wundt, Titchener sought to use introspection to accomplish this task. However, unlike Wundt who was interested in the whole of the conscious experience, Titchener was more concerned with the parts of the experience that made up the whole (Goodwin, 2008). Titchener's work suffered from the same criticism as Wundt's, and when Titchener died, so did structuralism.

Functionalism: The study of how the mind of an organism adapts to its current environment

FUNCTIONALISM. Around the same time that Titchener was developing structuralism, William James (1842–1910) and colleagues at the University of Chicago were developing the second school of thought in psychology; **functionalism**. Functionalism was a deliberate protest against the work of Wundt and Titchener. Functionalists believed that the work of Wundt and Titchener was narrow in scope and could not be applied to the real world. James and colleagues adapted their work from the work of Darwin and his principles of evolution. Specifically, rather than focusing on the conscious experience only, functionalism sought to study how the mind of an organism adapted to its current environment (Goodwin, 2008). This was a major change from Wundt and Titchener, who did not care about the outside environment, only the internal state. With the advent of functionalism, psychologists were able to expand the scope of psychology to children, animals, and the mentally impaired. These populations were not used with structuralism because researchers believed they were unable to be trained in introspection. Unfortunately, as with structuralism, functionalism lost ground around the 1920s with the death of Titchener and the introduction of behaviorism. However, some similarities do exist between functionalism and a contemporary perspective known as evolutionary psychology.

Psychoanalysis: A psychotherapeutic technique based on the belief that humans face psychological distress as a result of unconscious conflicts and desires (primarily sexual or aggressive) brought on during childhood

Psychoanalysis and Sigmund Freud

Sigmund Freud (1856–1939) is probably the most recognized name in psychology. Whether you are in the field or not, Freud is synonymous with psychology. Although his name is famous, there are mixed opinions as to his impact on the field. At roughly the same time as Wundt, Titchener, and James were working on their theories of psychology, Freud was heading in a different direction altogether. Whereas the other individuals were focused on learning about conscious experiences, Freud was more interested in the unconscious.

© Georgios Kollidas, 2014. Used under license from Shutterstock, Inc.

Freud graduated from the University of Vienna in 1881 with a medical degree and began work in neurology. Soon after starting his own practice, Freud developed the idea of a "talking cure." Freud believed individuals who suffered from psychological distress could be released from this distress by talking with a trained doctor. This process became the basis for Freud's theory called **psychoanalysis**. Psychoanalysis is a psychotherapeutic technique based on the belief that humans face psychological distress as a result of unconscious conflicts and desires (primarily sexual or aggressive) brought on during childhood. And it is these desires that influence negative behaviors exhibited in individuals. Freud's therapy was designed to bring these conflicts and desires from a patient's unconsciousness to their consciousness through discussion. Freud believed that once the patient was aware of the conflicts or desires, the patient would have a chance to resolve these issues (Hergenhahn & Henley, 2014).

At the time, Freud's theories and beliefs were groundbreaking and popular across the globe. Today, despite the prevalence of psychoanalysis in pop culture, very few psychologists subscribe to the foundations of Freud's psychoanalysis. Although some of Freud's theories (such as the impact of the childhood on adult behavior) were correct, much of Freud's original work has not been supported when tested empirically. In particular, researchers have been critical of Freud's theories for relying too much on unconscious sexual and aggressive desires, as well as for ignoring the impact of conscious decisions on behavior.

Behaviorism

In the early 1920s a major shift occurred in psychology with the introduction of behaviorism by John Watson (1878–1958). Watson and colleagues (such as B. F. Skinner, 1904–1990) believed psychology should move away from using subjective procedures (i.e., introspection) and begin to engage in objective procedures. Watson's solution was **behaviorism**. Behaviorism is the scientific study of the prediction and control of behavior. In behaviorism, anything that could not be observed, such as mental processes like thoughts and feelings, could not be studied.

Behaviorists were focused on how humans and animals acquired and modified behavior as a result of their environment, which they called learning. Behaviorist believed people's development is little more than a result of learning that occurs in their world. While seemingly similar to functionalism, behaviorism focused solely on the behavior and ignored the mind or mental interaction with the environment. However, behaviorist like Watson and Skinner differed on the type of learning that led to the development of people (Goodwin, 2008). Behaviorism was the dominant theory in American psychology until the early 1960s when other contemporary ideas began reshaping the psychological landscape.

Behaviorism: The scientific study of the prediction and control of behavior

Other Key Contributors

In addition to Wundt, Titchener, James, Freud, Watson, and Skinner, there were many notable early psychologists that helped to shape the field. Even though we do not have time to discuss all of them, we highlight a few important people in the following (Goodwin, 2008; Hergenhahn & Henley, 2014).

G. Stanley Hall (1844–1924)—Known by many in the field as "Mr. First," Hall is credited with starting the first experimental psychology lab in the United States, the first journal of psychology in the United States, founded APA (in 1892) and was its first president, and was the first to recognize adolescence as a separate stage of development.

- **James McKeen Cattell (1860–1944)**—Influenced by his work with Sir Francis Galton in eugenics, Cattell was the first to use the term "mental test" (although incorrectly as you will learn in later chapters). He spent much of his time professionalizing psychology producing many famous PhD students while serving as head of the psychology program at Columbia.

- **Mary Whiton Calkins (1863–1930)**—Based on a recommendation by William James, Calkins attended Harvard University successfully completing all requirements for a PhD in psychology. However, at the time Harvard did not accept women into graduate programs. Calkins never received her PhD despite her work in memory leading to breakthroughs in cognitive psychology. Calkins was recognized by her peers when she was elected the first female president of APA in 1905.

- **Christine Ladd-Franklin (1847–1930)**—Similar to Calkins, Ladd-Franklin completed all of her degree requirements for her PhD in mathematics but was not awarded the degree upon completion. Ladd-Franklin went on to develop the earliest theory of color vision, becoming the world authority on the topic until her death. Interestingly, 44 years after completing the requirement, Johns Hopkins University awarded Ladd-Franklin her PhD 4 years before her passing.

- **Margaret Washburn (1871–1939)**—Washburn was the first woman to earn a PhD in psychology; she received her degree in 1894 from Cornell University. She is best known for being a leading comparative psychologist and wrote the standard comparative text of its day. Washburn was also elected an APA president as well as to the National Science Academy.

- **Francis Sumner (1895–1954)**—Sumner was the first African American to receive a PhD in psychology, awarded in 1920 from Clark University under the direction of G. Stanley Hall. Long considered the father of African American psychology, Sumner established a psychology department at Howard University. At Howard, Sumner pushed the psychology department to become the most outstanding department at all historically Black universities, producing many notable students who would all make contributions to the field.

- **Mamie (1917–1983) and Kenneth (1914–2005) Clark**—The Clarks, both graduates of Howard University under Sumner, contributed to the field of psychology during the civil unrest of the 1960s. Mamie and Kenneth began working on the effects of segregation on children, empirically showing the psychological damage segregation inflicted during that time. Their work, along with others, was considered by the U.S. Supreme court in the decision *Brown v Board of Education.*

- **Jorge Isidore Sanchez (1906–1972)**—Sanchez is considered the father of Hispanic educational psychology. Sanchez's research was instrumental in showing the racial biases in intelligence testing. His methodologies and models are still used today in research in bilingualism and educational testing.

The Scientific Method: The Science of Psychology

The **scientific method** provides a framework for the systematic study of behavior and mental processes. There are six steps in the scientific method psychologists use when conducting research. The steps are: (a) problem identification, (b) hypothesis formation, (c) collection of data, (d) analysis of data, (e) conclusion, and (f) reporting of findings (Figure 1.2).

Scientific method: Framework for the systematic study of behavior and mental processes

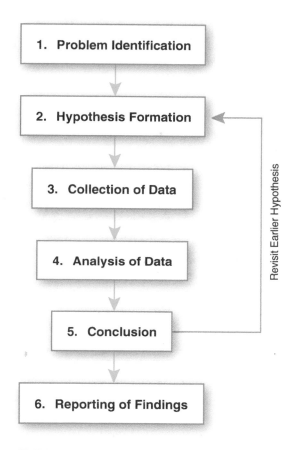

FIGURE 1.2

The first step in the scientific method is to identify the problem. This step involves identifying a topic to research, as well as doing an initial review of the literature to determine what previous research has been conducted on the topic. The second step in the scientific method is to formulate a hypothesis. A popular definition of a hypothesis is an educated guess. However, a more useful definition is that a hypothesis is a statement about the relationship between variables.

The third step is to collect data on the topic to test the hypothesis. To do this, researchers typically design an experiment or develop a study in which the variables of interest can be tested. The fourth step is to take the data collected and conduct data analysis. Data analysis involves the use of statistics. The results the statistical analysis yield are used to guide the fifth step, conclusion. The fifth step is very important in the research process. This is the step where a researcher revisits the hypothesis. At this point, the researcher, using the results from the analysis of the data, will make a judgment about the hypothesis. Based on the results of the study, a researcher will then decide to either support or reject the earlier hypothesis.

The final step is reporting your findings. Research must be shared in such a way that the experiment or study can be replicated. Replication occurs when a research experiment or study is reproduced using the exact methodology and procedure. Thus, when reporting findings, the procedure and methodology need to be clearly communicated, with no ambiguity. Researchers prefer to publish their findings in what is known as peer-reviewed sources. This means that other scholars have reviewed the content of the manuscript and judged it to be worthy of publication and free from error.

Nonexperimental (Descriptive) Research Methodologies

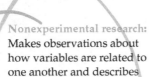

Nonexperimental research: Makes observations about how variables are related to one another and describes the findings

Correlational research methods: Provides information on the initial link between variables of interest

One way to differentiate among types of research is by describing if the research is experimental or nonexperimental. Experimental research involves the manipulation of a variable of interest and the assignment of participants to treatment conditions. **Nonexperimental research** does not rely on manipulating variables; rather, it makes observations about how variables are related to one another and describes the findings.

As mentioned, nonexperimental research does not manipulate variables of interest. However, even without direct manipulation, you can still explore relationships between variables using correlational research methods. **Correlational research methods** are very important to the field. This methodology provides us with information on the initial link between variables of interest.

When you have a correlational research method, your results will tell you if the two variables are related. Variables can be either positively or negatively related. Do not be confused by the labels of positive correlation and negative correlation. This does not mean that positive correlations are good and negative correlations are bad. Rather, positive correlations have variables that vary in the same direction and negative correlations have variables that vary in opposite directions.

To make this clear, we give some examples of positive and negative correlations. We have also provided the figure below to visually represent each type of correlation. Two variables that are positively correlated are years of education and salary. This is a positive correlation because as scores on one variable increase so too do scores on the second variable. Similarly, as scores on one variable decrease so too do scores on the second variable. In this situation, the greater number of years of education a person has, the higher the salary.

Arrows for Positive and Negative Correlation.

Conversely, the fewer number of years of education a person has, the lower the salary. In both instances, the two variables either increased or decreased together, making this a positive correlation.

With negative correlations, the two variables of interest are related to one another as well. However, as one variable increases, the other variable decreases, or as one variable decreases, the other variable increases. An example of a negative correlation is marital satisfaction and likelihood of divorce. As marital satisfaction increases, the likelihood of divorce decreases, and as marital satisfaction decreases, the likelihood of divorce increases.

As with any research method, there are advantages and disadvantages to examining correlations between variables. One major advantage of correlational research is that it allows us to make predictions. For example, if we know marital satisfaction and likelihood of divorce are negatively correlated, it can help us in counseling couples who are experiencing low marital satisfaction. Many times, examining correlations between variables is a great starting point to researching a topic. Plus, it is a useful method when conducting a true experiment would not be ethical.

This brings us to a limitation of the method—determining cause and effect. Did you know as ice cream sales increase, so do murder rates? This is a true correlation! So, should we stop buying ice cream so we can reduce the number of murders committed? Let's hope not! But we can ask ourselves questions to better understand the situation. When you have a correlation, you must think about the directionality of the correlation and ask yourself the following questions:

© HandmadePictures, 2014. Used under license from Shutterstock, Inc.

- Is X causing Y?
- Is Y causing X?
- Is there a third variable causing both X and Y to be related?

In the example of ice cream sales and murder rates, you would ask yourself the following questions:

- Does eating ice cream (X) cause you to commit murder (Y)?
- Does committing murder (Y) cause you to eat ice cream (X)?
- Is there a third variable that is causing ice cream sales (X) and murder rates (Y) to be related?

It really does not make sense that eating ice cream would cause you to commit murder or that murdering people would cause you to eat ice cream. However, it does make sense that a third variable (like heat) is related to both. Specifically, as it gets hotter, ice cream sales increase. Also, as it gets hotter, murder rates increase. Therefore, in this example, it is likely that a third variable was influencing both variables.

So far, we have provided you with introductory information that will be helpful as you learn about nonexperimental designs. Next we discuss naturalistic observation, case studies, and surveys. It is important to note that these nonexperimental designs can examine relationships among variables, as mentioned previously under correlational methodologies.

Naturalistic observation is when you observe people or animals in their natural settings. These observations can occur in the field (sometimes called

Naturalistic observation: Observe people or animals in their natural settings

© Ferenc Szelepcsenyi, 2014. Used under license from Shutterstock, Inc.Inc.

field studies) or in the laboratory (referred to as laboratory observations). One of the most famous naturalistic observations was conducted by Jane Goodall. In the summer of 1960, Goodall went to East Africa to live among the chimpanzee population. There were many aspects about chimpanzees that Goodall wanted to learn, such as if chimps used tools. She believed the best way to understand chimp behavior was to observe them in their natural environment. Goodall's work has led to numerous publications on the life of chimps. Another example of a naturalistic observation comes from developmental psychologists who routinely use laboratory observations to study children. Important developmental information has been gained by bringing children into the lab and observing their interactions with their moms and dads. Examples include information on attachment style and stages of development such as object permanence.

There are many advantages to this methodology. To begin with, the behavior being observed is natural and spontaneous. For the most part, participants being observed in naturalistic observations are just doing what they normally do in life. However, this method also has several disadvantages to be considered. One main disadvantage is how the observer changes people's behavior by his or her presence. Another disadvantage is that the researcher has to wait for events to occur. Goodall waited months before seeing chimps use tools. Researchers also need to be careful not to introduce bias in their observations. For example, researchers might be looking for a particular behavior and report "seeing it" when others would not. A well-known example of this has occurred with observation research of chimps using sign language. Some researchers reported seeing animals use sign language, while other researchers reported the animals were not signing. Finally, cause and effect cannot be determined from naturalistic observations.

Case study: An in-depth observation of an individual, animal, event, or treatment method

The next nonexperimental research method that we want to discuss is a **case study**. A case study is an in-depth observation of an individual, animal, event, or treatment method. Typically, an intensive observation is done and a detailed account is taken because the event is extremely rare and unusual. One example of a famous case study in the field is that of Phineas Gage. Phineas Gage provided us with information on the link between personality and parts of the brain. Specifically, in 1848, an explosion sent a tamping iron through Gage's skull. Surprisingly, Gage survived the explosion but his behavior changed greatly due to the damage in the frontal lobes of his brain. Researchers have long been interested in providing a detailed account of what took place and how Gage's behavior changed as a result.

The major advantage to case studies is we can study rare events that would be unethical to study otherwise. Therefore, case studies provide us with unique opportunities to better understand situations that we could not study experimentally. Despite this advantage, there are limitations to this method. First, we do not always know the cause of the behavior. Second, these unusual events might not influence everybody in the same manner. Furthermore, not all people would have experienced the same resulting behavior. Thus, when using case studies, it is important to keep in mind the limitations of the findings.

Survey research: A questionnaire is designed to obtain information regarding individuals' behaviors, attitudes, or opinions

The last type of nonexperimental research that we will cover in this chapter is **survey research.** Survey research is when a questionnaire is designed to obtain information regarding individuals' behaviors, attitudes, or opinions. This questionnaire can be administered in a variety of formats, but the most common format may be the written format. Questions are typed up and can be administered to participants in person by having them answer on paper or computer, through a mailed survey, and even over the internet. Another format of administering the questionnaire is via telephone. You can ask people questions verbally in person, which is known as a face-to-face interview, or gather a small group of people together to discuss the questions, which is known as a focus group. Each of these formats has its own advantages and disadvantages. A lengthy discussion of each is out of the scope of this book.

© zimmytws, 2014. Used under license from Shutterstock, Inc.

Experimental Research Methodologies

Experimental research involves the manipulation of a variable of interest and assignment of participants to treatment conditions. A **variable** is an event or characteristic with at least two possible values. For example, what would be the variable if we were to ask you, "How stressed are you about taking general psychology?." In this example, the condition with an assigned or attached value is your level of stress. Furthermore, the amount of stress you indicate in your answer is the value associated with the variable. There are two variables essential to research. These two variables are the independent variable and the dependent variable.

The **independent variable** (IV) is the variable in a study manipulated by the researcher. It is being manipulated because it is the variable the researcher believes will produce a change in his or her study. The other variable of interest is the dependent variable. A **dependent variable** (DV) is the variable within a study being observed or measured. Specifically, the dependent variable is the variable a researcher believes will change or will be influenced in the study. Usually, any change seen within the dependent variable is a result of the independent variable. In other words, any measureable change from the independent variable's influence will be seen in the dependent variable.

Let's look at an example. A pharmaceutical company has developed a new drug to help reduce the number of migraines experienced by individuals who report suffering from frequent migraines. To determine if the drug is effective, one group of participants takes the new drug daily and the other group does not. After 30 days, the participants report how many migraines they had during the time period. In this example, the independent variable was the new drug for migraines. It was manipulated by having some participants take the new drug daily and others

Experimental research: Involves the manipulation of a variable of interest and assignment of participants to treatment conditions

Variable: An event or characteristic with at least two possible values

Independent variable: Variable manipulated by the researcher

Dependent variable: Variable observed or measured

© 9nong, 2014. Used under license from Shutterstock, Inc.

not. The researchers at the pharmaceutical company manipulated the new drug because they believed it would reduce the frequency of migraines. The dependent variable was the number of migraines participants reported in the 30-day period. This was the variable the researchers measured and observed for change.

There is another type of variable used in research with some of the same qualities as the independent variable. This variable is known as a **subject variable**. A subject variable is a characteristic or attribute of a participant that can impact the participant's behavior or thoughts within a study. Subject variables are often traits specific to a participant, such as sex, age, or ethnicity, and these traits can influence the dependent variable. In the migraine example, the pharmaceutical company might also want to know if the new drug works equally well on men and women. Thus, sex of the participant could be a subject variable added to the study.

An independent variable will always have at least two conditions. These are referred to as treatment conditions. Typically, the treatment conditions are the experimental and the control group. The **experimental group** is the group exposed to the independent variable. In other words, the experimental group is the group of participants given the independent variable and is the group where we would expect to see a measureable change occur. The **control group** is the group of participants not exposed to the independent variable. This group does not receive the independent variable, and, therefore, we do not expect to see any measurable change in the participants.

Subject variable: Characteristic or attribute of a participant that can impact the participant's behavior or thoughts

Experimental group: Group exposed to the independent variable

Control group: Group of participants not exposed to the independent variable

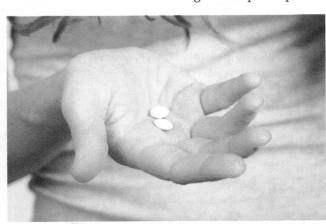

© Johan Larson, 2014. Used under license from Shutterstock, Inc.

Placebo control group: Participants are exposed to a placebo

Placebo: An inert substance or object

To revisit our earlier example, the group of participants who took the new migraine drug each day would be the experimental group. This is because those participants are exposed to the independent variable, the new drug. The participants who did not take the new drug daily would be the control group. This is because the participants are not exposed to the independent variable.

In addition to the experimental and control groups, there is another group often used as a treatment condition in research. This group is known as the placebo control group. The **placebo control group** is similar to the control group in that participants assigned to this condition are not exposed to the independent variable. However, the placebo control group is different from the control group because the participants are exposed to a placebo. A **placebo** is an inert substance or object similar to the independent variable but having no direct effect.

Essentially, the placebo control group acts as an insurance policy. Sometimes researchers see measurable changes in the experimental group that are not due to the independent variable but to the participant's belief that a change will occur. Therefore, the placebo control acts as a way for the researcher to determine how much measurable change is due to the independent variable and how much change is due to the participant's belief in a change occurring. If the pharmaceutical company wanted to be sure the reduced frequency of migraines was due to the new medicine and not participants' belief in the effectiveness of the medicine, the company could add a placebo control group to the research design. Participants in this group would take a daily pill. The participants would believe the pill to be the new drug but in reality it would be an inert substance like a sugar pill. The table below summarizes the different treatment conditions:

TREATMENT CONDITION	EXPOSURE
Experimental Group	Receives the new drug (IV)
Control Group	Does not receive the new drug (no IV)
Placebo Control Group	Receives the placebo (a sugar pill)

When conducting research, a researcher can have a single or double blind study. In a **single blind study**, the participant has no knowledge of the group to which he or she has been assigned—only the researcher knows. Although it is advantageous that the participant does not know to which group he or she has been assigned, there is a drawback. Specifically, the threat of demand characteristics may affect your study results. **Demand characteristics** are various hints and cues that participants use to tell themselves how the researcher wants them to behave, or at least how they think the researcher wants them to behave. If participants are responding to these demand characteristics, rather than the independent variable, this could explain the changes in the dependent variable.

However, in a **double blind study** neither the participant nor the researcher interacting with the participant knows into which experimental group the participant has been placed. Thus, you reduce the likelihood of the participant or experimenter behaving in a way that can influence the study, because neither knows which group the participant is in.

Single blind study: Only the researcher knows to which group the participant has been assigned

Demand characteristics: Hints and cues participants use to tell themselves how the researcher wants them to behave

Double blind study: Neither the participant nor the researcher knows to which group the participant has been assigned

Reliability and Validity

Regardless of the specific research methodology a psychologist might use for research, the discipline values the use of reliable and valid measures. Reliability of a variable is very important when conducting research. **Reliability** is the consistency of your measure to produce similar results on different occasions. Therefore, reliability is primarily concerned with being able to replicate or reproduce the findings. **Validity** is defined as the ability of your measurement to accurately measure what it is supposed to measure. This is different from reliability, which is about being able to replicate scores on future instances. To better understand these terms, let's look at an example.

Reliability: Consistency of your measure to produce similar results on different occasions

Validity: Ability of your measurement to accurately measure what it is supposed to measure

Remember the migraine drug example from earlier in the chapter? Researchers are currently working on this problem. Specifically, researchers are developing migraine drugs (independent variable) that are specifically designed to be more effective in reducing the number of migraines a person suffers in a month (dependent variable) as compared with current migraine medications. During the initial trials of the new "designer" migraine medication, the researchers saw a 63% drop in the number of

days a person had a migraine in a 30-day time period. These results were seen as extremely promising and thus the researchers are looking to continue the study (Norton, 2014).

If you were the researcher, how would you best determine the reliability of the measure (i.e., the effectiveness of the drug as measured by a reduction in migraine days)? The simplest way would be to expand the initial trial and conduct another study to see if you can produce similar results on a different occasion. Should the new "designer" drug show similar results again (i.e., a 63% or so drop), then you could argue the measure of reduction in migraine days is reliable since the obtained results in the second study are consistent with the initial study. However, should the change in the measure be significantly different on each occasion, then the measure would show low reliability.

Likewise, how would you determine the validity of the measure (i.e., the effectiveness of the drug)? On the surface, the reduction in the number of days one has a migraine is straightforward. And, if the drug reduces the days significantly, a researcher would argue the measure is valid. However, it could be the case the measure is missing the greater impact of the drug. Specifically, the drug may reduce the length of a migraine from a full day to a few hours. While this difference may result in the number of days without a migraine changing only slightly, the overall length of time in which a person suffers from a migraine may change dramatically. In this case, a researcher would say the measure of a reduction in the number of days is not valid and the measure should be length of time when assessing effectiveness of the drug.

Research Ethics

APA has developed a set of ethical guidelines all psychologists follow. These guidelines (most recently revised in 2010) are broken into 10 sections covering ethical issues: competence, human relations, assessment, therapy, and so on. For the purposes of this section, we will focus on a small part of Standard 8.0: Research and Publication and its 15 guidelines.

Institutional Review Boards. The first guideline for psychologists conducting research is that they secure permission from an institution (usually a college or university) before conducting their research. This institutional approval is typically given after going through the **Institutional Review Board (IRB)** process. An IRB is a committee that reviews proposals of intended research and evaluates if the research is ethical and if the rights of the participants are being protected. Although colleges and universities have IRBs that review all research conducted on campus, IRBs are not relegated to only the academic world. They can also be found in hospitals, government agencies, and private corporations. IRBs are a relatively new entity and have been developed, in part, because of past research that could be considered unethical.

Institutional Review Board (IRB) A committee that reviews proposals of intended research and evaluates if the research is ethical and if the rights of the participants are being protected

Informed Consent. When conducting research, it is very important that psychologists obtain informed consent (commonly referred to as a consent form) from those who participate in a research study. APA requires that the consent form address specific topics. To begin, your consent form should tell participants information about the research being conducted. It should also give the participants an estimate of how long it will take them to participate and a brief overview of what they will be required to do. The consent form should also clearly inform participants that they do not have to participate in the study. This means participation in the research is voluntary. Additionally, information regarding consequences to not participating or withdrawing from the study should be explained to the participant, as well as any potential risks or benefits of participating.

Furthermore, the informed consent should make clear to participants whether their responses are anonymous or confidential. Often, researchers and participants confuse these two concepts. When a study is **anonymous**, the researcher has ensured no identifying information is gathered and participants cannot be identified once the study is concluded. If a study is **confidential**, the participants can be identified by information that is gathered. However, this information is kept in a manner that participant responses are not shared with others and the participants cannot be identified. Finally, the consent form should close with information on how participants can contact the researcher(s) if they have questions.

Use of Deception in Research. Deception in research can occur in two ways, either as active deception or as passive deception. **Active deception** is deception by commission. In particular, this is deception that occurs when a researcher deliberately misleads a participant. This can happen when a researcher gives participants false information or when a researcher embeds a confederate into a study.

A **confederate** is a participant in the study but is also part of the research team. Confederates' participation is meant to influence other participants who are not members of the research team. In the famous study on conformity conducted by Asch (1951), he used confederates alongside participants to influence behavior. Specifically, Asch had confederates respond incorrectly to questions to see if "real" participants would conform to the incorrect answers, which they indeed did. Here, Asch actively deceived the participants to gain results for his study.

The other type of deception is passive deception. **Passive deception** is deception by omission. This type of deception occurs when a researcher withholds information about the nature of a study from the participants. For example, sometimes psychologists are prevented from explaining fully the purpose of their research design at the onset of a study. Doing so might change the way participants respond in the study. This occurs many times when researchers attempt to study concepts where participants are less likely to disclose their true behavior (e.g., cheating instances).

The topic of deception is continually debated to this day. Specifically, researchers and others have debated whether deception is helpful or harmful in research. APA states psychologists may use deception in research if it is needed to study a particular topic and if its use is justified by the knowledge gained. When deception is used, participants should be told about the deception as soon as possible and it should be clearly explained why this method was used and the anticipated benefits. Participants are given the opportunity to withdraw their data if desired. Although deception is permitted in special cases, APA has made it clear that psychologists are not allowed to deceive participants with regard to physical or emotional pain.

Anonymous research: Research that has ensured no identifying information is gathered and participants cannot be identified once the study is concluded

Confidential research: Research in which participants can be identified by information that is gathered. However, this information is kept in a manner that participant responses are not shared with others and the participants cannot be identified

Active deception: Active deception is deception by commission

Confederate: A participant in the study who is also part of the research team

Passive deception: Passive deception is deception by omission

Debriefing. In general, psychologists want to provide participants with information about the study immediately after the data are collected. If the results are not yet available, psychologists can provide participants with the contact information of the researcher so the participants can learn of the findings when they are prepared. Sometimes it is necessary to withhold a debriefing until all participants have completed the study. If this situation occurs, psychologists must be sure to reduce the risk of harm to the participants if debriefing is delayed. It is also important if psychologists know that a participant has been harmed during the study (either physically or emotionally) that they immediately try to minimize the harm.

Use of Animals in Research. Psychologists who conduct research with animals have additional government policies to be aware of than those we have discussed for humans. The purpose of this section is not to provide a detailed account of policies with animals. However, you should be aware that in addition to the APA guidelines, animal researchers also must follow local, state, and federal guidelines. If you are interested in learning more about research with animals, you can visit the website for the Institutional Animal Care and Use Committee (IACUC; www.unmc.edu/iacuc).

Approach of Textbook

Writing a textbook is a difficult and time-consuming task. Thus, you might wonder why the Department of Psychology at FHSU decided to do so. To begin, we frequently heard students express concerns about the length of standard textbooks on the market and the high price. We wanted our students to have a briefer textbook with accurate information at a reasonable price. Second, we wanted to have chapters written by faculty members who have extensive training, research experience, and/or teaching experience with the subject matter. Thus, you will find that each chapter is written by a different faculty member. We have provided a picture and a bio or fun facts about each faculty member. Finally, we wanted you to do well in the course. So, we have incorporated many student-friendly features in this textbook, which are presented in the following.

- **Relevant and Interesting Examples.** We provide you with many examples to help you understand key concepts. We use examples relating to your life and examples that are well known within the field of psychology. We also offer examples appealing to students with a broad range of backgrounds and interests. This includes traditional and nontraditional students, as well as those pertaining to the many different areas of interest in psychology. We hope by giving such examples you will find it easier to remember and apply the information.

- **Easy-to-Understand Definitions.** When introducing new terms, we avoid using technical or jargon-filled language. Rather, we explain the concept in easy-to-understand language. After you are comfortable with the new information, we illustrate how the term is used within the field. You will find new terms and concepts presented in bold font within the paragraphs and new terms also defined in the margins. This will help you to easily spot new information as you are reading the textbook.

- **Connections to the Faculty.** We want you to feel connected to the faculty members who contributed to this textbook. In the Contributor Biographies, you can learn more about the faculty member who contributed to the textbook.

Please feel free to share your comments about the textbook with me via email (jmbondsraacke@fhsu.edu). We hope that you enjoy learning about psychology in a complex world!

CHAPTER TWO

THE BIOLOGY OF BEHAVIOR

David Arndt
Fort Hays State University

LEARNING OBJECTIVES

- What are the principal biological advantages and disadvantages of humans relative to other species?
- What are the main components and functions of nerve cells?
- How do the most important neurotransmitters relate to behavior?
- How do drugs influence neurotransmitters and behavior?
- How is the human nervous system organized?
- What are the key brain structures and their functions?
- What is the nature and purpose of sleep?
- What functions might dreams serve?
- Is hypnosis a distinct state of consciousness?

> *Drinking without being thirsty and making love at any time, Madame, are the only things that distinguish us from other animals.*
>
> —Pierre-Augustin Caron de Beaumarchais,
> *The Marriage of Figaro*, Act 2, Scene 21, 1784

No, Monsieur de Beaumarchais, these are not the only things that distinguish us from other animals. And perhaps we are not, in all ways, the superior animal we flatter ourselves on being.

Take a bat, for instance: Many people think bats are blind, which they really are not. But their vision is not very good: It does not have to be. Spallanzani, an Italian priest, was fascinated by how bats seemed to be able to fly hectically about at what must be, for a bat, breakneck speed. Yet they never seem to break their necks on houses or trees even when they fly in the dark. When Spallanzani released blinded bats in a room crisscrossed with tiny silk threads, the bats zipped around the room without ever running into the threads. But when he plugged their ears, they smacked into everything in their way (Dijkgraaf, 1960).

We now know that as they fly, bats emit a series of high-pitched squeals that bounce predictably off the objects they encounter. Because sound travels at a relatively constant speed, it is a small trick for the bat to compute how far the sound has traveled to an object and back again. A small trick, but one that we humans find exceedingly difficult. Our **echolocation** capabilities are pretty limited compared with those of the bat.

The bat is not the only animal that is, in at least one sense, superior to us: Bears and dogs and even penguins can detect odors that we cannot; a golden eagle can, on a clear day, spot a green frog swimming in green water 6 inches below a murky green surface; the grizzly bear is physically stronger than we are; the antelope, faster; the dolphin, a more graceful swimmer.

The point is that we, and all other animals, behave as we do largely because of our different physiologies and our different nervous systems. The way in which our brains are "wired," along with the structure and function of the neural networks that comprise our brains, provide us answers to many questions regarding the biology of behavior.

Echolocation: The use of sound to localize objects, based on the amount of time it takes an echo to return to the sound source.

Evolution

We are *Homo sapiens*, the self-named *wise one*—a seemingly appropriate label given our well-developed "new" brains, our opposable thumbs, our upright gait, and our ability to communicate through the use of arbitrary symbols.

But we don't have clever thumbs just because we decided they would be an advantage; we did not invent our brains; we made no conscious decision to shift from a four-legged to a two-legged form of locomotion, thereby making our front legs obsolete and eventually changing their names to arms; nor did we, in council one day, decide that a language would be superior to the grunts and gestures we might previously have been using. Most scientists believe these revolutionary happenings resulted from **evolution** (Darwin, 1859). Evolution, the adaptive progression of species from their origins, might at first glance seem an inappropriate topic for a study of human behavior. We are, after all, concerned with understanding our current behavior. But perhaps something in evolution might help our understanding.[1] Certainly much in our behavior is related to biology; and much of our biology seems to be the product of evolutionary processes.

Evolution: A scientific theory that holds that present life forms have developed from preexisting species through a series of modifications governed by laws of natural selection and diversification of species.

Early Homo sapiens

Not only did *H. sapiens* survive, but the species thrived, although numbers grew very slowly at first, requiring more than 100,000 years to reach the first billion. This happened around 1800, but the second billion was reached in only around 100 years, and the next 100 years saw an increase of nearly 5 billion (U.S. Census Bureau, 2010a; Figure 2.2)!

In some ways, it is astonishing that our species of humans survived, as defenseless as we were against the fangs and claws of the large carnivorous predators of

---

[1] This is, in fact, the foundational idea of the perspective of evolutionary psychology. For a primer on this area of study go to the following url: http://www2.newpaltz.edu/~geherg/ep_expl.htm

For a more detailed primer go to this url instead: http://www.cep.ucsb.edu/primer.html

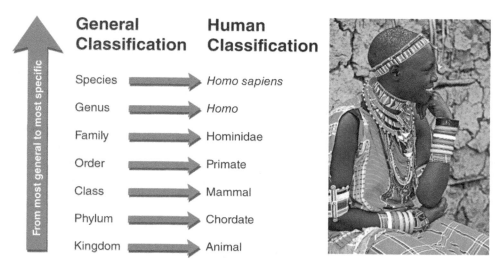

FIGURE 2.1 Biological classification of humans. We are the only species left of the genus *Homo*. But there are more than 300 known living primate species in the world.
Image on right: Photolibrary/Peter Arnold Images

those prehistoric times. We are a relatively slow species, endowed with unexceptional hearing and with a laughable sense of smell compared with that of many other species. Also, we are inadequately protected against both heat and cold, awkward at climbing trees or digging holes, clumsy in the water relative to dolphins, and incapable of flight without artificial means.

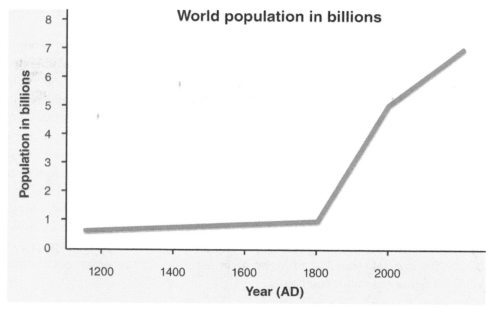

FIGURE 2.2 Approximate population growth for *Homo sapiens* on earth. The part of the graph to the left that is not shown would extend about 1 mile if it reached back to the time when humans first appeared.

Based on World Population Prospects: The 2008 Revision Population Database, United Nations Population Division. Retrieved July 20, 2010, from http://esa.un.org/unpd/wpp/index.htm; U.S. Census Bureau, International Data Base, June 2010 update. Retrieved June 20, 2010, from http://www.census.gov/ipc/www/idb/worldpopgraph.php

Useful though they may be for a variety of purposes, our fine opposable thumbs aren't our biggest evolutionary advantage: Our enormously complex brains are.

© Shvaygert Ekaterina, 2014. Used under license from Shutterstock, Inc.

Brain: A complex clustering of nerve cells that is centrally involved in coordinating activities and events in various parts of an organism. The human brain is reputedly the most complex structure in the universe.

Sapir-Whorf hypothesis: The belief that language is essential for and determines thought (strong form); or the belief that language limits but does not determine thought (weak form).

Nervous system: All parts of the body composed of nerve cells, the function of which is to transmit messages. The major components of the human nervous system are the brain, the spinal cord, receptor systems associated with the major senses, and other nerve cells implicated in the functioning of muscles and glands.

So, why have we *H. sapiens* thrived as a species? Why is the world population of humans growing at an extremely rapid rate compared to other species on this planet? The answer is that we are more intelligent! Prehistoric *H. sapiens* were not able to out-fight or outrun their prehistoric enemies; they outwitted them! An additional, but inconspicuous reason for our success is that we evolved to stand upright. And although becoming bipedal did not make us as fast as most four-legged animals, it freed our arms and hands for purposes other than locomotion. We became an ani-mal that could walk quite nicely on just two of its legs, freeing our arms for making tools, striking enemies while in full flight, making hand gestures to aid in communicating, and blowing our noses—an undertaking that was not at all hampered by the fine opposable thumbs that we now take for granted. Although many other primates also have opposable thumbs, no other animal can boast the manual dexterity that we have at our fingertips. And no other animal possesses as complex a **brain** as we have.

These adapted abilities are clues as to what tasks the mind of a *H. sapien* has developed to do, and how our brains have evolved into a system of "psychological faculties or mental modules" (Pinker, 1997).

BRAINS, LANGUAGE, AND THINKING

With such complex brains, we eventually were able to develop primitive tools, agricultural and hunting strategies, and inventions such as the wheel, the rocket, and the computer. But perhaps more important than all of those, the capacities of the human brain gave way to the development of language and culture.

Thinking and language are very closely related. In fact, a school of thought that was widely popular among anthropologists a few decades ago maintained that language is *essential* for, and determines, thought—a belief labeled the **Sapir-Whorf hypothesis**. This hypothesis maintains that different languages lead people to see the world differently and to think and behave differently (Whorf, 1956). For example, some early research suggested that the Inuit, who seemed to have many different words for snow, could actually perceive types of snow of which others were unaware. Similarly, cultures that had a different vocabulary for colors were thought to see colors differently. These beliefs have now been discredited (Pullum, 1991). Experimental research has not supported the Sapir-Whorf hypothesis (Koerner, 2000). It seems that language is not essential for thinking. For example, there is evidence of thinking among preverbal infants (Gleitman & Papafragou, 2005). And it is also true that adults sometimes think in terms of images or other symbols rather than with language.

EVOLUTION AND THE NERVOUS SYSTEM

The brain is part of our **nervous system**. In a simple sense, our nervous system is the electrical and chemical communication system within our bodies. It is because of our nervous system that our right hand knows what our left hand is doing, that our legs alternate rather than compete when we walk, and that we are sensitive to our environments. In fact, it is because of our nervous system we can even think about such matters; hence its tremendous importance in psychology.

The nervous systems of insects also provide an interesting evolutionary contrast to that of humans. In some insects, primitive clusters of nerve cells coordinate simple functions, such as a cockroach's brain telling it when and where to run (Bender, Pollack, & Ritzmann, 2010), but in many insects, there is no single "command area"—no brain to oversee all functions or to be aware of what is going on in all parts of the body. Cut off the head of a wasp and it will continue eating even though it has lost its abdomen and there's nowhere for the food to go. In much the same way, the male praying mantis will continue to copulate even as the female systematically devours him from the head down (Prokop & Vaclav, 2008).

The more advanced nervous systems of fish, reptiles, and mammals differ from these more primitive nervous systems. Not only is their functioning more complex, but their activity is coordinated by an increasingly larger brain. Furthermore, brains in more advanced animals have become highly specialized: A large portion of the bat's brain is devoted to hearing (essential for echolocation); the olfactory (smell) area of a dog's brain is far more developed than that of a human's brain; those parts of the brain that control rapid movement are more predominant in a bird's brain; and in humans, the area of the brain devoted to thinking is larger, proportional to the remainder of the brain, than in any other living creature (Figure 2.3). It is this brain, the command center of our nervous system, that is largely responsible for producing the behaviors and qualities we believe make us uniquely human.

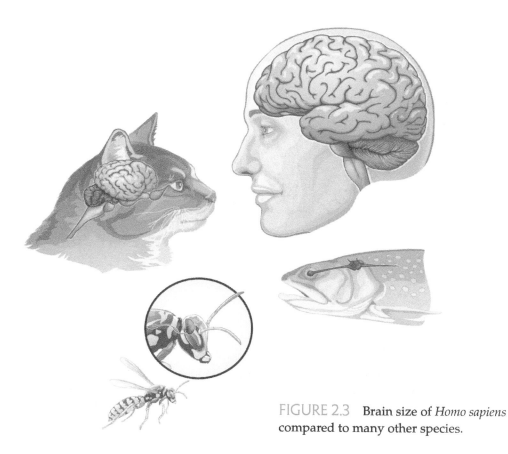

FIGURE 2.3   **Brain size of** *Homo sapiens* **compared to many other species.**

The Neuron

The human nervous system is a *communication* system; its function is to transmit messages (impulses). Many of the messages it transmits go from sensory **receptors** (such as the skin, eyes, nose, tongue, ears, muscles, joints, and tendons) to the command center (the brain). Impulses also go from the brain to what are termed **effectors** (such as muscular and glandular systems).

The cells that make up the nervous system, and whose specialized function is to transmit impulses, are called **neurons** (or *nerve cells*). Estimates vary widely, but scientists believe there are approximately 86 billion neurons in the human brain alone, with the bulk of these—some 69 billion—being in the part of the brain called the *cerebellum* (Azevedo et al., 2009). The spinal cord contains at least a billion more, and several billion more are concentrated in sensory receptors and in muscular and glandular *effector* systems. Other neurons are *connectors:* They serve as links between receptor and effector systems (Figure 2.4). Most of the connectors are located in the brain.

Like all other living cells, neurons consist of a nucleus and surrounding matter. This matter is made up of the cell body, **axon**, and **dendrites**. The axon of a neuron is surrounded by a protective coating, called a **myelin sheath** (made up of **glial cells**), which speeds up neuronal communication and provides an efficient mechanism for one neuron to talk to another neuron. Without this very important

Receptors: Specialized cells or groups of cells that respond to sensory stimulation.

Effector: A specialized cell or organ that carries out a response to a nerve impulse.

Neurons: A single nerve cell, the smallest unit of the nervous system and its basic structural unit. The function of the neuron is to transmit impulses, which are basically electrical but are made possible through chemical changes.

Axon: The elongated part of a nerve cell. Axons ordinarily transmit impulses from the cell body to adjoining dendrites.

Dendrites: Hair-like extensions emanating from the cell body of the neuron. Dendrites ordinarily receive impulses from adjoining axons.

Myelin sheath: An insulating, protective coating that surrounds nerve fibers and facilitates neural transmission.

Glial cells: Cells that support neural functioning. Among other functions, they clean out debris and form protective coatings around nerves.

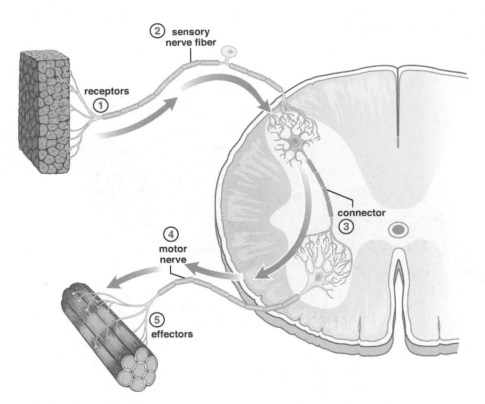

FIGURE 2.4 (A)   Schematic conception of the components of the sensorimotor arc. *Receptors* (1) in eyes, tactile organs, nose, ears, taste buds, and kinesthetic senses send signals (2) to *connectors* (3) in the spinal cord, brain, and other neural pathways. Signals are then sent (4) to *effectors* (5) in muscles and glands.

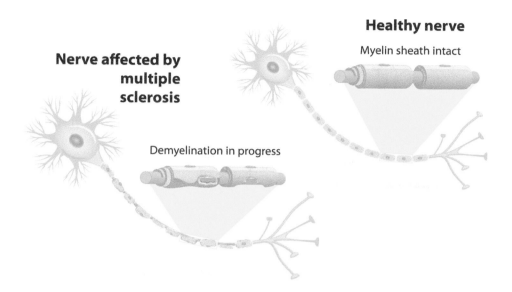

FIGURE 2.4 (B) Schematic conception of a healthy nerve cell and a nerve cell affected by multiple sclerosis.

© Designua, 2014. Used under license from Shutterstock, Inc.

myelin, your brain would not function properly. In extreme cases, our bodies can be tricked into attacking and destroying our own myelin, leading to what is known as *multiple sclerosis.* The destruction of myelin can also significantly affect the mind's ability to send messages to the muscles, which can lead to a loss of muscle control (Fields, 2008).

The axon is the elongated part of a neuron: It may be microscopically short or, as is the case for some neurons located in the spinal cord, as long as 2 or 3 feet! Dendrites are hairlike extensions emanating from the cell body of the neuron. These dendrites receive messages that other nerve cells, or neurons, send to them. The space between the ends of one cell's axon and another cell's dendrites is a **synapse**. At the synapse, one neuron can communicate with another neuron by sending little chemical messengers, called neurotransmitters (discussed in detail in a bit), across the synapse. The type and amount of these neurotransmitters can influence the likelihood of subsequent neural communication, which can alter our moods and behaviors. Bundles of neurons make up **nerves**. The typical configuration of a neuron is shown in Figure 2.5.

Neural Transmission

The transmission of impulses from neuron to neuron involves both electrical and chemical activity. Think of each neuron as a tiny battery that can generate an electrical impulse. Electricity is the flow of negatively charged particles (called *electrons*) toward a positively charged pole. In the neuron, electrical impulses operate in exactly the same way. A neuron at rest (*resting potential*) is like a charged battery with the switch off. Stimulation brings about a series of chemical changes that effectively open the switch, causing a flow of charged particles called an **action potential**. And about 2 milliseconds later, the neuron again regains its *resting potential*. But for a brief period,

Synapse: A microscopic gap between the end of an axon and an adjacent dendrite, axon, or other cell across which neural impulses (neurotransmitters) travel.

Nerve: Bundles of fibers consisting of neurons, whose functions is the transmission of neural impulses.

Action potential: A pulse-like electrical discharge along a neuron. Sequences of linked action potentials are the basis for the transmission of neural messages.

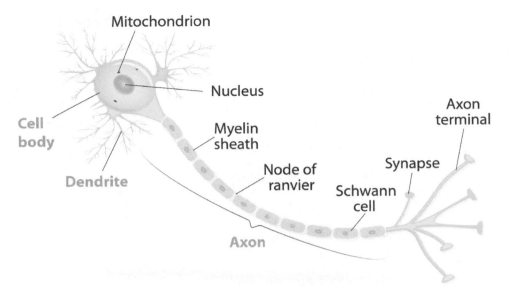

FIGURE 2.5   Anatomy of a typical human neuron. Neural transmission typically proceeds from the cell body, down the axon, across the synapse, and to the dendrites and cell bodies of adjacent cells.

© Designua, 2014. Used under license from Shutterstock, Inc.

Refractory period: A brief period after firing during which a neuron is "discharged" and is incapable of firing again.

Threshold: The minimum level of stimulation needed for a neuron to fire an action potential.

termed a **refractory period**, it is essentially discharged and therefore puts the neuron into a state that makes it physically impossible to produce another action potential until its normal resting potential is again achieved (Figure 2.6).

Note the electrical impulse involves the entire neuron and is equally strong throughout the neuron, hence the expression "all-or-none" firing. The level of stimulation needed for a neuron to fire is referred to as the **threshold**. Think of threshold as pulling a trigger on a gun, or a popcorn kernel about to pop. The amount of squeezing pressure you apply to the handle and trigger will eventually reach a level that causes the gun to fire. Likewise, the temperature inside a

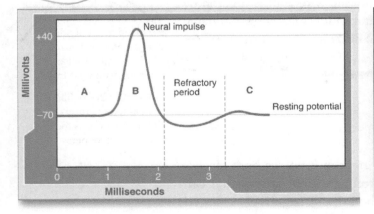

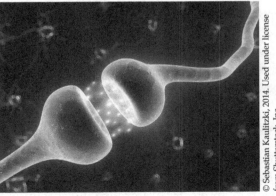

FIGURE 2.6   Representation of a neural impulse. At point A, there exists a state of readiness (*resting potential*). At B, a stimulus leads to an electrical impulse (*action potential*), which is followed immediately by a *refractory period* during which the cell cannot fire. A few milliseconds later, the cell is restored to its resting potential (charged) state. As shown in this photo of a synapse, certain chemical substances, as illustrated by the yellow and white dots located in this synapse, are the neurotransmitters (e.g., dopamine and serotonin), which play an important part in the "opening" of neural membranes to allow the passage of the electrical impulse.

kernel will eventually reach a temperature that will cause the kernel to pop. Both of these instances reach a time in which there is a point of no return: The level of stimulation will or will not cause the action potential (all-or-none firing). Just like a popcorn kernel or gun, the stimulation intensity applied to a neuron will or will not cause it to fire: It all depends on the intensity of the stimulus.

To illustrate the process of an action potential, imagine stubbing your toe on a piece of furniture. Unfortunately, axons are efficient transmitters of electrical signals, and you will soon feel pain as a result of the transmission from your toe to your brain. Unfortunately, the "pain" sensation will not reach your brain immediately. Although electricity travels at the speed of light (186,300 feet per second), the thinnest axons transmit impulses at only around 3 feet per second! Larger axons might transmit at speeds up to 10 feet per second (Kalat, 2009).

So, less than a second after you stub your toe, you will know that you did so, unless something has happened to disrupt the flow of electrical impulses in relevant nerves. That is basically what happens when your dentist uses *novocaine* to "freeze" you. Nothing is frozen in the literal sense, but novocaine does effectively block the flow of electrical impulses between neurons. So, pain signals are being sent, but nothing is reaching the end of the line. Basically, no matter how desperately the receptors in your tooth yell, "It hurts," the message simply does not get to your brain.

The process of neurotransmission is made possible by certain chemicals called **neurotransmitters**, which are released by neurons, changing the electrical potential of cells and thus leading to neural transmission. These chemicals are then reabsorbed by the releasing neuron—a process referred to as **reuptake**.

Of special interest in the treatment of a variety of emotional and physical disorders are drugs that have been developed to increase or impede the functioning of the neurotransmitters. **Agonists** increase the effectiveness of neurotransmitters, either by stimulating neurons to produce more, by increasing the sensitivity of receptor cells, or by preventing the *reuptake* of the neurotransmitter, thus making more available. **Antagonists** block or reduce the effects of a neurotransmitter.

Of the more than 100 different neurotransmitters that have now been identified, four are especially important in the study of psychology: dopamine, norepinephrine, acetylcholine, and serotonin.

DOPAMINE

Dopamine plays a key role in the functioning of neurons associated with pleasure and reinforcement. In fact, almost all abused drugs can attribute their abuse potential and feel-good effects to the increase in dopamine activity in certain areas of the brain. Some research (e.g., Asensio et al., 2010; Self & Staley, 2010) indicates individuals who normally have low levels of dopamine are more likely to become addicted. And in some cases, there appear to be genetic differences between addicts and non-addicts related to this neurotransmitter (Levran et al., 2009).

A disease associated with low dopamine levels in areas of the brain where dopamine is usually most concentrated is **Parkinson's disease**. It is characterized by uncontrollable shaking, generalized weakness, slow movements, constipation, sleep disturbances, and depression. On the other end of the spectrum, too much dopamine in different regions of the brain is thought to be a contributing factor to many of the positive symptoms of schizophrenia.

Neurotransmitters: Naturally produced chemicals that are released by nerve cells and that initiate or facilitate transmission of messages among nerve cells (e.g., serotonin, dopamine, norepinephrine, and acetylcholine).

Reuptake: The process by which a nerve cell recaptures some of the neurotransmitters it has released. Some medications and drugs function to increase neurotransmitter effectiveness by blocking reuptake.

Agonists: An agent or drug that enhances the activity of some naturally occurring substance. For example, cocaine is a dopamine agonist in that it appears to stimulate the activity of dopamine.

Antagonists: A drug that blocks the effectiveness of a neurotransmitter. For example, beta blockers are antagonists that reduce blood pressure by impeding receptivity of adrenaline receptors.

Dopamine: A neurotransmitter centrally involved with pleasure and reinforcement and also implicated in some instances of drug addiction as well as in conditions such as Parkinson's disease.

Parkinson's disease: A central nervous system disease characterized by tremors, slow movement, and other symptoms; associated with low dopamine levels in the brain.

Almost all abused drugs are effective because they increase the release of dopamine in the brain and/or prevent its reuptake. Dopamine function plays a key role in reinforcement and pleasure. Chocolate, too, as this child well knows, is associated with dopamine and other neurotransmitters linked with reinforcement.
© Marco Govel, 2014. Used under license from Shutterstock, Inc.

NOREPINEPHRINE

Norepinephrine: A neurotransmitter linked with arousal, memory, and learning. Anomalies in the functioning of the norepinephrine system may be linked to manifestations of depression. Also called *noradrenaline*.

Attention deficit hyperactivity disorder (ADHD): A disorder marked by excessive general activity for a child's age, attention problems, high impulsivity, and low frustration tolerance. Also termed *hyperactivity*.

The neurotransmitter **norepinephrine** (also called *noradrenaline*) increases blood pressure and triggers the release of glucose (sugar) from energy stores. Consequently, it is the neurotransmitter most closely linked with crises. In an emergency, parts of the brain are suddenly flooded with norepinephrine, a signal that prepares the body to respond, perhaps by fleeing, perhaps by fighting. If you have ever heard of, or experienced, an "adrenaline rush," norepinephrine is the primary neurotransmitter responsible for the feelings of the rush, which can accompany activities like skydiving or base jumping for some.

Norepinephrine is not just involved in extreme physical activities or flight-or-fight responses. Research indicates that norepinephrine levels may be implicated in some instances of **attention-deficit hyperactivity disorder (ADHD**; Bhaduri, Sarkar, Sionha, Chattopadhyay, & Mukhopadhyay, 2010). One of the effects of drugs (such as Ritalin) commonly used to treat ADHD is they act as norepinephrine/dopamine reuptake inhibitors, increasing available levels of norepinephrine and dopamine in the *synapse* (Cohen-Yavin et al., 2009). This improves the person's ability to concentrate and to think clearly about what is being focused on, thus alleviating one of the main symptoms of ADHD.

Some manifestations of depression are also linked with norepinephrine. Many common antidepressant drugs (e.g., *tricyclic antidepressants* such as Elavil, Norpramin, and Pamelor) are agonists that increase norepinephrine levels by blocking its reuptake (Craig, 2006). One of the effects of increased norepinephrine levels is a speeding up of neural activity, which counters the "slowing down" sensation that often accompanies depression. Interestingly, an overabundance of norepinephrine has been linked with *mania*, the opposite mood to depression (Narayan & Haddad, 2011).

ACETYLCHOLINE

Acetylcholine is a neurotransmitter involved in the largely unconscious functioning of the *autonomic* nervous system (concerned with functions such as heart and respiration rates). It is also importantly involved in conscious activity such as muscle movement, as well as in arousal, reinforcement, learning, and memory (Arnulf & Leu-Semenescu, 2009). It can also serve to increase the reactivity of neurons or to inhibit their responsiveness. Drugs that stimulate the acetylcholine system or that block its functioning have a variety of medical uses, including the treatment of Alzheimer's disease (Zhang et al., 2010).

The venom of a black widow spider acts as an *agonist* for acetylcholine. Meaning, when one gets bitten by a black widow spider, acetylcholine neurotransmitters and receptors are highly activated. This high activation and abnormally high release of acetylcholine can cause muscles to remain painfully contracted. Conversely, botulin (a poison found in small amounts in Botox treatments to get rid of wrinkles), is an antagonist for acetylcholine. *Antagonists* for acetylcholine can cause muscle paralysis (Gomez & Queiroz, 1982).

SEROTONIN

Serotonin is involved in neural transmission in much of the brain, especially in areas having to do with emotion. Its other functions include regulating sleep, appetite, and cognitive activity related to learning and memory (Pothakos et al., 2010). Depressed levels of serotonin have been linked with depression, aggression, and even violence. Accordingly, many antidepressants and anti-anxiety drugs are *agonists* that affect serotonin levels by acting as selective serotonin reuptake inhibitors, or SSRIs (Arnone, Horder, Cowen, & Harmer, 2009). Similar drugs are also sometimes used to control impulsive, violent behavior (Butler et al., 2010).

If you have a cat or kitten, you may sometimes wonder why it appears to follow things in the environment with its eyes that are not actually there. Although it is not known for certain, some researchers believe the kittens, and cats in general, have an abundance of serotonin neurotransmitters in their visual systems, leading to brief periods of hallucinations and other abnormal behaviors. These symptoms may be stemming from what is known as serotonin-induced feline hyperesthesia syndrome (Ciribassi, 2009). Interestingly, many psychedelic drugs, or hallucinogens, cause hallucinations by acting on serotonergic systems in the brain.

Serotonin is also present in some plants and seeds, including nuts from some walnut and hickory species, many of which are toxic or at least cause pain. In fact, pain is one of the side effects of large amounts of serotonin in the blood. Interestingly, wasp, toad, and stingray venoms contain serotonin, which serves to increase the painfulness of their stings (Fevzi, Ergin, Rivers, & Gençer, 2006; Ling, Clark, Erikson, & Trestrail, 2001).

The Psychobiology of Drugs

Various recreational and addictive drugs can provide ways of altering the biological mechanisms in our brain, and can effectively shape our reality. Most people do not develop crippling addictions to drugs because they can manage when and how much of a certain drug they should take. Like following

Acetylcholine: A neurotransmitter present in the peripheral as well as central nervous system, involved in voluntary activity as well as physiological functions (such as heart and respiration rates).

Serotonin: A neurotransmitter, the bulk of which is found in the gut, where it regulates intestinal activity. Too low levels of serotonin may be associated with depression.

a doctor's prescription, a person who experiences frequent mild headaches most likely does not become addicted to Advil or Tylenol. They don't *need* these pain killers to function properly throughout the day. Most people who use over-the-counter medication or other various prescriptions do not become **dependent** on these drugs.

Other people, however, do become dependent, and do need these substances to function properly, and at times, survive. These people more likely than not have become addicted to a **psychoactive drug**, a chemical substance that alters their perceptions and moods in such a way that either feels good to the user, and/or prevents the user from feeling bad. Here we briefly discuss a few of the more common psychoactive drugs, their effects on the brain and neurotransmitter systems, and how they can influence behavior. They are identified as being either a **stimulant** or a **depressant**. Stimulants are drugs that speed up bodily functions, whereas depressants are drugs that slow down bodily functions.[2]

NICOTINE

Nicotine is one of the most addicting stimulants. Not surprisingly, it is one of the most commonly used drugs in the world. People with a crippling addiction to nicotine generally resort to smoking as their primary route of administration. When a person smokes a cigarette, they feel the effects about as quickly and powerfully as heroin or cocaine. Unfortunately, this may be all it takes for one to get addicted, and attempts to quit within the first week of smoking often fail (DiFranza, 2008).

Nicotine acts on many different neurotransmitters to elicit its addicting properties. Two neurotransmitters involved with nicotine use are norepinephrine and dopamine, two that we discussed earlier in this chapter. Nicotine acts on norepinephrine to enhance mental efficiency and increase one's wakefulness, while also acting on dopamine, providing those crucial calming and reinforcing effects (Nowak, 1994).

COCAINE

Cocaine is another popular stimulant that influences dopamine levels in the brain. Cocaine produces reinforcing and addictive effects in its users by blocking the reuptake mechanisms of dopamine, serotonin, and norepinephrine (Ray & Ksir, 1990), resulting in more of these neurotransmitters left in the synapse, and the "feel good" feeling that follows. Cocaine is usually snorted in its powdered form, or smoked in its freebase form, known as crack cocaine, which results in a much stronger "high" in its users.

ALCOHOL

Alcohol is one of most commonly abused depressants. It slows neural processing and can disrupt memory formation if consumed in large quantities. Alcohol can also increase the chances of disinhibiting its users, or slowing the

Dependent: A state of being characterized by the compulsive desire to have a substance, such as a drug, in order to feel "normal" and postpone the effects of withdrawal.

Psychoactive drug: A chemical substance that has the ability to alter perception, mood, behavior, and/or physiological function.

Stimulant: A type of drug that speeds up physiological functions. Cocaine is an abused stimulant and it speeds up the heart rate.

Depressant: A type of drug that slows down physiological functions. Alcohol is a commonly abused depressant and it slows down respiration.

---

[2] Here is a link to an applet illustrating the effects of different drugs on the brain: http://learn.genetics.utah.edu/content/addiction/mouse/

brain activity involved in judgment and decision making. For example, both men and women are more likely to participate in casual or unprotected sex and experience unwanted sexual encounters while under the influence of alcohol (Presley et al., 1997).

Alcohol's ability to disrupt judgment and decision making makes alcohol even more dangerous when someone has used alcohol and gets behind the wheel of a car. Coupled with the effect of blurred vision that alcohol can cause, we can see why drunk driving is such a serious problem.

OPIATES

Opiates, specifically morphine and heroin, are two commonly abused depressants (psychoactive drugs that depress neural functioning). Morphine or heroin use leads to decreased respiratory function, slowed breathing, relaxation, and care-free pleasure as pain and anxiety subside.

Research done by Siegel (2001) has shown that opiate use and *tolerance* to opiate use is closely tied to environmental cues. For example, when researchers give repeated doses of heroin to rats in a specific environment, they eventually develop *tolerance* and need more of the drug to reach the same effects as before. This isn't surprising; however, if the researchers take the rat out of the environment that was usually paired with the opiate, and then give the rats the same dose of heroin as before, the rats overdose from the drug. What does this tell us? It tells us that these rats have *conditioned responses* that are elicited by the environment, which in a way "prepare" them for the drug. Without the environmental cues prior to drug taking, the rats are not expecting to the get the drug, their biological mechanisms used to fight the drug's effects are not there, and the likelihood of overdosing therefore increases.

Organization of the Nervous System

The **central nervous system (CNS)** consists of the brain and **spinal cord**. It is via the spinal cord that most of the major neural pathways conduct impulses between brain centers and various glandular, muscular, and sensory systems.

The system of neural networks that fan out from the CNS into various parts of the body is the **peripheral nervous system (PNS**; Figure 2.7). The peripheral nervous system is linked to all sensory organs and to the muscles and glands; it is also involved in physiological activities such as respiration, heart action, sweating, and crying.

Therefore, in a way, the CNS consists of the brain and spinal cord, while the PNS consists of everything else in the nervous system.

The peripheral nervous system has two divisions. The **somatic system** transmits impulses relating to sensations of heat, cold, pain, and pressure to the CNS. It also transmits impulses in the opposite direction, from the CNS to muscles involved in voluntary movement.

Central nervous system (CNS): The human nervous system, which includes the brain and the spinal cord.

Spinal cord: Main link between the brain and sensory and motor systems, closely involved in reflexes such as the knee-jerk reflex.

Peripheral nervous system (PNS): The neural networks that fan out from the central nervous system to various parts of the body.

Somatic system: Part of the peripheral nervous system concerned with bodily sensations and muscular movement.

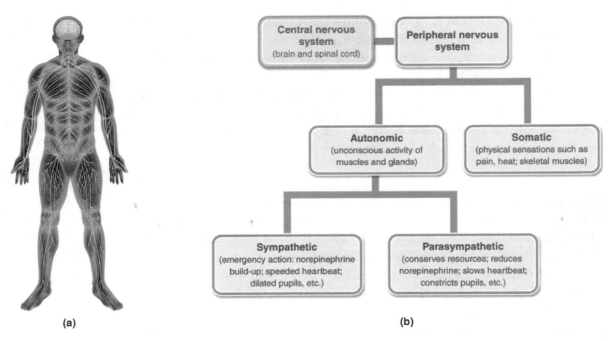

FIGURE 2.7   The human nervous system. Part (a) depicts the two major divisions of the nervous system: the central nervous system (bright orange) and the peripheral nervous system (darker). The organization and functions of each are described in (b).

(a) © BlueRingMedia, 2014. Used under license from Shutterstock, Inc.

Autonomic nervous system: That part of the peripheral nervous system that is not ordinarily under conscious control. It regulates physiological functions such as respiration, heart rate, temperature, and digestion and includes the sympathetic and parasympathetic systems.

Sympathetic nervous system: Part of the autonomic nervous system that instigates the physiological responses that accompany emotional behavior.

Adrenaline: Also called *epinephrine*. A substance produced by the adrenal glands, released in response to stress.

The **autonomic nervous system**, the other part of the peripheral nervous system, is directly involved in the action of muscles and glands that are automatic and involuntary. It includes the **sympathetic nervous system**, which is responsible for mobilizing the body's resources, particularly in emergency situations. It is your sympathetic nervous system that causes **adrenaline** to be pumped into your system. The result is that your heart beats faster, more blood rushes through your blood vessels, and you might tremble in anxiety, blush in shame, or respond with any of the other physiological changes that accompany intense emotion.

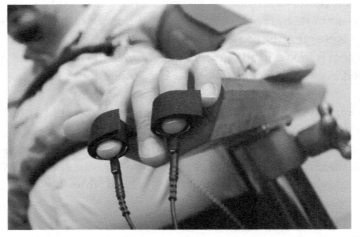

When we're anxious, as might happen when we lie to a police investigator, our sympathetic nervous system kicks up our heart rate, our palms start to sweat, and our breathing changes. We can't control these reactions, they are automatic, and the "lie-detector"—a polygraph machine that measures these changes—reveals our lie.

© pefostudio5, 2014. Used under license from Shutterstock, Inc.

Most of us have little control over our physiological reactions, a fact that led to the invention of the common lie-detector. This instrument is capable of detecting changes that result from activity of the autonomic nervous system. If you become anxious when you lie (as most people do), your sympathetic nervous system reacts accordingly. As a result, your palms start to sweat, your breathing changes, and your heart rate increases.

But your heart rate does not accelerate indefinitely, nor do you tremble more and more violently. The **parasympathetic nervous system**, the other part of the autonomic nervous system, slows your heart rate, steadies your trembling, increases your control over bowel and bladder functioning, and in other ways opposes some of the functions of the sympathetic nervous system. It is as though the parasympathetic nervous system serves to conserve bodily resources.

In sum, the sympathetic nervous system serves a "flight-or-fight" purpose, while the parasympathetic nervous system serves a "rest-and-digest" purpose.

The Endocrine System

The **endocrine system** is separate from the CNS, but it influences most of the organs, cells, and functions of the body. It includes glands that secrete **hormones** directly into the bloodstream and are therefore known as the ductless glands. Chief among them are the **pituitary gland**, which is frequently termed the "master" gland because of its role in regulating activity of other glands. The ductless glands also include the **adrenal glands** and the **gonads**.

The adrenal glands, which sit on top of the kidneys, are mainly responsible for releasing the hormone *adrenaline* in response to stress. The gonads include the testes, which produce male sex hormones such as *testosterone*, and the ovaries, which produce *estrogen* in females.

The Brain

The most important part of our CNS is our brain, which is arguably the single most complex structure in the entire known universe. We have known for some time this unimpressive-looking lump of grayish tissue is the very center of our ability to learn, feel, and think—it determines and defines our very essence. But we did not always know this. In fact, the ancient Egyptians considered the brain so unimportant that they did not bother to preserve it in their mummies, removing it instead through the left nostril (Blakemore, 1977). Only recently have modern discoveries revealed some secrets of the structures and functions of our brains, providing additional pieces to our human puzzle.

Studying Brain Functions

September 13, 1848, was an unlucky day for Phineas Gage, a railway worker on a rail line in Vermont. On that day, a tamping rod measuring 3 feet, 7 inches, shot out of a blasting hole and went through the left side of his face, through his brain, and out the top of his head! The blow hurled him to the ground. Most people would not survive such an extensive and serious blow to the head, but he quickly picked himself up, made his way to a cart, and went home.

Parasympathetic nervous system: Part of the autonomic nervous system that regulates physiological reactions that accommodate emotional reactions.

Endocrine system: A system of glands that secrete hormones whose functioning affects things such as growth, maturation, behavior, and emotion. Includes the pituitary, the adrenal glands, and the gonads.

Hormones: Chemicals that have a pronounced effect on growth, maturation, behavior, and emotions and that are produced by endocrine glands and secreted directly into the bloodstream.

Pituitary gland: A small endocrine gland found as a protrusion off the hypothalamus. The *master gland* involved in controlling functioning of other endocrine glands.

Adrenal glands: Endocrine glands situated at the top of the kidneys, involved in releasing hormones at times of stress.

Gonads: Hormone-producing sex glands. Testes in the male; ovaries in the female.

Phineas' physical recovery was rapid and apparently complete. Friends, family, and anyone who knew Phineas before his accident said that he became moody and selfish and prone to outbursts of violent temper—behaviors very uncharacteristic of him. His physician, Dr. John Harlow, and a Harvard surgeon named Dr. Henry Bigelow concluded that the damaged part of his brain was responsible for controlling various aspects of emotions and personality (Macmillan, 2000). In fact, prior to the development of modern brain scanning technology, performing case studies of individuals with brain injuries was one of the first ways that scientists discovered different functions of the brain, also called localization of function.

Based on the structure and cracks in Phineas Gage's skull, which is now housed at Warren's Anatomical Museum within Harvard Medical School's Countway Library of Medicine, it is believed that the tamping rod primarily damaged Phineas Gage's *frontal lobe*. However, as Macmillan (2008) points out, no one ever examined Phineas Gage's brain directly, so there really is no certainty about what structures were damaged as a result of his injury. Also, there seems to have been some exaggeration and contradiction in reports of his case: There is a strong likelihood he did not change as dramatically as has sometimes been reported. The fact that he later began to suffer seizures and eventually died as a result might indicate his recovery was far from complete.

BRAIN ABLATIONS

The problem with studying the brain using injuries such as those caused by tumors or by accidents is that these injuries don't usually have very specific effects. They often affect large parts of the brain, and investigators certainly cannot control who will have an accident—which makes for poor research.

Another approach is to deliberately cut out small portions of the brain and then see what the effects might be, also known as brain lesions. Understandably, this kind of research finds very few volunteers with healthy brains. Except where surgical procedures are required in cases of brain damage, epilepsy, tumors, or for other medical reasons, most of this research has been and has to be done with animals, primarily rats and mice.

A pioneer researcher in this area, Karl Lashley (1924), taught some rats how to run through a maze. He was convinced that different memories leave a trace in a tiny part of the brain, and he thought that if he cut out just the right part, the rat would no longer remember how to get through the maze. But Lashley never did find this memory trace (called an *engram*). It did not seem to matter what part of the brain he removed, or how much; the rat continued to run through the maze—although sometimes much more slowly. We now know that the kind of memories Lashley was studying were likely stored in parts of the brain he did not remove.

BRAIN STIMULATION

Another way of studying the brain is to stimulate different parts of it with electrodes or with chemicals. For example, Olds (1956) implanted electrodes in the brains of rats and accidentally discovered that stimulating part of the *hypothalamus*—now labeled the "pleasure center"—seemed to be extremely pleasurable for the rat. When the electrodes were connected to a lever so that rats could stimulate their own brain, many would pass up food to do so. One rat stimulated himself more than 2,000 times an hour for 24 consecutive hours! Even more telling is that Olds (1958) found out that these rats would also be willing to cross a painful electrified grid to get the opportunity to press a lever to stimulate their pleasure centers.

Stimulating the brain with electrodes is an invasive and difficult undertaking; chemical stimulation is much simpler. It is possible to administer different drugs (chemicals) and to observe their effects on the participant's behavior and their effects on the brain. For example, chemical stimulation of the brain reveals that the neurotransmitter dopamine is involved in neural activity associated with pleasure. Dopamine, as we previously learned, is a naturally occurring neurotransmitter. Normally, when it is released as a result of neural stimulation, it is quickly recaptured by affected neurons (Kalat, 2009). But certain drugs such as amphetamines and cocaine act as *agonists* by preventing the immediate reuptake of the dopamine so that *dopaminergic neurons* (neurons that use dopamine for neural transmission) stay active longer. Because dopamine is associated with neural activity in one of the brain's "pleasure" centers, the ultimate effect of cocaine is intensely pleasurable (Morcom et al., 2010).

The prolonged use of agonists such as cocaine, however, leads the brain to synthesize less dopamine naturally as it adapts to the drug. In a way, drugs that act on dopamine, such as cocaine, can trick the brain into thinking there is plenty of dopamine available, and that the dopamine systems are functioning just fine. But the brain is mistaken. After the artificial source of dopamine activity (the drug) is gone, the brain is left with a depleted amount of the neurotransmitter. As a result, the chronic drug user often experiences depression and other negative moods rather than pleasure when the effects of the drug begin to wear off (termed *withdrawal*). Also, dopamine receptor activity decreases with repeated drug use (termed drug *tolerance*) so that ever-increasing amounts of the drug are required to reach the same effect of the drug as before (Slomski, 2006). Tolerance and the presence of withdrawal symptoms are important indicators of addiction.

Electrical stimulation of the brain's pleasure centers, as well as natural reinforcers such as food, water, and sex, and substances such as nicotine and alcohol, all lead to the release of dopamine (Lajtha & Sershen, 2010). And all of these substances and activities are potentially addictive.

BRAIN IMAGING

The effect of chemicals on the brain is usually detected by means of one or more of the various sophisticated brain-imaging techniques researchers now have at their disposal. These include the **electroencephalogram (EEG)**, which provides recordings of brain electrical activity; **positron emission tomography (PET)**, which records changes in blood flow by responding to radioactive particles injected in the bloodstream; **functional magnetic resonance imaging (fMRI)**, which measures changes in magnetic fields related to blood oxygen level; and **magnetoencephalography (MEG)**, which detects incredibly small changes at the scalp in magnetic fields associated with neural activity. Note that these brain-imaging methods are used not only to study the effects of drugs, but also to look at brain activity during specific tasks. They are highly useful in studies of the brain's role in intellectual activities.

Electroencephalogram (EEG): An instrument used to measure electrical activity in the brain.

Positron emission tomography (PET): An imaging technique used extensively in medicine and in physiological and neurological research. Records changes in blood flow by detecting the distribution of radioactive particles injected in the bloodstream.

Functional magnetic resonance imaging (fMRI): A diagnostic imaging technique that detects extremely subtle changes in magnetic fields in the human body, allowing technicians to view real-time, computer-enhanced images of soft tissue. Used extensively to diagnose disease as well as to study neural activity in the brain.

Magnetoencephalogram (MEG): A recording of magnetic fields that correspond to electrical activity of the brain. MEG recordings are obtained at the scalp by means of a magnetoencephalograph to yield event-related fields (ERFs).

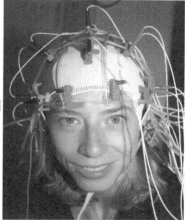

Electroencephalograms (EEGs) provide a nonintrusive way of studying brain functioning.

© Daniela Sachsenheimer, 2014. Used under license from Shutterstock, Inc.

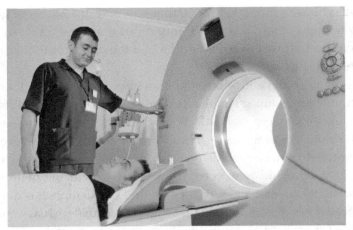

A technician for a magnetic resonance imaging (MRI) machine is ready to scan the brain of a patient. MRIs and fMRIs provide a noninvasive way to look inside the brain to view basic structures and activity.

© Levent Konuk, 2014. Used under license from Shutterstock, Inc.

Structures of the Brain

Physical examination of the brain reveals a grayish mass inside the skull (Figure 2.8). Some of its various structures are identifiable through this type of examination. But determining the functions of these structures is not so simple: The structures themselves present few clues to their functions.

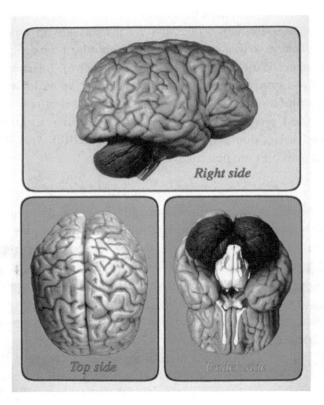

FIGURE 2.8   Top, right side, and under side view of the human brain. The outer covering of the brain is called the cerebral cortex.

Photolibrary/Imagestate Pictor

wed

HINDBRAIN

As shown in Figure 2.9, the human brain is normally divided into three basic parts: hindbrain, midbrain, and forebrain. These parts are thought to have evolved in that order, with the hindbrain being the oldest structure and the forebrain the most recent. Structures of the hindbrain and of the midbrain make up the **brain stem**—that part of the CNS that connects the spinal cord with higher brain structures.

The hindbrain is the lowest part of the brain in a person standing upright. It consists mainly of the **cerebellum** (the word means *small brain*), the **medulla**, and the **pons**.

Interestingly, although it is a small structure relative to the rest of the brain, the cerebellum contains approximately 80% of all the brain's neurons. Its main functions have to do with the balance and timing and coordination of motor movements. It is also involved in the recall of skills and habits. Musicians and others who practice motor skills extensively often have cerebellums that are larger than average (Hutchinson, Hui-Lin, Gaab, & Schlaug, 2003). Injury to the cerebellum

Brain stem: Part of the brain that connects the spinal cord with the higher brain centers. Includes the hindbrain (medulla, pons, cerebellum) and the midbrain (reticular formation).

Cerebellum: A major brain structure attached to the rear of the brain stem, the principal functions of which appear to be coordinating motor activity and maintaining balance.

Medulla: The lowest part of the brain, found at the very top of the spinal cord and containing nerve centers involved in regulating physiological activity such as breathing, digestion, and heart functioning.

Pons: A small brain structure that appears as a bulge at the front of medulla. Part of the brain stem involved in breathing and arousal.

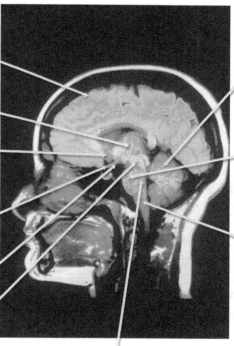

Cerebral cortex
sensation, language, speech, thinking, and motor activity

Limbic system

Thalamus:
"relay" center for sensory information

Hypothalamus:
regulation of endocrine gland activity relating to growth, sexual behavior, and other functions

Pituitary:
growth; regulation of other endocrine gland activity

Amygdala:
emotion, aggression, memory

Hippocampus:
learning and memory

Cerebellum:
control of rapid and habitual movements; coordination of motor activity; balance

Pons:
sleep and arousal; regulation of movement; respiration

Medulla:
physiological functions such as breathing, heart function, digestion

Reticular formation:
arousal center; sleep-wake control

Forebrain | Midbrain | Hindbrain

Brainstem

FIGURE 2.9   A sagittal (bisected front to back) view of the human brain showing major structures and some of their principal functions."

Photolibrary/Oxford Scientific (OSF)/Scott Camazine

Reticular formation:
(Reticular activating
system, RAS) That portion
of the brain stem assumed
to be responsible for the
physiological arousal of
the cortex as well as for
the control of sleeping and
waking.

Hypothalamus: A small
structure at the base
of the brain involved
in the functioning of
the autonomic nervous
system and in temperature
regulation.

Thalamus: A small brain
structure that serves as
a major relay center for
incoming sensory signals.

Limbic system: A grouping
of brain structures located
beneath the cerebral
cortex, associated mainly
with emotion, memory,
and reinforcement and
punishment.

Amygdala: A small
structure in the limbic
system (part of the
forebrain) that is involved
in emotion and aggression
and that plays an important
role in the processing and
storage of memories that
have to do with emotion.

Hippocampus: A limbic
system structure in the
forebrain, which is primarily
involved in learning and
memory.

Cerebrum: The main part
of the human brain,
consisting of the two
cerebral hemispheres and
covered by the cerebral
cortex.

Cerebral cortex: The
convoluted outer covering
of the cerebrum, the main
functions of which have
to do with higher mental
processes like thinking and
imagining.

can dramatically impair activities such as walking, playing the guitar, or catching
a ball.

The medulla is involved in physiological functions such as breathing, heart
functioning, and digestion. And the pons, which takes the form of a bulge at the
front of the medulla, serves as a link between the medulla and higher brain centers
(*pons* means bridge). The pons is importantly involved in sleep, the regulation of
movement, arousal, and respiration.

When substances, such as alcohol, cross through what is called the blood–
brain barrier, they can interrupt normal functioning of the hindbrain. This is what
police are indirectly measuring when they administer field sobriety tests for sus-
pected drunk drivers; they are seeing if the subject has ingested enough alcohol
to the point of affecting their cerebellum (involved in walking and balancing).
Furthermore, if the subject ingested so much alcohol to the point of unconsciousness, then the alcohol may have affected their medulla or pons (involved in breathing and heart rate), leading to life-threatening circumstances.

THE MIDBRAIN

The midbrain includes the **reticular formation**, found on the upper part of
the brain stem. This structure is involved in maintaining *arousal*, or degree of
alertness and motivation. It also contains nerve fibers associated with physical
movement. Associated nerves are *dopaminergic*, meaning that the main neurotransmitter involved in their activation is dopamine.

THE FOREBRAIN

The largest and most complex brain structure is the forebrain. It is also the
most important structure for understanding human thought, behavior, and
emotion. It includes the hypothalamus, the thalamus, and other structures of
the limbic system, as well as the cerebrum and cerebral cortex.

The **hypothalamus** is a bean-sized structure near the top of the brain stem.
It is mainly involved in regulating activity of the autonomic nervous system. In
a sense, the hypothalamus is a little like a thermostat; it oversees control of body
temperature (it plays a critical role in *homeostasis*), as well as hunger and thirst and
sleep–wake cycles. It is also involved in reactions to stress by initiating the signals
that lead to the release of adrenaline (fight-or-flight mechanisms).

The **thalamus** is found between the midbrain and the cerebral cortex. Its main
function is to act as a relay station for transmitting sensory signals to the cerebral
cortex. All sensations, except those having to do with smell, go through the thalamus. It is also involved in regulating sleep and consciousness.

The **limbic system** includes parts of the hypothalamus and various other
structures such as the **amygdala** and the **hippocampus**. Generally speaking, these
are structures involved in emotions. The hippocampus also plays an important
role in long-term memory. Alzheimer's disease and amnesia are both associated
with damage to the hippocampus (American Academy of Neurology, 2009).

The largest and most complex of our brain structures is the **cerebrum**, which
divides naturally into two halves, the left and right *cerebral hemispheres*. Its outer
covering, the **cerebral cortex**, is centrally involved in higher mental functioning.
This covering is highly convoluted and deeply fissured, the fissures resulting in

four natural divisions (*lobes*) in each of the hemispheres. These lobes have been separated by scientists based on the actual structure and function of these brain areas and what traits and behaviors they have been implicated in. These four lobes include the frontal lobe, parietal lobe, occipital lobe, and temporal lobe. There is also a right and a left hemisphere of each of these lobes (Figure 2.10).

At the front of the cerebral cortex are the **frontal lobes**, which are involved in motor activity as well as in higher thought processes. On either side are the **temporal lobes**, involved in language, speech, and hearing. The *auditory* cortex is the part of the temporal lobe concerned with hearing.

Just behind the temporal lobes are the **parietal lobes**, implicated in physical movement and in sensation and physical orientation. At the very back are the **occipital lobes**, involved in vision. The part of the occipital lobes involved in vision is referred to as the *visual cortex*.

It is important to note that the main tasks and responsibilities of each of these cerebral divisions are not very simple or clear. Most functions are carried out by more than one part of the brain. Note, too, that areas of these four lobes that are not involved directly in motor activity or sensation are nevertheless involved in higher mental processes such as think-

ing, remembering, learning, and speaking. These are referred to as **association areas of the brain.**

THE HEMISPHERES

Phineas Gage's accident provided some of the first crude evidence that the brain might be differentiated into separate functions, and since then, there has been other historical evidence as well. Paul Broca, a neurologist, was sent

Frontal lobes: Frontal part of the cerebral cortex, centrally involved in higher thought processes.

Temporal lobes: Cerebral structure located on either side of the cerebrum, associated primarily with speech, language, and hearing.

Parietal lobes: Cerebral lobes located just above the temporal lobes, between the frontal and occipital lobes. The parietal lobes are involved in sensation.

Occipital lobes: Part of the cerebral cortex located at the rear of the brain, involved in vision.

Association areas of the brain: Parts of the four cerebral lobes involved in higher mental processes like thinking, learning, and remembering.

Parts of the Human Brain

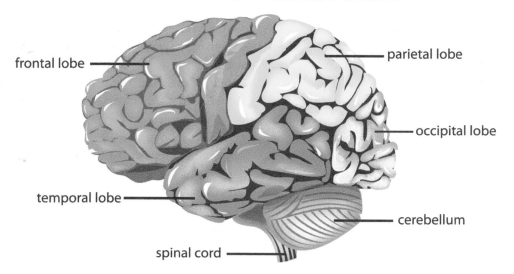

FIGURE 2.10 A left-side view of the cerebral cortex with the four right lobes labeled." Although each lobe is associated with certain functions, the lobes are highly integrated in terms of structure and function. The *corpus callosum* (not pictured) is primarily responsible for this integration.

a patient suffering from aphasia, a language disorder that we now know is linked to brain damage. The patient died within a few days and Broca performed an autopsy, discovering lesions in the left temporal lobe. The area of the lobe that was affected by these lesions is now known as Broca's region. Subsequent research has established that aphasia may be linked to lesions that are almost always on the left side of the brain. Lesions in the right half of the brain rarely disturb either *receptive* or *expressive* language functions, particularly in right-handed individuals, leading researchers to believe that language functions reside primarily in the left half of the brain in right-handed individuals and in most left-handed individuals (Holland et al., 2007).

There is evidence as well that the right hemisphere might be more involved with emotions as well as with music and art (Workman, Chilvers, Yeomans, & Taylor, 2006). These findings have led some to speculate that there are "right-brained" and "left-brained" individuals, distinguishable in terms of their major preoccupations and abilities. Thus, the "left-brained" would be expected to excel at verbal and logical tasks; the "right-brained" would be more artistic and more musical. This sort of speculation has led to the view that conventional education neglects the "right" brain because it emphasizes highly verbal, logical, scientific content and neglects more artistic and musical content. **Holistic education,** designed to educate both sides of the brain, is sometimes advocated as a remedy for this situation.

Unfortunately, much of what passes for information in this area is speculation and exaggeration rather than fact (Bruer, 2006). There is enormous overlap in the functions of the cerebral hemispheres. Nor are the hemispheres highly exclusive in their specializations. For example, although the left hemisphere is somewhat more involved in language production functions than is the right hemisphere, when the left hemisphere is injured, especially if the injury occurs early in life, the right hemisphere frequently takes over left hemisphere functions—a striking example of an important characteristic of the human brain: *plasticity*.

Brain plasticity is also evident in patients who suffer motor and language problems after brain damage resulting from a stroke. These patients often recover much of their previous functioning as other parts of the brain take over (Lazar et al., 2010). In extreme cases, *hemispherectomies* may need to be performed on individuals with life-threatening diseases or disorders. If these procedures are performed on a young child, their chances of recovering and maintaining their previous functioning are actually quite good. *Plasticity* makes it all possible.

Recovery of lost brain function may also result from **neurogenesis**—the formation of new neurons. Although most neurogenesis occurs during the prenatal period, it also continues into adulthood (Reynolds & Weiss, 1992). The finding of adult neurogenesis contradicts a long-held belief that we are born with a set number of neurons, and that we gradually lose them as we live our lives.

Biology of Consciousness

We humans are conscious of our awareness, and we can communicate this consciousness to others—as you and I are doing at this very moment. We have a **mind** made possible by our brain.

Holistic education: A label for educational approaches that attempt to remedy what is seen as the failure of traditional education to educate the whole brain—especially the right hemisphere, which is speculatively linked with music, art, and emotion.

Neurogenesis: The active production of new neurons. Most prevalent during the prenatal period but also occurs in adulthood.

Mind: A term referring primarily to human consciousness. Often defined as originating from or resulting in processes of the brain associated with activities like thinking, imagining, and perceiving.

Consciousness

If a neurosurgeon were to crack open the thick bony casing that protects your brain, would he uncover your mind? Perhaps, although he would not really *see* it; all he would see is a grayish lump of matter. But he might well presume that your *mind,* your *self-awareness,* resides in complex patterns of billions of interconnections that have formed among the neurons in your brain. And he might speculate, as he looks at this chunk of tissue, that at this very moment chemical and electrical changes and impulses swarm through many of the intricate patterns of neural networks. And some of these impulses will be associated with thoughts and feelings that you are now having: They will define your own private state of **consciousness.**

Consciousness, like *mind,* is a term with many meanings. The two terms are very closely related. *Mind* refers primarily to activities of the brain such as thinking and feeling that result in a sense of self; *consciousness* refers to an awareness of self and the environment.

In effect, there are two broad states of consciousness: sleeping and waking. In addition, there are *altered* states of consciousness that might result from certain drugs or perhaps from hypnosis.

Consciousness: Awareness of one's personal identity. Self-awareness. Awareness of mental processes like thinking, imagining, and feeling.

Sleep

Sleep, as you well know, is the state that ensues when you close your eyes and eventually lose immediate contact with your environment. It ends when you regain awareness of external events. But that does not mean you are completely unaware of your physical environment as you sleep. As you lie precariously on your bed, a few feet above your floor, you have little fear of falling. You casually assume that your body has some control over its movements during sleep and that it is responsive to signals indicating dangerous proximity to the edge of your sleeping platform. And if your baby cries in the middle of the night, you instantly awaken—strong evidence that you are not totally unconscious while you sleep; part of your brain remains alert.

Circadian Rhythms

We seem to be biologically prepared to sleep at night and to be active during the day—a phenomenon labeled a **circadian rhythm.** Circadian rhythms are daily cycles in biological and behavioral processes such as sleeping, temperature change, and the production of **melatonin.** Melatonin is a hormone closely tied to the regulation of sleep. It increases in the evening and during the night and decreases during the day. Melatonin is sometimes used to treat sleep disorders (Zee, 2010).

Although our sleep–wake cycles seem to be closely tied to the rising and setting of the sun, our ability to generate our own cycles becomes evident when we find ourselves in latitudes that have more or fewer hours of daylight. Other things being equal, we continue to sleep for approximately the same length of time and at about the same time each day. Even when participants are kept in surroundings

Circadian rhythm: A biological/behavioral cycle that is approximately 1 day long. It describes our sleep/wake and temperature cycles.

Melatonin: A natural hormone closely tied to sleep/wake cycles. Also called the sleep hormone.

that provide no clues about day and night, circadian rhythms tend to adjust to periods very close to 24 hours (Gronfier, Wright, Kronauer, & Czeisler, 2007).

Stages of Sleep

When early sleep researchers observed sleeping subjects, they saw that sleep involves eye closure, reduction of muscle tension, reduction of heart rate, lowering of blood pressure, slowing of respiration rate, and a marked decrease in body temperature. They also noticed people, and animals, don't seem to sleep uniformly and consistently. Sometimes sleepers breathe rapidly, moving and fidgeting as they sleep; at other times, breathing is regular and there is little twitching and jerking. Dogs, too, jerk and fidget and moan and even bark as they sleep. Based on these changes, researchers concluded that there are distinct stages in depth of sleep (Neubauer, 2009).

More recently, EEG recordings and observations of eye movements below closed eyelids have led researchers to describe four stages of sleep based on changes in brain activity. These four stages are followed by a period of rapid eye movements (REM; Figure 2.11).

EEG recordings indicate that when awake, the brain typically produces small, fast waves called **beta waves** (13 to 30 cycles per second), but these become slower, changing to **alpha waves** (8 to 12 cycles per second) as the individual relaxes. During Stage 1 sleep, different waves called **theta waves** (4 to 7 cycles per second) become evident, interspersed with spikes of rapid brain activity. Perhaps 10 minutes later, if not awakened first, the sleeper enters Stage 2 sleep, also marked by bursts of rapid brain activity called *sleep spindles*. Note that Stages 1 and 2 are very brief.

Beta waves: Typical shallow and rapid brain waves of person who is awake, having a frequency of 13 to 30 cycles per minute.

Alpha waves: Slower, deeper brain waves characteristic of deep relaxation, having a frequency of 8 to 13 cycles per second.

Theta waves: Slow brain waves (4 to 7 per second) characteristic of the early stages of sleep.

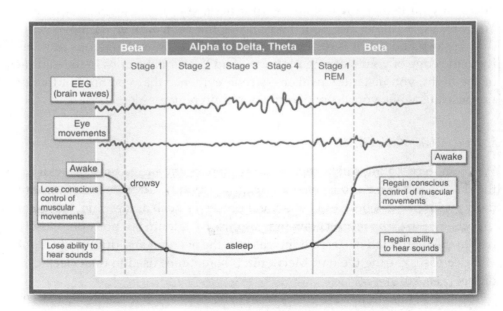

FIGURE 2.11   Physiological changes during sleep." Stage 1 REM sleep is sometimes labeled Stage 5 sleep, although brain waves during this stage are identical to those of Stage 1 sleep. The difference is that during this stage the rapid eye movements that typically accompany periods of dreaming are observed.

In Stage 3, body temperature and heart rate continue to decrease and **delta waves** (up to 4 cycles per second) begin to appear. These slow, deep waves are characteristic of Stage 4 sleep, often described as the *deepest* stage of sleep.

Interestingly, following Stage 4 sleep, a person will return to Stage 3, 2, and 1 (respectively) *before* entering the stage of **rapid eye movement sleep (REM sleep)**. It is during this stage that most of our dreaming takes place.

Between 20% and 25% of our normal sleep is spent in REM sleep, and the remaining 75% to 80% is spent in non-REM sleep (Stages 1–4).) There are some marked differences between these two sleep states, apart from their typical duration and the presence or absence of rapid eye movements. During REM sleep, physiological functions are very similar to those expected in a normal, awake person (hence this stage of sleep is often labeled **paradoxical sleep**): Heart rate ranges between 45 and 100 beats per minute, breathing is irregular, and EEG patterns are similar to those seen in quiet resting states with the eyes closed (alpha). However, voluntary muscle groups are typically in a state of paralysis during REM sleep. There is speculation this muscular paralysis is meant to keep the body from acting out violent dreams and possibly hurting itself or others.

In adults, REM sleep occurs fairly regularly at approximately 90-minute intervals and lasts for 25 minutes or more. It does not begin for 30 or more minutes following onset of sleep. If a person is awakened from non-REM sleep and kept awake for a few minutes, REM sleep will not begin for at least 30 minutes, even if the person had been in non-REM sleep for the last hour or more (Figure 2.12). Thus, it is possible to deprive subjects of REM sleep simply by waking them whenever rapid eye movements begin. Interestingly, if one is deprived of REM sleep,

Delta waves: Very slow brain waves (frequency of up to 4 per second) characteristic of deep sleep.

Rapid eye movement (REM) sleep: Sometimes referred to as the Stage 5 of sleep, the stage during which most of our dreaming occurs.

Paradoxical sleep: Another label for REM sleep, so called because during this stage of sleep physiological functions such as heart and respiration rate are very similar to those of a waking state.

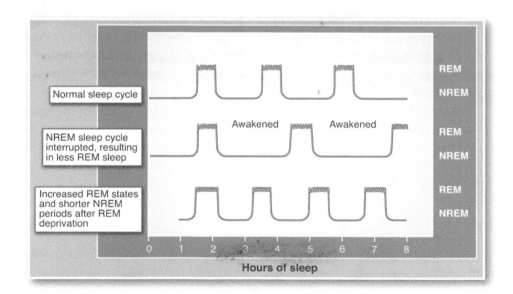

FIGURE 2.12   Cycles of REM/non-REM sleep." During a normal sleep cycle, REM sleep occurs fairly regularly at about 90-minute intervals and lasts for 25 minutes or more. If we are awakened from non-REM sleep, REM sleep will not begin for 30 minutes or more after the onset of sleep. If we are awakened during REM sleep (as in a dream-recording experiment), the result is shorter non-REM periods between REM states during the subsequent night.

they will advance more quickly into REM stage sleep the next time they fall asleep compared to someone not deprived of REM. Similarly, it is possible to deprive subjects of non-REM sleep. One of the results of this procedure is that subjects who are deprived of one type of sleep tend to make up for it during subsequent nights. A second effect of REM or non-REM deprivation is that subjects who are allowed only one type of sleep frequently feel and function as if they had not slept at all. It seems clear that we have a need for both types of sleep and that neither is more restful than the other in spite of the apparently greater reduction in rate of physiological functioning during non-REM sleep.

Why We Sleep

We still don't know for sure why we must sleep (*The Science of Sleep*, 2010). What we do know is that following prolonged periods of sleep deprivation our behavior becomes very bizarre, we suffer from hallucinations, our ability to respond appropriately to the environment is severely impeded, and we might eventually experience serious health problems, the most severe of which is death (Buysse, Strollo, Black, Zee, & Winkelman, 2008). No experiments have been conducted with human subjects that directly substantiate this last bit of speculation, although sleep deprivation of animals sometimes leads to their deaths (Newman, Paletz, Obermeyer, & Benca, 2009).

There are a number of theoretical explanations for sleep. One theory maintains it is necessary to repair physiological damage and maintain the body and mind in good working order. Evolutionary theory speculates sleep is an evolved mechanism, the usefulness of which lies in the fact that hidden sleeping animals are less likely to be preyed upon, particularly if their sleep cycles correspond with predation cycles. It also appears reasonable to suppose sleep might have evolved as a system for conserving energy (a hibernating bear may come to mind). Some researchers also suggest a select few stages of sleep, especially REM sleep, are important for consolidating memories and perhaps for resting important neural systems.

Research suggests that sleeping gives resting neurons the opportunity to repair the damage done to them throughout the day. Furthermore, there is evidence to suggest that sleep gives the body the opportunity to get rid of any damaged and irreparable the neurons that are beyond repair (Gilestro et al., 2009; Siegel, 2009; Vyazovskiy et al., 2008).

Dreams

Contrary to some beliefs, everybody dreams, but not everyone remembers dreams with equal clarity. In fact, most people remember only a small portion of what they dream, with women remembering their dreams more often than men (Schredl, 2010). Nor, as is popularly believed, and stated in Christopher Nolan's 2010 film, *Inception*, is a dream a condensed version of real-time events. Indications are that the amount of time that might have elapsed had dream events been real is very similar to the amount of time during which the dream occurred. Evidence that this is so is derived from tracings of eye movements, from verbalizations, or from movements corresponding to an event in a dream. Interestingly, in many cases, eye movements during dreams appear to actually scan dream objects. It is as though dreamers are actually looking at the dream scene or at the object for which they're reaching (Leclair-Visonneau, Oudiette, Gaymard, Leu-Semenescu, & Arnulf, 2010).

WHY WE DREAM

Psychologists are not certain why we dream. Nor can we easily investigate the effects of not dreaming because doing so requires the interruption of sleep and any observed effect could as well be due to sleep deprivation as to dream deprivation. Still, we have a number of dream theories.

1. *Dreams as symbols for disguised impulses.* Perhaps the best-known dream theory is one proposed by Sigmund Freud—sadly, a theory generally unsupported by any scientific research. Freud believed dreams represent disguised manifestations of unconscious impulses. He thought most of these impulses are linked to sexual desires, aggression, or other socially taboo inclinations. Hence they're disguised, even in dreams, as a form of self-protection or, more precisely, as a form of sleep protection. Were they not disguised, we would continually awaken horrified at our vile and base cravings. If the father we want to murder appears in a dream as a spider, we can step on that creature with no fear of self-reprisal. Only Freud and other gifted psychoanalysts would be expected to uncover what the spider represents.

2. *The threat-simulation theory of dreams.* Another dream theory suggests our dreams provide us with an opportunity to practice responding to threats. This might be why, as Revonsuo (2000) suggests, so many of our dreams and nightmares have to do with chasing or being chased. Revonsuo's *Threat Simulation Theory* argues that, even though our legs and arms might not be moving while we dream, we might still be practicing a variety of "fight and flight" responses. In support of this theory, there is evidence suggesting when we dream our brains often fire in ways highly similar to the way they might fire if we were awake and actually threatened.

3. *Dreams as cognitive tools.* There is also the possibility that dreaming may have a beneficial effect on cognitive functioning and attention (Cartwright, 2010). This is suggested by studies of partial and temporary dream deprivation, accomplished by waking individuals at the onset of REM periods. In the absence of dreams, explains Cartwright, the individual finds it difficult to attend to reality upon awakening.

Additional evidence that dreams might provide a cognitive benefit is found in the observation that when rats are placed in mazes during the day, their patterns of brain activity that night closely parallel their brain activity while they were in the maze (Ego-Stengel & Wilson, 2010). These authors suggest dreams provide us with an opportunity to sort our memories into those worth remembering and those we can afford to forget.

4. *Dreams as therapy.* Another current dream theory, somewhat reminiscent of Freud's, suggests that dreams are a form of therapy. Hartmann (2007) notes

dreams are often laden with emotion. As such, they provide an opportunity to confront difficult and surprising emotions and perhaps learn how to deal with them. Dreams allow us to think through our emotions.

In this connection, Cartwright (2010) notes the various dreams collected from a single individual on the same night typically present such a coherent pattern that it is impossible to believe dreams represent random happenings. She argues dreams may well have a therapeutic purpose, since they often appear to be directed toward the resolution of conflict-laden situations.

And, of course, there are those who believe dreams serve none of these functions—that they are simply the result of random brain activity, or what is referred to as *cortical noise*.

Hypnosis

Sleep—and the dreams that might then come—are one state of consciousness; being awake is the other. Does hypnosis represent a third, altered type of consciousness?

The answer is: perhaps. However, the final verdict is not yet in. We are not quite certain about **hypnosis**—not even certain whether or not we should investigate it: There has long been a faint odor of mysticism, magic, and pseudoscience about hypnosis. And, as scientists, we often fear and distrust such mysterious phenomena.

Hypnosis: A state characterized by heightened suggestibility (willingness to do and to believe what is suggested by the hypnotist).

Some Facts

Contrary to some popular misconceptions, hypnosis does not involve some powerful personality putting subjects into a state where, zombie-like, they have to obey. As defined by the American Psychological Association, hypnosis is a procedure in which subjects are given suggestions for "imaginative experiences" in which one person (the subject) is guided by another (the hypnotist) to respond to suggestions for changes in subjective experience, alterations in perception, sensation, emotion, thought or behavior" (*The Official Division 30 Definition and Description of Hypnosis*, 2010).

Basically, what happens in hypnosis is this: The hypnotist uses some form of what is termed *hypnotic induction* to heighten the **suggestibility** of the subject (Gafner, 2010). A common hypnotic induction technique, the *eye-fixation method*, uses an object to focus the subject's attention while the hypnotist speaks. Pocket watches were used extensively in 19th-century France and Germany and are often shown in graphic portrayals of hypnotists plying their trades. Of course, it is not an object that induces hypnosis, but the hypnotist's words. A very common induction technique does not ask subjects to fix their gaze on an object; it simply uses verbal directions to increase the subject's relaxation and suggestibility.

Suggestibility: A characteristic of a hypnotic state wherein subjects become exceedingly ready to believe whatever is suggested by the hypnotist and willing to perform whatever activities are asked of them.

A rather surprising discovery is that, in terms of physiological functioning, a hypnotic state is much closer to a waking state than to a sleep state. EEG waves are typically alpha, and respiration and heart rates may range from deep relaxation to strenuous physical activity. The single most striking feature of a hypnotic state is the willingness of subjects to do what is asked and the matter-of-factness that accompanies even the most bizarre behaviors requested of them.

Is Hypnosis a Different State of Consciousness?

Whether hypnosis is a different mental state or whether it simply involves imaginative role-playing remains uncertain and controversial (Revonsuo, Kallio, & Sikka, 2009). Much of the research examining this question has compared the performance of hypnotized subjects with that of others pretending to be hypnotized. Those who believe hypnosis represents a different state of consciousness try to find differences between the psychological processes of hypnotized and nonhypnotized persons; those who think hypnosis involves imaginative role-playing look for similarities.

Among other things, this research has sometimes found that *simulators* (participants who fake being hypnotized in hypnotism research studies) are often capable of many of the same impressive feats and deceptions as are hypnotized subjects, including total-body catalepsy (rigidity), apparent amnesia, age regression, hallucinations, and the ability to tolerate pain (anesthesia; Orne, 2009). These findings would seem to support the notion that hypnosis does not represent an altered state of consciousness.

Other psychologists believe that hypnosis can be partially explained as a social phenomenon. Specifically speaking, hypnotized subjects speak and behave as a good hypnotizable subject *ought* to behave. Furthermore, the authoritative presence of the hypnotist is believed to play an important role in influencing the behavior of the subject under hypnosis.

Nonetheless, there are interesting studies indicating that brain activity changes during hypnosis (Naish, 2010); simulators are not ordinarily able to alter their brain activity deliberately to please an investigator. For example, when hypnotized subjects are instructed to imagine black-and-white objects being brilliantly colored, activity in the part of the brain associated with color vision increases; this is not the case for nonhypnotized participants asked to imagine the same thing (Oakley & Halligan, 2010).

Applications of Hypnosis

There is evidence the use of hypnosis can be effective for a variety of medical procedures, including childbirth and even surgery. It has also been used successfully in dentistry (Brown, 2009).

A variety of psychotherapies also make use of hypnosis (Barber & Westland, 2011). For example, Almas and Landmark (2010) reviewed a large number of studies in which the use of hypnosis was effective in treating sexual problems.

Hypnosis has also been used in courtrooms in an attempt to help witnesses, and sometimes victims, recall details of a crime. However, because it is difficult to establish the veracity of what hypnotized individuals appear to remember, the use of hypnosis in court remains highly controversial (Lynn, Boycheva, Deming, Lilienfeld, & Hallquist, 2009).

The results of research that has attempted to determine whether hypnosis can be beneficial in the teaching–learning process remain somewhat uncertain. Some studies claim to have demonstrated that learning, motivation, and retention can sometimes be improved as a result of posthypnotic suggestion (Vernon, 2009). But other studies have failed to find differences between experimental groups and control groups, particularly when control groups are highly motivated. The most valid conclusion to be derived from a large number of related studies appears to be that hypnosis can be very effective in increasing motivation, but it does not increase intelligence or memory. There is also virtually no evidence it has any harmful effects, other than any indirect harm that may arise as a result of believing in hypnosis' sometimes grandiose and false claims of effectiveness.

Summary

Our species, *Homo sapien*, has evolved with certain physical limitations but with a remarkable brain and nervous system. The basic unit of our nervous system is the neuron. Neurons, through chemical and electrical activity, compose our communication systems, the intricate arrangements of which define our very essence.

The brain and spinal cord make up the central nervous system; the *peripheral* system includes the *somatic* system (concerned with bodily sensations) and the *autonomic* system (the *sympathetic* and *parasympathetic* systems concerned with unconscious physiological responses). The brain coordinates activity in these diverse systems. Its major divisions are the hindbrain (the *medulla, pons,* and *cerebellum,* involved in balance and locomotion, respiration, sleep, and arousal), the midbrain (the *reticular formation,* involved in arousal and motivation), and the forebrain (the *hypothalamus,* concerned with temperature regulation and circadian rhythms; the *thalamus,* a relay center; the *limbic system,* implicated in emotions; and the *cerebrum,* divided into the four cerebral lobes, which include the *visual* and *auditory cortices* and the *association areas of the brain*). The *brain stem* includes structures of both the hindbrain and the midbrain.

Biology prepares the human animal to learn and do certain things easily (learning languages; learning taste aversions) but makes other behaviors difficult (restraining our cravings for fat and sugar). Our consciousness seems to reside in patterns of activity in our brains. These patterns can change drastically while an organism is asleep or under hypnosis.

Sleep, of which there are two states, REM sleep (during which we do most of our dreaming) and non-REM sleep, is not a completely *unconscious* state. Stages of sleep are distinguishable by the nature of accompanying brain waves, ranging from small fast *beta* waves when awake, through *alpha, theta,* and *delta* waves (progressively slower and deeper). We don't know clearly why we sleep or why we dream, but we do know that deprivation has negative consequences.

Hypnosis is a procedure in which subjects are given suggestions for "imaginative experiences" that lead to "alterations in perception, sensation, emotion, thought, or behavior." Its hallmark is the desire of participants to obey the hypnotist's instructions. It is not clear whether hypnosis represents a different state of consciousness, but it has important implications in medicine and psychotherapy.

© Andresr, 2014. Used under license from Shutterstock, Inc.

CHAPTER THREE

SENSATION AND PERCEPTION

Dr. J. April Park and Dr. Trey Hill
Fort Hays State University

LEARNING OBJECTIVES

- Understand the differences between sensation and perception
- Explain the process from sensation to perception for each of the senses
- Identify the sensory receptors for each sense
- Understand the differences between top-down and bottom-up processing
- Explain how humans use different cues to infer visual depth
- Identify how perceptual illusions can tell us something about how perception works

The Basics of Sensation and Perception

Imagine it is your first day of general psychology. Upon arrival for class, you turn to the student to your right and exchange introductions. His name is Scott. After the introductions, your professor walks into class and begins lecturing. She lectures about the history of psychology and the wonderful things we know about the human mind. Accompanying the lecture are PowerPoint slides displayed on a projection screen at the front of the class. During the lecture you hang on your professor's every word, captivated by this newfound knowledge that psychological scientists have been discovering fascinating things for 150 years. Intermittently during the lecture, you jot down notes on a yellow legal pad. After about one hour the lecture concludes and you break for the day. As you sit in a cozy chair in the Memorial Union, you are amazed at the complexity of the human mind. However, as you will learn in this chapter, perhaps one of the most amazing aspects of human psychology is the

© wavebreakmedia, 2014. Used under license from Shutterstock, Inc.

intricate process known as *sensation and perception*, which constructs a seamless experience of reality, thus transforming a vastly large magnitude of physical energy from the environment (e.g., light waves, sound waves) into the perception of a normal college event (e.g., an opening-day lecture).

Sensation vs. Perception

The opening story describes an intricate process involving several processes. Therefore, we need to first break it down into smaller processes. Sensation and perception are these smaller processes. So, before describing how the human brain takes light and sound waves and constructs a seamless experience—as it does several hours each day—we must first discuss the differences between sensation and perception.

Sensation is best defined as the detection of some physical stimulus in the environment by one of your sensory organs. Do not be "thrown off" by the use of the word "stimulus." A stimulus is simply a scientific term for anything that acts on your own behavior or mental processes. A stimulus can be a shape on a computer screen, the smell of pizza, or even the words on the page you are currently reading. Stimuli (the plural of stimulus) lead to changes in your behavior (also called responses, as you will also learn in this book).

Perception, on the other hand, is your brain *making sense* of that physical stimulus from the world by organizing the stimulus into a representation of something useful. For example, the sensations of certain wavelengths of light, and a certain combination of smells may lead to the perception of an apple.

Sensation and perception are both important for what you might consider a normal, everyday experience, similar to the general psychology lecture described at the beginning of this chapter. Perception is not possible without sensation because the machinery used to gather physical stimuli from the environment is a crucial requirement. Imagine trying to estimate how much rain your hometown received without having a rain gauge. You could guess about the amount of rainfall, but you would probably not be very accurate. Similarly, you cannot perceive anything without first being able to register the environmental stimulus through sensation.

A great real-world example of this is the controversial topic of extrasensory perception, otherwise known as ESP. Extrasensory perception is the alleged ability to perceive something through the mind alone, but without reception of physical stimuli through any of the known senses. A classic example of ESP in practice includes psychics, whose claims to fame are centered on the ability to "know" things about a person that seem "unknowable." Professional skeptics, such as James Randi, have made careers out of debunking claims of ESP.[1] There is no known sense organ or mechanism that could pick up on someone else's thoughts. Thus, until evidence suggests otherwise, ESP is not scientifically supported (Moulton & Kosslyn, 2008).

Sensation: The detection of physical stimuli in the environment such as light waves, sound waves, pressure, or chemical molecules.

Perception: The detailed process of interpreting and making sense of a combination of sensations.

© BMJ, 2014. Used under license from Shutterstock, Inc.

---

[1] James Randi, or "The Amazing Randi" as he was known on stage, is a former illusionist now turned skeptic. Randi's foundation (http://www.randi.org/site/) is devoted to debunking pseudoscience such as ESP.

Once we have a way of detecting the physical stimuli from the environment (sensation), we will need a way to interpret those stimuli. For instance, even with a rain gauge, you will need some way to make sense of what a certain amount of water in a cylinder actually means. This illustrates the problem of sensation *without* perception. Although sensation is necessary, it is not by itself sufficient to account for a normal day's experiences.

The Process

To this point we have discussed the importance of both sensation and perception. However, getting from sensation to perception is also a fascinating and important step. The physical energy (stimulus) must be modified into a form the brain can use. This modification process is called **transduction**. Try this thought experiment: Below is the chemical structure for theobromine, a chemical contained in chocolate. What is appealing about the picture? If you are like most people, your answer is probably "nothing." There is nothing appealing about the chemical structure for theobromine.

Transduction: The process of converting a physical stimulus into a meaningful and useful neural signal capable of being interpreted by the brain.

However, when consumed in combination with other chemicals included in chocolate, your sensory receptors for taste analyze this exact chemical structure. So, how is it that a seemingly arbitrary chemical structure can result in such a pleasant experience as eating a piece of your favorite chocolate? The answer to this question is where transduction fits. Transduction changes the physical stimulus of chocolate—your taste buds recognizing that you are eating a sugary, high-calorie item—into a pleasurable experience you would very much like to repeat (the perception).

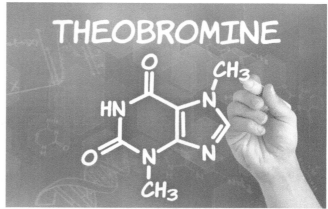

© Zerbor, 2014. Used under license from Shutterstock, Inc.

FIGURE 3.1 The process of sensation to perception.

Methods

Now that you know something about sensation and perception, we should clarify how modern psychological scientists study sensation and perception in participants. There are two basic methods of studying the sensation and perception of individuals, both involving measuring sensation's limits otherwise known as thresholds. Those methods are absolute threshold and difference threshold.

A person's **absolute threshold** is measured by taking the smallest amount of a stimulus and gradually increasing its strength until a person correctly guesses the stimulus's presence 50% of the time. For example, imagine we are measuring

Absolute threshold: A method used to study the limits of sensation; the smallest amount of a physical stimulus that can be correctly detected 50% of the time.

someone's absolute threshold for vision. As psychologists, we would begin by presenting the faintest possible light to a participant. At first the participant will probably not perceive the light; it is below the person's threshold. However, the psychologist will gradually increase the intensity of the light until the person correctly indicates that the light is present.

This minimum amount of a stimulus's intensity that can be detected is known as the absolute threshold. Each of the senses we discuss in subsequent sections of this chapter has its own absolute threshold, which is directly related to our own sensitivity to different types of physical stimuli in the environment; for instance, human olfaction is far less sensitive than that of canines, partly due to a deterioration in olfaction's relative importance during the course of human evolution (Gilad, Wiebe, Przeworski, Lancet, & Pääbo, 2004).

Difference threshold: A method used to study the sensitivity of sensation; the smallest difference between two stimuli that can be correctly detected 50% of the time; this is also called the just-noticeable difference.

A **difference threshold** is estimated by comparing the intensity of two stimuli, and gradually increasing the difference between their intensities until a difference can be detected by the person. For instance, imagine holding two pieces of fruit of approximately the same weight. You will probably not be able to tell a difference in their weights because of the similarity. However, if we begin increasing the weight of one piece of fruit, the difference will also increase. Due to this increased difference between the two pieces of fruit, there will be a point at which you can accurately detect the difference. This point is called the difference threshold, also known as the just noticeable difference (JND).

© VeryUlissa, 2014. Used under license from Shutterstock, Inc.

A fascinating aspect of the difference threshold is that it is not fixed, but relative. For example, if a researcher places a 10-pound weight in your left hand and a 5-pound weight in your right hand, you will probably be able to accurately indicate there is a difference in weight. However, if we put 50 pounds in your left hand and 45 pounds in your right hand, you will have a much more difficult task of accurately indicating the difference in weight. Why would this happen? The difference in both examples is 5 pounds. **Weber's law—** derived by Ernst Weber—suggests the difference threshold between

Weber's law: A principle in sensation that suggests that the size of the difference threshold is relative to the strength of the original stimulus.

two stimuli is relative to the size of the original stimulus. In the weight example described previously, Weber's law would predict that the 5 pound difference is easier to detect in the first example because 5 pounds is 50% of the weight in your left hand as opposed to being only 10% of the weight in your left hand when carrying 50 pounds. Give this a try the next time you are at the gym!

Adaptation

Sensory adaption: A decline in a sensation's sensitivity resulting from the presence of a constant stimulus.

The sensitivity of sensory receptors can also be affected by the duration of a stimulus. For example, imagine walking across campus to reach a class on a sunny day. While walking, you have been in constant sunlight for the duration of a few minutes. When you arrive to class a few minutes late, the room appears pitch black and you stumble over backpacks and empty chairs before you find your seat. After sitting in class a few minutes, everything seems to be more visible. You even smile as another tardy student stumbles to his or her seat. This example illustrates something called **sensory adaptation**. Our sensory receptors become less sensitive when exposed to a constant stimulus for a certain amount of time. For example, our sensory receptors for vision become less sensitive after prolonged, constant exposure to sunlight. When the sunlight is removed by walking into a dark classroom, our sensory receptors are much less sensitive to the minimal amount of light, thus making the room appear very dark.

The Senses

Vision

Our ability to "accurately" see the world around us is perhaps one of the most important abilities humans possess; the word *accurately* is placed in quotes for reasons you will discover later in this chapter when we discuss the topic of perception.

When Scott looked at the PowerPoint presentation in class in the opening story, he was using his sensation of vision to register the information on the screen. This sensation is also important in your own life as you currently try to read this paragraph. As with all types of sensation, vision requires a stimulus from the environment. The stimulus involved in human vision is physical energy in the form of light waves.

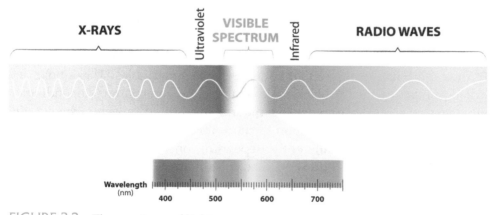

FIGURE 3.2 The spectrum of light.

© Designua, 2014. Used under license from Shutterstock, Inc.

Light Waves

Light, such as a lamp or rays from the sun, is actually composed of waves. These waves are analogous to waves in an ocean and may have a similar pattern if we view them from a side profile. Waves of light can be very different, and these differences correspond to our perceptions of different colors and their intensity. Also, humans are only capable of registering a certain amount of the possible spectrum of light. Going back to the rain gauge metaphor, the rain gauge is wonderful at catching rain. However, other forms of precipitation may not be as accurately registered. For example, thick snow may not be as easily measured in a narrow rain gauge, and hail may not fit into the opening at the top of the rain gauge. Of course, this does not mean heavy snow and hail are nonexistent in the world. We know from experience those forms of precipitation occur. Similarly, there are many forms of visible light (e.g., ultraviolet, infrared) that cannot be sensed by the human eye, but may be sensed by other species (e.g., bees, snakes).

© Gladskikh Tatiana, 2014. Used under license from Shutterstock, Inc.

The wavelength of a light wave—the distance from peak to peak—is the physical property of the light wave stimulus that we would perceive as color. Red has a longer wavelength than blue. The amplitude of a light wave—the vertical distance from peak to trough (the low point)—is the physical property of a light wave that corresponds to the brightness, or intensity, of a color; "hot" pink's amplitude is much larger than that of salmon, but the two may have similar wavelengths.

The particular wavelength of light is dictated by the object that the light is bouncing off; a wavelength of light associated with the perception of red is reflected off an apple and a fire truck.

From the World to the Eye

Light waves bounce off objects in the physical world and enter our mental world through small holes at the front of the eyes. The colorful area of the eye that is documented on your driver's license is called the iris, and it is the fibrous muscular structure that contains these small holes. These holes are called pupils, and are the black circles that expand and contract depending on whether you are inside or outside in the sun. In addition, law enforcement officers sometimes use pupil dilation to check for consumption of drugs; pupils will dilate or constrict differently depending on the specific type of drug induced (Richman, McAndrew, Decker, & Mullaney, 2004).

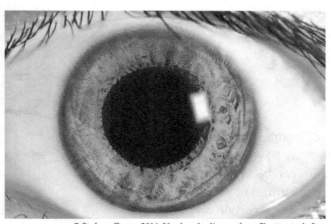

© Stefano Garau, 2014. Used under license from Shutterstock, Inc.

Keep in mind that these black circles are not structures at all. In fact, they are literally just holes in the structure of your eye, but they fall directly behind a covering called the cornea. The pupils appear black because there is no reflected light inside of the eye.

Light waves travel through the opening in the front of the eye (the pupil) and are processed on a structure at the back of the eye. This structure is crucial for human vision. Its name: the retina. As you learned earlier in this chapter, each of the senses requires a specific type of sensory receptor, designed to process a specific type of physical stimulus from the environment. The sensory receptor for vision is called a **photoreceptor** and many of these photoreceptors rest on the structure called the **retina**.

Rods and Cones

The photoreceptors are not created equal, however. Different types of photoreceptors may process light waves in different ways and with different clarity. There are two basic types of photoreceptors in the human eye: rods and cones. **Rods** are rod shaped and better at processing dim light, which may be experienced at dusk or at night. The acuity—or HD-ness—of rod-based vision is fairly low, though. If we could somehow watch a movie made entirely with rods it would be blurry and black and white. This does not mean that rods are useless. Rods require less light to function, and therefore they are wonderful assets when we are trying to see something (a tiger, perhaps) in the failing light at the end of the day.

Cones are cone shaped and are specialized to process colorful images in very high detail. Keep in mind that there is a tradeoff, though. Cones also require substantial light in order to properly work. For example, do you find it difficult to determine the colors of objects and read fine print in a dimly lit classroom? If so, it is because your cones—which are necessary for achieving color vision and high acuity—require large amounts of light in order to properly function.

Photoreceptor: A type of sensory receptor specifically for vision, which is located on the retina at the back of the eye.

Retina: A light-sensitive membrane at the back of the eye that contains the sensory receptors for vision.

Rods: A specific group of photoreceptors that are specialized to process dim light and are useful for night vision and peripheral vision.

Cones: A specific group of photoreceptors that are specialized to process color and are useful for daylight vision and high visual acuity.

Human Eye Anatomy

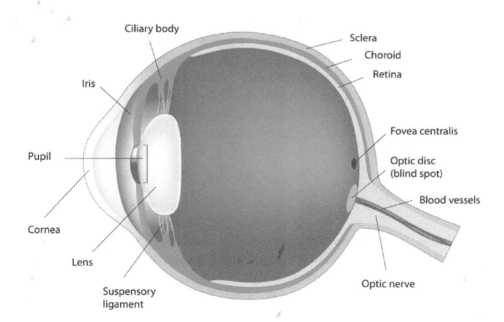

FIGURE 3.3   Diagram of the human eye.
© Alila Medical Media, 2014. Used under license from Shutterstock, Inc.

Fovea: An area at the center of the retina that contains the highest density of cones; visual acuity is highest in this region.

Optic nerve: A large bundle of axons that leave the back of the eye and carries visual information to the visual cortex of the brain.

Blind spot: A gap in the retina due to the exit of the optic nerve where no photoreceptors are located; this causes a blind spot in the visual field during sensation.

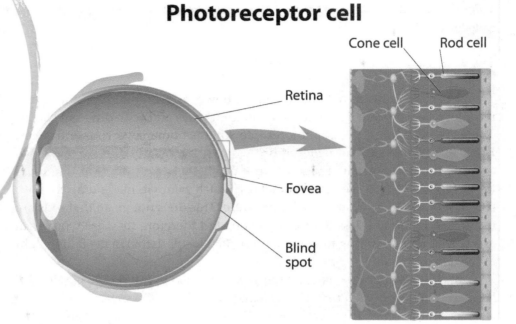

FIGURE 3.4   Photoreceptor cells in retina of human eye.
© Designua, 2014. Used under license from Shutterstock, Inc.

Cones and rods are also distributed on the surface of the retina in very different ways. Suppose we took the retina out of the eye and flattened it on a table. We could then look at the number of cones and rods in different locations on the retina. What we would find is that cones are mostly located in the **fovea**, an area on the retina associated with the center of vision. When we look at an object, the center of that object is located in the fovea on our retina. The number of cones significantly decreases as we move from the fovea toward the edges of the retina. These edges of the retina contain far more rods than cones.

© victorass, 2014. Used under license from Shutterstock, Inc.

From the Eye to the Brain

There is also an interesting quirk about the retina that is a result of the specific way the human eye is constructed. Notice in the figure that there is a hole in the retina where the **optic nerve** must exit the inside of the eye. In this location there are zero rods *or* cones. Therefore, the point at which the optic nerve leaves the eye—the **blind spot**—is quite literally not sensitive to light waves because there are no photoreceptors on that part of the retina. However, amazingly, you do not walk around with the perception of blind spots in your visual field. Instead, neighboring photoreceptors help fill in the empty areas in perception. To illustrate the blind spot, close your left eye and stare at the star in Figure 3.5. Gradually move forward or backward and you will notice something amazing. The red circle to the right will seem to disappear! This is because that image has moved into the blind spot in your right eye.

FIGURE 3.5 Blind spot example.

After leaving the eye, the optic nerves meet in the brain at a point called the **optic chiasm**. Here, the optic nerve from each eye splits into two smaller bundles of axons—one for the right and left visual fields of each eye—and is sent to different regions of the brain for higher-order perception.

Optic chiasm: The point in the brain at which the optic nerves from each eye meet and partly cross over to the other side of the brain.

Audition (Hearing)

Hearing, or audition, is an important sensation used in creating the perceptual experience we call reality. While sitting through a college lecture, most people are able to discern the different sounds being projected from the professor and interpret them as words, sentences, and coherent thoughts. However, the initial process of detecting, amplifying, and processing sound is what we must first discuss.

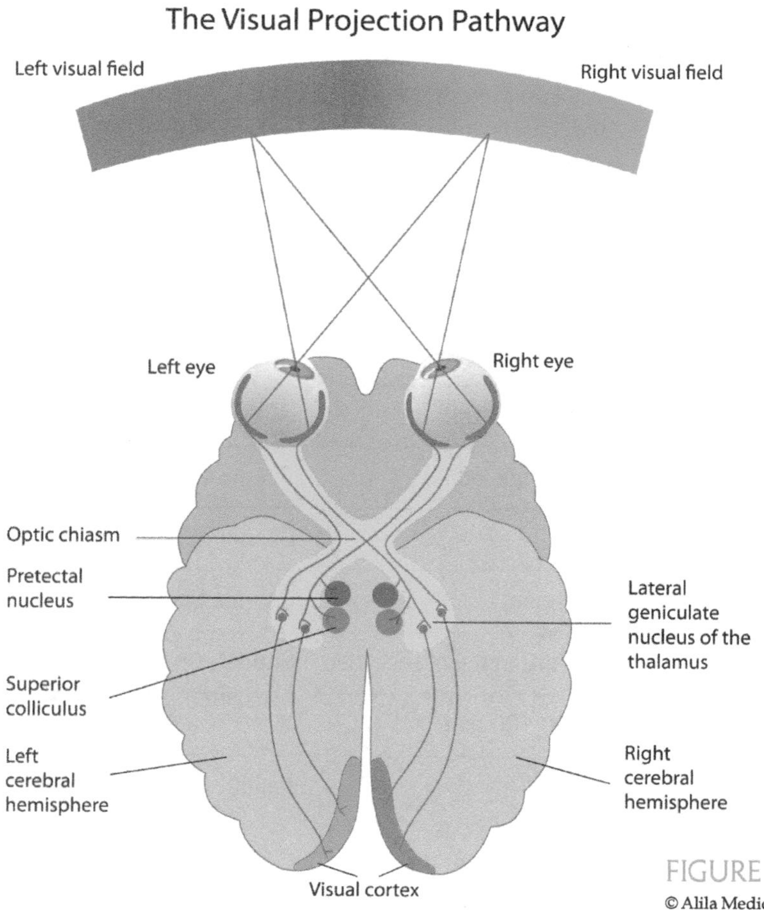

The Visual Projection Pathway

Left visual field

Right visual field

Left eye

Right eye

Optic chiasm

Pretectal nucleus

Superior colliculus

Left cerebral hemisphere

Lateral geniculate nucleus of the thalamus

Right cerebral hemisphere

Visual cortex

FIGURE 3.6 The visual projection pathway.

© Alila Medical Media, 2014. Used under license from Shutterstock, Inc.

Sound Waves

Decibel: The scientific unit of measurement for loudness.

Similar to vision, the physical stimulus for audition comes in the form of a wave: a sound wave. Sound waves are produced by vibrating molecules in the air or water. The vibrating molecules are the result of something else in the environment vibrating at a certain frequency (e.g., a guitar string, vocal chords).

The properties of sound waves dictate our perceptions of sounds in the environment. Properties of waves we have already discussed—wavelength and amplitude—can be used to describe certain qualities of sound. Amplitude for sound waves corresponds to the perception of loudness, with higher amplitudes of sound waves indicating louder noises. Wavelength in sound waves corresponds to pitch, the relative highness or lowness of a sound. So, a tug boat horn may have a high amplitude value but a low wavelength value. The sound of fingernails softly being raked across a chalkboard may have a low amplitude value but a high wavelength value.

The scientific measurement used to describe the loudness of a particular sound is called a **decibel**. The decibel level is set to have a minimum of 0, which is the lowest sound audible to the human ear. You can also think of the 0 decibel level as the absolute threshold for audition. Decibel levels are also able to provide information about the relative safety of certain amounts of loudness. Some sounds, such as those normally experienced during a conversation, are perfectly safe even after prolonged exposure. Other decibel levels are dangerous to the structures in the ear involved in sensing sound. For example, fans of the National Football League's Seattle Seahawks set the world record for decibel level at a sporting event in 2013 by collectively creating a sound wave registering at 137.6 decibels, a level just below that of a jet engine. This level of loudness would be dangerous even for short durations.

DECIBALS	EVENT	DANGER
0	Lowest audible sound	
30	Whispering in a library	
65	Normal conversation	
85	City traffic inside a car	Danger with prolonged exposure
105	Lawnmover	Danger after 2 hours of exposure
125	Balloon popping	Sounds become painful
137	Loudest sporting event recorded	Short-term exposure may cause permanent hearing loss
140	Jet engine at 100 feet	
160	Shotgun blast	Instant perforation of eardrum

FIGURE 3.7   Various events and their associated levels of loudness.

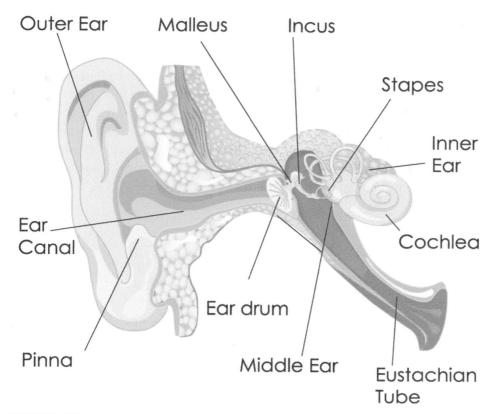

FIGURE 3.8   Diagram of the human ear.
© snapgalleria, 2014. Used under license from Shutterstock, Inc.

From the World to the Ear

Have you ever wondered why we have these "satellite dishes" on each side of our head? Part of the answer to that question involves the ability of the **pinna**, what we normally just refer to as "ears," to collect sound waves from the environment. After collecting these sound waves, the outer ear funnels them down through the ear canal right up to the **eardrum**. Similar to a drum used to make music, the eardrum is a thin membrane stretching over the inside of the ear canal. As sound waves come into contact with the eardrum, the eardrum vibrates at the same frequency as the sound waves in the ear canal. Occasionally, either due to infection, or to loud noises, the eardrum may rupture. This is typically a painful experience, but the outlook is normally very good; ruptured eardrums usually heal within only a few months, and any hearing loss due to the rupture is most often short-lived.

Pinna: The outer funnel-shaped structure of the ear; normally, this is what people refer to as their ear.

Eardrum: The thin membrane at the end of the ear canal that vibrates at a specific frequency when bombarded by sound waves.

Sound waves are then transferred from the eardrum to three tiny bones that constitute the middle ear. The tiny bones are the malleus (hammer), incus (anvil), and stapes (stirrup). Together, the function of these tiny bones is to amplify the sound waves coming into contact with the eardrum, and to send the amplified sound waves to the inner ear for processing.

The middle ear sends sound waves to the inner ear through a tiny structure similar to the eardrum. This structure is called the oval window and is the "front gate" to the **cochlea**. The cochlea—derived from the Greek word for snail—is the

Cochlea: The spiral structure in the inner ear that contains both fluid and the basilar membrane; the latter houses sensory receptors for audition.

location where transduction of sound waves finally begins to occur. The cochlea is essentially a fluid-filled tube that is coiled inside the inner ear. As amplified sound waves travel through the fluid in the cochlea, a structure called the basilar membrane begins to ripple as well. Attached to the basilar membrane are the sensory receptors for sound. These sensory receptors are called **hair cells**. As the basilar membrane bends due to sound waves, so too do the hair cells. As these hair cells bend with the sound waves, the physical energy is transduced into neural impulses sent from the auditory nerve to the appropriate parts of the brain for higher-order processing. Thus, the stimuli (sound waves) are finally converted to information the brain can use through the process of transduction in the cochlea.

Hair cells: Thin, hair-like structures that are the sensory receptors for audition; these are located on the basilar membrane inside the cochlea.

Olfaction (Smelling)

If you have ever had the privilege of taking a college course at 10:30 A.M., you have probably experienced a feeling of hunger in the minutes prior to the end of class. You may sprint to student union to get lunch, but as you arrive you may be overwhelmed by the vast number of smells coming from every direction. How this process works is the focus of our next section.

As you know by this point in the chapter, every sense must detect a specific physical stimulus from the environment. For vision and audition, this physical stimulus came in the form of a wave of physical energy. For olfaction, the stimulus comes in the form of chemical molecules in the air, which are released by the substance we are smelling (e.g., chemical molecules released by a bar of chocolate).

These chemical molecules enter the nostrils and stimulate the olfactory receptors that are located at the top of the nasal cavity. Once these olfactory receptors are stimulated, the neural signals are sent through the porous part of the skull at the top of the nasal cavity and on to the olfactory bulb. The olfactory bulb, which resides inside the skull, sends messages to other parts of the brain for higher-order processing and perception of the specific odor.

At this point in time, hundreds of specific olfactory receptors have been identified, each responsible for responding to certain chemical molecules (Gottfried, 2010). However, the seemingly large number of olfactory receptors is far fewer than the many thousands of distinct smells humans are capable of detecting. So, there does not seem to be a one-to-one correspondence between olfactory receptor types and specific smells. Instead, research has shown that the thousands of distinct smells we are capable of detecting are actually the result of a specific combination of activation for several types of olfactory receptors (Shepherd, 2006). For example, when we smell chocolate, the "chocolate" olfactory receptors are not activated; there are no "chocolate"

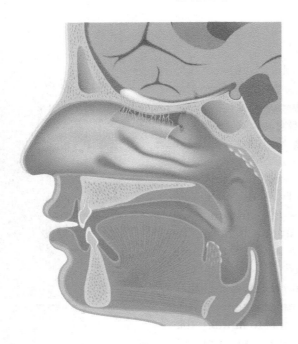

Olfactory Nerve

FIGURE 3.9   Diagram of the human olfactory bulb.
© Alila Medical Media, 2014. Used under license from Shutterstock, Inc.

receptors. Instead, several different receptors are activated, and this specific combination of receptor activation leads to the perception of the smell of chocolate.

As humans, our olfactory sensitivity is directly related to the number of total olfactory receptor cells in the nasal cavity. Although humans have approximately 10 million olfactory receptor cells, and a very good sense of smell, many dogs have approximately 200 million olfactory receptor cells, and a much better sense of smell (Sela & Sobel, 2010). Dog owners realize this discrepancy in sense of smell any time they are taking their pet for a walk; dogs tend to smell things that humans are not capable of sensing, which can lead to incredibly long walks! However, some research suggests that humans may be better at olfaction that previously thought (Porter et al., 2007).

Gustation (Taste)

In our story at the beginning of this chapter we asked you to imagine sitting down in the student union. Now, also imagine that you decide to get something to eat in the food court. The sensation of taste—scientifically known as *gustation*—is the focus of our next section.

Our story of the sensation of taste begins with the physical stimulus for gustation. The stimuli are various chemicals contained in food we consume. Saliva in the mouth breaks down food and releases these chemicals, which are then free to be processed by the sensory receptors for gustation. The sensory receptors for gustation are located on your **taste buds**.

The human tongue contains many thousands of bumps and grooves. Inside these grooves are taste buds, and each taste bud contains several gustation receptors. The gustation receptors are slightly specialized for certain types of taste; each receptor is *most* sensitive to one particular taste and *less* sensitive to the other types of taste. When these receptors are activated by certain chemicals in the saliva, the receptors send signals to the thalamus, and then to various parts of the brain for higher-order processing.

Taste buds: The sensory receptors for gustation that are located deep within porous structures on the tongue; there are five basic types of taste buds.

There are five basic types of taste: sweet, salty, sour, bitter, and umami. We can think of each type of taste serving a particular function. Things that are sweet tend to be sugar- and calorie-rich foods that are desirable to eat, especially when humans were living as hunter–gatherers. Salty foods are high in sodium, which was a scarce resource in ancestral environments. Sour and bitter tastes may have served as a cue that something is undesirable about the food, thus making the person not want to eat that particular food item. Umami, a relatively newly discovered taste, is associated with foods high in protein such as meat.[2]

One interesting aspect of our sensation for taste is that it can also illustrate the occasional mismatch between the present day and the environments our senses were design to navigate. For example, humans evolved to desire sweet and salty foods because sugar and salt are highly useful in small amounts, and they were also highly scarce prior to the rise of modern technology. However, technological advancement is much faster than the process of evolution. So, there is a mismatch. We still desire sugar and salt as if they were scarce, but many people throughout

[2] There is an interesting group known collectively as "supertasters." Here is a link to a video on supertasters: https://www.youtube.com/watch?v=Hd_mxyMAJJY

the world can easily walk down the street and purchase ice cream and French fries, which are packed with sugar and salt. This insatiable appetite for items that are easily available may contribute to modern problems such as obesity and type 2 diabetes.

Touch

Our sense of touch is very important because it gives our brain information about environmental stimuli that are directly in contact with the skin. If something is touching our skin, we definitely want to know about it!

The physical stimulus for touch comes in the form of any force enacting pressure on the surface of the skin. The sensory receptors for touch are called **Pacinean corpuscles**, which are located just below the surface of the skin. These Pacinean corpuscles sense pressure being exerted on the surface of the skin and send neural messages to the appropriate parts of the brain for processing.

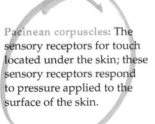

Pacinean corpuscles: The sensory receptors for touch located under the skin; these sensory receptors respond to pressure applied to the surface of the skin.

Interestingly, Pacinean corpuscles are distributed with different frequencies throughout the body. This difference in distribution is reflected through the different levels of sensitivity for different parts of your body. For example, our faces, hands, and feet are highly sensitive to touch. This is partly due to the fact that there are many more Pacinean corpuscles in these areas. In contrast, our elbows and knees are less sensitive because they have fewer Pacinean corpuscles just below the surface of the skin.

Perception

Earlier in this chapter we learned about the basic transduction process for different sensory systems. Our contact with the world typically starts with information reception from our sensory receptors (e.g., rods and cones for the visual information) and ends with meaningful interpretation of the environment based on a higher level of information integration at the brain level (e.g., occipital lobe for visual information). Perception is what enables us to effectively interact with the environment. It is "the acquisition and processing of sensory information in order to see, hear, taste, or feel objects in the world; also guides an organism's actions with respect to those objects" (Sekuler & Blake, 2002, p. 621).

In an effort to efficiently gather meaningful and useful information, perception allows us to be selective and even occasionally ignore unimportant information. In this restructuring process, you will see the world guided by your perception, which may be different from your friend's view. For example, take a look at Figure 3.10 on the left. What do you see? You might see two human heads, in profile, facing each other. Conversely, you might see a single vase. It is possible to see both features as well. The process of sensation does not tell us whether to focus on the background or on the front figure. It is perception that enables us to evaluate the visual stimulus and produce a meaningful answer for this illustration. On a side note, it is a quite common *misbelief* that what you see (the figure or the ground) says something about you (the viewer). These ambiguous

FIGURE 3.10   Figures vs. background.
© Ye Liew, 2014. Used under license from Shutterstock, Inc.

figures are designed to be interpreted in two different ways simultaneously; your first focal point will shape the outline of the figure and allow you to see either a face or a vase.

Two Worldviews

Solipcism vs. Naïve Realism

As we have seen, individuals are guided by their own perceptions and form their own realities or "each individual's personal theory of reality" (Blake & Sekuler, 2005, p. 10). People will react to the environment based on the information and experience gathered by perception. What are the bases for perception? Traditionally there have been two philosophical views on the relation between perception and reality (Blake & Sekuler, 2005).

The first extreme view is **solipsism**, which states the world exists as one chooses to see it (Colvin, 1905). The world is completely filtered through and determined by the viewer's conscious state and may be different from the objective state of this world. The other extreme end of this argument is called naïve realism. **Naïve realism** postulates that the world should exist in only one form and therefore all the viewers should see the world identically (or as it is).

These two worldviews can bring interesting philosophical debates though it is beyond this chapter's scope to find an answer to this question. Before we move on to the next topic, take a look at the Necker Cube in Figure 3.11. This figure is designed to create a visual illusion from you and is an impossible object. Most people see this cube as facing this object parallel to your horizontal viewpoint at first. In this case, the left face is the front of this cube. However, you can also change your viewpoint and see this cube from the top. Once you shift your viewpoint, the lower-left face suddenly disappears. Do you think there is a more correct way to see this cube, or does it simply depend on how one chooses to see it?

Solipsism: A philosophical idea that states the world exists by the viewer's conscious state and may be different from the objective state of this world.

Naïve realism: A philosophical idea that states the world should exist in only one form and therefore all the viewers should see the world as it exists.

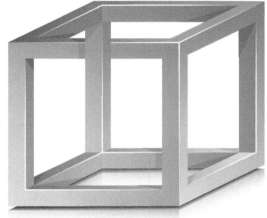

FIGURE 3.11   Ambiguous Necker cube.
© Yuriy Vlasenko, 2014. Used under license from Shutterstock, Inc.

Top-Down Processing vs. Bottom-Up Processing

Given that perception is a way of processing information, we have to think about commonly mentioned information processing approaches: top-down and bottom-up processing. **Top-down processing** emphasized the importance of the context and cognitive structures we have. It is "processing influenced by the individual's knowledge and expectations rather than simply by the stimulus itself" (Eysenck & Keane, 2005, p. 2). Different from the objective transduction of neuronal impulses (sensation), more often our perception is filtered by (organized by) our past experience and expectation and top-down processing will be relevant.

Bottom-up processing, on the other hand, is more focused on gathering information from individual stimuli. For example, if we are only using bottom-up

Top-down processing: An information-gathering process starting from an individual's knowledge, expectations, and prior experiences.

Bottom-up processing: An information-gathering process starting from each individual stimulus.

FIGURE 3.12   Composition of the alphabet A.

FIGURE 3.13   Duck vs. rabbit.

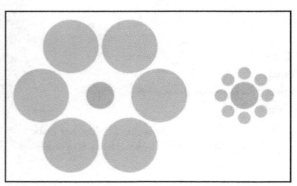

FIGURE 3.14   Ebbinghaus illusion.

processing, we might have a difficult time figuring out that "A" and "a" are the same letter in the alphabet. The letter "A" is composed with three lines in the first example (see Figure 3.12), but the second example "a" looks quite different from the prototype. However, in both cases, most of us will be able to interpret both letters as the alphabet "A" based on our previous experience and knowledge.

The same principle applies when interpreting Figure 3.13. If we only rely on bottom-up processing, we will not be able to see the whole picture since you are only focused on individual stimulus. Luckily, most of us use top-down processing as well and are able to see either a rabbit or a duck in Figure 3.13. Figure 3.14 demonstrates the same idea in a slightly different way. To your naked eye, which of the two circles looks bigger to you? Is it the inner circle on the left side, or the inner circle on the right side? If the inner circle to your right seems bigger to you, you are relying on top-down processing. The two inner circles, which are exactly the same size, have different context (surrounding) information. The inner circle on the right is surrounded by much smaller circles and thus appears much larger than the inner circle on the left, which is surrounded by much larger circles. If you only use bottom-up processing, you will not experience this optical illusion.

Which do you think is a better way of understanding and making sense of the world? Should bottom-up processing be a superior way than top-down processing (or vice versa)? Or do you think both are equally valuable ways of organizing events occurring around us? Keep this in mind as we go through the rest of the perception process.

Importance of Attention in the Perceptual Process

When you are looking for your blue sedan at a shopping mall parking lot, you will first focus on all the blue cars and narrow down your search. You will ignore all the SUVs for the same reason. Likewise, we often get help from attention to recognize and locate particular objects. In a way, object perception is a goal-driven process. There is a plethora of information around us and it is neither practical nor meaningful to process all of the sensory input. That is why we need a selective filter known as **attention**. The term attention refers to "a large set of selective mechanisms that enable us to focus on some stimulus at the expense of others" (Wolfe et al., 2012, p. 217).

Attention: A concentrated mental effort that functions as a filter to ignore unimportant events and focus on important events.

Attention, or concentrated mental effort, is crucial in the beginning of perception. Imagine driving on a highway. If you decide to text your friend while driving, you might be too engaged in the conversation and might not see a road construction warning sign.

Simons and Chabris (1999) devised a very simple, yet powerful, experiment to test this phenomenon in a more controlled environment. Participants watched a short video and were given a specific instruction to count the number of passes that individuals wearing white shirts made in the video. In the middle of the video, a confederate in a gorilla suit walks across people passing the ball. At the end of the study, participants were asked if they saw a gorilla. Results showed half of the respondents were not aware the presence of the gorilla! (You can visit Simons and Chabris's website at http://www.theinvisible gorilla.com/videos.html to check out the video and test it your-

© Stripsa, 2014. Used under license from Shutterstock, Inc.

self.) Similar to what might happen to you while texting and driving, this study clearly shows the importance of attention as a precursor of perception. When you do not (or fail to) allocate attention, you can miss quite obvious scene changes or a big gorilla. The unpredictability of an event or diverted attention will result in failure of accurate scene detection (as if we are blind to that event) for a short time. This phenomenon is known as **inattentional blindness** (Mack & Rock, 1998). This concept clearly shows the importance of attention in our perceptual process.

Inattentional blindness: Diverted attention resulting in failure of accurate scene detection as if we are blind to that event.

So far we have walked through a few important concepts related to our perceptual processes and fundamental differences between perception and sensation. Unlike sensational process, the context surrounding individual stimulus as well as your personal expectations and experience will shape your perceptual process. We will continue to examine how these neuronal signals (sensory input) are assembled in the higher level of brain.

Perceptual Procedure at the Brain Level

The first steps in sensation will allow us to objectively register sensory inputs. If the input were visual information, these neural signals have to be carried to the visual cortex in our brain before we can see things meaningfully. In this chapter, we take a closer look at how visual and auditory neural signals are projected in our brain.

Visual Cortex

The information processed through rods and cones will eventually be projected to the back of our brain known as the **occipital lobe** (Wolfe et al., 2012).

Occipital lobe: The part of our brain responsible for processing the visual information.

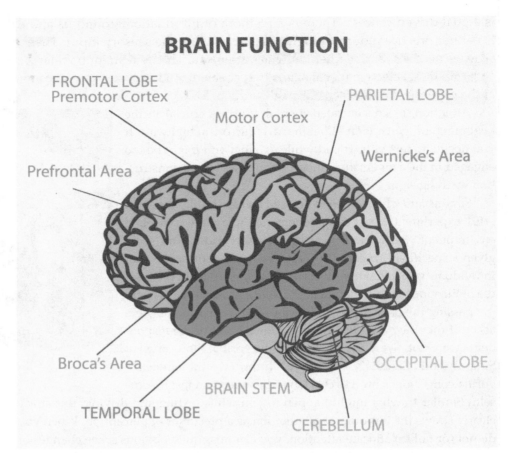

FIGURE 3.15   Human brain areas.
© okili77, 2014. Used under license from Shutterstock, Inc.

This is where all the visual information will first be processed in our brain (Figure 3.15).

The occipital lobe is further localized based on the types of visual information we receive. For example, when you see a red apple flying across a gym, you are processing three types of visual information: a color (red), an object (apple), and a movement (flying across). The primary visual cortex can be subdivided into five different sections depending on its primary function (Coren, Ward, & Enns, 2004). Going back to our apple example, the area in the brain known as V4 will concentrate on processing the color information, and V1 on the object's form, whereas another area—V5—will be better equipped to interpret and gather the visual information about global movements. We will not go into too much detail about the segregation of the visual cortex but will take a look at how visual stimuli are processed in our visual cortex.

The primary visual cortex also processes retinal images in a very specialized way through M and P pathways. The **magnocellular pathway** (or M pathway) receives information from M ganglion cells about peripheral vision and therefore low spatial resolution images from the retina (Palmer, 1999; Zeki, 1993). The **parvocellular pathway** (or P pathway) receives information from P ganglion cells about central vision and therefore high spatial resolution images. These separate pathways serve as the anatomical basis for more localized visual information processing even at an earlier stage (Chaudhuri, 2011; Wolfe et al., 2012).

Magnocellular pathway: A visual pathway for peripheral vision and low spatial resolution images from the retina.

Parvocellular pathway: A visual pathway for central vision and high spatial resolution images.

The Visual Projection Pathway

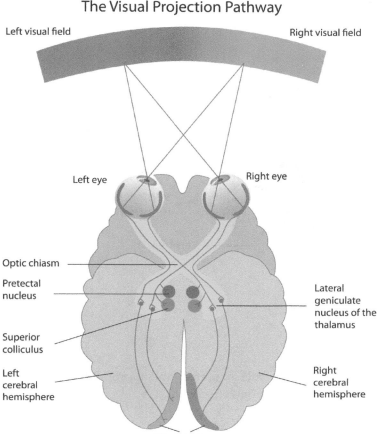

FIGURE 3.16 The visual projection pathway.
© Alila Medical Media, 2014. Used under license from Shutterstock, Inc.

In the primary visual cortex, retinal images that crossed over the optic chiasm will once again be separated. Ultimately, retinal images from the left visual field are transmitted to the right hemisphere and images from the right visual field are transmitted to the left hemisphere (Figure 3.16). This is known as the contralerality of visual processing and shows that each side of the brain hemisphere processes the images from the opposite side of the visual field (e.g., Rodieck, 1998; Rosenzweig, Leiman, & Breedlove, 1999).

We have seen how the initial stage of visual information processing is done somewhat separately through different pathways. However, later in the perceptual process it is combined again to provide a meaningful and wholesome picture. There are two main streams of processing that start from the occipital lobe (V1, to be specific). The pathway going into the temporal lobe is known as the **"what" pathway** and responds to and integrates information about the size, color, and/or the identity of the object (Husain & Jackson, 2001; Posner, 1980). The other pathway, which goes into the parietal lobe, is called the **"where" pathway**. As you can presume from the name, the parietal pathway helps you find the location of an object. Visual cortex areas are localized based on their primary responsibilities in the earlier stage of processing. In the higher level of processing, these local areas

"what" pathway: A visual pathway projected into the temporal lobe that responds to and integrates information about the size, color, and/or the identity of an object.

"where" pathway: A visual pathway projected into the parietal lobe that integrates information about the location of an object.

Parts of the Human Brain

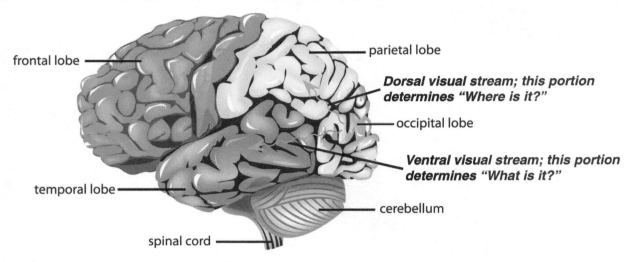

FIGURE 3.17   Where" vs. "what" visual pathways.
© Matthew Cole, 2014. Used under license from Shutterstock, Inc.

communicate with each other to convey the appropriate meaning to the visual images and allow us to respond effectively.

Perceptual Aspects of Vision

Visual Illusion

Perception of the visual information involves your conscious awareness. Nonetheless, we are not sensitive enough to acknowledge the neuronal connections continuously made in our brain during the process. This process is a highly efficient and organized process to help us provide meanings to the scenes around us and to allow us to make appropriate judgment based on the sources of the information. For example, if you see a friendly face, you might decide to approach the person to say hello or, conversely, an unfriendly face may make you decide to avoid another person. During this delicate process, our brain makes a great deal of assumptions based on our expectations and past experiences. Perception attempts to find useful ways to make the most of our surroundings, sometimes even at the cost of misrepresentation of the visual stimulus (Blake & Sekuler, 2005). This is why we experience optical illusions. Take a look at Figure 3.18. There are five black horizontal blocks and in the middle there seems to be two gray blocks occluding some parts of the black blocks. Take a closer look at the shades of those two gray blocks. Would you believe that those gray blocks are the same luminance (brightness or in this case shade)? Due to the surroundings—black for the

FIGURE 3.18   Relative luminance.
© diskoVisnja, 2014. Used under license from Shutterstock, Inc.

left gray block and white for the right gray block—the left gray block seems to be much lighter than the right gray block. Though the sensory procedure involves an objective processing of the visual information, our brain is making an assumption about the context and changes the overall perception of the shades or the colors. In other words, the information you receive from your eyes about left and right gray blocks is exactly the same. However, the context information around the stimuli will make your brain "think" and come to a conclusion that these two blocks do not have the same luminance.

A different optical illusion founded in a similar principle is shown in Figure 3.19. In Figure 3.19, three individuals are the same height. However, the vanishing point (where the straight lines are converging in one corner) allows you to experience a sense of distance between these individuals and perceive the individual closer to the vanishing point as being further away from you compared to the individual to the far left. This is why the individual standing to the far right seems taller than the other two, although all three are the same height.

Gestalt psychologists proposed that people tend to follow a simple rule to organize objects (i.e., Law of Pragnanz). The members of the Gestalt school articulated the importance of context and holistic understanding of the world rather than dissecting the environment by an individual stimulus (Wolfe et al., 2012). Though they did not explicitly emphasize the role of the assumptions the brain makes, Gestalt principles delineate how we identify and group visual elements. During this perceptual procedure, our brain will find the most efficient way to interpret the visual input and may trick us to believe a phantom existence of a stimulus. To see illusory contours, go to http://perceptualstuff.org/illuscont.html.

FIGURE 3.19   Linear perspective and relative height.
© Darq, 2014. Used under license from Shutterstock, Inc.

FIGURE 3.20   Monocular depth cue: Occlusion.
© Matthew Cole, 2014. Used under license from Shutterstock, Inc.

Depth Perception

Occlusion: A phenomenon in which an object closer to a viewer appears to block another object that is farther away from the viewer.

Depth perception can also be the evidence for another level of information integration process. If you recall the sensory procedure of vision, humans should see the world as two-dimensional images from the retinal images. However, we all see the world as three-dimensions. In other words, we use diverse depth cues around us to access the depth information (Blake & Sekuler, 2005). In Figure 3.20, we perceive the dog as being closer to us because it appears to be similar in size compared to the trees behind it (when in real life a tree should be bigger than a dog). Furthermore, the dog is obscuring some parts of the grass and trees. We make the assumption that an object blocking something is closer to us than the object being blocked and extract depth information from those cues. This concept is known as **occlusion**. Occlusion is just one example of monocular depth cues. We can also estimate depth by using multiple cues and sometimes experience visual illusion because of this practice (Figure 3.21).

Though we can receive plenty of depth information by using one eye (monocular cues), we get more sophisticated information by using both of our eyes (binocular cues). Because your left and right eyes cover slightly different visual fields, the images from the left and right eyes are slightly different (binocular disparity) and provide the information for depth perception.

FIGURE 3.21   Three-dimensional chalk drawing illusion.
© hipproductions, 2014. Used under license from Shutterstock, Inc.

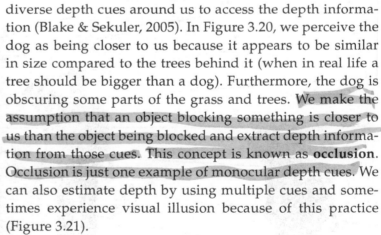

Auditory Cortex

Sound waves or sound information is useful for locating, identifying, and reacting to objects around us. The transduction process in the auditory sensory receptors (e.g., hair cells) codes and transmits the basic sound inputs to the brain. The **auditory cortex** then assembles these neural signals into meaningful sounds, such as your friend's voice or a siren from an ambulance. Similar to our visual information processing, perception of sound information involves a higher-order acoustic information processing. In sum, once the basic auditory input (sound wave) is registered by the hair cells, it is transmitted to the primary auditory cortex, which is the temporal lobe (Figure 3.22).

Auditory cortex: The part of our brain that is primarily responsible for processing the auditory information.

The neuronal signals from our hair cells in the cochlea reach both the left and right side of the temporal lobe earlier in the process and this early integration of sound input is useful to locate the sound source (Wolfe et al., 2012). Similar to the localization of the visual cortex, the auditory cortex processes sound waves in a segregated manner based on the types of auditory information before the information reaches the higher order integration center. From a certain distance, you can trace the direction of an aircraft judging by the sound of its engine. In this example, the two pieces of sound information are about the object (aircraft) and about its trajectory (direction). The auditory cortex then combines information

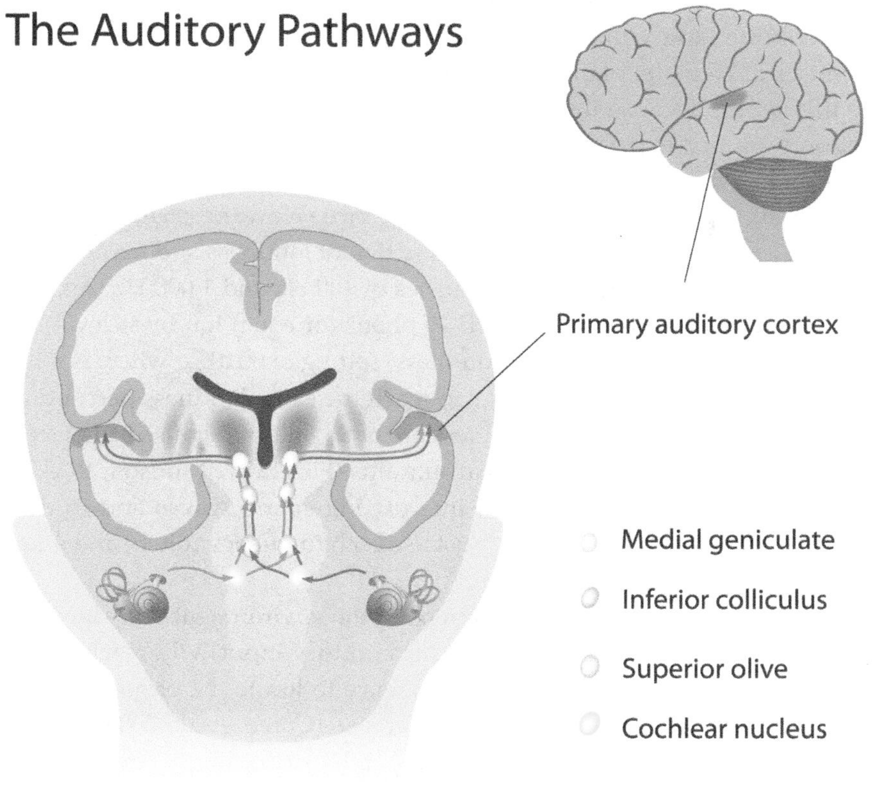

The Auditory Pathways

Primary auditory cortex

Medial geniculate

Inferior colliculus

Superior olive

Cochlear nucleus

FIGURE 3.22 The auditory pathways.

about "what" and "where" separately and uses two pathways for each function similar to the visual "what" and "where" pathways (Rauschecker & Tian, 2000). Two main processing streams start from the primary auditory cortex and send one projection to the temporal lobe (what pathway) to concentrate on identification of objects. The other projection is sent to the parietal lobe (where pathway) to process the locations of sounds more in depth.

In addition, the auditory cortex has areas specializing in speech language input such as voice. Speech sounds are given extensive attention in our auditory cortex, such as the left auditory cortex areas (Belin, Zatorre, Lafaille, Ahad, & Pike, 2000; Zatorre, Belin, & Penhune, 2002). Interesting facts are shown with stroke patients. Patients with brain damages in certain areas have shown distinct deficits in speech language production and comprehension. These two brain areas are known as Broca's and Wernicke's areas, named after the surgeons who first discovered these areas (Coren et al., 2004).

Perceptual Aspects of Audition

Early psychophysists such as Ernst Weber (1795–1878) and Gustav Fehner (1801–1887) argued that there is a difference between the objective intensity of physical stimulus and people's subjective experience of this stimulus. For example, when you listen to music through a headphone you can either increase or decrease the sound volume. However, if the music is too loud you might not notice the difference in volume when you increase the intensity of the volume. You will have a similar perception of sounds at the opposite extreme end. Weber explained this perceptual experience in relation to a difference threshold. Because the physical intensity of a stimulus has a logarithmic function with our experience, a greater sound intensity will be needed at the higher end of the sound wave spectrum for us to notice a difference (production of JND). This notion is captured in the **equal loudness contours**.

Equal loudness contours: Lines measuring the function of loudness and frequencies of sound waves.

Equal loudness contours show the function of loudness and frequencies. Let's say you are comparing the two frequencies of 100 Hz and 1,000 Hz. According to the equal loudness contours, to reach 40 phons (or equal loudness level), an 100-Hz stimulus requires an intensity (loudness) setting of 60 dB_{SPL} whereas a 1,000 Hz only requires an intensity of 40 dB_{SPL} to reach the same loudness perception. This represents how frequency and loudness are both collectively used to perceive the sound waves and experience physical stimulus (Fletcher & Munson, 1933; Gulick, Gescheider, & Frisina, 1989). When interpreting sound waves and to detect an increase or decrease in sounds, we must use both frequency (pitch) and amplitude (loudness) information.

Sound comes from different locations in the environment and since we have one ear on each side, the sound wave (or auditory input) will reach each ear at a slightly different time. We use this difference to locate the origin of the sound. This is known as the interaural time difference (Coren et al., 2004; Wolfe et al., 2012). One source of sound information (e.g., intensity or frequency) is not enough to accurately localize sound. That is why we have to collectively process various pieces of information about a sound's source.

Summary

We opened this chapter by asking you to imagine a very simple activity: listening to a lecture and going to the student union following class. However, as we have described throughout this chapter, the underlying psychological processes that are occurring during these seemingly simple events are far from simple. Many years of scientific research conducted by psychologists have helped us understand that our experience of a continuous world is driven by two processes: sensation and perception.

Sensation is a process of registering environmental stimuli from the external world, and perception is the process of making sense of those environmental stimuli. Our sensation and perception processes have evolved to help us navigate the world very well. However, as we have discussed in the sections about illusions, sometimes our brains misinterpret physical stimuli.

These illusions should not lead us to the conclusion that humans are flawed, but they should point to the fact that the world is an unimaginably complex place, and that through the processes of sensation and perception, our minds do a very good job of guiding us through the world unscathed . . . with only a few mistakes here and there. We hope you take a moment to reflect on the amazing complexity of human sensation and perception the next time you do something mundanely uninteresting, such as sitting and reflecting about the grandeur of the human mind.

CHAPTER FOUR

LEARNING

© Sergey Nivens, 2014. Used under license
from Shutterstock, Inc.

LEARNING OBJECTIVES

- Define learning
- Explain the key concepts of behaviorism
- Differentiate between classical and operant conditioning
- Identify various schedules of reinforcement and impact on behavior
- Analyze limitations of behavioristic explanations
- List the key principles of cognitive psychology
- Define the term, reciprocal determinism
- Apply learning principles to everyday life

Uncle Abner said that the person that had took a bull by the tail once had learnt sixty or seventy times as much as a person that hadn't.

—Mark Twain, Tom Sawyer Abroad, 1894

My grandfather once took a bull by the tail as my cousins and I watched from the other side of the split-rail fence. He was trying to get him into the chute so he could load him on the truck and take him over to have a go at Mr. Tremblay's cows.

Grandpa's bull wasn't real anxious to get into that chute. He ignored all the little piles of oats cleverly pointing up into the truck; he refused to be led by rope or coaxed from behind; and when Grandpa sicced the dog on him, the bull snorted and the dog went yelping through the gap between the rails.

So Grandpa hitched up his pants and spat on the ground and then he took the bull by the tail and turned him to face the chute and yelled, "Git!" and the bull took four or five quick steps and it looked like he was gonna git right straight up the chute and we thought, Wow, Grandpa's a smart one . . .

But no, quick as you can spit, the bull yanked his tail out of Grandpa's hands, whirled around, lowered his head, and lifted my grandpa clear over the fence.

What Is Learning?

Had our grandfather learned 60 or 70 times as much as a guy who never grabbed a bull by the tail? Maybe. Certainly, he learned not to grab a bull by the tail. And he also learned, as we found out the next day, that if you put a handsome cow in the truck to begin with, you don't have to grab the bull by the tail or sic the dog on him: He'll just sashay right up into the truck by himself.

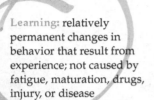

Learning: relatively permanent changes in behavior that result from experience; not caused by fatigue, maturation, drugs, injury, or disease

Learning, psychology tells us, consists of changes in behavior—changes such as no longer grabbing a bull by the tail. But not all changes in behavior are examples of learning. Some changes are temporary; they might result from fatigue or from the use of drugs. Other changes appear to be mainly due to physical maturation; still others might result from injury or disease of the brain or other parts of the nervous system.

Learning is defined as *relatively permanent changes in behavior that result from experience but are not caused by fatigue, maturation, drugs, injury, or disease* (Figure 4.1). Strictly speaking, however, it is not the changes in behavior themselves that define learning; the changes are simply evidence that learning has occurred. Learning is what happens to the organism as a result of experience.

Although we look at behavior—at actual performance—for evidence that learning has occurred, changes in behavior are not always apparent following experiences that might be presumed to have led to learning. In many cases there will be no evidence of learning until an opportunity to display a behavior is presented; and in some cases, that opportunity may never occur. It might forever remain latent (meaning potential but not apparent).

Approaches to Learning

Learning is not easily separated from other major topics in psychology. Changes in behavior are centrally involved in many aspects of psychology, including motivation, personality, perception, development, and even mental disorders. We are not simple, highly predictable organisms with static and unchanging patterns of behavior. We profit from experience—and that defines learning.

Not surprisingly, most of the first psychologists devoted considerable effort to discovering the laws and principles of learning. As we saw in Chapter 1, these early efforts, especially in the United States, rejected the more philosophical and intuitive approach of an earlier age. Instead, they embraced a scientific approach—an approach concerned mainly with the objective and observable aspects of human functioning. The most important pieces of the puzzle, these early psychologists thought, would have to do with the rules that govern relationships between stimuli (observable conditions that can give rise to behavior) and responses (actual, observable behavior).

Learning is a change in behavior (or the potential for behavior) as a result of experience. Such as learning not to grab a bull by the tail.

© patrimonio designs ltd, 2014. Used under license from Shutterstock, Inc.

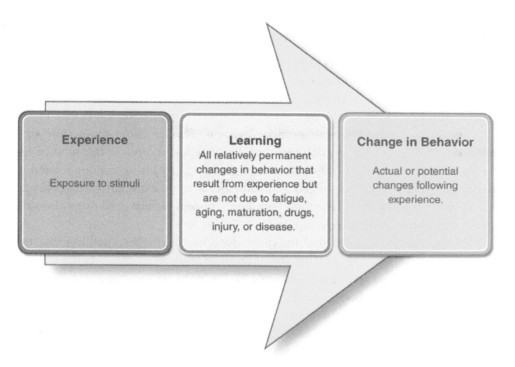

FIGURE 4.1 Evidence of learning is found in actual or potential changes in behavior as a result of experience. But learning itself is an invisible, internal neurological process.

Because they deal with observable *behaviors*, the theories that resulted from early psychologists are labeled **behavioristic theories**. Sometimes they're also referred to as *S-R* or *associationistic* theories because they deal mainly with associations between **stimuli** and **responses**. And although the early psychologists have sometimes been accused of leading to a mechanistic and incomplete description of human learning, they have contributed a great deal to our understanding that continues to be both valid and valuable.

A second major group of learning theories are **cognitive theories**. They are concerned less with the objective aspects of behavior than with more *mental* processes such as thinking, imagining, anticipating, problem solving, decision making, and perceiving.

Behavioristic Approaches

An American with the melodic name Edwin Twitmyer was actually the first person known to have reported the principle of *classical conditioning*. He discovered it while doing research for his doctoral dissertation, publishing his findings in 1902. In 1904, he even presented these findings to the American Psychological Association (when William James was its president) as a paper entitled "Knee Jerks without Stimulation of the Patellar Tendon" (Twitmyer, 1905). But nobody paid any attention.

Behavioristic theories: Theories concerned with objective evidence of behavior rather than with consciousness and mind.

Stimulus (*pl.* stimuli): A physical stimulus is any change in the physical environment capable of exciting a sense organ. Stimuli can also be internal events such as glandular secretions or even thoughts.

Response: A muscular, glandular, or mental reaction to a stimulus.

Cognitive theories: Theories that look at intellectual processes such as those involved in thinking, problem solving, imagining, and anticipating.

Classical Conditioning

And then about a year later, a Russian by the name of Ivan Pavlov presented essentially the same findings—only he had used dogs as subjects whereas Twitmyer had used humans. Nobody knows Twitmyer's name today, but everybody knows Pavlov's.

Ironically, the discovery that made Pavlov so famous came about almost by accident. Pavlov was a physiologist, not a psychologist, and at the time of his lucky discovery, he was busily investigating and measuring secretions related to digestion. That's when he noticed that some of his more experienced dogs began to salivate whenever they saw their handlers. The less experienced dogs also salivated, but only when given food.

Pavlov rightly guessed that his older dogs had learned something that the more naive dogs had yet to learn: The older dogs learned to associate the sight of a handler (stimulus) with food (Figure 4.2). But only one of these stimuli, food, would normally lead to salivation. So, in a sense, what the dogs had learned was to substitute one stimulus (handler) for another (food). Not surprisingly, this kind of learning is sometimes called *learning through stimulus substitution*; its more common label is **classical conditioning.**

That the dog has *learned* something is clear: there has been a change in behavior (specifically, in the response to the handler) as a result of experience (repeated pairing of the handler and food). That is, a previously neutral stimulus (sight of handler) now leads to a response ordinarily associated with another stimulus (food). This defines *classical conditioning.*

classical conditioning: learning through stimulus substitution as a result of repeated pairings of an unconditioned stimulus with a conditioned stimulus

PAVLOV'S EXPERIMENTS

To clarify the laws of classical conditioning, Pavlov devised a series of experiments (Pavlov, 1927). In the best known of these, a dog is placed in a

FIGURE 4.2   What Pavlov first noticed was that the sight of the handler was enough to cause experienced dogs to salivate. He later paired other stimuli, such as bells and buzzers, with the presentation of food to study the details of classical conditioning.

FIGURE 4.3 Pavlov's dogs were placed in harnesses such as the one shown. Saliva dropping through the tube activates the balancing mechanism so that the amount of salivation is recorded on the revolving drum. In this demonstration, presentation of food is paired with a light that shines through the window.
© Time & Life Pictures/Getty Images

harness-like contraption similar to the one shown in Figure 4.3. The apparatus allows food powder to be inserted directly into the dog's mouth or to be dropped into a dish in front of the dog. The salivation that occurs when food powder is placed in the dog's mouth is an unlearned response and is therefore an **unconditioned response (UR)**. The stimulus of food powder that gives rise to the UR is an **unconditioned stimulus (US)**.

Most animals, including humans, are born with a number of these simple, prewired (meaning they don't have to be learned) stimulus–response associations called **reflexes**. More complex behaviors that are also unlearned are **instincts**. That we blink when something brushes our eye is a reflex—as is our tendency to salivate in response to food, to withdraw from painful stimulation, and to jerk the knee in response to a sharp blow below the kneecap.

In Pavlov's conditioning demonstration, the trainer arranged for a buzzer to sound as food powder was inserted into the dog's mouth. This procedure was repeated a number of times. After a while, the trainer simply sounded the buzzer without providing any food powder. And the dog still salivated. The animal was been conditioned to respond to a buzzer, termed a **conditioned stimulus (CS)**, by salivating, a **conditioned response (CR)** (Figure 4.4).

ACQUISITION

Several factors are directly related to the ease with which a classically conditioned response can be acquired. One is the distinctiveness of the CS. Not surprisingly, a stimulus that is easily discriminated from other stimulation will more easily become associated with a response.

unconditioned response (UR): the automatic, unlearned response an organism gives when the US is presented

unconditioned stimulus (US): a stimulus that elicits an automatic, unlearned response from an organism

reflexes: stimulus–response associations

instincts: complex unlearned, behaviors

conditioned stimulus: a once neutral stimulus that becomes conditioned after repeated pairings with the US

conditioned response: previously the UR that is now given in response to the CS

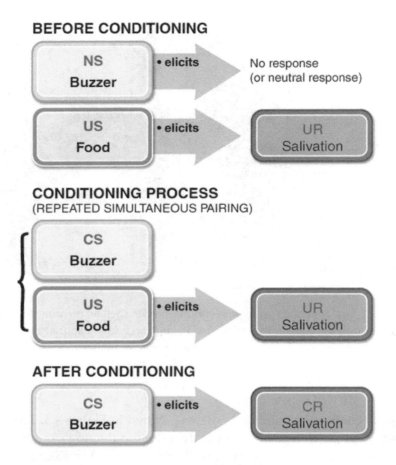

FIGURE 4.4   Classical conditioning. Initially, the stimulus (buzzer) does not elicit salivation. After repeated pairings of this stimulus with the unconditioned stimulus (food), the buzzer has become a conditioned stimulus that now elicits a conditioned response (salivation).

A second critically important factor is the temporal relationship between the conditioned and the unconditioned stimuli. The ideal situation, *delayed* (or *forward-order*) *conditioning,* presents the conditioned stimulus before the unconditioned stimulus, with the CS continuing during the presentation of the US (Hussaini, Komischke, Menzel, & Lachnit, 2007). In the classical Pavlovian experiment, for example, the fastest learning occurred when the buzzer sounded just before the presentation of food powder and continued while the food powder was injected into the dog's mouth. Other alternatives are to have the CS begin and end before the US, termed *trace conditioning;* to present the US and the CS simultaneously (*simultaneous conditioning*); or to present the US prior to the CS (*backward conditioning*). Figure 4.5 summarizes the relationship of these temporal factors to classical conditioning.

As noted, fastest learning typically occurs when the conditioned stimulus precedes the unconditioned stimulus (forward-order conditioning). The opposite situation, backward conditioning, in which the conditioned stimulus follows the unconditioned stimulus, has generally not resulted in learning except under very specific circumstances. For example, presenting a dog with food and then later ringing a bell does not normally lead the dog to salivate in response to the bell.

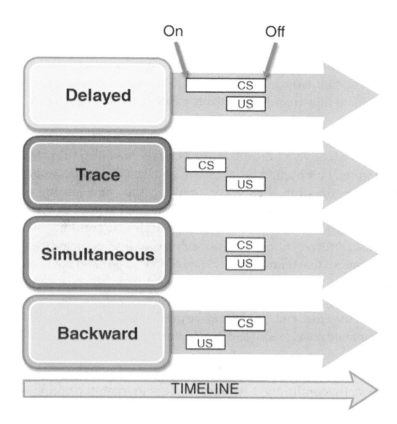

FIGURE 4.5 Unconditioned stimulus (US)–conditioned stimulus (CS) pairing sequences are shown here in the order of effectiveness. Conditioning takes place most quickly in the delayed sequence where the CS (buzzer) precedes the US (food powder) and continues throughout the time the US is presented.

Backward conditioning can sometimes be effective, however. For example, Minnier, Misanin, and Hinderliter (2007) successfully conditioned taste aversions in rats by injecting them with lithium chloride (which makes them sick—a US) either 15 or 45 minutes *before* they were allowed to drink sweetened water (the CS). Most rats who experienced the 15-minute delay later avoided the sweetened water.

Keith-Lucas and Guttman (1975) conditioned rats to avoid a plastic toy by shocking them electrically and then placing a plastic hedgehog-like toy in their cages. A significant number of rats exposed to the hedgehog 1, 5, or 10 seconds after receiving the electric shock displayed avoidance behavior the following day. Backward conditioning had been established after a single trial—unlike Pavlov's dog, who required many trials before learning.

The significance of these results is not simply that they illustrate that backward conditioning can be accomplished. More important, they illustrate that many organisms have biological predispositions to learn behaviors that have survival value. Rats are prepared to learn to avoid strange objects such as plastic hedgehogs. And many preyed-upon animals, as Griffin and Galef (2005) point out, are highly prepared to learn about predators. That a warbler flies like the devil when a dark shadow sweeps by may well be because the shadow has previously been preceded by signs of alarm among other warblers, one of whom might have succumbed to a swift-flying merlin or a sharp-shinned hawk. And, as we saw in Chapter 2, humans seem to be prepared to learn strong taste aversions—which is useful when the tastes you learn to avoid belong to objects that might kill you if you ate them. Similarly, many people acquire fear of snakes, insects, and other potentially dangerous creatures relatively easily (Öhman et al., 2007).

GENERALIZATION AND DISCRIMINATION

A dog trained to salivate in response to a buzzer may also salivate in response to a bell, a gong, or a human imitation of a buzzer. This phenomenon is called **stimulus generalization.** It involves making the same responses to different but related stimuli. An opposite phenomenon, **stimulus discrimination,** involves making different responses to highly similar stimuli.

Watanabe (2010) conditioned a group of pigeons by reinforcing them when they pecked at paintings that human judges had labeled "good" and not reinforcing them when they pecked at others judged "bad." When these pigeons were later shown new paintings, they *generalized* what they had learned, pecking the "good" paintings far more often than the "bad." As Watanabe puts it, "the results showed that pigeons could discriminate novel 'good' and 'bad' paintings" (2010, p. 75).

EXTINCTION AND RECOVERY

Many classically conditioned responses are remarkably durable. A dog conditioned to salivate in response to a tone and then left to do nothing but dog things for many months will immediately salivate when he is brought back into the laboratory and he hears the bell.

stimulus generalization: involves making the same responses to different but related stimuli

stimulus discrimination: involves making different responses to highly similar stimuli

extinction: process by which classically conditioned responses are eliminated

Classical conditioning is sometimes a good explanation for unconscious emotional learning—like acquiring a fear (or a love) of dogs.

© Rob Hainer, 2014. Used under license from Shutterstock, Inc.

But classically conditioned responses can be eliminated—a process called **extinction.** Extinction requires that the experimenter present the conditioned stimulus repeatedly without the unconditioned stimulus. For example, if Pavlov's well-conditioned dog heard the tone repeatedly but it was never again paired with food, it would soon stop salivating in response to the tone.

Once a classically conditioned response has been extinguished, it can be reacquired much more easily than was initially the case. A dog who has learned to salivate in response to a tone and whose conditioned response is later extinguished, will learn to salivate again after only one or two pairings of tone and food powder. In fact, an extinguished response sometimes recurs in the absence of any training. This phenomenon, termed *spontaneous recovery*, illustrates that behaviors that are apparently extinguished are not necessarily completely forgotten.

CONTIGUITY

When I was 5 years old, my grandfather's dog bit me. I remember it as a vicious attack, although I suspect it really wasn't that bad. I haven't been bitten by a dog since, and I have raised and loved various dogs.

But last week my truck broke down on the way to the lake and I had to walk into a farmyard for assistance. When the farm dog came bounding across the field, barking, I tasted fear, as I have on many other occasions since I was 5. I'm conditioned to fear strange dogs; I have no control over my physiological reactions when I meet one.

Why does an emotional (or other) response such as fear become conditioned to a particular stimulus (or class of stimuli)? Pavlov's explanation is that the simultaneous or near-simultaneous presentation of a stimulus and a response leads to the formation of a neural link between the two. In this view, what is most important in the conditioning situation is the **contiguity** (closeness in time) of the stimulus and response. A contiguity explanation of classical conditioning maintains that the stimuli associated with "dog" (appearance, smell, sound, movement) were also associated with my initial fear response. Thus the sight, sound, or smell of a dog continues to plague me in my otherwise peaceful adult life.

contiguity: closeness in time of the stimulus and response

BLOCKING

Although contiguity might appear to be an adequate explanation for what happened to Pavlov's dogs, and perhaps for my fear of strange dogs, there are some relatively simple experimental situations that it does not explain. For example, Kamin (1969) paired a noise and a light (two unconditioned stimuli) with electric shock (a conditioned stimulus) administered to the feet of a group of rats (we'll call them the A group). In this study, the light and noise were turned on, and immediately afterward the rats were shocked. Classical conditioning theory would clearly predict that after the light and noise are paired often enough with the shock, either the light or the noise alone would cause an avoidance reaction in the rat. The prediction is correct.

But now Kamin threw a twist into the procedure. First he conditioned a group of rats by pairing only noise and electric shock (this is the B group). Then, once these rats showed a well-conditioned fear response to the noise, he conditioned them exactly as he had the A group, this time pairing both light and noise.

Recall that the A-group rats responded with fear to both the light and the noise. The B group rats also responded with fear to the noise. Strikingly, however, they showed no fear in response to the light in spite of the fact that they were conditioned in exactly the same way as the A group—but only after they had already been conditioned to the noise alone. It seems that for the B-group rats, learning that noise means shock *blocked* them from learning that light might also mean shock—a phenomenon appropriately labeled **blocking** (Figure 4.6).

Blocking: A phenomenon in classical conditioning in which conditioning to a specific stimulus becomes difficult or impossible because of prior

Contiguity does not explain blocking. Clearly, if conditioning depends only on the simultaneous presentation of stimulus and response, there is no reason why both groups of animals should not have learned the same things.

One explanation for blocking is this: Whenever something new happens to an animal, it immediately searches its memory to see what events could have been used to predict it. When a lynx leaps at a rabbit and narrowly misses, the terrified rabbit scans its memory banks for immediately preceding events. Maybe it remembers a looming shadow, the thudding of padded footfalls, the stink of hungry lynx. And forever after, it flees from footfalls and shadows and hot stenches.

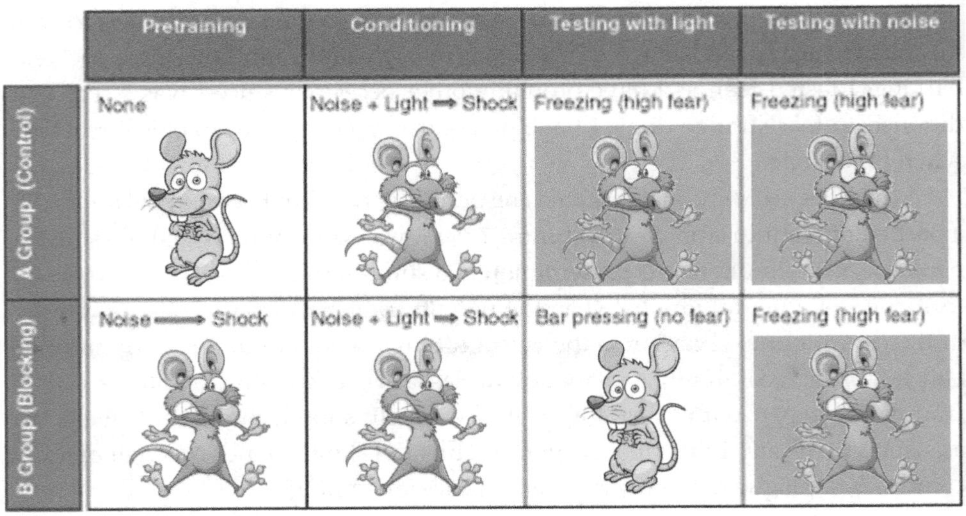

	Pretraining	Conditioning	Testing with light	Testing with noise
A Group (Control)	None	Noise + Light → Shock	Freezing (high fear)	Freezing (high fear)
B Group (Blocking)	Noise → Shock	Noise + Light → Shock	Bar pressing (no fear)	Freezing (high fear)

FIGURE 4.6   Kamin's study of blocking. A-group rats, exposed to both noise and light followed by a shock, subsequently react strongly to the light alone. But B-group rats, who have previously learned that noise means shock, fail to learn that light might also mean shock.

Images used under license from Shutterstock, Inc.

So when a rat receives a mild foot shock, it scans its memory to see what just preceded the event. The A-group rat notes that both light and noise always come before the shock, and so it freezes whenever it hears the noise or sees the light. But the B-group rat, who already knows that noise means shock, learns absolutely nothing new when later exposed to both noise and light followed by shock. Once the rat has learned that noise means shock, it no longer needs to pay attention to other stimuli.

CONSEQUENCES

Learning is a fundamentally adaptive process: Changes in behavior are what allow organisms to survive. Clearly, we, like any other animal, need to remember what is edible and where to find it; we need to recognize potential enemies; we need to stay away from electric shocks. Put another way, we have to learn what goes with what—what the most likely outcomes of our behavior are.

One explanation for classical conditioning says, in effect, that what is learned is not a simple pairing of stimulus and response as a function of contiguity, but the establishment of relationships between stimuli. This explanation holds that what is important in a conditioning situation is the information a stimulus provides about the probability of other events. When a dog salivates in response to a tone, it is because the tone now predicts food. In the blocking experiments, animals who have learned that stimulus A means shock find it difficult to learn that B also means shock. That's because when A and B are subsequently paired, there is no new information provided by stimulus B.

Operant Conditioning

Classical conditioning theorists were not especially concerned with consequences; they studied relationships among stimuli and responses. But a second form of conditioning, **operant conditioning**, is built around the importance of behavior's consequences. Operant conditioning is closely associated with B. F. Skinner (1953, 1969, 1971, 1989), one of the most influential psychologists of this age. He dealt with a large and important piece of the puzzle.

Skinner noted that although classical conditioning explains some simple forms of learning where responses are associated with observable stimuli (termed **respondent** behavior), most of our behaviors are of a different kind. Behaviors such as walking, jumping, listening to music, writing a letter, and so on are more deliberate; they are seldom associated with a specific stimulus the way salivation might be. These behaviors appear more voluntary. Skinner calls them **operants** because they are operations that are performed on the environment rather than in response to it. Classical conditioning does not provide an easy explanation for behaviors such as deciding to go for a walk or, at a simpler level, a dog learning to sit or roll over.

operant conditioning: (Skinner) describes changes in the probability of a response as a function of its consequences

Respondent: A response elicited by a known, specific stimulus. An unconditioned response.

Operant: An apparently voluntary response emitted by an organism.

THE SKINNER BOX

In his investigations, Skinner used a highly innovative piece of equipment now known as a **Skinner box**. Typically, this *experimental chamber* is a small, cagelike structure with a metal grid for a floor. At one end is a lever; above it, a light; below it, a small tray. Outside the structure are various mechanical or electronic devices designed so that if the lever inside the cage is pushed down, the light will go on, a click will be heard (if someone is listening), and a food pellet will drop into the tray.

Skinner box: an experimental chamber used in operant conditioning experiments

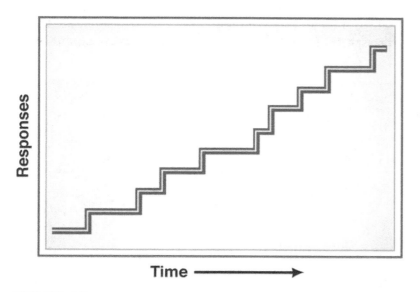

FIGURE 4.7   The photo shows B. F. Skinner with a rat in a Skinner box. The graph is a typical learning curve recorded on a revolving drum. The drum revolves at a constant speed, and each depression of the lever causes the recording pen to move up a notch. Steepness of the curve reveals response rate.

Photo © Time & Life Pictures/Getty Images

When a naive rat is placed in this box, it does not respond as predictably as a dog in Pavlov's harness. Its behaviors are more deliberate, perhaps more accidental. It does not know about Skinner boxes and food trays. It needs to be *magazine trained*. In a typical magazine training session, the experimenter depresses a button that releases a food pellet into the tray. At the same time, there is an audible clicking sound. Eventually the rat is drawn to the tray, perhaps by the smell of the pellet, perhaps only out of curiosity. Now the experimenter releases another food pellet, the rat hears the click, eats the pellet, hears another click, runs over to eat another pellet . . . In a very short period of time, the rat has been magazine trained.

Now the experimenter stops rewarding the rat unless it depresses the lever near the food tray. Most rats will eventually do so in the course of sniffing around and exploring. And when they do, they hear the tell-tale click and immediately rush over to the food tray. Very shortly, the rat will have learned to depress the lever. And if a light is paired with the presentation of food, the rat may eventually learn to depress the lever simply to see the light go on (Figure 4.7).

THE BASIC OPERANT CONDITIONING MODEL

All of the basic elements of Skinner's theory of operant conditioning are found in the rat-in-Skinner-box demonstration. The bar pressing is an operant—an emitted behavior. The food is a **reinforcer; reinforcement** is its effect. Any stimulus (condition or consequence) that increases the probability of a response is said to be reinforcing. In the Skinner box the light, too, may be a reinforcer.

Reinforcer: any stimulus condition or consequence that increases the probability of a response

Reinforcement: The effect of a reinforcer.

Discriminative stimulus (SD): Skinner's term for the features of a situation that an organism can discriminate to distinguish between occasions that might be reinforced or not reinforced.

What happens to a rat in the Skinner box may be described simply: A naive rat placed in this situation eventually emits a specific operant (bar pressing); the operant is reinforced; the probability of the operant occurring again increases with each reinforced repetition. When placed in the same situation on another occasion, the rat may begin to emit the operant immediately. The rat has learned associations not only between the operant and reinforcement, but also between the operant and specific aspects of the situation—called **discriminative stimuli (SD)**.

© Dudarev Mikhail, 2014. Used under license from Shutterstock, Inc.

© Petr Jilek, 2014. Used under license from Shutterstock, Inc.

© Sunny studio, 2014. Used under license from Shutterstock, Inc.

Nope, you can't get me to fetch a stick or read a book. Those aren't things we cows do! It seems that organisms are biologically "prepared" to learn certain things and not others.

These discriminative stimuli might include things such as the sight and smell of the inside of the cage. They are stimuli that allow the rat to discriminate between this situation and others where the operant is impossible or will not be reinforced. To some extent, the operant is now controlled by discriminative stimuli as well as by its consequences.

In brief, Skinner's explanation of learning is based not on associations that might be formed between stimuli as a function of their co-occurrence (classical conditioning), but on associations that are established between a behavior and its consequences. Any other distinctive stimulus that happens to be present at the time of those consequences may also come to be associated with the operant.

The basic law of operant conditioning is the **law of effect**, first proposed by Edward Thorndike (1898). This law states that behaviors that are followed by reinforcement (Thorndike called them "satisfying states of affairs") are more likely to be repeated. Conversely, behaviors that are not followed by reinforcement (that lead to "annoyers," in Thorndike's words) are less likely to recur.

law of effect: behaviors followed by reinforcement are more likely to be repeated and behaviors not followed by reinforcement are less likely to recur.

SHAPING

If you wanted to train a rat to depress a lever, you might not have to do much more than sit by the Skinner box and watch while the rat sniffs around, eventually depresses the lever, eats, depresses the lever again, eats, and on and on. In short order, your rat will rush over and begin working the lever as soon as you put it in the cage.

But what if someone asked you to train a cow to sit on a chair? Do you think, if you put a chair in the cow's pen, she might eventually sit on it and you could then reward her with a nice bale of timothy hay?

Not too likely. But operant conditioning does suggest a way of teaching animals very complex behaviors. This is done by reinforcing small sequential steps in a chain of behaviors that will ultimately lead to the desired final behavior—a process called **shaping**. The animal (or person) does not learn a complete final response at once, but is reinforced instead for behaviors that come progressively closer to that response—hence the phrase *differential reinforcement of successive approximations*. Using *shaping* techniques, pigeons have been taught to bowl, chickens to play baseball, mules to dive into shallow waters from precarious heights, and pigs to point pheasants.

shaping: reinforcing small sequential steps in a chain of behaviors, leading to the desired final behavior

Shaping can be a useful technique for toilet-training infants. For example, in the first phase of a potty-training study described by Smeets, Lancioni, Ball, and Oliva (1985), whenever infants "strained" as though they were about to soil their diapers, mothers or research assistants tapped on a nearby potty and called or touched the infant. This first phase of the *shaping* procedure was designed to draw the child's attention to the potty and to reinforce the infant for paying attention to it—after which the infant was placed on that piece of equipment.

In the second phase, the potty was kept within reach of the child so that when signs of imminent defecation or urination appeared, the infant could be guided to grab the potty before being placed on it. And in the third phase, the potty was placed further away so that self-initiated movement toward the potty could be reinforced. By then, many of the infants had learned to crawl toward the potty.

Throughout all three phases, mothers and attendants reinforced the infants, primarily through smiling, verbal praise, and other gestures of approval. And all were toilet trained before they had learned to walk.

Schedules of Reinforcement

Skinner's primary interest had been discovering the relationships between behavior and its consequences. His investigations with rats and pigeons quickly revealed that the way in which reinforcement is given (the *schedule of reinforcement*) is an important factor in determining responses.

The experimenter has several alternatives: Every correct response (called a "trial") might be reinforced (*continuous reinforcement*) or only some responses might be rewarded (*partial* or *intermittent reinforcement*). In turn, partial reinforcement can be based on a proportion of trials (*ratio reinforcement*) or on the passage of time (*interval reinforcement*). Furthermore, reinforcement can be regular (fixed), or irregular (random or variable; Figure 4.8).

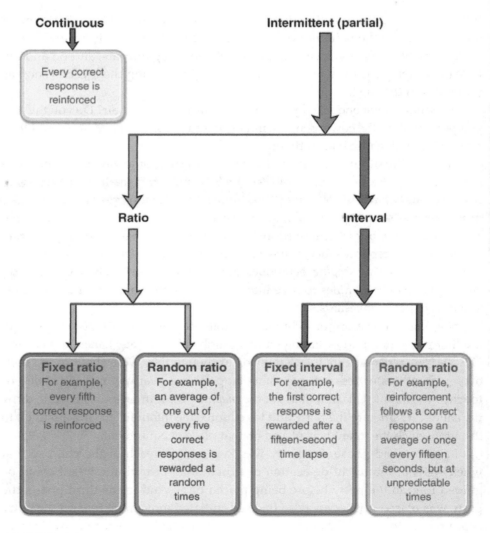

FIGURE 4.8   Schedules of reinforcement. Each type of schedule tends to generate a predictable pattern of responding.

EFFECTS OF DIFFERENT SCHEDULES

The effects of different schedules of reinforcement are evident in three different *dependent* variables: rate of learning (*acquisition rate*); rate of responding; and rate of forgetting (*extinction rate*). The *independent* variable in studies of operant conditioning is the experimenter's control of reinforcement (the schedule of reinforcement).

Initial learning—that is, rate of acquisition—is usually more rapid when every correct response is reinforced (a continuous schedule). If only some responses are reinforced (intermittent schedule), learning tends to be slower and more haphazard.

If, after initial learning, the experimenter continues to reinforce every correct response with food, the animal may respond at a high rate for a while, but will eventually become satiated and stop responding. Hence, the best training combination for an animal is usually a continuous schedule initially, followed by an intermittent schedule.

With intermittent schedules, rate of responding seems to be closely tied to expectations the animal might develop about how and when it will receive reinforcement. For example, under variable schedules, when it is difficult to predict when the reward will occur, rate of responding tends to be high and relatively unvarying. But under a fixed-interval schedule, when reinforcement occurs after the first correct responses following a predetermined time lapse, rate of responding tends to drop off dramatically immediately after reinforcement and picks up again just before the end of the time interval (Figure 4.9).

Rate of extinction, which is the cessation of a response following withdrawal of reinforcement, is also a function of schedule of reinforcement. Extinction is typically more rapid with a continuous schedule than with intermittent schedules. And of the intermittent schedules, variable ratio schedules typically result in the longest extinction times—a fact that has not escaped the attention of slot-machine programmers. Skinner reports the case of one pigeon that, after complete withdrawal of reinforcement, emitted more than 10,000 pecks before extinction was complete.

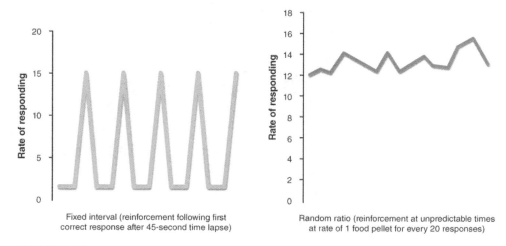

Fixed interval (reinforcement following first correct response after 45-second time lapse)

Random ratio (reinforcement at unpredictable times at rate of 1 food pellet for every 20 responses)

FIGURE 4.9 Idealized graphs showing the effects of two reinforcement schedules on rate of responding.

TYPES OF REINFORCEMENT

The fact that a pigeon would wear its beak to a frazzle before giving up an apparently unreinforced behavior may be evidence that reinforcement is not nearly as simple or as obvious as these few pages might suggest. We really have no basis for concluding that pecking itself is not a rewarding activity for the pigeon and that it requires no extrinsic reinforcement to be maintained. As we saw in Chapter 2, pigeons are biologically programmed to peck—as pigs are to root and humans are to explore. These activities don't necessarily require **extrinsic reinforcement**.

Extrinsic reinforcement includes the variety of external stimuli that might increase the probability of a behavior. In contrast, **intrinsic reinforcement** may be loosely defined as satisfaction, pleasure, or reward that is inherent in a behavior and that is therefore independent of external rewards. The satisfaction that people sometimes derive from their work is a form of intrinsic reinforcement; the money and the praise that might also result are forms of extrinsic reinforcement.

Skinner distinguishes between two broad classes of reinforcers. **Primary reinforcers** are stimuli that are rewarding for most people, most of the time, without anybody having had to learn that they are rewarding. They include food, drink, sleep, comfort, and sex.

Secondary reinforcers include the wide range of stimuli that may not be reinforcing initially but that eventually become reinforcing as a function of having been associated with other reinforcers. Thus, secondary reinforcers are learned; primary reinforcers are not. Social prestige, praise, money, and applause are very powerful secondary reinforcers.

In general, reinforcement is any stimulus (situation) that increases the probability of a response occurring. If the stimulus increases the probability of a behavior it follows, it is a **positive reinforcer**. Food pellets in the rat's cage are examples of positive reinforcers. So is the applause a performer receives, the money a worker gets paid, and the satisfaction a student gets from learning.

Extrinsic reinforcement: reinforcement to increase a behavior in the future that comes from an external source (e.g., reading to earn a reward)

Intrinsic reinforcement: reinforcement to increase a behavior in the future that comes from an internal source (e.g., reading because one loves to read)

Primary reinforcers: stimuli that are naturally rewarding for an organism.

Secondary reinforcers: stimuli that may not be reinforcing initially but that eventually become reinforcing as a function of having been associated with other reinforcers.

positive reinforcer: pleasing or positive stimulus is given and consequently, the probability that the behavior will be repeated is increased

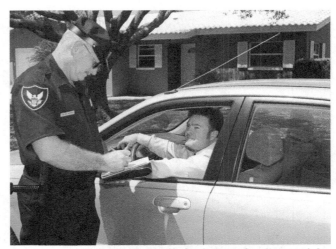

Operant conditioning is based on the consequences of behavior. They can be positive and reinforcing, as when this young lad is given his medal. Or they can be negative, as this driver is discovering.

But some reinforcers are effective not when they are *added* to a situation, but rather when they are *removed*. For example, if a mild electric current is turned on in the rat's cage and then is turned off when the rat depresses the lever, the result might be an increase in the probability that the rat will subsequently press the lever. In this case, turning off the electric current is an example of a **negative reinforcer**. In much the same way, the removal of pain might be a negative reinforcer for taking some medication, even as the alleviation of withdrawal symptoms might be a negative reinforcer for continued drug use.

The important point is that reinforcement is defined in terms of its *effects* rather than in terms of the characteristics of the reinforcing stimuli used. And the effect of reinforcement, by definition, is to *increase* the probability of a behavior. A positive reinforcer does so when it *follows* a behavior; a negative reinforcer does so when it is *removed* following a behavior.

negative reinforcer: unwanted or painful stimulus is removed and consequently, the probability that the behavior will be repeated is increased

PUNISHMENT

Negative reinforcement is often confused with punishment, although the two are quite different. Negative reinforcement increases the probability of a response; the intended effect of punishment is precisely the opposite.

In essence, the consequences of behavior can involve the removal or presentation of stimuli that are pleasant or unpleasant (noxious). This presents the four distinct possibilities that are relevant to operant learning: positive reinforcement, negative reinforcement, and two types of punishment (Figure 4.10). There are countless illustrations of each of these possibilities in human behavior: Josephine is complimented on a new hairstyle (the addition of a pleasant stimulus; positive reinforcement); a pill relieves Norbert's headache (removal of an unpleasant stimulus: negative reinforcement); Arnaldo is reprimanded for losing his homework (addition of an unpleasant stimulus: punishment); Ronald has his jelly beans confiscated for throwing one in the goldfish bowl (removal of a pleasant stimulus; punishment).

	Pleasant Stimulus (Appetitive)	**Unpleasant Stimulus (Aversive)**
Added to the situation after a response (Behavior strengthened)	**Positive reinforcement (reward)** [Bobby is given 10 bucks for getting an A in math]	**Punishment** [Bobby is given detention for talking in class] (Behavior weakened)
Taken away from a situation after a response (Behavior weakened)	**Punishment** [Bobby has his ten dollars taken away for painting his sister]	**Negative reinforcement (relief)** [Bobby is let out of detention when he promises to be quiet] (Behavior strengthened)

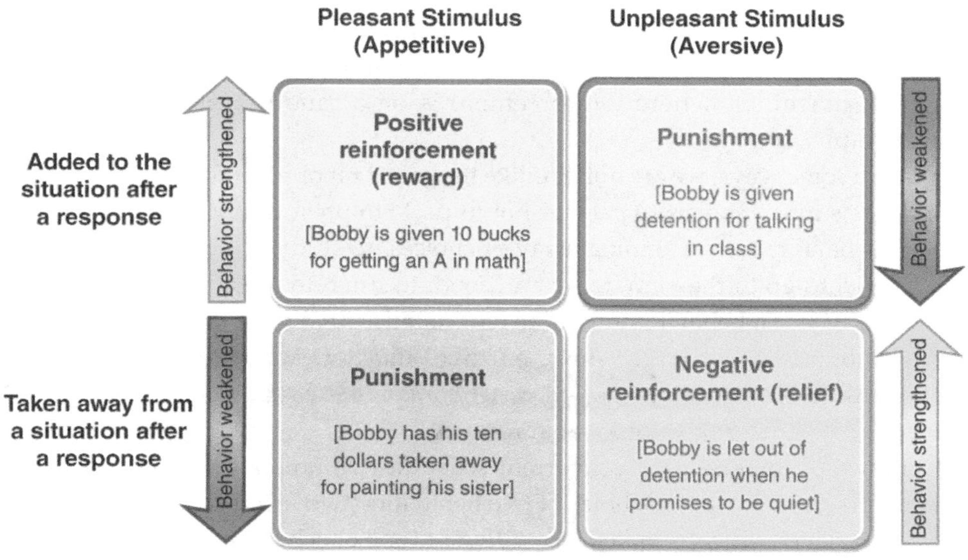

FIGURE 4.10 Reinforcement and punishment.

THE ETHICS OF PUNISHMENT

Is punishment ethical? Is it even effective? Or does it just teach us to be sneakier? Psychology offers some tentative answers.

First, punishment is not always effective in eliminating undesirable behavior. Certainly, it is not nearly as effective as reinforcement is in bringing about more desirable behavior.

Second, punishment often leads to undesirable emotional side effects sometimes associated with the punisher rather than with the punished behavior. For example, punishment might lead a child to dislike and fear the punisher, and might result in efforts to avoid punishment rather than efforts to avoid the transgressions for which the punishment was administered.

Third, punishment does not present a guide for desirable behavior; instead, it emphasizes undesirable behavior.

Finally, some research indicates that punishment sometimes has effects opposite to those intended. For example, Mulvaney and Mebert (2007) found that physical punishment of young children actually increased maladjustment and misbehavior later in life.

Note that most of these objections apply mainly to physical punishment and not to other forms of punishment. These other forms of punishment (verbal reprimands, loss of privileges) have long been considered legitimate and effective means of controlling behavior. There are instances when punishment appears to be effective in suppressing destructive, aggressive, and dangerous behavior in children (and sometimes in adults as well).

Verbal reprimands and loss of privileges are legitimate and effective forms of punishment not subject to the same objections as physical punishment.

© wavebreakmedia, 2014. Used under license from Shutterstock, Inc.

OPERANT CONDITIONING AND HUMAN BEHAVIOR

Human behavior is seldom as simple as the pecking of a pigeon or bar pressing of a rat. Still, many of the results of investigations with these animals generalize easily to our behavior. There is no denying the effectiveness of rewards and punishments in our lives. The persistence with which people play slot machines, where reinforcement is on a random ratio schedule, is one example.

But in some ways, we are quite unlike the caged rat or pigeon. Neither of these animals has much choice: to peck or not to peck; to press or not to press. We, on the other hand, have a stunning array of choices: to study or not to study, to go to a movie, to go to the gym, to text a friend, to listen to music, and on and on. And each of these behaviors might be associated with a very different type and schedule of reinforcement. In short, our lives illustrate what are called **concurrent schedules of reinforcement**—a variety of options, each linked with different kinds and schedules of possible reinforcement.

Studies of the effects of concurrent schedules on animal behavior typically present the animal with the choice of two behaviors (two levers to press; two keys to peck), each of which is linked to a different type or schedule of reinforcement. In a study of a new drug treatment for cocaine addiction, for example, rats had a choice of lever A, which would lead to a small dose of intravenously administered

Concurrent schedule of reinforcement: A situation in which two or more different reinforcement schedules, each typically related to a different behavior, are presented at the same time.

cocaine, or lever B, which would provide a highly palatable food as a reinforcer (Thomsen et al., 2008). The rat preferred the drug.

Other studies indicate that, when given choices, rats and pigeons typically match their responses to maximize the likelihood of reward (Herrnstein, 1997). Not surprisingly, studies with humans lead to much the same conclusion. In experimental situations where participants can choose between different behaviors with different probabilities of reward, they try to maximize the payout (Borrero, Frank, & Hausman, 2009).

A Transition to Cognitivism

Historically, behavioristic theory has recognized two general classes of behaviors, respondent and operant (elicited or emitted) and two general sets of rules and principles to account for each of these. One set relates to classical conditioning; the other, to operant conditioning.

Classical conditioning theory has been found most useful for explaining learning involving autonomic and reflexive reactions, such as those associated with emotional responses, over which we ordinarily have no conscious control.

Operant conditioning had generally been thought to apply to all behaviors that were not respondent—that is, to all behaviors that were not elicited by specific, identifiable stimuli but that simply occurred and could then presumably be brought under the control of reinforcement. Whereas classical conditioning appealed to principles of contiguity, operant conditioning invoked the law of effect: The consequences of behavior determine the probability of future occurrence or of change.

Problems for Traditional Behaviorism

Early behaviorists had hoped to discover laws of learning that would prove sufficiently general to explain most human behaviors. Unfortunately, behavior did not prove to be as simple as behavioristic theory might have indicated. Even animals sometimes behave in ways that are troublesome for traditional conceptions of behaviorism. The Brelands, two of Skinner's students, trained some 6,000 animals to perform a bunch of stunning animal tricks. But then many of these animals began to "misbehave," reverting to their more natural inclinations—a phenomenon called *instinctive drift*.

Instinctive drift presents a problem for traditional operant theory. It is now apparent that not all behaviors can be conditioned and maintained by schedules of reinforcement, that there is some degree of competition between unlearned, biologically based tendencies and the conditioning of related behaviors.

There are other examples of what are labeled *biological constraints* that have a clear effect on what an organism learns. Behaviors that are highly probable and relatively easy are typically those that have high adaptive value. Among humans, these might include behaviors such as avoiding bitter-tasting substances so that we don't poison ourselves, or learning a language so we can communicate. Among animals, behaviors such as pecking in birds and nosing around levers in rats are examples of highly probable, biologically based learning.

Organisms are *prepared* to learn certain things and *contraprepared* to learn others. Thus, it is almost impossible to teach a rat to depress a lever to escape an electric shock (Bolles, 1970). A rat's natural response to danger is to fight, flee, freeze, or become frantic; it is not to approach a lever and depress it. Therefore, a rat can be trained to jump to escape shock. The ease with which this is accomplished demonstrates preparedness. That the rat cannot be trained to depress a lever to escape a shock illustrates contrapreparedness. As Guthrie (1935) put it, "We cannot teach cows to retrieve a stick because this is one of the things that cows do not do" (p. 45).

Insight

Bertrand Russell (1927) made the interesting observation that U.S. and German rats must be quite different. "Animals studied by Americans rush about frantically, with an incredible display of hustle and pep, and at last achieve the desired result by chance," he wrote, adding, "Animals observed by Germans sit still and think, and at last evolve the solution out of their inner consciousness" (p. 33).

He was referring to the fact that U.S. psychology was then largely dominated by the behavioristic notion that responses are learned as a result of the reinforcement of a "correct" response that occurs through trial and error (i.e., by chance). At the same time, some German psychologists were working on different parts of the human puzzle.

One of these psychologists, Wolfgang Köhler, spent 4 years in the Canary Islands during World War I trying to frustrate apes with a pair of problems: the "stick" problem and the "box" problem. Both problems are essentially the same; only the solutions differ. In both, an ape finds itself unable to reach a tantalizing piece of fruit, either because it is too high or because it is outside the cage beyond reach. In the "stick" problem, the solution involves inserting a small stick inside a larger one to reach the fruit. In the "box" problem, the ape has to place boxes one on top of the other (Figure 4.11).

© Time & Life Pictures/Getty Images

© Everett Collection, 2014. Used under license from Shutterstock, Inc.

FIGURE 4.11   In the box problem, the chimp piles boxes to reach some fruit—a process involving insight, claimed Köhler. Playing chess, too, requires insight.

The solution, insists Köhler (1927), does not involve trial and error, although some of that type of behavior might be displayed in the early stages. When the ape realizes that none of its customary behaviors is likely to obtain the bananas, it may sit for a while, apparently pondering the problem. And then, bingo, it leaps up, quickly joins the sticks or piles the boxes, and reaches for the prize.

That, according to Köhler, is **insight**, the sudden recognition of relationships among elements of a problem. It is a complex, largely unconscious process, not easily amenable to scientific examination.

insight: the sudden recognition of relationships among elements of a problem.

The behaviorists were hard-pressed to explain the behavior of Köhler's apes. Many were tempted to assume that the apes simply tried a number of apelike actions, eventually resorting to combinations of these when none of the simple behaviors was rewarded. Staunch behaviorists would assume that the ape's recognition of the solution would not occur until the fruit was in hand.

Many psychologists, however, were reluctant to accept behavioristic explanations for insight, a phenomenon that is common enough among our species that its existence is difficult to deny. And in time, the lowly rat was allowed to contribute in a small way to the study of insight.

In a pioneering study, Tolman and Honzik (1930) allowed a rat to become totally familiar with a maze in which there were several routes to the goal. Once the rat has learned the maze, barriers were placed so that the rat had to choose one of the alternatives. Typically, a rat will always select the shortest route—and the next shortest if that one is later blocked. The behaviorist assumption is that the rats developed a preference for the shortest routes as a result of receiving reinforcement more quickly when they follow these routes than when they stupidly meander through lengthy detours.

The maze, shown in Figure 4.12, has three alternatives. Path 1 is the most direct and is almost invariably chosen when there are no barriers. When there is a barrier at A, the rat would be expected to choose alternative 2. This is, in fact, the case some 93% of the time. When the barrier is at B, rats might again be expected

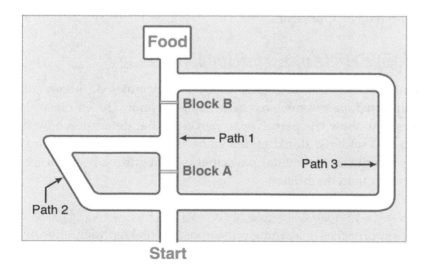

FIGURE 4.12 In the Tolman and Honzik (1930) blocked-path study, rats that had learned this maze almost invariably selected path 3 when path 1 was blocked at B. It seemed they somehow knew that the barrier at B also blocked the much shorter path 2.

to select path 2 since its opening is not blocked. They don't. These clever rats now run all the way around path 3, despite the fact that they should still have a higher preference for path 2. One explanation is simply that they have developed a *cognitive map*—a mental representation—of the entire maze, and that they understand that a barrier at B also blocks route 2.

Other studies have shown that a rat will learn a maze even without any tangible reinforcement. Rats who are allowed to explore a maze without food learn the maze considerably more quickly than naive rats when food is later introduced. Such observations indicate that rats, too, have some understanding of their environments that goes beyond the formation of simple associations among stimuli, responses, and rewards.

And we humans, too, form *cognitive* maps that allow us to navigate in our environment. In doing so, report Foo, Warren, Duchon, and Tarr (2005), we tend to rely heavily on our recollection of landmarks and their positions relative to each other and to our preferred paths. Forming mental representations of our worlds is a uniquely *cognitive* activity.

Cognitive Approaches

Instinctive drift, delayed taste aversion, cognitive maps, and insightful learning present serious problems for traditional behavioristic theories. And if behaviorism does not explain the simpler behaviors of animals, then the presumably more complex behaviors of humans might be even less well explained. If even animals have concepts and apparent thought processes, psychology should perhaps concern itself with these as well as with more easily observed and described behaviors.

Enter **cognitivism**, an approach concerned mainly with intellectual events such as problem solving, information processing, thinking, and imagining. It is an approach that has sometimes rejected behaviorism as overly mechanistic and incomplete. Behaviorism does not deal well with thinking—with *cognition*. For that, we need other approaches.

Cognitivism: an approach concerned mainly with intellectual events such as problem solving, information processing, thinking, and imagining.

The Main Beliefs of Cognitive Psychology

The dominant metaphor in cognitive psychology, notes Garnham (2009), is a computer-based, *information processing (IP)* metaphor. The emphasis is on the processes that allow the perceiver to perceive, that determine how the actor acts, and that underlie thinking, remembering, solving problems, and so on. Not surprisingly, experimental participants in cognitive research tend to be human rather than nonhuman.

LEARNING INVOLVES MENTAL REPRESENTATION
Cognitive approaches to learning presuppose mental representation and information processing. The behaviorist view, as we saw, tends to describe learning as a largely unconscious process where factors such as repetition, contiguity, and reinforcement push the organism this way and that. In contrast, the cognitive view describes an organism that is more *thoughtful*, that can mentally

imagine and anticipate the consequences of behavior. In this view, the learner is not a passive receiver of information, pushed and prodded by stimuli and their consequences. Instead, the learner actively participates in the learning process, discovering, organizing, and using strategies to maximize learning and reward.

LEARNERS ARE NOT IDENTICAL

Behaviorism sees all learners as relatively equal in terms of their susceptibility to the effects of reward and punishment. In contrast, cognitivism emphasizes that learners are different. Individuals come with different background information, different inclinations and motives, different genetic characteristics, and different cultural origins. As a result, even in the same situation, individuals often learn very different things

NEW LEARNING BUILDS ON PREVIOUS LEARNING

The importance of individual differences among learners rests partly on the fact that new learning is often highly dependent upon previously acquired knowledge and skills. Take 100 naive rats; most of them can easily be *conditioned* to depress a small lever. But take 100 15-year-olds, and perhaps only a handful will be ready to understand the mysteries of quantum theory.

As we see in later chapters, for most important topics in human psychology (such as memory, motivation, and social learning), the continuing search for pieces of the puzzle has taken a largely cognitive turn.

Bandura's Social Cognitive Theory

You cannot, in any simple sense, *condition* someone to learn quantum physics. Still, explains Albert Bandura (1997), we learn many things through conditioning. It is clear that we are highly responsive to reinforcement—and perhaps to punishment as well. What is not so clear in most accounts of human learning through operant conditioning is just how operants come about in the first place.

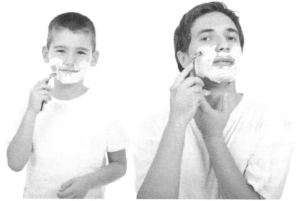

Imitation is a powerful teacher among children. And sometimes among animals, too.

observational learning:
Bandura's theory involving learning through observing and imitating models

Model: A pattern for behavior that can be copied by someone. Also refers to descriptions of objects or phenomena. In science, models often serve as a sort of mental guide.

Imitation: Copying behavior. To imitate a person's behavior is simply to use that person's behavior as a pattern.

Social cognitive theory: An explanation of learning and behavior that emphasizes the role of social reinforcement and imitation as well as the importance of the cognitive processes that allow people to imagine and to anticipate.

Symbolic model: A model other than a real-life person. For example, books, television, and written instructions are important symbolic models.

Direct reinforcement: Results from the consequences of the act itself.

vicarious reinforcement: When you see someone doing something repeatedly, you unconsciously assume that the behavior must be reinforcing for that person.

triadic reciprocal determinism: describes the three principal features of our social cognitive realities: our personal factors (our personalities, our intentions, what we know and feel); our actions (our actual behaviors); and our environments (both the social and physical aspects of our world).

Bar pressing and key pecking are simple behaviors that are highly likely to occur in a given situation. A complex human behavior such as driving a car is not likely to appear fully formed, ready to be reinforced. And *shaping* such a complex behavior by reinforcing behaviors that slowly approximate the complete sequence of required behaviors would be a highly ineffective way of learning.

Nor do we learn complex behaviors such as how to drive a car through trial and error. We learn many of these complex behaviors, explains Bandura, through **observational learning**—that is, by observing and imitating **models**. And, in a sense, learning through **imitation** is a form of operant learning in that the imitative behavior is like an operant that is learned as a result of being reinforced.

A large number of studies indicate that social imitation is a powerful teacher among humans: Even children as young as 2 or 3 imitate and learn from each other. Moreover, a number of investigations show that monkeys, dogs, birds, and dolphins can learn a variety of relatively complex behaviors by observing their trained fellow animals (Ferrari et al., 2009; Miller, Rayburn-Reeves, & Zentall, 2009).

MODELS

In Bandura's **social cognitive theory**, models are not limited to people who might be imitated by others; they include **symbolic models** as well. Symbolic models are any representation or pattern that can copied, such as oral or written instructions, pictures, book characters, mental images, cartoon or film characters, and television actors.

Models provide the imitator with two kinds of information: how to perform an act, and what the likely consequences of doing so are. And if the observer now imitates the behavior, there is a possibility of two different kinds of reinforcement. **Direct reinforcement** results from the consequences of the act itself. If 10-month-old Norbert is given a glass of milk when, in trying to imitate his sister, he says, "mwuff" (Norbert's best attempt at "milk"), he may soon learn to say "mwuff" whenever he is thirsty.

The other source of reinforcement is *secondhand*, labeled **vicarious reinforcement**. When you see someone doing something repeatedly, you unconsciously assume that the behavior must be reinforcing for that person. You might now imitate this behavior and continue to produce it even in the absence of any direct reinforcement.

RECIPROCAL DETERMINISM

There is little doubt that we engage in many behaviors because of the reinforcing consequences of so doing. But reinforcement does not control us blindly, explains Bandura (1997); its effects depend largely on our *awareness* of the relationship between our behavior and its outcomes. What is fundamentally important is our ability to figure out cause-and-effect relationships and to anticipate the outcomes of our behaviors.

Not only can we anticipate and imagine the consequences of our behavior and therefore govern ourselves accordingly, but we can also deliberately select and arrange our environments. That we are both products and producers of our environment is the basis of Bandura's concept of **triadic reciprocal determinism**.

In this view, there are three principal features of our social cognitive realities: our personal factors (our personalities, our intentions, what we know and feel); our actions (our actual behaviors); and our environments (both the social and physical aspects of our world). These three factors affect each other reciprocally. For example, a harsh, demanding environment might alter Joe's personality, making him bitter and cynical. This might change his behavior, driving him to more selfish acts. These actions might destroy friendships, thus changing important aspects of his social environment. And the changing social environment, in turn, might further affect his personality and his behavior.

On the other hand, instead of making him bitter and cynical, a tough environment might lead Joe to rally his friends that they might struggle together to ease their lot. The reciprocal influence of person, action, and environment might be no less in this case, but the outcomes might be vastly different (Figure 4.13).

EFFECTS OF IMITATION

Through observational learning, we learn three different classes of behaviors, explain Bandura and Walters (1963): We learn brand new behaviors (**modeling effect**); we learn to suppress or stop suppressing deviant behaviors (**inhibitory/disinhibitory effect**); and we learn to engage in behaviors similar but not identical to the model's behavior (**eliciting effect**; Table 4.1).

HUMANS AS AGENTS OF THEIR OWN BEHAVIORS

Some of our behaviors, such as our classically conditioned fears, are under the control of stimuli. Others, like our highly reinforced imitations, are controlled more by their consequences. And a third group of behaviors are controlled by cognitive activities such as thinking and imagining. Bandura labels these three behavior control systems *stimulus control, outcome control,* and *symbolic control.*

In the end, although stimuli and outcomes might affect our behaviors, it is the symbolic control system that is most important in Bandura's description. We are

Modeling effect: The type of imitative behavior that involves learning a novel response.

Inhibitory/disinhibitory effect: The type of imitative behavior that results either in the suppression (inhibition) or appearance (disinhibition) of previously acquired deviant behavior.

Eliciting effect: Imitative behavior in which the observer does not copy the model's responses but simply behaves in a related manner.

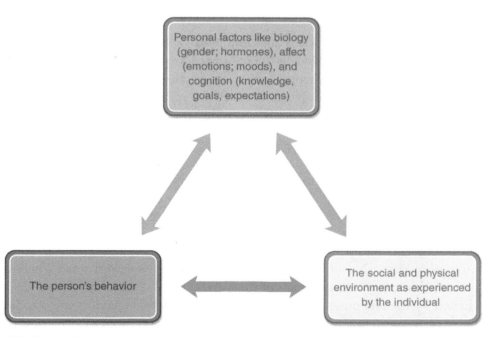

FIGURE 4.13 Bandura's notion of triadic reciprocal determinism. Behavior, the person, and the environment all mutually influence and change each other.

TABLE 4.1   **Three Effects of Imitation: Bandura's Theory**

TYPE OF EFFECT	DESCRIPTION	ILLUSTRATION
Modeling Effect	Acquiring a new behavior as a result of observing a model.	After watching a mixed martial arts program, Jenna tries out a few novel moves on her young brother, Liam.
Inhibitory-Disinhibitory Effect	Stopping or starting some deviant behavior after seeing a model punished or rewarded for similar behavior.	After watching Jenna, Nora, who already knew all of Jenna's moves but hadn't used them in a long time, now tries a few of them on her sister (disinhibitory effect). Nora abandons her pummeling of her sister when Liam's mother responds to his wailing and takes Jenna's smartphone away (inhibitory effect).
Eliciting Effect	Engaging in behavior related to that of a model.	Robin tries to learn to play the guitar after her cousin is applauded for singing at the family reunion.

not simply pawns pushed hither and yon by rewards and punishments and classically conditioned reflexes. We are in charge, Bandura (2001) insists: We are agents of our own actions.

Being agents of our own actions requires three things: First, it requires *intentionality*. If someone bumps into you, causing you to spill your latte on your friend, you would not be considered an agent of *that* action. But if you deliberately threw your coffee at said friend, you would be the agent of *that* action.

Second, intentionality implies *forethought*. It is the ability to symbolize that allows you to foresee the consequences of the actions you intend. You could not intend to amuse your friend with your behavior unless you could foresee the effects of tossing your coffee.

Finally, being agents of our actions implies being able to reflect on them and to reflect on ourselves and especially on our own effectiveness—on our **self-efficacy**. Self-efficacy, as we see in Chapter 6, is a very important concept in human motivation. Our estimates of our personal effectiveness, of our likelihood of success, have a lot to do with what we choose to do and how much effort we are willing to expend doing it.

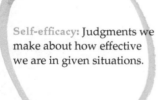

Self-efficacy: Judgments we make about how effective we are in given situations.

Practical Applications of Learning Principles

There are countless, everyday, intuitive applications of classical and operant conditioning principles and of Bandura's social-cognitive theory. People are controlled and manipulated by organizations and by other people, sometimes quite unconsciously—although often consciously as well. Performers' behaviors are shaped by the responses of their audience; the behavior of teachers is shaped by the responses of their students; consumers' behaviors are affected by advertising media; models are used to influence consumers; drug addicts are reinforced by the effects of the drugs they take. Even criminals are reinforced by the outcomes of their behaviors.

Applications of Behaviorism

Findings in behaviorism have led to the development of a variety of practical applications in fields such as education and psychotherapy. For example, many teachers use systematic reinforcement programs to foster learning or to prevent or correct deviant behavior.

General instructional recommendations that derive from conditioning principles suggest that teachers should:

- Try to maximize pleasant unconditioned stimuli in their classrooms. This might involve making sure learners are comfortable, that surroundings are colorful and upbeat, and that no individual is faced with overwhelming demands. At the same time, teachers need to minimize the unpleasant aspects of being a student to reduce the number and potency of negative unconditioned stimuli in the classroom.
- Use punishment—especially corporal punishment—sparingly as it is not very effective for eliminating undesirable behavior and even less effective for teaching desirable behavior.
- Be aware of what is being paired with what in the classroom, so as not to inadvertently condition undesirable behaviors. If the teacher smiles when Johnny does something outrageous—or if his classmates all laugh— doing outrageous things may well be what Johnny learns.
- Limit the use of repetition without reinforcement; it does little to improve learning.
- Emphasize positive rather than aversive methods of control.

The systematic application of learning principles to change behavior is labeled **behavior modification**. Behavior modification is widely used in schools and institutions for children with behavioral and emotional problems, as well as in the treatment of mental disorders. Essentially, it involves the deliberate and systematic use of reinforcement, and sometimes punishment, to modify behavior.

Two behavior modification techniques are described in Chapter 9. One, *systematic desensitization*, is widely used to treat phobias (intense, debilitating fears). Basically, it involves conditioning a relaxation response that conflicts with the fear responses characteristic of phobias. The other, *aversive conditioning*, is sometimes used to treat drug or alcohol addiction. It attempts to attach negative, avoidance responses to the use of these substances, perhaps by using stimuli such as electric shock or nausea-inducing drugs.

Applications of Cognitivism

Cognitivism typically views the learner as an active, information-processing being, capable of imagining and anticipating the consequences of behavior, and essentially responsible for his or her own actions, as well as for *constructing* his or her own view of the world. This orientation lends itself especially well to **discovery learning**. This is a learner-centered approach where content is not organized by the teacher and presented in a relatively final form. Instead, learners are expected to investigate and discover for themselves, and to *construct* their own mental representations—hence the current expression for discovery and other related approaches, widely used in educational circles: **constructivism**.

behavior modification: systematic application of learning principles to change behavior

Discovery learning: A learner-centered approach to teaching in which the acquisition of new knowledge comes about largely through the learner's own efforts.

Constructivism: A general term for student-centered approaches to teaching, such as discovery-oriented approaches, reciprocal learning, or cooperative instruction—so called because of their assumption that learners should build (construct) knowledge for themselves.

A cognitive view of the learner also supports approaches designed not so much to teach students specific content, but more to teach them *how* to learn—to make self-regulated learners of them. To this end, cognitively oriented educational psychologists suggest that teachers should develop problem-solving skills in students—for example, by giving them practice with the five-step strategy for general problem solving suggested by Bransford and Stein (1993). The five steps are easily remembered with the acronym IDEAL:

- Identify problems and opportunities
- Define goals and represent the problem
- Explore possible strategies
- Anticipate outcomes and act
- Look back and learn

reciprocal teaching:
a method designed
to improve reading
comprehension

cognitive apprenticeship:
novice learners are paired
with older learners,
teachers, or parents who
serve as mentors and
guides.

There are a wide variety of specific, cognitively based approaches to teaching, including **reciprocal teaching**, a method designed to improve reading comprehension, and **cognitive apprenticeship**, where novice learners are paired with older learners, teachers, or parents who serve as mentors and guides. There are also various programs designed to develop cognitive strategies, as well as to help learners become aware of their own use of cognitive strategies, to reflect on them, to evaluate their effectiveness, and to change them as needed.

We are all players of what Flavell (1985) calls *the game of cognition.* It is a strategic game—a game for which we need to have mastered the strategies that allow us to understand and make sense of information, to organize it and process it, to recall it when we need it, and to use it in the best way possible. Most of us learn cognitive strategies incidentally in the course of learning other things. Now cognitive psychology suggests there should be concerted attempts to make sure all learners develop the best cognitive strategies possible.

Some people play the game of cognition very badly.

Some play it extraordinarily well.

Summary

Learning is a relatively permanent change in behavior resulting from experience but not including the effects of fatigue, maturation, drugs, injury, or disease. Two behavioristic approaches to learning are classical and operant conditioning. Classical conditioning (Pavlov) describes learning through stimulus substitution as a result of repeated pairings of an unconditioned stimulus with a conditioned stimulus; whereas, operant conditioning (Skinner) describes changes in the probability of a response as a function of its consequences. Behaviorism, however, was not able to explain and predict many aspects of behavior. Thus, a cognitive approach to psychology soon developed. This approaches focused on an individual's ability to be self-aware, anticipate the consequences of behavior, and guide actions accordingly. Some principles of the behavioristic approach such as behavior modification are still used today.

CHAPTER FIVE

MEMORY AND INTELLIGENCE

Dr. Joe Engler, Dr. J. April Park, and Dr. Trey Hill
Fort Hays State University

LEARNING OBJECTIVES

- Understand the different types of memory and their hierarchical organization
- Discover the process by which information to goes from sensory to long-term memory (LTM)
- Explain the process of encoding, storage, and retrieval
- Identify some applications of LTM
- Discover some LTM problems, such as false memories
- Learn how to improve memory
- Discover the historical beginning of intelligence tests
- Learn how to calculate IQ
- Understand different theories of intelligence
- Identify some cultural differences in intelligence testing
- Understand genetic and environmental determinants of a person's intelligence

Imagine being asked to participate in a psychological experiment. You arrive for the experiment to find a psychologist sitting at a table with several pieces of paper, some multicolored blocks, pencils, and booklets. Directly across from the psychologist is your chair. You sit down and begin performing various mental tasks that the psychologist directs you to do. Some of the mental tasks have you maneuver blocks into specific patterns as directed by the psychologist. As you get a design correct, each subsequent design becomes more difficult to master. On a separate task, the psychologist asks you to repeat a short string of numbers back, in reverse order. Again, this task is simple in the beginning but becomes more difficult as you get each string of numbers correct.

The task described above is loosely based on modern intelligence tests. As you can imagine, part of this chapter will discuss the historical development and modern definition of intelligence. However, directly tied to the concept of intelligence is that of memory. For some practicing psychologists (e.g., school psychologists, clinical psychologists), intelligence is enormously important. For researchers, especially cognitive psychologists, the study and understanding of memory are foundational to an understanding of the human mind. However, for every individual person, irrespective of occupation, the existence of both memory and intelligence are crucial for normal life. In this chapter, we will discuss both topics in detail. Enjoy!

Memory

The Basics of Memory

Everything we are, in our conscious experience, is dependent upon memory. Think about this for a few moments: How would you answer the question, "Who are you?" Most people would begin their answer by stating their name, and then stating their occupation, and then personal interests. These pieces of information—names, occupations, and personal interests—collectively account for our ideas of who we are. Moreover, these pieces of information are all memories that were encoded, stored, and in the present moment retrieved when someone asks for your name, occupation, or interests. Without memory we would live in a constant state of rediscovery, whereby every instance would be newly learned, even if the instance had occurred several hundred times. And thus, the question of who we are could plausibly be answered differently each day.

© CHAIWATPHOTOS, 2014. Used under license from Shutterstock, Inc.

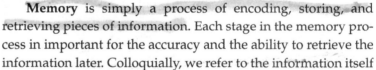

Memory is simply a process of encoding, storing, and retrieving pieces of information. Each stage in the memory process in important for the accuracy and the ability to retrieve the information later. Colloquially, we refer to the information itself as a "memory." For example, I may have a memory of my PhD graduation. The ability to bring that particular memory into my cognitive awareness depends on encoding, storage, and retrieval.

Memory: The process of encoding, storage, and retrieval of any piece of information obtained through conscious experience; a memory can also be an individual instance of encoded, stored, and retrieved information.

To illustrate the process of memory, imagine that you are a scientist conducting interviews for your research on the long-term effects of watching too much reality television. As a scientist, you need a lot of data! Another name for data is simply *information*. As participants come to your experiment they are handed a questionnaire that asks various questions about how often they watch reality television. Now, the questions on the questionnaire are very important for real scientists, but the limiting of questions also draws a nice parallel with the process of encoding.

There is a finite but unimaginably large amount of information that can be gathered and stored in the human mind, just as there are an almost infinite number of questions a scientist can ask about reality television. However, as humans, and as scientists, we must pick the most important information and change it to a form we can use. For example, if I ask a question such as, "Do you enjoy reality television?" participants may write things such as "absolutely!," or "No, it is the bane of human existence." These are informative, but I need numbers in order to analyze the data. So, we must transform the information into a useful form that can be stored. The process of **encoding** changes information into a form that can be used later, perhaps during some important task.

After encoding occurs, the information must then be stored in the mind. This component of the memory process is titled **storage**. For the psychologists studying reality television, these data may be stored on a flash drive, or as paper copies in a filing cabinet. The organization of how these files (memories) are stored is important for the last step: retrieval.

Retrieval occurs when we pull some of the information stored in memory back to conscious awareness. For the psychologists this would be like taking data from the filing cabinet in order to analyze it, or write a report about it. For example, if someone asks you about your third grade teacher, the memories for this period of your life are most likely not active in conscious awareness. Rather, they must be retrieved from storage.

Encoding: The process of transforming experienced information into a form that can be later stored and used by the brain.

Storage: The process of storing.

Retrieval: The process of recognizing and then correctly recalling a piece of information from storage in long-term memory.

Sensory memory: A form of memory that holds large amounts of sensory information such as sights and sounds for a very brief amount of time, normally only a few seconds.

Memory Structures (STM- WM and LTM)

So far, we have discussed the process of encoding → storage → retrieval to illustrate how information gets to conscious awareness. However, this process is a little more complicated. To begin, there are three basic types of memory, not just one as we have discussed thus far. The stage model of memory suggests the process of encoding → storage → retrieval is integrated into these three different levels of memory. These levels are sensory memory, short-term memory, and long-term memory.

Sensory memory is a very short duration type of memory that helps construct a continuous perceptual world rather than thousands of isolated segments. We have different types of sensory memory for the different senses humans possess. For example, sensory memory for vision is also called iconic memory, whereas sensory memory for audition is sometimes called echoic memory. The duration and capacity of sensory memory were partly discovered by a series of interesting experiments conducted by George Sperling (Sperling, 1960).

In his experiments, Sperling briefly presented participants with a display consisting of rows of letters similar to Figure 5.1. Each display was visible for 1/20 of 1 second, and was followed by a short duration of time—no more than 1 second. After this short duration, the participants would hear a low-, medium-, or high-pitched tone indicating that they should try to recall their visual memory for either the bottom, medium, or top row of letters.

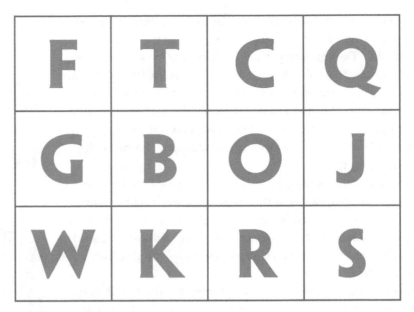

FIGURE 5.1   Example stimulus shown to participants in Sperling's classic 1960 study.

In his classic experiment, Sperling discovered after about 1/3 of 1 second, participants were unable to recall letters in the rows. This demonstrated sensory memory may have a large capacity, but its duration is quite limited (e.g., 1/3 second). Years of research after Sperling's study have demonstrated sensory memory's capacity is quite large, but its duration ranges from 1/4 to only a few seconds.

Unlike other types of memory we discuss in the sections to follow, sensory memory cannot be retained for a longer duration through the process of rehearsal (e.g., studying). Instead, sensory memory seems to happen automatically, without awareness, and is very difficult to manipulate through psychological techniques. Further, sensory memory captures a very large amount of information. This information must be selected and sent to conscious awareness. In order to send certain pieces of sensory information to conscious awareness, we must focus—pay attention to—that specific information. Thus, attention is the gateway from sensory memory to conscious awareness.

The conscious awareness we have been discussing to this point is more formally termed **short-term memory**, at least for those of us who study human memory processes. Another term for short-term memory is "**working memory**." The name "working memory" illustrates qualities of this memory stage by point to its global function, rather than simply its duration relative to long-term memory.

Short-term, or working, memory can be imagined as a desktop on which you do homework. A desk is only a certain size; therefore, the capacity of books, papers, pencils, and so forth that can be held on the desk is quite certainly limited. To further illustrate the roles of short-term memory, it is important to discuss what it is not: it is not a long-term storage space. Imagine in your room you have a desktop (short-term memory) that can be useful for reading books and taking notes. You may also stack papers on your desk in order to remind you they need to be read. Short-term memory, like a desktop, is useful for putting a

Short-term memory: A type of temporary memory used to hold information long enough for an individual to process it, and make sense of it; also called *working memory.*

Working memory: The Baddeley model describing how information is processed in short-term memory by means of a control system (central executive system) and systems that maintain verbal material (phonological loop) and visual material (visual-spatial sketch pad).

limited amount of information right in front of you (in conscious awareness) so it can be manipulated. People use short-term memory to think about certain items, events, or people, with the assumption that this newly retrieved information may be used to guide future behavior; in fact, contemporary research may suggest the evolutionary function of memory is to plan for future events (Klein, Robertson, & Delton, 2010; Nairne, Pandeirada, Gregory, & Van Arsdall, 2008).

As previously mentioned, short-term memory has a limited capacity. For example, try this on your friend or roommate: Take a look at Figure 5.2 containing various numbers of digits. Beginning at Row 1 and, moving from left to right, read aloud one digit per second until you reach the end of the row. After stating the digits, ask your "participant" to repeat back that number of digits. This is a simple test of short-term memory.

Research conducted by George Miller (1956) demonstrated the same pattern your participant will probably demonstrate: that accuracy of recalling the string of digits decreases as more digits are added (going from Row 1 to Row 4). To be specific, Miller discovered humans have a short-term memory capacity of approximately seven plus or minus two items. So, we seem to be capable of holding five to nine different items for a short amount of time. Contemporary research has examined this "magic number seven" idea more carefully. The results of highly controlled studies seem to suggest that short-term memory actually has a smaller capacity: four plus or minus one (Cowan, 2001, 2010).

Short-term memory also has a limited duration, as does sensory memory. However, the duration for short-term memory is much longer. On average, the amount of time a piece of information will remain in short-term memory—without rehearsal—is 20 seconds. The "without rehearsal" piece of this statement is very important. By using different rehearsal techniques people can retain information in short-term memory for much longer.

ROW 1	16 7 9 7 1
ROW 2	27 7 2 4 2 5
ROW 3	37 4 2 9 7 8 3
ROW 4	42 7 9 4 6 3 5 9

FIGURE 5.2 Sample stimulus used to test a person's short-term memory capacity.

FIGURE 5.3   Idealized process from sensory memory to long-term memory (LTM).

Until this point in the chapter, we have discussed short-term memory as though it is a singular unit. However, research by Alan Baddeley led to the formulation of the Baddeley working memory model of short-term memory (Figure 5.4). According to Baddeley, short-term memory is divided into three components: the visuospatial sketchpad, the phonological loop, and the central executive. The **visuospatial sketchpad** is specialized to process visual and spatial information, as the name implies. For example, if you ask a veteran student where a certain building is located on campus, the student may provide verbal instructions on where to go. As you hear the verbal instructions, you may be creating a mental map of where to go. This spatial organization of a campus's layout on your small mental "desktop" is performed, according to Baddeley, using the visuospatial sketchpad.

The verbal instructions provided by the veteran student are processed by the **phonological loop,** which is specialized for auditory and verbal information. This is also the part of short-term memory assumed to be used during most traditional memory tasks, such as remembering word lists. The **central executive** of short-term memory acts as a type of CEO. It organizes and integrates the specialized processing of the visuospatial sketchpad and phonological loop prior to encoding the information into long-term memory. The central executive also plays a key role in dictating when retrieval from long-term memory will occur, and which information will be retrieved.

Once information is in short-term memory after leaving sensory memory, it has the potential to become stored in long-term memory. Encoding, as mentioned earlier, helps move information from its temporary state in short-term memory to

Visuospatial sketchpad: A part of Alan Baddeley's working memory model specialized to process visual and spatial information.

Phonological loop: A part of Alan Baddeley's working memory model specialized to process verbal and auditory information.

Central executive: A part of Alan Baddeley's working memory model responsible for coordinating the input and output of information to working memory, as well as to integrate the separate pieces of information from the visuospatial sketchpad and phonological loop; the "CEO" of working memory.

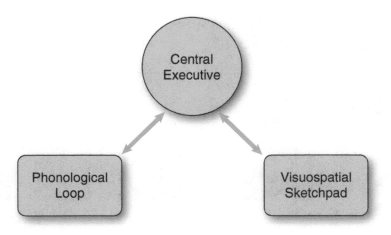

FIGURE 5.4   Baddeley's working memory model.

a much longer lasting state in long-term memory. This process is also sometimes called **rehearsal**. There are two main types of rehearsal that can be used to get information into long-term memory—they are called maintenance rehearsal and elaborative rehearsal. **Maintenance rehearsal** is a very shallow level of processing. A good example of maintenance rehearsal is simply rote memorization, or saying a phone number over and over again to yourself. If, for example, you are using maintenance rehearsal to try and remember a term such as classical conditioning, you might simply memorize the definition from your textbook by stating it to yourself many times.

Elaborative rehearsal is a much deeper level of processing that is more effective at storing information into long-term memory. Elaborative processing works by trying to create connections between the newly acquired information and existing information already present in long-term memory. For example, if you were using elaborative rehearsal to try and remember classical conditioning, you might think about the temporal layout of the process of classical conditioning. You might also think of several examples of classical conditioning from your own life, and you might try to imagine new situations to which classical conditioning could be applied. All of these events use already-existing information in long-term memory in order to more efficiently encode new information into long-term memory.

Long-Term Memory (And Application)

Who is your favorite childhood cartoon character? Do you remember what classical conditioning is? What happened at your 16th birthday? Do you know how to ride a bicycle? If you can answer these questions, you are successfully retrieving appropriate information from your **long-term memory system**. Later in this chapter we see how these questions require you to find sources from different types of long-term memory. Successfully encoded memories, partly through rehearsals, transition from working memory to a much longer-term storage capacity known as long-term memory. Unlike short-term (working) memory, long-term memory allows the information to be retrieved at longer delays (Anderson, 1990). Thus, in theory, long-term memory can store an infinite amount of information as long as we want. Then, we can retrieve the content any time we want. In reality, however, our long-term memory system is not perfect; we will take a look at a few examples later.

Think about how your USB flash drive works. You can open a new Word document, make edits, and save it for later uses. You can save as much as the storage size (2 GB, 16 GB, or 64 GB) allows you and sometimes you might use more than one flash drive. What would happen if you do not remember the specific sub-folder where you last saved your working document? You might have to spend hours trying to scan through multiple flash drives and folders within. To avoid this unnecessary waste searching, it will be beneficial to organize the contents based on some criteria. Likewise, long-term memories seem to have several sub-types. Atkinson and Shiffrin (1968) were among the first researchers to argue for diverse long-term memory types. Later, numerous lab studies (e.g., Jacoby, Toth, & Yonelinas, 1993; Schacter & Tulving, 1994) successfully differentiated between at least 3 and 4 long-term memory systems (Figure 5.5).

Rehearsal: The process of repeatedly introducing new information in order to retain the information in short-term memory, or to introduce into long-term memory.

Maintenance rehearsal: A relatively shallow level of rehearsal typically characterized by repeating something many times (e.g., repeating a phone number in your head).

Elaborative rehearsal: A type of rehearsal in which a person actively tries to tie new information to pre-existing information already in long-term memory. The net effect is to increase the likelihood that the new information is retained in long-term memory.

Long-term memory: One of the human memory systems that can store information for a long-period of time.

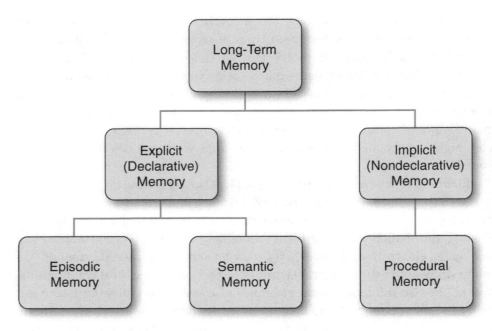

FIGURE 5.5   Different types of long-term memory.

EXPLICIT MEMORY

Explicit memory is conscious recollection of facts or experiences (Graf & Schacter, 1985). It requires you to consciously think about general knowledge about this world and specific concepts (semantic memory), or may involve your conscious access to your personal experiences that took place at a specific time in a certain place (episodic memory). It is possible for you to have semantic memory of camping (e.g., an outdoor activity in the forest) by learning its definition but if you have never camped, you will not have episodic memory. For some of you, it is possible to have experienced camping before reading it in a book. You might remember one summer night when you were sitting by a bonfire making s'mores with your cousins at a camping site. In this case, you have built your episodic memory first and have gained knowledge about what camping is (semantic memory) based on that experience (Figure 5.6).

Semantic memory is similar to a reservoir of facts and knowledge about this world. It shows how words, concepts, languages (e.g., verbal symbols), and their relations are woven together to provide an understanding of facts (Tulving, 1972). **Episodic memory** enables us to remember, "a specific moment in one's personal past and consciously recollects some prior episode or state" (Wheeler, Stuss, & Tulving, 1997, p. 333). Semantic and episodic memories are conceptually distinct, and recent brain-damaged patients are providing more vivid evidence supporting the differences between the two memory systems. Episodic memory seems to be more vulnerable to neuronal deterioration and showed a greater severity in anterograde amnesia (failure to form new memories since the onset of the damage-inducing event) than semantic memory (Tulving, 2002).

Explicit memory: A type of long-term memory; conscious memory about facts or experiences.

Semantic memory: A type of long-term memory (explicit memory, to be exact); it is one's general knowledge about the world and specific concepts.

Episodic memory: A type of long-term memory (explicit memory, to be exact); conscious recollection of one's personal experiences that took place at a specific time in a certain place.

FIGURE 5.6   Episodic (left) and semantic (right) memory about camping.

In addition, these two memory systems seem to be processed in different brain areas. Episodic memory depends on the hippocampal area, whereas semantic memory is primarily concentrated in the underlying cortices (Vargha-Khadem et al., 1997; Figure 5.7).

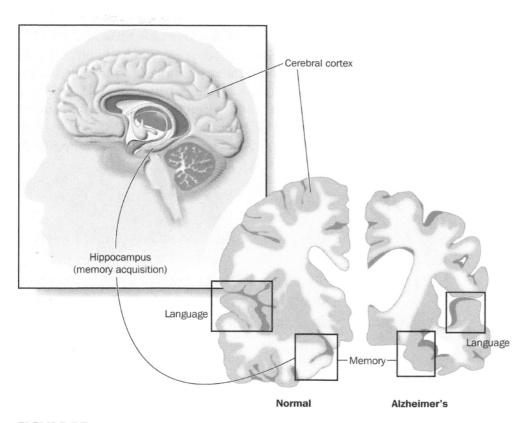

FIGURE 5.7   Hippocampus area.

© studioVin, 2014. Used under license
from Shutterstock, Inc.

© Tribalium, 2014. Used under license
from Shutterstock, Inc.

FIGURE 5.8   Semantic (left) vs. procedural (right) memory.

IMPLICIT MEMORY

Implicit memory: A type of long-term memory; memory about how to perform a task (usually accessed unconsciously).

Unlike explicit memory, **implicit memory** is unconsciously accessible and it is generally easier to demonstrate or perform this memory than to explain it. Imagine you have to teach someone how to tie a knot only by words. It will be much easier to teach someone by showing your performance. In other words, implicit memory is shown when "performance on a task is facilitated in the absence of conscious recollection" (Graf & Schacter, 1985, p. 501). One type of implicit memory is known as procedural memory, which involves learning of motor and cognitive skills (Schacter, Wagner, & Buckner, 2000). In the next section, we discuss procedural memory and some evidence that supports the difference between procedural and semantic memory systems.

WHAT MEMORY RESEARCHERS LEARNED FROM H. M.

"Right now I'm wondering, have I done or said anything amiss? You see, at this moment everything looks unclear to me, but what happened just before? That's what worries me. It's like waking from a dream; I just don't remember. Every day is alone in itself, whatever enjoyment I've had, and whatever sorrow I've had."

—Henry Gustav Molaison, aka H. M. (1926–2008)

Amnesia patient H. M. is one of the most famous patients in memory research. At the age of 10 H. M. started having minor seizures and by 16 he was having so many epileptic seizures that they began to seriously debilitate him. H. M. ended up receiving brain surgery that included bilateral removal of the hippocampus and part of the temporal lobes in treatment of seizures (Corkin, 1984).

After the surgery, H. M. maintained a normal I.Q. score and digit span, and was able to carry out a normal conversation (Scoville & Milner, 1957). However, just a few minutes after speaking with someone, he had no memory of having a conversation. H. M. seemed to have lost the ability to transfer information into long-term memory. Despite serious anterograde amnesia (lack of ability to remember after the amnesia-inducing events such as brain surgery or brain damage) related to explicit memory, H. M. still preserved the ability to learn procedural memory. For example, H. M. was given instructions to learn a star-tracing task (tracing an outline of a star) only by using a reflection in the mirror. He showed a typical normal learning curve (getting better after 3–4 sessions) and therefore demonstrated his procedural memory. However, he had no conscious recollection of having ever learned the task before (Milner, 1970). Case studies with H. M. greatly advanced our understanding of the difference between short-term and long-term memory, as well as the difference between explicit and implicit (procedural, to be exact) memory systems. We now know, and we owe this to H. M., the importance of the hippocampal area and the medial temporal lobe as long-term memory consolidation places.

As shown by H. M., amnesia patients and other brain-damaged patients suffer from different kinds of memory loss. However, memory loss is not always a neurological concern but a truly natural event that occurs to healthy normal people.

Forgetting

You might first think forgetting is inconvenient. Imagine you don't have to study at all because you have such a perfect memory. Wouldn't that be nice! However, it can be a blessing and a curse to be able to remember everything. Earlier in this chapter we learned that people form a meaning-based conceptual map to form long-term memory, which allows us to remember things later. But why do we forget?

One can argue that we have limited storage and when we learn new things, old things have to be deleted (forgotten) to make room for the new materials. Others might think (e.g., Freud) we forget things because certain memories are too big of a threat to our reality identity. Though there are many different ways to argue why we forget, here we will look at the interference theory.

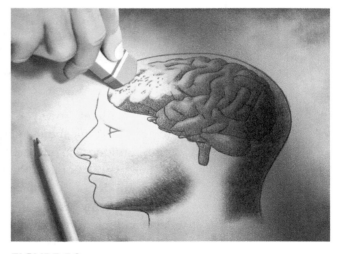

FIGURE 5.9   Forgetting.
© Andrea Danti, 2014. Used under license from Shutterstock, Inc.

INTERFERENCE THEORY

Interference theory is currently the dominating theory to explain forgetting (Eysenk & Keane, 2005). First, interference can happen because new materials are competing with something you used to know and interferes with the old information. This is known as retroactive interference, a "disruption of memory by learning other material during the retention interval" (Eysenk & Keane,

Interference theory: A theory of forgetting which suggests most forgetting is the result of an interaction between new and previously learned information, leading either to a failure to learn new material, or a forgetting of past material.

2005, p. 563). You can think of this as an overwriting model. New information writes over what you had known previously and interferes with old materials.

Interference can happen in an opposite way. Old materials can compete with new things we are trying to learn. This type of interference is known as proactive interference, a "disruption of memory by previous learning, often of similar materials" (Eysenk & Keane, 2005, p.564). We can understand this as a force-of-habit model. For example, your email portal regularly requests you change your password for security purposes. Next time you log on to your email you might type in your old password and make an error. Old information has become a habit and interferes with the new material.

Why does it happen? One possible explanation is retrieval cue competition between target words (the words that you are asked to remember) and similar nontarget words (distractor words that are similar to the target words, but that you are not asked to remember; Lustig, & Hasher, 2001). When target information is not consolidated, seemingly similar targets can compete and result in interference at a retrieval cue. In this context, (memory) consolidation is "the process lasting for several hours or possible even days which fixes information in long-term memory" (Eysenk & Keane, 2005, p. 225).

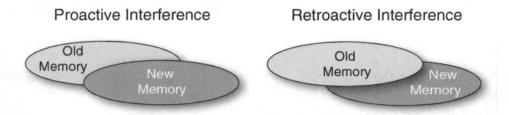

FIGURE 5.10   Proactive (left) and retroactive (right) interference.

In our lives, however, interference is not the only obstacle for accurate memory recall. Think about a penny. Most of us have used a penny and would show a high confidence in our ability to accurately recall (or recognize) a penny. Contrary to our expectation, in Nickerson and Adams's (1979) study, most participants failed to identify the correct penny among 15 different versions of U.S. penny. This surprising result suggests there is little correlation between your confidence level and memory accuracy. If the accuracy of long-term memories does not measure up to our expectation, what makes us forget things so easily? There is no one absolute answer to this question, but we will review a few characteristics of our long-term memory.

SEVEN DEADLY SINS OF MEMORY

Schacter (1999) discussed the forgetful nature of our long-term memory with following seven characteristics.

1. **Absent-mindedness:** This refers to the breakage between your memory and your attention. Attention is required to encode the information accurately, and inattention will lead to a failure of proper encoding. This can sometimes happen due to distractions, and if it happens, you may have to repeat the same task. For example, let's think about our absent-minded

professor Dr. Jones. While talking to a friend on her cellphone, Dr. Jones complains how her memory has gotten worse lately. Dr. Jones then says, "For example, at this very moment, I can't even remember where I put my cell phone!," forgetting she was using the exact device she "misplaced." This illustrates the concept of absent-mindedness.

2. **Transience:** Despite our effort, memory tends to diminish quickly. It describes the temporal nature of our memory. Rehearsal or repeat can be useful in overcoming transience.

3. **Blocking:** Blocking is also known as the tip-of-the-tongue phenomenon—when you feel and try to remember things but cannot articulate it. It happens because of the inaccessibility of stored information. If you want to try this yourself, pull out a piece of paper and write down the names of the seven dwarves from the story of Snow White. Can you remember all of their names? If you can picture their faces and feel you know their names but just can't articulate them, you are experiencing the tip-of-the-tongue phenomenon!

4. **Misattribution:** This refers to the confusion of the original source of information. You might have a general scheme of an event, but have difficulty remembering when and where it had happened. You might remember Tim as the person who borrowed a book from you a year ago, when in fact it was Paul.

5. **Suggestibility:** Due to the constructive nature of our memory system, leading words or suggestions from others can alter and bias our memory. See the section on memory reconstruction for further information on suggestibility.

6. **Bias:** Current personal experiences or events can cloud how we remember similar events that happened in the past.

7. **Persistence:** According to Schacter, negative events tend to linger longer than neutral or positive memories. Other studies have shown better memory for emotionally (any emotions) intense information (Ashcraft & Radvansky, 2010).

Memory Reconstruction

Human memory is a fascinating construct though it has several limitations such as the seven weaknesses we have just reviewed. Long-term memory is malleable; it can be surprisingly easy to implant a new memory or alter one's existing memory. In a series of studies, Loftus and colleagues provided strong evidence that the human memory system does not work as a recording device but rather is susceptible to changes. In one study, Loftus and Palmer (1974) showed a short video describing a car accident to participants. Later she asked the participants to estimate the speed of the cars by using leading verbs such as, "How fast were the cars going when they contacted (in other conditions, the word "contacted" was replaced by *hit, bumped into, collided with, smashed into* each other?" The results showed that participants' memory about the

FIGURE 5.11   Car accidents and estimated speed.
© GraphicGeoff, 2014. Used under license from Shutterstock, Inc.

speed of cars systematically increased in relation to the severity of the leading verb. For example, if the lead word was "smashed," the estimated speed was a little over 40 mph. On the other hand, when "contacted" was used as the lead word, the estimated speed was around 31 mph.

Additionally, Loftus (1975) found implanting a new false memory was not as difficult as one might think. She used a similar paradigm as in her previous study and showed another short video involving a car accident. Later Loftus asked one group of participants, "How fast was the white sports car going when it passed the barn while traveling along the country road?" There was no barn shown in the film. The other group received the same question without the leading word ("How fast was the white sports car going while traveling along the country road?"). Participants were brought back to the lab a week later and were asked whether they remember seeing a barn in the film. Surprisingly, 17% of the participants in the leading-word condition answered that they saw a barn. These results show the long-term memory system may not be as accurate as we wish and can be changed by a simple leading question.

What would happen if we apply memory reconstruction to eyewitness testimony? Since eyewitness testimonies are so critical in legal procedures (either false or true), would witnesses' long-term memory be free from this reconstructive nature? Unfortunately, study results imply the answer is no. This bias worsened when there was a weapon involved in the crime scene (Loftus, 1979). The unexpectedness of the crime and the brevity of the scene with the combination of a life-threatening weapon seemed to consume most of the victim's attention. As a result, victims showed poorer memory recall (or recognition) for other important details.[1]

[1] Go to the following website for an interesting TED Talk by Elizabeth Loftus on the fallibility of memory: http://www.ted.com/talks/elizabeth_loftus_the_fiction_of_memory

Long-Lasting Memories

As we have seen so far, long-term memories are not perfect. However, there seem to be special events immune from forgetting. For example, people still vividly recall the 9/11 terrorist attack or the Sandy Hook elementary shooting because both were very emotional and had an impact in our lives to a certain degree. Memories formed by "very important, dramatic, and surprising public or personal events" are known as **flashbulb memories** (Eysenk & Keane, 2005, p. 272). For example, people tend to remember clearly when they heard the news, where they were, how they felt at the time, and whom they were with. In addition, due to the nature of the events, flashbulb memories are frequently rehearsed and have personal importance (Conway et al., 1994).

Flashbulb memories are typically long lasting, precise, and accurate (Brown & Kulik, 1977). It seems people have surprisingly accurate time-stamped memory for certain events. It is therefore quite natural to be curious why flashbulb memories are exceptionally resistant to forgetting. To examine the mechanism behind flashbulb memory, Conway and colleagues (1994) asked U.K. and non-U.K. groups their memory about Margaret Thatcher's (a former Prime Minister of the United Kingdom from 1979 to 1990) resignation. At the time of the study, her resignation was quite unexpected and considered historic by most British people. Both U.K. and non-U.K. groups were tested three to four times (within 10 days of the resignation, 14 days, around 350 days; a small group was tested again after 26 months of the resignation) for the flashbulb memory formation. If flashbulb memories are similar to any other types of long-term memory, people should show a typical forgetting curve and not be able to retain many concrete details about the event.

> Flashbulb memories: A type of long-term memory. Memories formed by dramatic and surprising public or personal events; typically known to be immune from forgetting.

© Ken Tannenbaum, 2014. Used under license from Shutterstock, Inc.

© Gina Jacobs, 2014. Used under license from Shutterstock, Inc.

FIGURE 5.12   9/11 attack (left) and massacre at Sandy Hook Elementary School (right).

Contrary, Conway's result showed that 86% of U.K. group showed very detailed memories about Thatcher's resignation even after 26 months; only 29% of the non-U.K. group showed the similar level of flashbulb memories.

The differences between U.K. and non-U.K. groups hint at the critical role of prior knowledge and rehearsal in flashbulb memory. U.K. participants who would have had more interest about Thatcher would be more likely to talk about the resignation frequently with their colleagues or family in their daily lives. In addition, her resignation received great media exposure, which made it easier for people to follow media reports (Conway et al., 1994) and give a greater chance for repeated encoding of the information.

Improving Memory

Based on what we have learned, what can we do to make the results benefit our own memory? Particularly, there are a few useful strategies for successful studying habits. Repeat the materials. As several studies showed, proper encoding and repetition help maintain the information for a longer period of time. In addition, when you repeat the materials, leave some space between your study sessions. New materials are more vulnerable to forgetting, so repeat the process to consolidate that information. Next, make the materials meaningful. Information that goes through elaborative rehearsal is processed deeply and more deeply processed information is typically remembered better (Craik & Lockhart, 1972). Lastly, minimize interference if possible. If you are studying two similar contents, leave some time between the two rather than working on them back to back. Devising your own memory aid (mnemonic device) can be useful to retain the information for a long time. These are only a few tips but numerous studies persistently showed effective results so they may be worth trying!

Intelligence

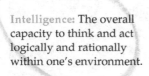

Intelligence: The overall capacity to think and act logically and rationally within one's environment.

Intelligence and intelligence testing has been one of the most studied and controversial constructs in the history of psychology (Wasserman, 2012). On the one hand, it has been extremely useful in identifying individual strengths and weaknesses by providing additional information on how to best teach struggling

© iQoncept, 2014. Used under license from Shutterstock, Inc.

students. On the other hand, it has been used to segregate and label individuals that, in turn, has produced devastating effects. Because of this, many professionals have debated intelligence tests in relation to their use and misuse, which has led to an ongoing debate about their appropriateness. To make matters even more difficult, psychologists have not been able to agree on an operational definition of intelligence.

Typically, when somebody mentions the word *intelligent*, you automatically equate it with the word smart. That is, people often view somebody who is intelligent as somebody who is smart. As you will see throughout the remainder of this chapter, there are a number of misconceptions and misunderstandings that need to be resolved by psychologists in the field today. My hope is that through further discussion in this text, you will garner a better understanding of what intelligence is and is not. That way, we can move away from answering the question, "Is this person smart?" to "How is this person smart?" By doing so, you will begin to understand that each individual has different skills and abilities that make him or her unique. The application of these skills and abilities to life situations is in turn what many use to determine the success of an individual.

History and Development

To gain a better perspective on intelligence, it is important to understand its historical underpinnings. Although the concept of intelligence can be traced back thousands of years to ancient philosophers, it was not until the late 19th to early 20th centuries that intelligence was quantifiably measured. Moreover, there were different events that sparked an interest into the need for intelligence testing. The first event was the advent of compulsory schools (Fagan & Wise, 2007). Simply put, compulsory schools meant children were mandated to attend school. By having compulsory school laws, schools were flooded with both students with and without disabilities. For the first time, educational systems were responsible for educating all children. This mandate presented an opportunity to utilize intelligence testing to identify whether students needed special education services (Wasserman, 2012).

Due to the demand to educate all students, Alfred Binet designed a test to measure intelligence among children. Because of this, he is often referred to as the "father" of the intelligence tests (Foschi & Cicciola, 2006). Binet collaborated with Theodore Simon and created a scale for intelligence in 1905. Although Binet used his scale to delve deeper into his understanding of intelligence, the test was primarily used to identify and treat individuals who were experiencing difficulties within the educational system (Nicolas & Levine, 2012). That is, Binet and Simon's first test was used to identify whether children could be educated within the traditional confines of a school building. To better understand how such results were achieved, it is important to gain a better understanding of the construct of the test.

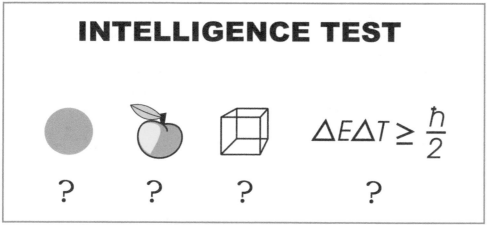

© Amitofo, 2014. Used under license from Shutterstock, Inc.

The Binet–Simon Scale was designed so that test items increased in level of difficulty related to age. As you can expect, a 10-year-old should be capable of completing more complex tasks than a 7 year old. This is the genesis of the concept of mental age. A child's overall intelligence was calculated by dividing the child's mental age by chronological age and multiplying the results by 100. Here would be the mathematical calculation for the child:

$$7 \text{ (mental age)} / 10 \text{ (chronological age)} \times 100 = 70 \text{ (IQ)}$$

Therefore, if students were demonstrating problem-solving abilities consistent with their chronological ages, they would be thought of as average intellect.

© HolyCrazyLazy, 2014. Used under license from Shutterstock, Inc.

Conversely, if a child was performing problem-solving abilities much lower than his or her chronological age (per the example above), they would have been thought of as intellectually inferior. Thus, the results of the test were used to give each student a classification describing the student's abilities and for making a determination as to the best placement for education. Currently, an IQ of 100 is considered average.

After the design of the Binet–Simon Scale, the popularity of intelligence tests began to rise due to the practicality of their use (Gottfredson & Saklofske, 2009). In 1910 Henry Goddard revised the Binet–Simon Scale for use within the United States. Also, in 1916 Lewis Terman (of Stanford University) revised and extended the work of Binet and Simon into adulthood to create the Stanford–Binet Intelligence Scale (Boake, 2002). One of the major changes made to the Binet–Simon Scale was that Terman introduced the term **intelligence quotient** (IQ) rather than using **mental age**. Within a few years, the Stanford–Binet Intelligence Scale was widely used throughout the United States. Currently, the Stanford-Binet Intelligence Scale is on its fifth revision and is viewed as one of the top intelligence tests used by practicing psychologists today. As mentioned, the practicality and popularity of intelligence tests created a lot of interest within the psychological field. This became particularly evident around the commencement of World War I.

© daughter, 2014. Used under license from Shutterstock, Inc.

Intelligence quotient: The global score derived from standardized intelligence tests.

Mental age: The age given at which a child is currently performing intellectually.

Army Alpha: The test given to literate military personnel to determine rank.

Army Beta: The nonverbal test given to illiterate military personnel to determine rank.

Prior to World War I, the United States' military lacked preparedness (Wasserman, 2012). Thus, Robert Yerkes created a taskforce to extend the use of intelligence testing from strictly education into the military (Boake, 2002). Yerkes and colleagues created two group-administered intelligence tests: **Army Alpha** and **Army Beta**. Both intelligence tests were used to assess incoming soldiers on their ability to serve the military and move into leadership positions. The two tests differed, however, in that Army Beta was administered to those who were illiterate or had language-based deficiencies. The Army Alpha was administered to those that were literate. In sum, over 2,000,000 soldiers were evaluated; during this time, intelligence testing grew largely in popularity within educational and noneducational settings (Sattler, 2008).

In 1939, David Wechsler introduced the Wechsler–Bellevue Intelligence Scale. Approximately 20 years prior, Wechsler received training as a psychological examiner and worked extensively with Army personnel that had failed both the Alpha and Beta intelligence tests (Boake, 2002). Therefore, it is no coincidence that the Wechsler–Bellevue Intelligence Scale was largely derived from the Army Alpha and Army Beta subtests (Sattler, 2008). That is, Wechsler did not design subtests from scratch, but rather utilized and modified a number of subtests that were currently in use on other measures of intelligence. Furthermore, Wechsler wanted to extend intelligence testing to adult populations that currently could not be assessed using the Stanford–Binet. Currently, there are four different Wechsler intelligence tests (Wechsler Preschool and Primary Scale of Intelligence–Fourth Edition, Wechsler Intelligence Scale for Children–Fifth Edition, Wechsler Adult Intelligence Scale–Fourth Edition, and Wechsler Nonverbal Ability Scales) widely used for intellectual assessment. Although the Stanford–Binet–Fifth Edition and the Wechsler scales are the more popular intelligence tests, it is important to note that a number of other intelligence tests exist and have demonstrated utility.

Right now, you may be wondering why there are so many intelligence tests. Remember at the beginning of this chapter when we said that psychologists have not been able to operationally define intelligence? Hence, a number of theories have been proposed throughout the previous century in an attempt to answer that question. One of the largest contributions to the overall understanding of intellectual theories is the use of statistics utilizing factor analysis. Further, factor analysis assists in identifying the number of factors that exist within a data set. Although the following is not an exhaustive list of contemporary theories, you will no doubt have a better understanding about how particular theorists would describe intelligence.

Contemporary Theories

CHARLES SPEARMAN

One of the first theories of intelligence was proposed by Charles Spearman when statistically analyzing performance on intelligence tests. Spearman noted there were large positive correlations among different test scores (Wasserman, 2012). This lead Spearman to argue that all the individual test scores were measuring one similar construct. He described this construct as **psychometric g**, which is commonly called general intelligence. Moreover, psychometric g is a global measure of an individual's overall ability, and is highly predictive of intellectual performance. Psychometric g is widely accepted by many psychologists in the field today. Spearman contended that there was one factor related to overall intelligence; other psychologists disagreed.

Psychometric g: A term coined by Spearmen regarding a person's general or overall intelligence.

LEWIS THURSTONE

It is no surprise that many psychologists disagreed with Spearman's perspective on psychometric g. In contrast to Spearman's view on intelligence, Thurstone contended that intelligence is not derived from a single factor (g) but rather seven equally weighted abilities (Sattler, 2008). These primary mental abilities consisted of:

1. **word fluency**—the ability to generate as many words as possible about a given topic, either semantic or phonemic.

2. **verbal comprehension**—the ability to understand verbal and written language in the form of questions, reading analogies, verbal fluency, similarities, and word usage and retrieval.

3. **spatial visualization**—the ability to mentally manipulate and analyze both two- and three-dimensional visual information.

4. **number facility**—the ability to carry out mathematical operations quickly, accurately, and internally and being able to use numbers in mathematical problems.

5. **associative memory**—the ability to learn new information through repetition and the relationship between unrelated situations.

6. **reasoning**—ability in all three types: inductive, deductive, and arithmetic.

7. **perceptual speed**—the capacity to quickly and accurately compare letters, symbols, or pictures, in two similar visual spaces.

ROBERT STERNBERG

Sternberg contented intelligence is best understood and defined by those who adapt successfully within their environment. Furthermore, Sternberg believed individuals could use their intelligence to adapt and shape their external environment to achieve success. Sternberg purposed a triarchic theory of successful intelligence, which was comprised of analytical, practical, and creative intelligence.

1. **analytical intelligence**—used while analyzing, evaluating, criticizing, reasoning, and judging

2. **practical intelligence**—used when implying, implementing, and using the intelligence

3. **creative intelligence**—used when discovering, inventing, and creating

Sternberg's triarchic theory of successful intelligence suggests individuals are not limited to just strength or one of the three areas of intelligence. Rather, individuals need to identify their strengths and use those to overcome their weaknesses to succeed and adapt within the context of their environment.

HOWARD GARDNER

A recent theory of intelligence is Howard Gardner's Multiple Intelligence Theory. Gardner believed intelligence is much more broadly defined than through a single IQ score or psychometric g. Rather, intelligence can be best described and understood through multiple abilities. Consequently, Gardner proposed a theory of **multiple intelligences**. His theory posits there are at least eight different types of intelligences:

Multiple intelligences: A theory suggesting that intelligence is a product of a number of abilities rather than one ability.

1. **logical-mathematical intelligence**—the ability to detect patterns, think logically, reason deductively, and carry out mathematical operations

2. **linguistic intelligence**—involves the mastery of spoken and written language to express oneself or remember things

3. **spatial intelligence**—involves the potential for recognizing and manipulating patterns of both wide spaces and confined spaces

4. **musical intelligence**—the capacity to recognize and compose musical pitches, tones, rhythms, and patterns and to use them for performance or composition

5. **bodily–kinesthetic intelligence**—involves the use of parts of the body or the whole body to solve problems or create products

6. **interpersonal intelligence**—the ability to recognize the intentions, feelings, and motivations of others

7. **intrapersonal intelligence**—the ability to understand oneself and use that information to regulate one's own life

8. **naturalistic intelligence**—the ability to discriminate patterns in nature

CATTELL–HORN–CARROLL

Currently, one of the most researched and widely accepted theories of intelligence is the Cattell–Horn–Carroll, or CHC, model (Schenider & McGrew, 2012). The **CHC Theory of Intelligence** is actually an integration of Cattell and Horn's and Carroll's models of intelligence. Originally, Cattell determined psychometric g could be broken down into two different broad abilities Gc and Gf. Thus, overall intelligence (*g*) is a combination of Gc (crystallized intelligence) and Gf (fluid intelligence). Horn expanded on Cattell's model and discovered, through factor analysis (advanced statistics), that there were many more broad abilities that could be aggregated to ascertain psychometric g. The combination of Cattell and Horn's work led Carroll to further investigate the statistical structure of intelligence.

> CHC Theory of Intelligence: The most researched and widely supported theory of intelligence.

Carroll added to the work of Cattell and Horn through additional factor analytic studies. He concluded that intelligence can be thought of, and supported, as a three-stratum model. Stratum III consists of an overall general ability (psychometric *g*). Stratum II consists of a number of broad abilities. These broad abilities are those uncovered by Cattell and Horn. Currently, most commonly administered intelligence tests measure approximately seven broad abilities. Those abilities are:

1. **crystalized intelligence (Gc)**—depth and breadth of knowledge and skills that are valued by one's culture

2. **fluid intelligence (Gf)**—the deliberate but flexible control of attention to solve novel problems that cannot be performed by relying exclusively on previously learned information

3. **short-term memory (Gsm)**—the ability to encode, maintain, and manipulate information in one's immediate awareness

4. **long-term storage and retrieval (Glr)**—the ability to store information and fluently retrieve it later through association

5. **processing speed (Gs)**—the ability to quickly perform automatic, routine cognitive tasks, particularly when pressured to maintain focused concentration

6. **visual processing (Gv)**—the ability to analyze and synthesize visual stimuli

7. **auditory processing (Ga)**—the ability to analyze and synthesize auditory stimuli

Further, Carroll concluded broad abilities were comprised of a combination of narrow abilities. Narrow abilities were identified at Stratum I. Currently, there are approximately 90 narrow abilities that have been identified.

Carroll's work at identifying a three-stratum model of intelligence has been extremely influential for psychologists and scholars alike. It has provided a foundation for the understanding of what intelligence is and is not. Also, it has provided a common language to aid in the design and interpretation of intelligence tests. That is, most intelligence tests use factor analysis to determine whether the test has items that represent many of the broad abilities proposed by the contemporary CHC theory.

Genetic and Environmental Influences

© iQoncept, 2014. Used under license from Shutterstock, Inc.

Across decades, researchers have attempted to identify the exact influence of genetics and environment on intelligence (Sattler, 2008). Some of the questions have been answered, yet many other questions remain. For the purpose of this text, it is important to know you are not born with a level of intelligence. That is, intelligence is *not* innately given to each individual and can change throughout one's lifetime. Rather, you are born with a genetic predisposition or genotype that is expressed through interactions with your environment or your phenotype. One way in which psychological researchers have examined the relationship between intelligence and genetic/environmental influences is through twin studies. Specifically, researchers have measured intellectual ability of both monozygotic and dizygotic twins to identify the similarities and differences.

A plethora of research has been conducted to identify whether monozygotic twins (100% same genetics) have higher correlational coefficients than dizygotic twins (50% same genetics). There has been a convergence of data suggesting monozygotic twins have more similar IQs than dizygotic twins (Bartels, Rietveld, Van Baal, & Boomsma, 2002). This suggests that, in fact, genetic predispositions do affect IQ test scores. If genetic predispositions, however, accounted for 100% of the similarity in monozygotic twins, one would expect IQ scores to remain stable and similar across time. On the contrary, research shows the correlational coefficients between monozygotic twins decreases over time (Sundet, Eriksen, & Tambs, 2008). This provides evidence as to the effects of the environment on IQ test scores. Nobody truly knows the exact percentage genetics or environment play in overall IQ scores; however, it is widely agreed that both do influence IQ test scores. Therefore, intelligence is not a fixed number.

Rather, it is a manifestation of your genotype as it interacts with your phenotype throughout development.

To better understand the relationship between genetics and environment, please consider the following analogy. Each and every person is born with an "intellectual can." The size or capacity of the can is different for each person. The size of your "intellectual can" can be described as your genetic predisposition for acquiring intellectual abilities. Now, envision water being poured into each "intellectual can." The water represents environmental experiences and influences. Collectively, the amount of your "intellectual can" that is filled with water can be described as your overall intelligence. In theory, somebody with a larger capacity and greater amounts of experiences will demonstrate a much higher amount of intelligence than someone born with a smaller amount of capacity and the same experiences. Conversely, it is entirely possible for one individual born with a smaller "intellectual can" but vast amounts of experiences to have a higher level of intelligence than another individual with a much larger can with very few experiences.

Cultural Differences

As you can see from the history of intelligence testing and lack of an operational definition of intelligence, scrutiny can and does exist within the psychology profession. That is, intelligence and intelligence testing are ripe with controversy. If, as a psychologist, one cannot define intelligence, the floodgate is open for those who disagree with the results. This has never been as evident as it is in the field of education where multiple levels of litigation have ensued. Dating back to the second half of the 20th century, multiple landmark court cases have attempted to answer the question, "Are intelligence tests **culturally biased**?" This question arose because children from ethnic minorities were being classified for special education at a rate much higher than their overall percentage within the United State population. Judges have ruled in such cases yielding different interpretations. In *Larry P. v. Riles,* the judge concluded intelligence tests are racially and culturally biased. Conversely, in *Parents in Action on Special Education v. Joseph P. Hannon,* the federal court ruled intelligence tests are not culturally biased. These conflicting views have made it difficult to answer the question "Are intelligence tests culturally biased?" Rather, they have sparked a call for those familiar with intelligence testing to make judgments about their application with different ethnic groups (Sattler, 2008).

Culturally biased: A term used when an intelligence test gives an unfair advantage to White, affluent, male test takers.

These seminal cases have created a political "hot potato" resulting in polarizing viewpoints as to the use of intellectual tests for ethnic minorities. The aforementioned litigation have presented the opportunity for psychologists to dissect intelligence tests specifically looking at their psychometric properties. An effective test, for example, must consistently yield the same results (reliability) and also must accurately measure what it purports to measure (validity). Advancement in statistical methods

and analyses has allowed researchers to answer these questions as well as iden-tify a hierarchical model (another statistical analysis) of intelligence. Results of such analyses should be able to identify whether intelligence tests are culturally biased. That is, if intelligence tests are consistent in their measurement across eth-nic groups, they are not assumed to be culturally biased. The consensus is that intelligence tests are psychometrically fair (Gottfredson & Saklofske, 2009). The question remains, "Why are there group differences in IQ scores across racial/ethnic groups?"

To this point, we have touched on sensitive issues as to whether current intel-ligence tests are culturally biased. Current psychologists would often argue "no"; however, others might argue "yes." It is important to differentiate between cultur-ally biased and culturally loaded. In fact, intelligence tests are culturally loaded (Sattler, 2008). Therefore, all intelligence tests have some degree of relationship with the culture in which they were designed. Tests that are largely language based can be considered to have high cultural loadings, whereas tests that require visual–spatial processing may be less **culturally loaded**. Moreover, it would be virtually impossible to eliminate any influence of culture that exists within an intelligence test. Therefore, it is entirely possible that different levels of cultural exposure could result in group differences in IQ scores. This, along with many other explanations, must be taken into account through interpretation by a psy-chologist. For example, we would never recommend giving a largely language-based intelligence test to somebody who just moved to the United States from a non-English speaking country. Thus, intelligence test scores must be interpreted within the context that they are achieved.

Culturally loaded: A term used when many of the items on the intelligence test are derived from the mainstream culture.

Intelligence Conclusions

To this point, you have learned much more about the psychological construct of intelligence and current theories attempting to explain what intelligence is and is not. You also have learned about some of the controversy surrounding intel-ligence, specifically intelligence tests. What we would like you to understand is that all current theories are essentially inaccurate (Horn & Blankson, 2012). Theories are designed to be picked apart and put together to make a better theory. This is the basic nature of science. This has and will continue to occur as our understanding of intelligence evolves. In the past century, we have seen many benefits of using intelligence tests to predict successes, but we have also seen some of their drawbacks as well. If the continued use of intelligence tests is to label and segregate individuals, the same negative outcomes that have had detrimental effects on the profession will continue to exist. If, however, results of the tests are used to identify individual strengths and weaknesses, intelli-gence tests will continue to be a valuable asset to society. Our hopes would be that we continue to have these difficult discussions about their utility and how to make more accurate predictions using their results.

Summary

In this chapter we have discussed the complicated and fascinating processes involved in memory, as well as the interesting work that has occurred over the past century in order to fully understand human intelligence. These two psychological topics—memory and intelligence—are closely intertwined. Together they have helped us inhabit every corner of the planet. What does the future hold? It is difficult to tell, but any major accomplishments of our species, whether good or bad, will undoubtedly also be due to the both our ability to encode, store, and retrieve information (memory), and our ability to rationally engage and navigate the environment (intelligence).

© AntonioDiaz, 2014. Used under license from Shutterstock, Inc.

CHAPTER SIX

MOTIVATION AND EMOTION

Dr. Joe Engler
Fort Hays State University

LEARNING OBJECTIVES

- Define motivation
- Differentiate between instincts and reflexes
- Explain the relationship between needs and drives
- Describe Maslow's hierarchy of human needs
- Define cognitive dissonance theory
- Assess the relationship between achievement motivation and attribution theory
- Recognize the importance of self-efficacy
- Recall the main theories of emotion
- Explain how arousal relates to behavior
- List common eating disorders

We would frequently be ashamed of our good deeds if people saw all of the motives that produced them.

—Francois De La Rochefoucauld

© szefei, 2014. Used under license from Shutterstock, Inc.

Monsieur De La Rochefoucauld may have had a point.

Although television news programs and other media tend to focus on many of the negative acts of society, there really is no shortage of good deeds occurring on a daily basis. For example, people spend tens of billions of dollars each year on gifts; politicians generously give their time to charitable events; friends buy each other dinner or carry each other's grocery bags.

On the surface it appears that good deeds are all motivated by selfless love and generosity. Ultimately, this is how you would want the society in which you reside to behave. It is entirely possible, however, that the acts in which we engage are not motived by selfless love and generosity.

Adapted from *Psychology: The Human Puzzle* by Guy R. Lefrancois. Copyright © 2012 Bridgepoint Education. Reprinted by permission.

© juniart, 2014. Used under license from Shutterstock, Inc.

Is it possible that the real motives for these behaviors are not always what they seem? Do we sometimes give gifts mainly because we want something in return? When Evelyn says she will buy dinner for Edward because he helped her study, is that truly her motive? Or is her motive the hope that he will invite her on his yacht? Does Robert carry his friend's bag because he is younger and stronger and genuinely likes to help? Or is he driven by the urge to have a look at what's inside? How likely is it that the fund-raising politician is moved more by a desire to be reelected than by basic charitable impulses? These questions, along with many more, have caused debates among professionals as to why people are motivated to do the things that they do.

Further, the questions remain: How many of our behaviors are driven by their apparent motives, and how many of our behaviors are not driven by their apparent motives, but by ulterior motives?

What Is Motivation?

A Definition

Motivation: Conscious and unconscious forces that instigate, direct, and control our behavior.

The forces that drive us to action define **motivation**. The term derives from the Latin verb *movere*, which means "to move." Hence motivation deals with the forces, conscious or otherwise, that underlie our behaviors. Moreover, the "why" we engage in the behavior we do is motivation. Further, motivation theorists try to understand why we do certain things and not others, what instigates behavior, and what stops behaviors.

Motives are very closely tied to emotions. Clearly, complex combinations of feelings such as hate, fear, love, disgust, anger, and on and on are the reasons for much of what we do.

Ulterior Motives

By definition, ulterior motives are hidden: They are motives of which, as De La Rochefoucauld suggests, we would be ashamed were they made public. In fact, there is the possibility some of our ulterior motives are so well hidden even we don't recognize them.

Historically, psychology has not concerned itself much with ulterior motives; it prefers pieces of the puzzle that are more easily exposed—motives such as hunger and sex and our need for affection and achievement. But in its search for the forces that drive our behavior, it sometimes uncovers hidden motives.

Physiological and Behavioristic Approaches

Early theorists looked at biology and behaviorism for their explanations of motivation. It seemed to them that certain basic instincts and drives we inherit might account for much of our behavior.

Instincts

After all, they reasoned, we are animals, and many animal behaviors appear to be biologically determined. For example, migration in birds and butterflies, spawning and nesting in fish and fowl, and mating in mouse and man and woman are all examples of biologically determined behaviors. These complex behaviors, labeled **instincts**, are *common* to all members of a species, are apparently unlearned, and are little affected by experience (Figure 6.1).

Instincts: An innate tendency.

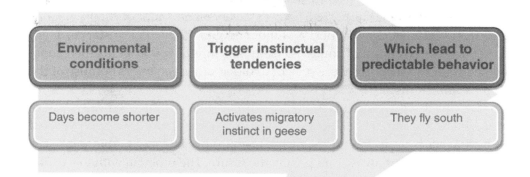

Environmental conditions	**Trigger instinctual tendencies**	**Which lead to predictable behavior**
Days become shorter	Activates migratory instinct in geese	They fly south

FIGURE 6.1 The instinct model. It is no longer a popular explanation for human behavior.

Photo © J. Marijs, 2014. Used under license from Shutterstock, Inc.

Many theorists, including William James (1890/1950), listed an enormous number of human instincts, among which were tendencies toward jealousy, cleanliness, clasping, biting, sucking, and even kleptomania (the urge to steal)! At one point, Bernard (1924) counted more than 6,000 human instincts. The problem with Bernard's count was that most of these tendencies are not instincts at all. That is, they're not *common* to all members of our species, and they don't remain unchanged by experience. Furthermore, lists of instincts explain very little about human behaviors. To say we are jealous because we have a jealousy instinct does nothing to explain our jealousy: It merely labels it. This is what is called the **nominal fallacy**—the assumption that naming something explains it.

The nominal fallacy is not uncommon in psychology. To say, for example, that Robert sets fires because he has *pyromania* or that Sandra has trouble learning because she has a learning disability or that Nora does not eat because she has *anorexia* does not explain a single one of these behaviors: It merely labels it. To attribute fighting to an aggressive instinct is, in the final analysis, no more revealing than to say that people fight because they fight.

Although instincts are now studied in relation to animal rather than human behavior, many psychologists contend that inherited biological tendencies play an important role in human behavior. As we saw in Chapter 2, for example, evolutionary psychologists point out that biology "prepares" us to learn certain things such as language or aversions to bitter-tasting and possibly poisonous foods, or fear of snakes. Others suggest that our tendencies toward aggressiveness and toward eating too much of the wrong things may also have a biological basis (van Honk, Harmon-Jones, Morgan, & Schutter, 2010).

Psychological Hedonism

Another explanation of motivation is a historical approach resting on the appealing and obviously true idea that people usually behave so as to achieve pleasure and to avoid pain. This notion, labeled **psychological hedonism**, or the *pain–pleasure principle*, seems, at first glance, to be a good explanation for human behavior, supported both by science and by anecdotal evidence (Riediger, Schmiedek, Wagner, & Lindenberger, 2009). For instance, I am sure that you can think of countless examples in which you performed some behavior for the sheer pleasure of it, or avoided other behaviors because of the unpleasant results.

But, by itself, psychological hedonism explains nothing. Basically it says that whatever we do, we do because doing so is pleasurable now or is expected to lead to pleasure in the future, or because it moves us away from pain or is expected to move us away from pain in the future. The problem with this explanation is it does not lead to any valid predictions or explanations unless pain and pleasure can be defined beforehand. Also, there appear to be differences between what one person defines as pleasurable and painful. Further, these are subjective states and not easily defined. If The Great Magician Mammoon eats broken bottles, we must assume that he, too, is driven toward pleasure and away from pain, but we might have been hard pressed to predict his glass-eating behavior in the first place.

Nominal fallacy: The assumption that naming something explains it.

Psychological hedonism: An approach to explaining human behavior suggesting that humans act in a way to achieve pleasure and avoid pain.

FIGURE 6.2   The drive-reduction model of motivation.

Needs and Drives

Still, there are clearly some common elements in our estimates of what is pleasant and unpleasant. As we saw in Chapter 4, certain stimuli, including food, drink, praise, and $50 bills, are likely to be positive reinforcers and increase the probability of performing a particular behavior. These are stimuli that satisfy our various *needs*. Hence, they are motivating and provide a behavioristic explanation for our actions.

PHYSIOLOGICAL NEEDS

One way of looking at needs is to say they *drive* behavior. Thus, the need for food gives rise to a hunger **drive**; for drink, to a thirst drive; and for sex, to a sex drive. These are basic **physiological needs**. From a hedonistic point of view, satisfaction of a basic need may be described as pleasurable and failure to satisfy a need as unpleasant.

Drive: Cause to move.

Physiological needs: Basic needs to satisfy internal functions of an organism.

It is clear that physiological drives are related to actual needs with respect to hunger and thirst. Deprivation of food and water leads to detectable physiological changes that are responsible for our awareness of these needs. Drinking or eating then leads to a reduction in the drive—hence the label **drive reduction**. But that there is more to hunger and thirst than simple physiology and drive reduction is also clear. As we see later, a host of external stimuli, as well as cognitive and emotional states, contribute to our eating and drinking behaviors (Figure 6.2). This gives rise to exactly how complex particular behaviors such as eating and drinking are to explain.

© luchschen, 2014. Used under license from Shutterstock, Inc.

With respect to sex, the picture is much murkier. Sexual deprivation is not accompanied by tissue changes, although sexual urges are clearly influenced by hormonal factors. Perhaps much more important for humans, however, are the varieties of other factors—cognitive, emotional, perceptual, and cultural—that are inextricably linked with sexual behavior.

Drive reduction: Behaviors that reduce an individual's drive.

PSYCHOLOGICAL NEEDS

Although the basic physiological needs seem clear, there is less agreement about what our **psychological needs** are. Likely candidates include the need for affection, belonging, achievement, independence, social recognition, and self-esteem.

Psychological needs: The need for affection, belonging, achievement, independence, social recognition and self-esteem.

Research supports the notion that outcomes such as emotional well-being and academic achievement are linked with satisfied psychological needs (Faye & Sharpe, 2008). However, unlike physiological drives that can be assumed to be common to most individuals, it is not entirely clear that everyone has the same psychological needs. In fact, many of these needs appear to be at least partly, if not entirely, learned. Consequently, some people seem to have a higher need for acceptance, achievement, or love than others.

Note, too, physiological needs can be entirely satisfied at least temporarily. You can eat or drink until you absolutely don't want any more. Psychological needs, on the other hand, are not so easily satisfied. Few people are ever totally sated with love, achievement, or affection.

One of the weaknesses of earlier drive-reduction explanations is they attributed behavior to tensions accompanying inner states that are subsequently reduced as a result of appropriate behaviors. For example, the drive-reduction explanation suggests that you engage in a behavior to satisfy an inner need or internal state. But even hunger is not entirely an internal state. If it were, people would always eat only as much as required to activate the physiological mechanism that says, "Whoa, you've had enough." But no, many people eat far more if the food *looks* and *tastes* especially good.

And some eat more if they're given a small appetizer first, even though the appetizer should have begun to *reduce* the hunger drive. Even rats will run a little faster toward the goal box when given a taste of food beforehand (Zeaman, 1949; Figure 6.3). Why? Because the food has incentive value; it provides the rat with **incentive motivation.** Basically, *incentive* relates to the subjective value of a goal or reward. The higher the value, the greater is the incentive; hence the more motivating the goal or reward.

Different goals have different incentive value. For example, monkeys typically work harder to obtain a banana than a piece of lettuce (Harlow, 1953)—and humans willingly pay more for a steak or a lobster than for a bowl of soup. These have more incentive value for us. Nor do we have to be given a taste beforehand, gifted as we are with imaginations; we can anticipate the consequences of our behavior. And there is little doubt our anticipations are powerful influences in directing our activities. Anticipation underlines the importance of the cognitive aspects of motivation.

Incentive motivation: The notion that the greater the subjective value of an item or reward, the more someone is motivated to achieve the item or reward.

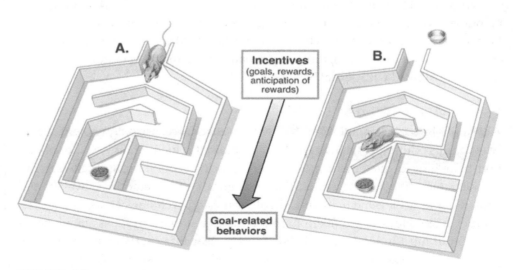

FIGURE 6.3   Drives alone cannot explain some behaviors. In Zeaman's 1949 study, rats that had already been given some food (b) performed better on a maze they knew led to food than did presumably hungrier rats (a).

Maslow's Hierarchy

Maslow (1970) suggests human actions may be accounted for by two systems of needs: the basic needs, and the **metaneeds.** The basic needs are called *deficiency needs* because when they are unsatisfied, they lead to behaviors designed to satisfy them. They include both physiological needs (food, drink) and psychological needs (security, love, and self-esteem).

Metaneeds are higher-level needs; they include cognitive needs, aesthetic needs, and the need for self-fulfillment. They're called *growth needs* because activities relating to them don't result from deficiencies, but from the organism's tendency toward growth.

According to Maslow, needs are hierarchically arranged as shown in Figure 6.4. What this means is that lower-level needs must be satisfied before higher-level needs are attended to. Thus, it is unlikely that a starving person would be attending to cognitive growth needs rather than the basic physiological need for food (Harper & Guilbault, 2008; Figure 6.4). Once the basic needs are met, however, that same individual may begin to focus on the growth needs.

Metaneeds: Higher-level needs related to an organism's tendency toward growth.

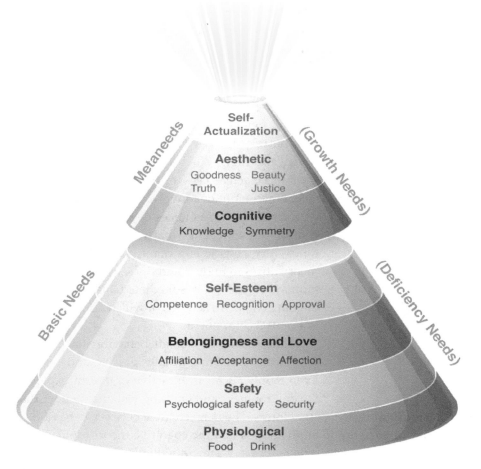

FIGURE 6.4 Maslow's hierarchy of needs. That the pyramid is open shows that self-actualization is a never-ending process.

© morrison, 2014. Used under license from Shutterstock, Inc.

To better understand Maslow's hierarchy of needs, consider the example of being stranded on a deserted island. What would be your first priority? How about your second priority? My guess is that your first priority would align with the physiological needs such as food, water, warmth, and rest. After these were satisfied, my assumption would be that you would seek safety. This is precisely what Maslow was describing when he created the hierarchy of needs.

Maslow was concerned with developing a theory that would encompass the more "human" qualities of behavior that define our "higher nature." We have an overpowering tendency toward growth, explains Maslow. This defines our very essence and is absolutely fundamental to mental health and happiness. The highest and most important of our growth needs is the need for **self-actualization** (discussed in Chapter 8).

Self-actualization: An ongoing process in which an organism attempts to reach its potential.

Unlike the more basic needs, the satisfaction of which can be ensured through appropriate activities (e.g., eating), self-actualization, as a need, is never satisfied. Self-actualization is rarely an achieved state but more an ongoing process. Depiction of Maslow's theory as a triangle is misleading, explains Rowan (1998), because it implies an end point to personal growth. Hence the open triangle in Figure 6.4.

Cognitive Views

Some early behavioristic positions tended to view us as passive victims of forces over which we have little control. Motives were seen as internal or external prods that pushed us this way and that.

Cognitive positions present a more active view of the human animal. They take into account the wealth of human emotions involved in behavior, dealing

© Fabio Berti, 2014. Used under license from Shutterstock, Inc.

with emotions not as forces over which we have no control, but as feelings that we actively and sometimes very consciously manipulate. The cognitive theorist tries to understand the sequence of ongoing human behavior as it is mediated and controlled by ongoing cognitive activity, of which affect (emotion) is a central component.

Note, however, not all behavioristic positions view the organism as totally passive and reactive. Even Skinner's rat is an active organism exploring the environment and emitting responses rather than simply reacting blindly to external forces. The main contrast between behavioristic and cognitive approaches to motivation is that the cognitive theorist looks at the role of rewards and punishments in terms of the individual's understanding and anticipation. In so doing, cognitive theories take into account what might well be the single most powerful explanatory concept in human motivation: our ability to delay gratification. Moreover, the ability to delay gratification is something that separates human beings from many other animal species. For example, I understand that if I do my job, my employer will reward me with a paycheck every 2 weeks. Because of this, I show up to work on time prepared for my duties. I know that if I perform these duties to a specific standard, I will be compensated for my efforts. Now, imagine telling dogs that if they do not chew on anything in the house, you will reward them with a treat in 2 weeks! Dogs do not have the cognitive abilities to understand the passage of time. Doing so involves thinking, imagining, and self-verbalization—some uniquely human activities.

Cognitive Dissonance Theory

Festinger and Carlsmith (1959) asked college students to perform an extremely boring and apparently pointless task as part of an experiment. They were then divided into three groups, one of which did nothing further, serving as a control group. The remaining two groups were asked to help the experimenter by lying to some new participants, telling them that the experiment was interesting, exciting, and useful. All agreed to do so. For their services, one group of participants was paid $20; the other group, ignorant of how much the others had been paid, was given a single dollar.

After members of these two groups had each spoken to the "new" participants (actually confederates of the investigators), they were interviewed to uncover their true feelings about the experiment. Not surprisingly, the control group still found the experiment boring and useless. The $20 group also found it boring; they hadn't changed their minds. Strikingly, however, the group who had been paid a single dollar now thought the experiment was useful and quite interesting (Figure 6.5).

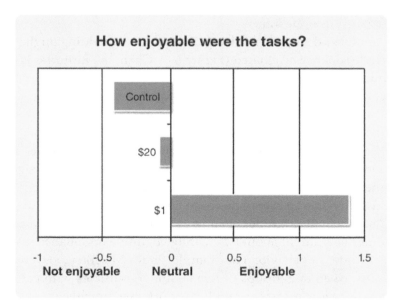

FIGURE 6.5   Cognitive dissonance and "forced compliance." In the Festinger and Carlsmith study, the group paid only $1 to lie experienced dissonance (conflict) about lying, and convinced themselves the task was really quite enjoyable. The group paid $20 felt justified in lying, experienced little dissonance, and continued to believe the experience had been boring.

Why should those who are paid a single dollar change their minds and the well-paid group, not? The answer, explains Festinger (1957), lies in the theory of **cognitive dissonance**. It predicts that whenever there is conflict between cognitions (e.g., conflicting information about behavior, beliefs, values, and desires), people will try to reduce the conflict. Cognitive dissonance (cognitive conflict) may arise when people do things contrary to their beliefs, when they compromise principles, or when they observe people doing things they don't expect of them.

Cognitive dissonance: A conflict between cognitions.

In the Festinger and Carlsmith experiment, participants experienced dissonance because they told a lie. But if they were well paid for telling the lie, there was little dissonance because the behavior seemed justified. So those paid $20 did not change their minds about how boring the task was. But those who were paid very little money had less justification for lying; they therefore experienced more dissonance. Changing attitude is one of the easiest ways of reducing dissonance—which is precisely what happened.

Cognitive dissonance theory contradicts the saying, "The grass is greener on the other side of the fence." When participants are given a choice between two relatively equal options, the one they select is the one they later rank as most desirable. Why? Cognitive dissonance theory provides an easy explanation: Whatever conflict results from having had to make an uncertain choice is quickly reduced when participants become convinced they've made the best choice. It should not be surprising that people who buy houses, cars, and other objects that require major decisions immediately begin to exaggerate the positive aspects of their choices. They are simply reducing dissonance or guarding against its appearance.

There are several ways of reducing dissonance, depending on the behavior from which dissonance originated (Figure 6.6). Changing attitudes is one common method, illustrated in the experiments just described. A second method involves changing behavior. Those individuals who stop smoking, for example, reduce dissonance created by their smoking by changing their behaviors.

Distorting information or perceptions can also reduce dissonance. When Gibbons, Eggleston, and Benthin (1997) interviewed individuals who had stopped smoking but later started again, they found that they had significantly distorted their perception of the risks associated with smoking.

Cognitive dissonance theory has become a relatively common approach to therapy. Changes in the attitudes of patients with eating disorders or addictions can sometimes be brought about by creating cognitive dissonance to stimulate change in attitudes or behavior. For example, Smith-Machin (2009) created cognitive dissonance among groups of female undergraduates with eating disorders using discussion, exercises, and homework assignments aimed primarily at countering cultural pressures and beliefs about women's bodies. She found significant reductions in dieting behaviors and *bulimic* symptoms among these women (*bulimia* and other eating disorders are discussed later in this chapter).

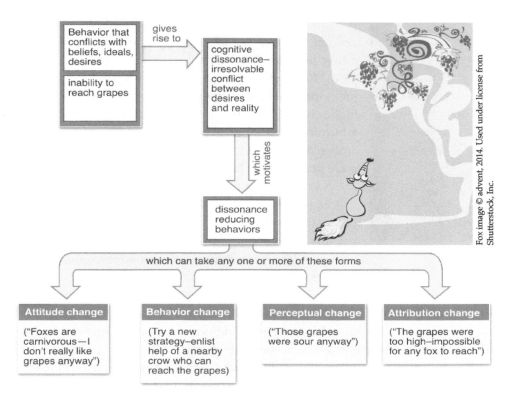

FIGURE 6.6 A model of cognitive dissonance. Everyone occasionally experiences conflicts between beliefs or desires and reality. There are many ways of trying to reduce cognitive dissonance.

Achievement Motivation

There are two competing forces in achievement behavior: the desire to excel and do well, and an opposing fear of failure. Those who fear failure too much are less likely to seek out challenging and difficult undertakings. Failure, as this girl is discovering, is often uncomfortable.

The urges that propel us toward achievement are complex and not easily defined or measured, although their influence can be extremely powerful. Those urges can vary widely from one individual to another. Some people have a strong drive to excel, to meet some inner standard of excellence, to do well. These people have a high **need for achievement (nAch)**; others, not so much.

A classic example can be related to academic performance. For some, the strong desire to excel can only be met by having the top grade in the class. That is, an A in the class is not good enough. Rather, their standard of excellence is maintained from being at the top of the class. Others may be perfectly content passing a class with a D.

© Lucky Business, 2014. Used under license from Shutterstock, Inc.

Need for achievement: A strong desire to excel, meet some inner standard of excellence, and do well.

© Olivier Le Moal, 2014. Used under license from Shutterstock, Inc.

McClelland and his associates' pioneering investigations of the need for achievement revealed several interesting findings (McClelland, Atkinson, Clark, & Lowell, 1953). First, and least surprising, those with the highest measured need for achievement typically achieve at a higher level. But this is not always the case; just having a burning drive to achieve and succeed brings no guarantees. Sometimes those more intelligent, more talented, more persistent, or luckier are the highest achievers.

Another interesting finding from this research is that children with high nAch scores tend to be moderate risk takers; those with lower scores tend to be either very low risk takers or very high risk takers. McClelland (1958) had young children play a ring-toss game where they could stand as close to the target as they wanted, and they would win prizes for accurate tosses. High-need achievers tended to stand a moderate distance away. But low-need achievers either ensured success by standing very close to the target or ensured failure by standing very far away. When there is very little probability of success, failure carries little stigma.

There are two competing forces involved in achievement behavior, explains McClelland: One is the desire to achieve success; the other is a fear of failure. What happens is that achievement-oriented behavior is a combined function of approach tendencies (resulting from a desire to achieve) and avoidance tendencies (resulting from fear of failure).

Attribution Theory

Why should we fear failure? Because failure might say something about what we are like: It might reflect badly on our estimates of ourselves.

We don't all react the same way to our successes and failures, explains Weiner (2008). Some of us believe we do well or poorly because we are intelligent or not so intelligent; others think they are just lucky or unlucky. **Attribution theory**, which we discuss again in Chapter 10, looks at these issues.

LOCUS OF CONTROL

Our attributions, says Weiner, depend on our **locus of control**; that is, on whether we are *internally oriented* or *externally oriented*. These are also described as internal and external loci of control, respectively. If I am internally oriented, I tend to take responsibility for the consequences of my own actions, attributing them either to my ability or to effort, both of which are under my control. But if I am externally oriented, I attribute success or failure to factors that are not under my control, such as the difficulty of the tasks I face or luck. Because these factors are not under personal control, the externally oriented individual does not accept responsibility for either success or failure. For example, an externally oriented individual attributes a good grade on an exam as the teacher made the test easy rather than giving him- or herself credit for studying. Conversely, an internally oriented individual attributes a good grade on an exam as a product of studying hard and preparing well for the exam.

Attribution theory: The attempt to attach meaning to ourselves or others.

Locus of control: Whether we internally or externally attribute our successes or failures.

Weiner also differentiates between causes that are stable and those that are unstable, as well as controllability. Ability and task difficulty are stable factors; that is, they don't vary for a given task and a given individual. Effort, however, can be high or low; and luck can be present or absent. Thus, these are unstable variables (Figure 6.7).

ATTRIBUTIONS AND NEED FOR ACHIEVEMENT

One of the striking and consistent findings from attribution studies is that people who are high in need achievement are much more likely to attribute outcomes to internal factors for which they have personal responsibility. They are likely to think that ability and effort—or lack thereof—are responsible for their successes and failures.

When they are successful, individuals low in measured need for achievement may attribute success to any of the four causal factors. That is, they might conclude they succeeded because they worked hard (effort), they are intelligent (ability), the task was exceptionally easy (difficulty), or they were just fortunate (luck).

However, when those individuals who are low in need for achievement are not successful, they are more likely to attribute the outcome to lack of ability. They see failure as reflecting on their abilities. That, explains Dweck (2006), is because they naively believe that intelligence is fixed and unchanging, a belief that, as we saw in Chapter 5, is a myth. But even if it is a myth, this belief (the **entity theory**) shapes goals and efforts. Those who are convinced that intelligence is fixed often

Entity theory: The belief that intelligence is fixed and unchanging.

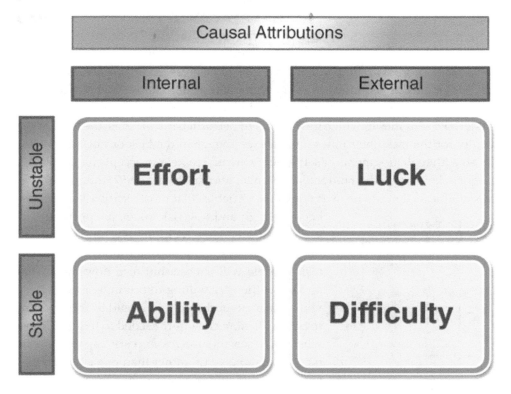

FIGURE 6.7 Four important possible attributions for success and failure. Our explanations for why we succeed or fail can be internal or external; they can also invoke causes that are stable or unstable.

go to great lengths to convince people that they have a lot of it. Or they struggle to hide the fact that they don't have very much. What happens in either case is that the individual avoids challenges that might expose weaknesses.

If, on the other hand, you believe that intelligence is malleable, that it can be improved with effort (the **incremental theory**), you will develop what Dweck labels a *growth mindset*. Knowing that you can develop astonishing skills and talents if you work at it, you will be willing to accept challenges that would stagger others (Dweck & Grant, 2008).

Incremental theory: The belief that intelligence is malleable and can be improved upon with effort.

Self-Efficacy

Our personal opinions of how competent we are in different situations—our judgments of self-efficacy—are important in determining what tasks we choose and how much effort we put into them. High self-efficacy judgments ensure that this female will not be intimidated by the formulas behind her.

© racorn, 2014. Used under license from Shutterstock, Inc.

Attribution theory presents an active view of people. We don't simply behave; we actively evaluate our behaviors and try to make sense of them. When we fail or succeed, we try to understand the reasons why. Depending on our predispositions, our personality characteristics, and our previous histories, we ascribe causes to specific factors.

Basic to our attributions is what we think of our personal competence—in Bandura's (1997) terms, our **self-efficacy** judgments. These are evaluations we make of our personal effectiveness in different situations. Those with high self-efficacy see themselves as capable and effective.

Self-efficacy: Our belief of personal competence.

Judgments of self-efficacy are instrumental in determining what people do; hence, they are important as motives. Under most circumstances, people don't undertake activities in which they expect to perform badly. That is, the level of difficulty for the task determines whether we engage in the task or not. In contrast, those with high judgments of self-efficacy are more likely to accept challenges that might help validate their judgments. Slanger and Rudestam (1997) found that level of self-efficacy judgments was one of the variables that most clearly differentiated between high and low risk takers in sports such as sky-diving, kayaking, rock climbing, and skiing.

© phloxii, 2014. Used under license from Shutterstock, Inc.

Self-efficacy judgments determine not only what tasks people will choose, but also how much time and effort they are willing to put in. For example, if you are a great mechanic, you would be more willing to put in the time and effort needed to fix a car. Those who don't see themselves as very capable are far more likely to give up rather than persist when they encounter difficulties. That's one of the reasons why self-efficacy judgments are so important in schools. Williams and Williams (2010), for example, found a significant relationship between math achievement and self-efficacy in a study that looked at students in 33 different schools. Those who have higher levels of self-efficacy are more likely to work through difficult problems. As you can see, self-efficacy is critical for success in the schools. A school system is designed to continually challenge students through the presentation of new, more difficult information. If a student has low self-efficacy, the very purpose of school will not be accomplished as this student will be more likely to give up and not learn new material.

SOURCES OF SELF-EFFICACY JUDGMENTS

Not only does high self-efficacy contribute to high achievement, but there is a sort of *reciprocal determinism* at play in the sense that high achievement, in turn, contributes to a heightened sense of competence. In fact, direct experiences of success or failure (termed *enactive* because they result from our own actions) are probably the most important sources of information we have about our competence. Thus, enactive learning occurs through completing a task by yourself. For self-efficacy to remain strong, one must complete tasks over and over making minimal mistakes. By doing so, minor mistakes often are of little impact to your judgments of self-efficacy.

Second, we learn about our effectiveness from *vicarious* (secondhand) sources—that is, through the observations of others. For example, when learning math in school, the teacher may do multiple problems on the board. She may intentionally make mistakes and demonstrate how to correct those mistakes. Thus, vicarious learning is very important in that it allows a novice to learn many nuances of the task through the observation of an expert. I know many individuals feel more confident completing a task after they have seen it performed. A third source of influence is *persuasion*. If others express faith in your abilities, if they continually urge, "Why don't you try? I know you can do it," you might, in the end, come to believe just a little more in your effectiveness and competence.

Finally, explains Bandura (1997), *emotions* can have a direct impact on your estimates of capability. Under conditions of extreme arousal, for example, you might decide that you are capable of outrunning a threatening gorilla or of swimming across a river to save a baby. And if an activity makes you feel especially good, you are more likely to conclude that you're good at it than if it makes you feel frustrated and unhappy (Figure 6.8).

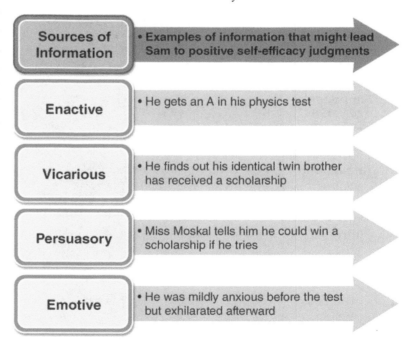

FIGURE 6.8   Sources of information that influence our judgment of personal effectiveness and competence.

EFFICACY AND EXPECTANCY-VALUE THEORY

We are not simple creatures, you and I; our motives expose themselves easily to the probing psychologist trying to find another piece of the puzzle. No matter how overwhelmingly positive our judgments of self-efficacy and how high our expectations of success, there are other factors at play. Our choices, explain Eccles and Wigfield (2002), and our persistence and performance, are profoundly influenced by the *value* of the outcome we expect. And the cost of the activity, in terms of amount of effort required, sacrifices entailed, and other opportunities given up, also has to be taken into account. This is the basis of Eccles's **expectancy-value theory** (Wigfield, Tonks, & Klauda, 2009).

Expectancy-value theory: The belief that motivation is determined by the expectancy of success and the value of the reward.

Expectancy, in this theory, is similar to a judgment of self-efficacy; it is defined by the individual's belief about how well he or she will do on a task. *Value* is a combined function of four factors: the personal importance of the task in terms of how it fits into the individual's plans and self-image (*attainment value*); its *intrinsic value* based on the personal satisfaction the person gets from doing the task; its *utility value*, which has to do with what the task contributes to short- and long-term goals; and its *cost* in terms of the amount of effort required, the probability of failure, associated stress, conflicting options, and so on.

In short, it's as though we make choices based on a sort of mental calculus. If either the expectancy (our ability to successfully perform a task), or the value (what we get out of performing a task), are inconsistent with our expectations, we will not engage in a task. Consider the following example. For some, the motivation of money is extremely appealing. If I told you that you would be given a million dollars for completing a task, you probably would be highly motivated to engage in the task. If I told you that the task was learning to speak Japanese fluently within 10 minutes, you would immediately dismiss the task (assuming all people fluent in Japanese previously were excluded from participating). The reason for this is that your expectancy would be that you will not be capable of performing the task. While the money would be nice, the probability of being successful would be zero, meaning that it would be a waste of time to participate. The important factors in our calculation include our expectations of success, our judgments of our effectiveness and competence (our self-efficacy), and the values and costs associated with each of the various options (Figure 6.9).

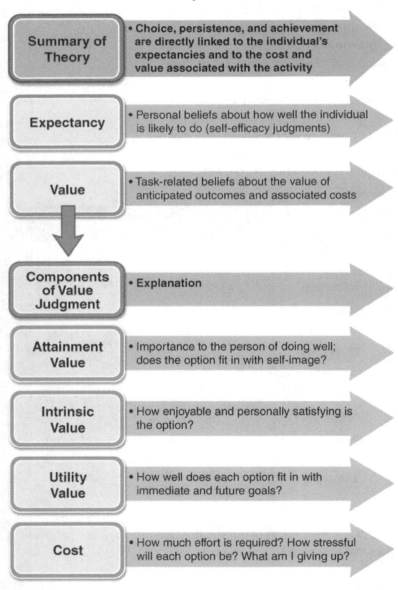

FIGURE 6.9　Eccles's expectancy-value theory of motivation, a sort of mental calculus we use to guide our choices and our efforts.

Emotions

In situations of high arousal, the body's physiological systems prepare the individual to respond. If arousal becomes too high, panic may result and the effectiveness of behavior may drop. Some studies indicate that many soldiers under attack fail to fire their rifles. Some even run away.

The mental calculus that is the basis of Eccles's *expectancy-value theory* describes a cognitive side of human motivation. It tries to explain how we choose among different options, how we decide on goals and actions.

There is another side to human motivation. It has to do with the fact that, as Turner and Goodin (2008) explain, when we succeed in attaining a goal, we feel positive **emotions**; failure can lead to negative emotions. For all of us, we can think of memories related to extreme happiness. Examples may include, graduating from high school, getting a job, or the birth of a child. All of these examples also relate to why we engage in certain behaviors. Hence emotions are a fundamental part of human motivation. And some of the physiological aspects of emotion can be detected and measured. These are the changes that define **arousal**.

© Oleg Zabielin, 2014. Used under license from Shutterstock, Inc.

Arousal

The term *arousal* has both physiological and psychological meaning. As a physiological term, it refers to activity of the *sympathetic nervous system*. Remember, the sympathetic nervous system is activated for your "fight or flight" response. Physiological arousal ranges from states of very low activity such as those characteristic of sleep or deep comas (alpha, theta, or delta waves; low **electrodermal response**, or electrical conductivity of the skin; low respiration and heart rates), to very high activity such as might be characteristic of extreme anger, fear or panic.

As a psychological term, *arousal* refers to the alertness or vigilance of the organism and to the emotions accompanying physiological arousal. Thus, an individual at a very low level of arousal might be asleep; a moderately aroused individual is alert and attentive; one who is extremely aroused may be in a state of extreme emotion. Given these three states, it seems that the moderately aroused individual would perform the best on a variety of tasks.

© YanLev, 2014. Used under license from Shutterstock, Inc.

© Mert Toker, 2014. Used under license from Shutterstock, Inc.

THE YERKES–DODSON LAW

The effectiveness of our behavior is closely tied to arousal level. At very low levels of arousal, such as when you are asleep or almost asleep, you might have trouble responding to the simplest question. But if what later awakens you is the fact that your house is on fire, you might immediately become so highly aroused that your responses to this same question would not be any more appropriate. High arousal, evident in increasing anxiety and sometimes even fear or panic, explains why some highly competent students do poorly in tense oral or written examinations. As you have probably experienced, when your arousal is virtually nonexistent, or when your arousal was hypervigilant, you probably could not perform tasks to the best of your ability.

Emotions: Motives.

Arousal: To excite.

Electrodermal response: Electrical conductivity of the skin.

Further, considerable research indicates that anxiety reduces school performance (Chen, 2009).

It seems, explained Yerkes and Dodson (1908) more than a century ago, that there is a level of arousal at which behavior is most effective. A lower or higher level of arousal is associated with increasingly ineffective behavior. This observation, now known as the **Yerkes–Dodson Law**, has been widely accepted in psychology (Landers, 2007; Figure 6.10).

Yerkes–Dodson Law: A law stating that there is an optimal level of arousal and performance.

NEED FOR STIMULATION

In a classic experiment, Hebb and his colleagues (Hebb, 1972; Heron, 1957) paid college students to do absolutely nothing. For as long as they wanted, they lay on a cot, getting up only to go to the bathroom and to sit on the edge of their cots at mealtime. The remainder of the time they lay down, their ears covered with U-shaped foam pillows, their eyes with translucent visors, their hands with cardboard cuffs. Overhead, a fan hummed constantly to mask any other noises. Although they could hear, see, and feel, their stimulus world was unchanging.

This was the first of a large number of studies on sensory deprivation. For example, in a recent demonstration, the BBC (U.K.) arranged for six volunteers to spend 48 hours alone in totally darkened nuclear bunkers (Total Isolation, 2008). The outcome in this demonstration was highly consistent with previous studies, most of which found that participants typically cannot endure such isolation for very long. In the original experiment, 2 days was the usual duration. In conditions of more extreme deprivation—where, for example, participants are immersed in brine solutions in silence and darkness, floating unattended—length of stay is considerably shorter.

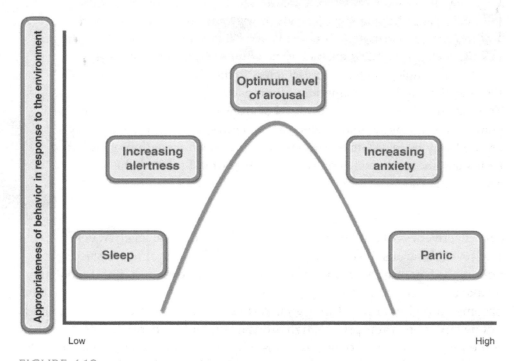

FIGURE 6.10   The Yerkes–Dodson law. As arousal increases, performance becomes more effective until an optimal level is reached. Increases in arousal beyond this level lead to decreasingly effective behavior.

Among the striking findings from these studies is the observation that most participants eventually experience some impairment of perceptual and intellectual functioning. Tasks that are very simple before isolation become extremely difficult and sometimes impossible after prolonged sensory deprivation. In the BBC demonstration, one participant's performance on simple memory tasks had dropped by 36%. In addition, many isolation participants experienced emotional changes and rapidly fluctuating moods ranging from nervousness and irritability to anger or fear.

The most striking finding involves the appearance of hallucinations among some sensory deprivation participants (Mason & Brady, 2009). These uncontrolled "apparitions," typically visual, are mildly amusing at first and can be gotten rid of if the participant wishes. Later, however, they become more pronounced, less amusing, and quite persistent. Three of the six participants in the BBC study reported hallucinations involving objects such as snakes, zebras, and oysters; and a fourth became convinced that her sheets were soaking wet.

Sensory deprivation research strongly suggests humans have a need for variety in sensory stimulation. If this is so, perhaps some of our otherwise unexplainable behaviors might be accounted for—behaviors such as curiosity and exploration. That we have a need for stimulation is the basis for an **arousal theory** of motivation.

Arousal theory: A theory stating that individuals behave in a way to maintain an optimal level of arousal.

AROUSAL THEORY

Arousal theory is premised on two assumptions (Hebb, 1972). The first, already mentioned, is the *Yerkes–Dodson Law*—the belief that there is an optimal level of arousal for different behaviors and that this level varies both for different individuals and for different behaviors. For example, playing well in an intense, physical sporting activity such as football may require that players be "psyched up" (highly aroused). The same level of arousal may be a detriment in a highly cognitive task like writing an examination.

The second assumption is individuals behave so as to maintain an optimal level of arousal. This is evident, for example, in highly arousing situations where an intensely frightened individual tries to escape or change the situation. The consequences of escaping from an angry mob will surely be a reduction of arousal.

The assumption is double edged, however: It predicts not only that people behave so as to reduce arousal when it is too high, but also that they will attempt to increase arousal when it's inappropriately low. Evidence of this is clear in sensory deprivation studies, where participants whistle, sing, talk to themselves, try desperately to engage the experimenter in conversation whenever food is brought in, and otherwise try to increase the amount of stimulation they are receiving. This could explain why when you are alone in a quiet place, you may instinctively feel the need to turn on the television or listen to the radio. Doing so increases your level of arousal to an optimal state. One of the effects of sensory stimulation is to increase arousal.

SOURCES OF AROUSAL

The physiological changes that accompany arousal are brought about by activity of the *autonomic nervous system,* which is not ordinarily under the individual's conscious control. We cannot easily "will" our skins to become more

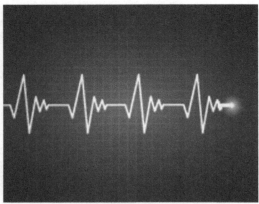

© Ramona Kaulitzki, 2014. Used under license from Shutterstock, Inc.

conductive to electricity, our hearts to beat faster, and our brain-wave activity to change.

Still, there are ways in which we can control these changes. For example, simply imagining highly arousing scenes, or seeing them depicted in pictures, films, or words, can clearly increase physiological arousal. Hence one source of arousal is internal, cognitive activity.

A second obvious source of arousal is external stimulation. The sheer amount of stimulation, however, may not be especially important. In the original isolation experiments there was considerable sensory stimulation, including the sound of a fan, the pressure of the cardboard cuffs, sensations relating to clothing and diffuse light, and perhaps even tastes inside the mouth and vague odors in the environment. But this stimulation was constant and unchanging, and arousal level consequently dropped dramatically. Recordings of participants during isolation indicate that their brain-wave functioning was more like that of the deeper stages of sleep than like that of participants who are awake (Zubek, 1973).

The types of stimulation that appear to cause the greatest arousal are those associated with emotion. At one extreme, emotion-laden experiences can increase arousal dramatically, as is evident in panic situations.

In general, the most arousing stimuli are those capturing interest and attention—that is, stimuli that are surprising, novel, meaningful, ambiguous, or complex (Berlyne, 1960). These qualities of stimuli are linked with emotions such as interest and excitement; their opposites are associated with boredom and apathy. All these emotions are closely linked with motivation.

What Is an Emotion?

Emotions have presented a great deal of difficulty for psychologists. They cannot easily be defined or described; they are difficult to measure; their physiological bases don't clearly differentiate among them. Yet they are a fundamental part of being human. In fact, it is difficult to imagine any human experience that does not involve emotions.

Emotions (or *affect*) have two broad dimensions. The first is intensity, which, for most emotions, can range from low to high. Thus, anger might range from annoyance to rage; disgust, from mild aversion to utter revulsion; joy, from contentment to absolute ecstasy.

Emotions vary not only in intensity, but also in terms of whether they are positive or negative. Joy, love, happiness, and interest are generally positive feelings; fear, anger, rage, and disgust are generally negative feelings.

Emotion can be defined as the "feeling" or "affective" component of human behavior, where *feeling* describes a subjective state that can be pleasant or unpleasant, as well as intense or mild. In addition, emotion entails detectable physiological changes and is sometimes accompanied by predictable behaviors. For example, imagine a time when you became extremely angry. Think about what was happening from a physiological and behavioral perspective. My guess is that your anger was generally accompanied by increased heart and respiration rates as well as other physiological changes, and it may also be evident in changes in facial expressions, voice, and body language.

There are several thousand words referring to emotion in the English language, so it is very difficult to agree on the precise number of different emotions of which we are capable. Many psychologists have tried to summarize our emotions with lists of *basic* emotions. For example, Izard (2009) suggests we can easily distinguish among six distinct emotions: sadness, anger, disgust, fear, interest, and joy/happiness. Others, such as Parrott (2004), divide basic emotions into related secondary and tertiary emotions. For example, secondary emotions related to joy include cheerfulness, zest, contentment, pride, optimism, enthrallment, and relief. And each of these secondary emotions might be described more precisely in terms of a tertiary emotion. For example, cheerfulness brings with it the possibility of many other emotions, including amusement, bliss, gaiety, glee, jolliness, joviality, delight, satisfaction, and ecstasy.

Not only have we not agreed about how many emotions we have; we cannot always agree about whether a given emotion is positive or negative. Consider the element of surprise. On one hand, we have all been pleasantly surprised. This may occur when you find out that you received a birthday gift or present. On the other hand, we have all been surprised when somebody has jumped around a corner and scared us. Therefore, you may wonder, is surprise pleasant or unpleasant? In fact, we cannot really say because emotion is not a property of stimulation, but a property of our subjective reaction to stimulation. By subjective, we refer to the individual's interpretation to the reaction of the stimulation.

© arka38, 2014. Used under license from Shutterstock, Inc.

EMOTIONAL EXPRESSION

To define an emotion is to speak about what we presume to be the subjective experience of being in that emotional state. Emotion, however, has other dimensions. Among the most important of these for human interaction is its expression. Emotions can be expressed in behavior, as, for example, when you run from an angry competitor or chase after something you want. In these examples, the motivational component of the emotion is clear. Most emotions may be seen as having approach or avoidance tendencies, although these will not always be expressed overtly.

Emotions may also be expressed verbally. Much of the richness of human conversation derives from the expression and interpretation of emotion. So, too, our books, movies, and art forms play on and with our emotions.

Emotions are expressed nonverbally as well, and they have been extensively studied as manifestations of facial expression. Ekman (2005) and others have noted that there appear to be a number of emotional expressions that are innate and common to all members of our species. Raising the eyebrows is a quasi-universal expression of greeting or acknowledgment; smiling, a universal gesture of approval and friendliness.

Many emotional expressions, however, are learned and culture specific. Klineberg (1938) examined some Chinese novels to discover how their authors describe emotional expression. It might seem strange to us that sticking out the tongue means surprise; clapping the hands indicates anxiety or disappointment; and scratching the ears shows happiness. The Chinese might be equally surprised to find us frowning when we are puzzled, chewing our lips in concentration, pounding fist in palm to signal determination or anger, and wetting our lips in anticipation.

Theories of Emotion

In addition to how we experience and express it, we know that emotion is related to activity of the autonomic nervous system, as we saw earlier in this chapter. Popular literature abounds with descriptions of physiological activity that are so meaningful, given their contexts, that the reader need not be told anything more about the nature or intensity of the emotion. "My heart beat fast/stood still/quaked/shivered/jumped/rattled in my throat/stopped." "My hair stood on end." "Shivers ran up my spine." "My hands were cold/clammy/perspired/trembled/shook."

THE JAMES–LANGE THEORY

Early theorists made much of these physiological changes. William James (1890/1950) went so far as to say that emotion results from them, an idea developed simultaneously by a Danish psychologist, Lange. As a result, the theory came to be known as the *James–Lange theory*. In essence, it maintains that an emotion-related stimulus gives rise to certain physiological changes and the individual perceives these physiological changes and then interprets them as an emotion. As James (1890/1950) put it, "We feel sorry because we cry . . . afraid because we tremble" (p. 1,006).

THE CANNON–BARD THEORY

Two other researchers, Cannon (1929, 1939) and Bard, objected to the James–Lange theory. They thought our awareness of physiological changes is too slow to explain how we can instantly react to emotion-laden situations. Besides, physiological changes, such as increased heart rate, that accompany different emotions don't appear to differentiate among them. For example, increased heart rate may occur when an individual is happy or when fearful. Also, Cannon had demonstrated with cats that if he cut nerves linking the brain to those parts of the body most obviously involved in emotional reactions, the cats still behaved as though they "felt" emotion. So Cannon and Bard proposed the *Cannon–Bard theory*.

The Cannon–Bard theory suggests when an individual perceives an emotion-related situation or object, the *hypothalamus* sends messages both to the cortex, where the emotion is felt, and to the body, where physiological reactions take place. As a result, awareness of emotion and awareness of physiological changes are independent, although they result from the same source of stimulation. It is the organism's awareness of the emotional significance of an experience that gives rise to an emotion.

SCHACHTER'S TWO-FACTOR THEORY

It turns out that both the James–Lange and the Cannon–Bard theories are probably at least partly right. In an early study, Maranon (1924) injected human participants with epinephrine, a compound very similar to noradrenaline, and found that while they experienced physiological reactions similar to those that accompany intense emotion, they did not feel any specific emotion.

Schachter later replicated the Maranon studies to try to clarify the relationship between physiological changes and cognitions in producing emotional states (Schachter & Singer, 1962). Participants in an experiment were told they would receive injections of a new drug that would improve their performance on a test of visual perception. Some participants received injections of epinephrine; the others received a placebo. After the injections, they were given one of three types of information about the effects of the drug. The *informed* group was told what the actual effects of the drug might be and how long these effects normally last; the *ignorant* group was told that the drug would have absolutely no side effects; and the *misinformed* group was told that a slight numbness and itchiness might result.

Members of each group were then assigned to one of two experimental conditions, or to a control group. The control group waited quietly for a period of time, and members were then questioned about their emotional reactions. Not surprisingly, they reported no particular emotion, as had been the case in the earlier Maranon studies.

In one experimental group, the *euphoria* group, participants were left to wait in a room with another individual who was introduced to them as a fellow participant. In fact this person was a confederate of the experimenters who had been instructed to perform a standardized "euphoric-manic" routine—dancing, playing basketball with crumpled pieces of paper, making little projectiles and launching them with rubber bands, playing with a hula hoop, and otherwise trying to convey the impression that this was really a lot of fun.

In the second experimental group, the *anger* group, participants were left with a confederate and were asked to fill out a long and intensely personal questionnaire while waiting. It asked about the personal hygiene of every member of the subject's family—how often they took a bath and brushed their teeth, and who had the most disagreeable body odor; participants weren't allowed to answer "no" or "none." One question read: "With how many men (other than your father) has your mother had extramarital relationships? 4 and under—: 5–9—: 10 and over—." The confederate, acting according to precise directions, became progressively angrier while completing the questionnaire, finally crumpling it up and leaving the room.

Following this, all participants were individually interviewed to uncover their emotional reactions. Results were as follows: Participants who were uninformed or misinformed and who had received epinephrine exhibited and felt anger or euphoria, depending on the experimental condition; informed participants and those individuals who had received placebos typically did not.

Schachter's explanation for these findings is the basis of his *two-factor theory of emotion:* One factor is an undifferentiated state of physiological arousal that underlies all emotions—as James had argued. The second factor is the individual's interpretation of arousal in light of what caused it. Thus, participants who had a logical explanation for their physiological states (the informed group) experienced no emotion. They simply labeled their physiological states according to the explanations given by the experimenter. Those who had been misinformed or not informed attributed their physiological states to emotions they thought they should be feeling and labeled these emotions according to the confederate's behavior. In short, although physiological changes are clearly involved in emotional reaction, the individual's cognitive label for the change determines the nature of the emotion (Figure 6.11).

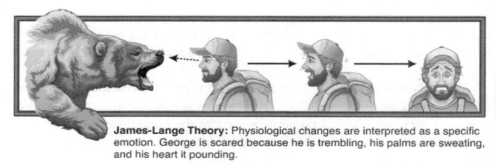

James-Lange Theory: Physiological changes are interpreted as a specific emotion. George is scared because he is trembling, his palms are sweating, and his heart it pounding.

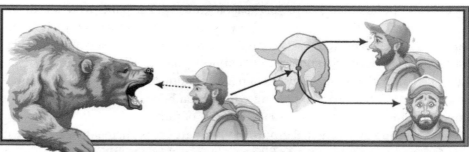

Cannon-Bard Theory: George's fear results from his understanding, mediated through the hypothalamus which has sent messages to his cortex as well as his autonomic nervous system, that this is a dangerous bear.

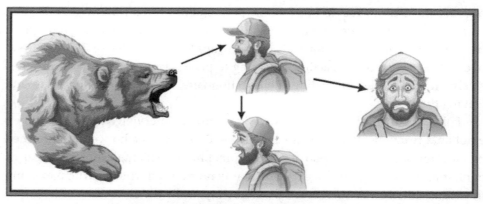

Schacter Two-Factor Theory: George is scared because he is aroused and he interprets his arousal as being caused by the danger in this situation.

FIGURE 6.11   Three historical explanations of emotion.

RECENT THEORIES

Both the Cannon–Bard theory and Schachter's two-factor theory hold that the nature and intensity of an emotion depend largely on the individual's conscious understanding of the emotional significance of an event. These are, in a sense, *attribution* theories of motivation. Both emphasize that it is the individual's *conscious* understanding of the meaning of a situation (or of the reasons for physiological arousal) that determines the emotion (Moors, 2009).

Some theorists point out, however, that not all emotional reactions require a conscious understanding of a situation. Scherer (2005), for example, argues emotional responses can also result from *unconscious* cognitive activity. Someone experiencing a classically conditioned fear response, for example, might not always have a clear, conscious explanation for the accompanying emotion.

Other theorists have proposed emotional responses are represented in the brain in complex, linked networks that can be activated by a wide range of related stimuli (Lewis, 2005). These emotional responses may well have been classically conditioned in the first place. The behaviorist John Watson (1930) suggested many decades ago that infants are born with three basic emotional reactions: fear, rage, and love. Each of these is elicited by specific stimuli as an unlearned reflex. For example, stroking the

© wavebreakmedia, 2014. Used under license from Shutterstock, Inc.

infant evokes emotions related to love; confining the infant might elicit rage; and fear can be brought about by loud noises. Over time, these emotions become classically conditioned to a wide range of other stimuli (see Chapter 2). What happens is that whenever an individual has an emotional experience, information about the situation, the individual's behavior, and a variety of other related details is stored in memory and linked with other related emotions. As a result, previously neutral stimuli can come to have emotional significance for an individual.

THE DUAL-PATHWAY MODEL FOR FEAR

The notion that there are unconscious as well as conscious processes involved in emotional reactions has led to an important model of emotional processing of fear-related stimuli: the *dual-pathway model.* What this model says, in effect, is that there are two systems involved in fear reactions. One is unconscious and faster; the other is conscious and slower (LeDoux, 2010).

When you see an avalanche come barreling down on you, visual and auditory stimuli race to your thalamus. From there, the information forks out into the two paths of this dual-pathway system. One path streaks to the amygdala—that part of the brain directly involved with fear and danger—and leads you to react almost instantly. Meanwhile, the other path carries information to the cortex, allowing you to interpret the situation more thoroughly (Figure 6.12). A fraction of a second later, you might decide your initial reaction was unwarranted, that this *looked like* an avalanche but was just a few snowflakes on the periphery of your vision and you can relax.

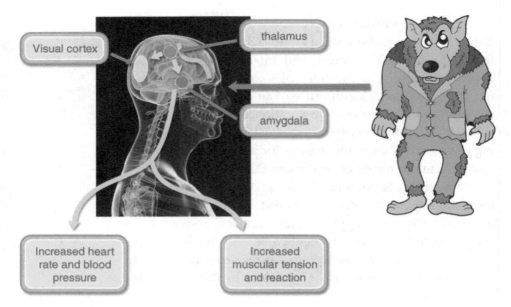

FIGURE 6.12   The dual-pathway fear system. Signals associated with fear are first processed in the thalamus. From there, signals streak toward the amygdala, giving rise to immediate physiological and muscular reactions. Signals also go to the visual cortex, where they are interpreted more carefully. Now the individual, who has already started to run, might decide it is only a trained wolf

Photo courtesy of Thinkstock/iStockphoto, Thinkstock/Hemera.

GENDER DIFFERENCES FOR DISPLAYING EMOTIONS

Think back to your childhood and how you displayed emotions. My guess is that there will be significant differences between how boys and girls displayed their emotions. That is, boys probably externalized (expressed outwardly) their emotions more often than girls. Conversely, girls probably internalized (expressed inwardly) their emotions more often than boys. Why is this? The answer is likely that biology and society may contribute to gender differences in expressing emotions. That is, the combination of internal differences (i.e., testosterone/estrogen levels), paired with socially identified constructs (i.e., boys don't cry) may lead to differences in emotional expression.

When considering the culture of the United States, it is no surprise that emotions are expressed differently between genders. Within our culture, boys are often taught to be the "protectors" while girls are taught to be the "nurturers." This is especially evident by the toys relegated to each gender and may eventually develop into role expectations as children age. If girls are always encouraged to play with dolls, is it any wonder that they develop into "motherly" figures? Conversely, if boys are encouraged to engage in physical activities, is it any wonder that they develop aggressive tendencies?

Emotional Control

In a sense, our emotions control us: They make us do things. When we speak of experiences that have moved us, we speak of things that have evoked profound emotion. We can as easily speak of the emotions themselves as being moving, for novelists have not yet counted all the things we do in the name of passion. Love is a motive as surely as is hunger; so too are hate and fear and the vast array of more subtle, less passionate emotions.

But we are not necessarily prisoners of our emotions. Even very young infants can do things to control their emotions. When 8-month-old Jessica is frightened, she might suck her thumb, bury her face in her mother's lap, or close her eyes and make the bad thing go away.

But we adults are wiser. We know closing our eyes seldom makes bad things disappear. We have our own ways of controlling emotions. In the first place, our *successful intelligence* encourages us to seek out situations likely to lead to pleasant emotions and avoid those with unpleasant possibilities.

THE BRAIN AND EMOTIONS

There are more extreme forms of control as well. As we saw in Chapter 2, the sometimes dramatic mood-altering effects of drugs is one; electrical or surgical brain intervention is another. For example, early studies showed that something similar to rage could be evoked in cats, dogs, primates, and other animals by stimulating appropriate areas of their brains (Flynn, 1967). These studies also showed that violent emotional reactions could be completely inhibited in these animals.

Demonstrating his confidence in such procedures, Delgado (1969) entered a bull ring armed only with a radio transmitter. The bull facing him, menacingly angry, had radio-activated electrodes implanted in his brain. He charged! But with a flourish and a flick of the switch, Delgado stopped him dead in his tracks. The bull had been turned into an apparently docile and friendly beast. What was being controlled, however, is not clear. Whether Delgado's bull had actually become docile, whether it was just confused, or whether its motor system was paralyzed remains uncertain.

Research with humans also indicates that certain parts of the brain, especially of the limbic system, are closely involved in emotional reactions. For example, Koelsch (2010) showed that music, which can evoke very strong emotions, reliably leads to activation of virtually all limbic structures.

Odors, which often evoke strong emotions, also lead to activation of the limbic system. Schredl and associates (2009) stimulated 15 sleeping participants during rapid-eye-movement (REM) sleep with one of two smells: hydrogen sulphide (a rotten egg smell) or phenyl ethyl alcohol (the smell of roses). Not only did these smells lead to activation of the limbic system, but they also affected the content of the participants' dreams. The authors suggest it might be valuable to study the effect that olfactory stimuli conditioned to pleasant reactions might have on nightmares.

Among limbic system structures that are involved in interpreting emotions and in guiding behavior in appropriate directions, the amygdala is especially important in processing fear

LIMBIC SYSTEM STRUCTURES

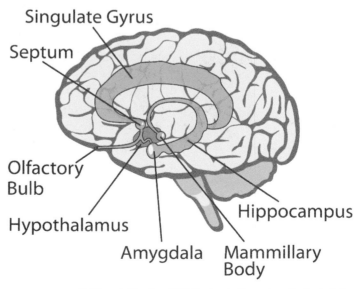

Singulate Gyrus

Septum

Olfactory Bulb

Hypothalamus

Amygdala

Mammillary Body

Hippocampus

reactions (Bush, Schafe, & LeDoux, 2009). There is some suggestion that impairment of amygdala functioning in individuals may be linked to psychopathology and, consequently, to criminal behavior. Such individuals may be unemotional, callous, and fearless, and more prone to committing acts of violence without fear of consequences (DeLisi, Umphress, & Vaughn, 2009).

The amygdala and other structures of the limbic system, such as the hypothalamus, are involved not only in fear reactions but also in the recognition of emotional expression (Batista & Freitas-Magalhaes, 2009). Individuals with impaired limbic system functioning—as sometimes happens as a result of diseases such as Parkinsonism or alcoholism—may have difficulty interpreting the meaning of facial expressions (Marinkovic et al., 2009).

Not surprisingly, brain surgery can also be used to control emotional reactions. It has sometimes been used with mentally disturbed people for whom all other forms of therapy have been unsuccessful. The practice of removing parts of the cortex (for example, *prefrontal lobotomy* or *eucotomy*), once relatively common, has largely been abandoned since the discovery that very small lesions have many of the same positive effects without the same side effects. Rosemary Kennedy, sister of President John F. Kennedy, was left permanently incapacitated after a eucotomy (Feldman, 2001).

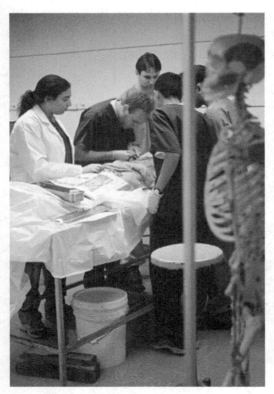

In this human anatomy class, it's likely that at least some students are using cognitive disengagement strategies to lessen the potential emotional impact of the situation.

Photolibrary/Peter Arnold Images/The Medical File/
Michelle Del Guercio

COGNITIVE CONTROL OF EMOTIONS

In this human anatomy class, it's likely that at least some students are using cognitive disengagement strategies to lessen the potential emotional impact of the situation.

It is possible that, at least to some degree, we are masters of our emotions and not their prisoners. In an experiment conducted by Lazarus and his associates, participants were exposed to films of woodshop accidents (Koriat, Melkman, Averill, & Lazarus, 1972). In the films, one man lacerates the tips of his fingers, another cuts off a finger, and a third is skewered through the midsection by a plank propelled from a circular saw. He dies.

Some participants were asked to detach themselves from events in the film; others were asked to involve themselves. In neither case were they told how to do this. Heart rate changes were recorded for every individual during presentation of the film, and reports were obtained of subjective emotional states. Significantly, participants who were asked to detach themselves from the film had much lower emotional reaction in terms of both their heart rates and self-reports. Those who were told to involve themselves experienced profound emotional reactions.

When questioned about their strategies, a majority of the involvement group said they imagined they were the person to whom the accidents were happening, or they attempted to relate the accidents to other accidents they might have witnessed or in which friends or relatives had been involved. Members of the detachment group pretended that the events had been "staged" for the filming, or paid particular attention to the technical details of the film.

The cognitive control of emotions is an important coping mechanism, explains Lazarus (1974, 1999). For example, a study of patients before and after surgery revealed that those who adopted detachment strategies, not wanting to know details of their surgery or symptoms of recovery or complications, experienced more rapid and smoother recoveries than patients who were more involved. Lazarus speculates that paying undue attention to possible signs of complications, or even to signs of recovery, is probably associated with more anxiety (stress) and is negatively associated with recovery. In Lazarus's view, cognitive activity does a great deal to control emotional states.

Emotion is seldom a single, identifiable response to a given situation; more often it is a complex of responses. Moreover, this complex shifts continually. Anger turns into despair; grief into elation; rage into apathy; joy into sorrow; anxiety into relief. Emotions ebb and flow as we appraise our situations, our relationships with people and things, our probabilities of attaining or not attaining goals. The fundamental point is that we are the ones doing the appraising; the emotion resides not in the situation but in our appraisal of it. Furthermore, we exercise control over our appraisals, sometimes deliberately reducing emotional reaction, as may be the case with anger or fear, sometimes purposely enhancing it, as with love or joy.

Hunger and Sex Drive

Some of the more obvious emotions and motives have been extensively investigated—especially negative emotions such as anxiety, fear, and stress and the more basic motives, including hunger and sex. In the remainder of this chapter, we look at hunger and sex; Chapter 9 looks at anxiety and fear in relation to mental health; and in Chapter 10, we look at a powerful sex-related social emotion: love.

Hunger Stimuli

Subjectively, hunger may be described as the bodily sensations that result from not eating for a period of time. Such sensations range from mild discomfort (the gentle growling of a hollow belly) to severe pain (the tortured pangs of intense hunger). Normally, death by starvation is preceded by cessation of hunger pains.

Hunger is a function of certain physiological mechanisms related to survival. It's also a function of taste, smell, appearance, and learning, and it doesn't always relate to nutrition.

© ElenaGaak, 2014. Used under license from Shutterstock, Inc.

STOMACH CONTRACTIONS

For many years most psychologists and physiologists believed hunger results directly from the actions of an empty or nearly empty stomach. So do we eat because the stomach is empty and it begins to contract? Early theorists thought this might be the case. Cannon and Washburn (1912) developed an ingenious test to look at this question. Washburn swallowed a balloon that was then inflated inside his stomach. The balloon was connected to a recorder so that stomach contractions could be measured. Whenever he felt a hunger pang, Washburn depressed a key to record the event.

After a while, Washburn's stomach contracted, although he sometimes had to wait a long time for this to happen. At about the same time, he thought he felt hunger. But that piece of the puzzle did not really fit. It turns out that even people with no stomachs get hungry and that hunger persists even when neural pathways from the stomach to the brain are cut. There have now been many experiments with "gastric" balloons (Schachter, 1971). Contractions may sometimes be involved in sensations of hunger, but sometimes not, and it is likely that the duodenum (upper part of the small intestine) is even more involved.

THE ROLE OF THE BRAIN

The brain, too, plays a key role in hunger motivation. Satisfying hunger is highly rewarding. It leads to a pleasant state that can easily become conditioned to various situations—for example, to the taste and smell of food, to its appearance, and to other situational factors. In fact, argues Panksepp (2010), the positive emotional states that accompany eating, in the same way as those that accompany drug use, may be very important in explaining addictions.

Using magnetic resonance imaging (MRI) recordings, Martin and associates (2010) found significantly increased brain activity in the limbic systems (*medial prefrontal cortex*) of participants when they simply looked at images of food. Interestingly, obese participants displayed more brain activity than normal participants both before and after a meal. This activity, the authors suggest, is closely related to food motivation.

It has been known for some time that certain parts of the hypothalamus are involved in eating behavior. Patients with tumors or other injury on the hypothalamus sometimes overeat and consequently become obese (Rowell & Faruqui, 2010). And MRI studies now indicate that the cerebellum, too, is closely involved in controlling hunger, perhaps via its connections with the hypothalamus (Zhu & Wang, 2008).

TASTE AND SMELL

Taste and smell, too, clearly contribute to food motivation, as is dramatically illustrated in studies using the black blowfly. When this fly is given a choice between a totally nonnutritive sugar substitute and a more nutritious alternative, it insists on eating the sweeter substance. And it will continue to do so until it starves to death (Dethier, 1976).

Like the blowfly, we often prefer tasty over less tasty food, regardless of nutritional value, although when we are really hungry, taste becomes less important than the immediate availability of food (Hoefling & Strack, 2010). The evidence suggests as

we become hungrier, we pay more attention to food cues. When participants are asked to detect specific rapidly presented visual targets that are randomly inserted among other images, hungry participants are easily distracted by food-related images (Piech, Pastorino, & Zald, 2010).

METABOLIC FACTORS

Hunger is a complex motive, tied not only to the body's need for food and to brain activity but also to various metabolic factors. For example, as levels of glucose (a form of sugar) in the blood drop, hunger increases; as blood glucose levels rise, there is a decline in hunger. But the relationship between blood sugar level and hunger is not quite so simple because participants who are given sugar substitutes such as aspartame don't subsequently eat more than participants given sucrose, although their measured blood-glucose levels are significantly lower (Anton et al., 2010).

Many hormones and chemicals alter hunger. For example, fat cells produce *leptin,* a hormone that signals the hypothalamus to reduce appetite. Mice that lack the gene for leptin typically become obese. When they examined children's metabolic profiles, Eriksson and associates (2010) found that leptin was the best predictor of being overweight among 8-year-old children.

Another chemical related to hunger control is cannabinoid (THC or *tetrahydrocannabinoid*), the active ingredient in marijuana. There is considerable nonanecdotal evidence, both with rats and humans, that THC increases hunger and leads to overeating, even in satiated organisms. There is also evidence of differences in cannabinoid sensitivity between some obese people and others of normal weight. Drugs that counter the effects of cannabinoids are occasionally successful in combating obesity, although many of these also have negative side effects (Bermudez-Silva, Viveros, McPartland, & de Fonseca, 2010).

Obesity

Unfortunately, our hunger control systems don't always work perfectly. Overeating, termed **hyperphagia**, is one possibility that may result in *obesity*. **Obesity** is a global problem. Estimates are that about 15% of the world's population—slightly more than 1 billion people—and more than one third of the adult U.S. population are obese (Figure 6.13). Americans now spend about $60 billion a year in efforts to lose weight, mostly on drugs, physicians, weight-reducing programs, patent weight-reducing medications, and weight-reducing literature (*Worldometers*, 2010). An impressive 30% of all those who seriously attempt to lose weight will be substantially successful. Sadly, only 6% of these—hence fewer than 2% of all who try to lose weight—will maintain their reduced weights for any length of time.

A variety of factors may be at play in obesity. Metabolic factors, such as a malfunctioning pituitary gland or hypothalamus, account for a small number of cases. Genetic tendencies are also involved, and a handful of gene defects have now been identified as causing severe obesity (Farooqi, 2010). But the fact that incidence of obesity among children in the United States has nearly doubled since 1980 suggests that environmental factors may be more important (*Obesity Rates Continue to*

Hyperphagia: Overeating.

Obesity: Medical condition related to being overweight.

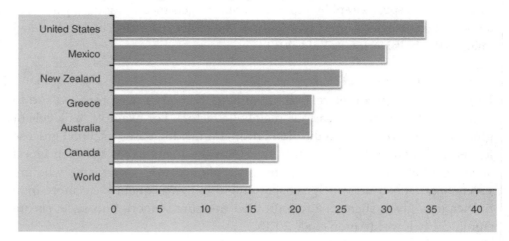

Percentage of adult population considered obese

FIGURE 6.13   Percentage of adult population with a body mass index over 30, based on health estimates rather than self-reported data. Based on U.S. Bureau of the Census, 2010, Table 1306. Retrieved August 20, 2010, from http://www.census.gov/compendia/statab/2010/tables/10s1306.pdf

Climb, 2007). This may be due to situational factors such as socioeconomic status, cost of healthy foods, or even lack of time needed to cook meals. Next time you are at a grocery store, compare the cost of something rich in nutritional value such as fruit to something with lower nutritional value such as pasta noodles. The difference is huge! It is unlikely, however, that our genes have changed significantly in just a few decades.

The most important factors that underlie obesity include the overwhelming popularity and availability of calorie-dense, high-sugar, and high-fat foods, coupled with an increasingly sedentary lifestyle among children. And, as Must and Anderson (2010) point out, by the time children have reached adolescence, detrimental eating and exercise habits have been repeated and reinforced so often that they are very difficult to change.

Aphagia: Undereating.

Anorexia nervosa: Psychological disorder characterized by being significantly underweight.

Bulimia nervosa: Psychological disorder characterized by binging and purging.

Binge-eating disorder: Psychological disorder characterized by excessive binging, however, the individual does not engage in purging behaviors.

Anorexia, Bulimia, and Binge Eating Disorder

Malfunctions of our hunger control systems may be evident in overeating (**hyperphagia**); they may also be manifested in undereating (termed **aphagia**). Clinically, they may lead to one of three eating disorders: **anorexia nervosa**, commonly shortened to *anorexia;* **bulimia nervosa**; and **binge-eating disorder**.

Anorexia is classified by the Diagnostic and *Statisical Manual of Mental Disorders,* Fifth Edition (*DSM-5*) as an eating disorder. Its symptoms include unwillingness or inability to eat and eventual emaciation. It is often characterized by a significantly distorted body image and is sometimes fatal. Its possible causes include cultural standards that glamorize thinness, family and peer pressure, and occasionally genetic factors and psychological issues such as low self-esteem or depression. It is most common among adolescent girls (Keel, Eddy, Thomas, & Schwartz, 2010).

Moreover, individuals with anorexia often experience fear associated with gaining weight. Therefore, to regulate their emotions, they will engage in minimal amounts of food intake.

Literally, *bulimia* means "ox hunger." It is not clear whether it is intended to mean as hungry as a bull or hungry enough to eat the entire bull. Its main characteristics are recurrent episodes of often secretive and guilt-ridden binge eating at least once a week over a period of 3 months. Binges are typically followed by compensating behaviors, including self-induced vomiting (purging) and sometimes the use of laxatives or diuretics to combat weight gain. Purging can have damaging effects. For example, quickly purging after eating a meal may not provide the nutritional value that your body needs. Additionally, frequent vomiting may rot your teeth. Bulimia is most common among adolescent girls.

Obesity is a complex problem. After gastric bypass surgery for severe obesity, Beverley Keating, pictured here with her husband Doug and son Eldon Burke, regained half the weight she had lost. She claims she was not psychologically ready to be thin.
Photolibrary/Peter Arnold Images/The Medical File/Rich Frishman

Binge-eating disorder is also marked by episodes of excessive compulsive eating but, unlike bulimia, does not involve purging or other attempts to get rid of excess calories. As a result, whereas individuals with bulimia are often very thin or of normal weight, those with binge eating disorder are often obese. For example, in one binge, an individual may consume thousands of calories!

There are a variety of possible therapies for anorexia, bulimia, and binge-eating disorder, including cognitive therapies (Murphy, Straebler, Cooper, & Fairburn, 2010), behavior therapies (Kroger et al., 2010), drug therapies, and sometimes even hospitalization.

CAUSES

Interestingly, these three eating disorders often manifest at different ages. Anorexia appears earliest, peaking at around age 14, and then again around age 18. Bulimia peaks somewhat later, at around age 19, and often occurs among girls who were previously anorectic. Binge eating disorder appears even later, at around age 25 (Keel et al., 2010).

As we saw, various factors are related to greater risk of eating disorders, including genetic background, emotional disorders, brain injury and disease, and metabolic malfunction. But perhaps more important than any of these factors are cultural pressures stemming from what Saguy and Gruys (2010) describe as the American media's glorification of excessive thinness. In a sense, we equate being thin with high social status; we make a moral virtue of it—an observation that is reflected in the fact that the average waist sizes of Miss America pageant winners decreased from around 26 inches in 1921 to below 24 inches by 1986 (Freese & Meland, 2002). By the same token, we associate fatness with lower status; we make of it the sins of gluttony and sloth.

These are some of the many pieces of the obesity puzzle. But we don't yet know for sure if we have all the pieces or just how they go together.

Sexual Motivation

Nor do we completely understand sexual motivation, another powerful biological motive. Unlike hunger and thirst, sex is not necessary for the individual's survival; but it is clearly essential for the survival of the species. Nor is it a simple motive, easily explained by a lack or deficiency. If you do not eat, you eventually become very hungry. In contrast, the relationship between the sex drive and lack of sex is not quite so clear.

HORMONAL FACTORS

Estrogen: Female sex hormone.

Androgens: Male sex hormone.

What does seem clear is that hormonal factors are closely linked to sexual urges. At puberty, when the body begins to produce the sex hormones—mainly **estrogen** among females and **androgens** (mainly testosterone) among males—sexual drive increases dramatically. And injections of sex hormones are known to increase sexual drive (Meletis & Wood, 2009).

CULTURAL AND OTHER FACTORS

But hormones are only part of the story. In fact, when the organs that produce sex hormones, the *ovaries* in women and the *testes* in men, are removed, sex drive does not necessarily disappear. Even nonhuman primates display sexual motivation that seems to be independent of hormones. Giles (2008) summarizes a number of studies that have shown that nonhuman primates that have been castrated continue to display both sexual interest and activity. Similarly, women who have had their ovaries removed typically experience little change in sex drive.

Sexual motivation has a number of cultural and learned components as well, as is clear from looking at the sometimes dramatically different sexual behaviors of different cultures. Hence, aspects of sexual motivation are clearly learned. Cultural standards play an important role in determining what we find sexually arousing, even as they define sexual behaviors that are acceptable.

And for humans, perhaps one of the greatest sexual motives of all is love—a topic that science has sometimes found awkward. It is a piece of the puzzle that we examine in Chapter 10.

Summary

In this chapter, we discussed the topic of motivation. Motivation deals with the conscious and unconscious forces that instigate, direct, and control our behavior. We looked at explaining motivation from both the physiological and behavioristic approaches. The hedonistic principle (we seek pleasure and try to avoid pain) and need-drive theory support the behavioristic notion that satisfying needs is reinforcing. Most important is the *incentive* value of goals, linked with our ability to imagine and anticipate the consequences of our actions. Next, we discussed Maslow's hierarchy of needs. Maslow suggests we are driven by low-level basic (deficiency) needs and higher-level (growth) needs, hierarchically arranged so that higher-level needs are not attended to until lower-level needs have been satisfied. The highest human need is the need for self-actualization. Finally in the area of motivation, we looked at cognitive views and defined important terms including cognitive dissonance theory, achievement motivation theory, attribution theory, and expectancy-value theory.

This chapter also covered emotions. Emotions are motives; we are driven toward positive emotions and away from negative emotions. Intensity of emotions is reflected in physiological arousal. Our need for stimulation and our efforts to combat boredom reflect the principle (Yerkes–Dodson Law) that there is an optimal level of arousal for most tasks. Intensity of emotions is reflected in arousal level; the nature of the emotion has to do with cognitive interpretation. We covered three theories on emotion including the James–Lang theory, the Cannon–Bard theory, and Schachter's two-factor theory. The James–Lange theory of emotion says you feel an emotion because of your physiological reactions. The Cannon–Bard theory says, no, emotion and physiological reaction are separate; you feel an emotion because of your cognitive interpretation. Schachter's two-factor theory says the physiological reaction is basic to the emotion, but its nature is determined by the cognitive attribution the individual makes. The limbic system is closely involved in emotions. Finally, we discussed hunger and sex drives. Hunger control has to do with stomach sensations, changes in blood sugar level, hormonal and chemical signals (many of which affect the limbic system and especially the thalamus), and a host of learned factors associated with the taste, smell, and appearance of food and with cultural values associated with food and with body appearance. Malfunctions of hunger control systems can result in obesity or in eating disorders such as anorexia, bulimia, or binge eating disorder. Sex drive is related to hormonal, cultural, and other factors, sometimes including love.

CHAPTER SEVEN

DEVELOPMENTAL PSYCHOLOGY

Dr. Janett Naylor-Tincknell
Fort Hays State University

LEARNING OBJECTIVES

- Recall the major areas of study within developmental psychology
- Explain how research conducted by developmental psychologists changes across the lifespan
- Describe how prenatal development progresses
- Identify possible negative outcomes due to environmental exposure to hazardous substances
- State the changes in cognitive functioning that occur in childhood and adolescence
- Assess how attachment in early life affects later development
- Describe the outcomes of different parenting styles
- Analyze how families have changed across the last century
- Explain how the sense of morality develops according to Kohlberg
- Based on Erikson's theory of psychosocial development, differentiate between how life crises are successfully and unsuccessfully resolved.

PERIOD OF DEVELOPMENT	AGE RANGE
Prenatal	Conception–birth
Infancy	Birth–2 years
Toddlerhood	2–4 years
Preschool	4–6 years
Early Childhood	6–8 or 9 years
Middle Childhood	8 or 9 years–puberty
Adolescence	Puberty–18 years
Early Adulthood	18–35 or 40 years
Middle Adulthood	35 or 40 years to 60 or 65 years
Late Adulthood	60 or 65 years+

What Is Developmental Psychology?

Developmental psychology: The study of change across the life span.

Developmental psychology can be defined as the study of change across the life span. Changes in skills and behaviors come in many forms including increases, decreases, and changes in type. For example, changes in expressions of aggression (behaviors directed at harming others; Parke & Slaby, 1983) occur across the life span. The manner in which aggression is displayed changes across childhood and adolescence, as well as increases and decreases in the frequency of particular aggressive displays. Early forms of aggression among 12-month-old infants typically involve tugging and pulling on toys between peers (May et al., 2011). Physical aggression displays like hitting and pushing begin around 18 months and increase in frequency until about 2 to 3 years of age. However, as language skills improve, physical aggression decreases and verbal aggression increases (taunting and name calling). The incidents of biting and hitting decrease throughout childhood, while social exclusion and verbal insults increase through adolescence.

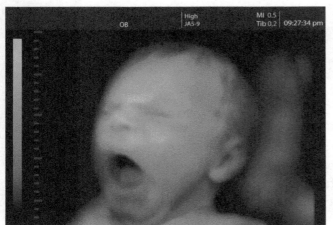

© Valentina Razumova, 2014. Used under license from Shutterstock, Inc.

The change of aggression displays in type and frequency across childhood and adolescence is only one area of study for developmental psychologists. Developmental psychology is divided into three main domains of study: biological, cognitive, and social and emotional development. Biological development pertains to changes in body, brain, perception, motor capabilities, and health, while cognitive development pertains to changes in thought processes, intellectual abilities, and learning styles. Social and emotional development relate to the development of emotions, self-understanding, interpersonal skills, relationships, and moral reasoning.

Cross-sectional design: Research design that collects information from different groups of people of different ages.

Longitudinal design: Research design that collects information from the same group of people across time.

Studying change across time requires a different set of data collection techniques, as well as different methodological designs. To collect information from people with no or limited language skills, researchers typically rely on observations, reports from others, and physiological assessments like movement tracking, eye scans, and brain waves. If language skills are present, interviews and self-reports are possible. These data collection techniques can be used separately or together in complex methodological designs.

To gain information about change across time, participants must be compared at different points in development. One methodological design is called the **cross-sectional design**. Using this design, researchers would collect the same information using the same data collection techniques from different groups of people. For example, researchers may interview a group of 8-year-old children, a different group of 16-year-old adolescents, and a

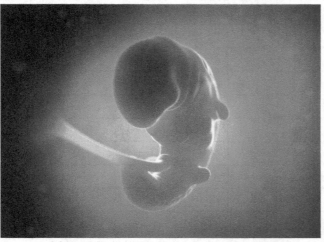

© Sebastian Kaulitzki, 2014. Used under license from Shutterstock, Inc.

different group of 32-year-old adults. In contrast, the **longitudinal design** follows the same group of people across time. Using the same example, researchers would interview children when they were 8 years old, then again when they were 16-year-old adolescents, and then again when they were 32-year-old adults. Both designs show change across time but in various ways. The cross-sectional design provides snap-shots of different developmental periods, whereas the longitudinal design provides information about individual pathways of change.

Now that we have briefly discussed the unique terms and research methods of developmental psychology, let's investigate topics within the three domains of biological, cognitive, and social/emotional development. Within the domain of biological development, we cover prenatal and physical development. Next, we explore Piaget's theory of cognitive development. Finally, we learn about several key ideas related to social/emotional development, including attachment, temperament, parenting, morality, and Erikson's theory of psychosocial development.

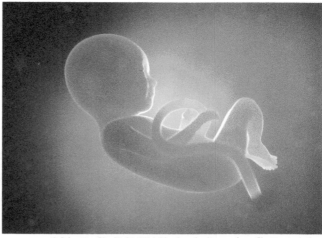

© Sebastian Kaulitzki, 2014. Used under license from Shutterstock, Inc.

Prenatal Development

Prenatal development begins with conception and ends with the birth. The process of prenatal development is best understood in three stages: germinal period, embryonic period, and fetal period. The **germinal period** begins with conception, when sperm fertilize eggs, and ends when the zygote implants in the uterine wall about 2 weeks later. Conception takes place in the fallopian tubes after which fertilized eggs start to divide rapidly and travels down the fallopian tubes to the uterus. Once landing safely on the uterine lining, the zygote attaches to the uterine wall and becomes dependent on the mother for nourishment.

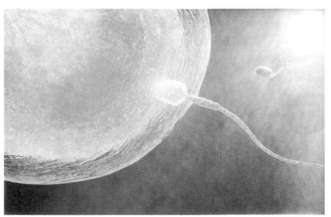

© Giovanni Cancemi, 2014. Used under license from Shutterstock, Inc.

During the next 6 weeks of prenatal development, the embryonic period, the most rapid development occurs. The foundations of all the major structures of the body are formed making this the most critical period of development. Although not all systems are functioning, the cells are differentiating and migrating to form the bases for all the major organ systems. For example, at about 5 to 6 weeks, the fetus's nose, mouth, and palate are beginning to form and by the 8th week the nose, mouth, and palate are almost fully formed. Sexual differentiation begins at the end of the embryonic period with the development of external genitalia. At this time, the sex of the developing organism may be visible using ultrasound technology.

The fetal period is the longest stage of prenatal development, lasting from week 8 of pregnancy until birth, and is a time of continued growth and preparation

Prenatal development: Period of development from conception to birth.

Germinal period: First period of prenatal development from conception to implantation

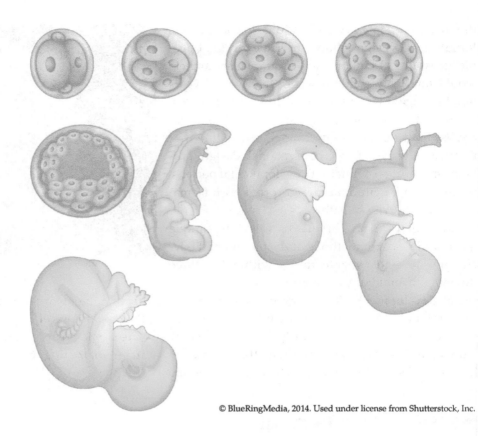

© BlueRingMedia, 2014. Used under license from Shutterstock, Inc.

Process of delivery: The three-stage process of giving birth.

Dilation and effacement: The first stage of the process of delivery in which the fetus turns head down and the cervix begins to expand.

Delivery: The second stage of the process of delivery in which the fetus passes through the birth canal.

Birth of the placenta: The third stage of the process of delivery in which the placenta and other supporting structures detach from uterine wall and pass through the birth canal.

of the fetus for birth. The organ systems are more organized and, across the entire 7-month period, the organ systems begin to function. The fetus can gain more than 5 pounds and grow more than 7 inches. Some of the weight added during this time is due to general development but also during this time, the fetus is putting on a fat layer that will help regulate the body's temperature after birth. As the fetus approaches the time of delivery, movement becomes more difficult because of lack of space. In the final weeks, the fetus prepares for delivery by turning upside down and moving further down in the womb.

The **process of delivery** begins with contractions and ends with the birth of the baby. The first stage of the birth process, **dilation and effacement**, is the longest stage lasting, on average, from 12 to 14 hours. Contractions begin to become more frequent and intense causing the cervix to widen and thin to allow the fetus to pass through the birth canal. Once the cervix is open and prepared, the fetus is ready to be born. **Delivery**, the second stage of the birth process, can last about 50 minutes (with decreasing duration with each subsequent birth). Contractions are extremely intense causing the mother to feel the need to push with the abdominal muscles. The contractions and pushing force the fetus out of the birth canal. The final stage of the birth process is the **birth of the placenta**, where the mother expels the amniotic sac and placenta. With only a few contractions and pushes, the placenta detaches from the uterine wall in about 5 to 10 minutes.

Stages of Childbirth

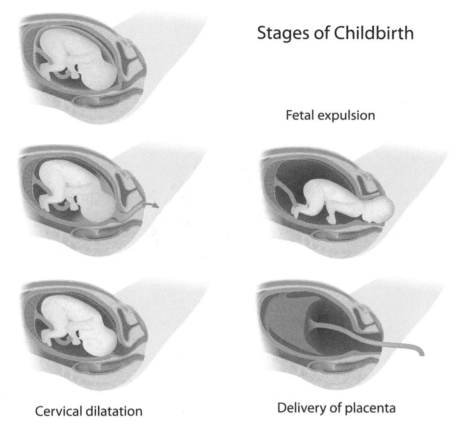

Fetal expulsion

Cervical dilatation

Delivery of placenta

© Alila Medical Media, 2014. Used under license from Shutterstock, Inc.

Once in the world, babies are assessed using the APGAR Scale (Bregman, 2005) at 1 minute and then again at 5 minutes after birth on the following five items: activity level, pulse, grimace (reflex response), appearance, and respiration. Babies can receive 0 to 2 points for each item or 10 points total. Scores between 7 and 10 are within the normal range. Babies in the normal range will be cleaned

APGAR Score

	SCORE = 0	SCORE = 1	SCORE = 2
Activity Level	None	Some Bending of Arms and Legs	Bent Arms and Legs That Resist Extension
Pulse	None	Less Than 100	Re Than 100
Grimace	No Response to Stimuli	Minor Grimace or Weak Cry When Stimulated	Cry or Pull Away When Stimulated
Appearance	Blue or Pale All Over	Blue or Pale in Extremities	Pink Body and Extremities
Respiration	None	Weak, Irregular, Gasping	Strong Cry

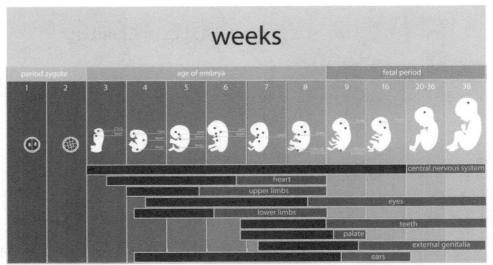

weeks

period zygote		age of embrya						fetal period			
1	2	3	4	5	6	7	8	9	16	20-36	38

central nervous system

heart

upper limbs

lower limbs

eyes

teeth

palate

external genitalia

ears

© Dragana Gerasimoski, 2014. Used under license from Shutterstock, Inc.

and kept warm; it is unlikely that medical intervention will be needed. Scores between 4 and 6 indicate some medical intervention may be needed, such as suction and oxygen. Scores below 4 mean babies are in need of immediate medical interventions to save their lives.

Prenatal development can be negatively impacted by external agents called teratogens. Teratogens are any substances ingested, consumed, or experienced by the mother that can cross the placental barrier and damage the developing organism during pregnancy. These substances can be: (a) environmental influences like mercury, radiation, and lead; (b) legal drugs such as alcohol, cigarettes or second-hand smoke, and prescription or over-the-counter drugs; (c) illegal drugs such as marijuana, cocaine, and methamphetamines; and (d) maternal factors like disease, stress, age, and nutrition.

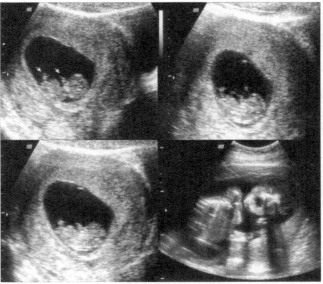

© dodda, 2014. Used under license from Shutterstock, Inc.

The impact of teratogens on prenatal development depends on the timing of exposure. Teratogens cause the most negative outcomes when they are ingested during the sensitive period when the major systems are still being formed and are most vulnerable to damage. Additional factors in the impact of teratogens are the genetics of the mother and developing organism, the amount of teratogen ingested, and the number of teratogens ingested. For example, more negative consequences are possible if several teratogens are ingested versus if one teratogen is ingested. In addition, the mother consuming five alcoholic drinks can have more negative impact than the mother consuming one alcoholic beverage.

The negative consequences of teratogens can range in severity and type and can be expressed in a variety of developmental issues from physical changes, cognitive delays, emotional and behavioral problems, and medical issues. For example, fetal alcohol spectrum disorder (FASD) is a result of women drinking alcohol during pregnancy. Symptoms of FASD include changes in facial features resulting in small eyes, an absent or flattened groove above the lip (philturm), and a thin upper lip, as well as varying degrees of intellectual disabilities, attentional problems, and hyperactivity (Sokol et al., 2003). Despite the possible negative outcomes of teratogens, most prenatal development

© Rick's Photography, 2014. Used under license from Shutterstock, Inc.

occurs without incident because developing organisms are resilient. For optimal prenatal development, it is recommended that parents are aware of possible teratogens and take steps to reduce to eliminate their impact. For more information on how to remain healthy during pregnancy or to learn more about possible teratogens, visit the National Institutes of Health's website athttp://www.nlm.nih.gov/medlineplus/pregnancy.html

Physical Development

To help with survival in the first few months after birth, newborns come into the world with an array of reflexes they can use to manipulate the world around them. Most of these reflexes will disappear within the first 6 months of life when newborns gain control of their motor skills. Several reflexes are dominant in those first few months. The sucking reflex (when something touches the mouth, newborns close their lips and begin to suck) disappears after about 2 months but is necessary for newborns to acquire sustenance. When placed on their stomachs, newborns' legs will begin to move as if trying to crawl. This reflex, the crawling reflex, helps provide a foundation for future mobility. Not all reflexes, however, are as useful. For example, researchers are unsure of the function of the Babinski reflex, which is when the sides of newborns' feet are stroked; they point their big toe out and curl up the other toes. How this reflex promotes survival is still unclear but all babies are born with this skill.

© Aaron Amat, 2014. Used under license from Shutterstock, Inc.

Newborn Reflexes

Newborns also use their senses to manipulate the world around them. At birth, the senses of smell, taste, hearing, and touch are fully developed. However, vision still has much development to become similar to adult visual abilities. When born, infants' visual acuity is about 20/400, which means they can see clearly at 20 feet what adult vision can normally see at 400 feet (Balaban & Reisenauer, 2005). Visual acuity levels similar to adults are not developed until about 6 months to 3 years (Slater, Field, & Hernandez-Reif, 2007), with visual development continuing into adolescence. Therefore, for the first few months of life, infants can see basic colors and shapes but lack the details of objects.

Infants' visual attention centers on contrasts and faces to understand the visual world. In general infants prefer moderately complex color contrast patterns, like those found in checkerboard patterns. In early infancy, babies lack the visual acuity to see complex patterns and therefore, prefer to look at bold, moderately

© Kritchanut, 2014. Used under license
from Shutterstock, Inc.

© Herr Biter, 2014. Used under license
from Shutterstock, Inc.

REFLEX	DESCRIPTION	WHEN REFLEX DISAPPEARS
Sucking Reflex	When something touches the roof of his mouth, his lips close and he sucks.	About 2 Months
Crawling Reflex	When places on her stomach, she will make crawling motions.	About 2 Months
Babinski Reflex	When the sides of her feet are stroked, she points her big toe and curls up other toes.	About 4 Months
Stepping Reflex	When supporting his weight and his feet touch the ground, he will make a walking motion.	About 3 Months
Rooting Reflex	When her cheek is stroked, she will turn her head toward the touch and open her mouth.	About 4 Months
Gag Reflex	Gag response to prevent choking.	Never Disappears

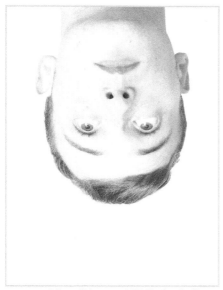

© Lasse Kristensen, 2014. Used under license
from Shutterstock, Inc.

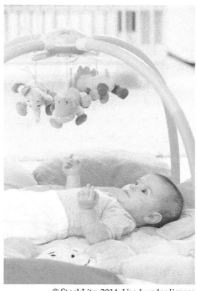

© StockLite, 2014. Used under license
from Shutterstock, Inc.

complex patterns (Banks & Ginsburg, 1985). Additionally, infants prefer to look at naturally arranged faces rather than faces that have been rearranged or are upside-down (Cassia, Turati, & Simion, 2004), indicating that infants understand the basic face structure and expect structure in patterned objects. Finally, infants use motion to help detect object size and color (Spelke & Hermer, 1996). These three concepts may help explain why infants become so fascinated with brightly colored mobiles.

Cephalocaudal: Pattern of development from head to toe.

Proximodistal: Pattern of development from core out to appendages.

Hearing is fully developed in the womb, so infants are very familiar with the sound of their mothers' voices and remember their voices later as infants (DeCasper & Fifer, 1987). Infants are also able to recognize their mothers' smell within the first few days of life (MacFarlane, 2008), prefer the sweet taste of their mothers' breast milk (Mennella, Griffin, & Beauchamp, 2004), and are soothed by the soft touch of skin-to-skin contact (Gray, Watt, & Blass, 2000).

At birth, infants have comparatively large heads, large eyes, small noses, small mouths, and fluffy cheeks to that of older children and adults. These proportions make infants especially attractive to adults and promote nurturing. As infants grow, these baby-like facial characteristics diminish. During the first 2 years of life, infants grow rapidly, putting on weight and getting taller. These bodily changes follow predictable patterns. Most early physical development occurs from head to toe, using the **cephalocaudal** (from the Greek for "head to tail") pattern of development. For example, infants will gain the ability to hold their heads up before they can sit up without support and will sit up without support before they can walk.

© Flashon Studio, 2014. Used under license from Shutterstock, Inc.

The other pattern of development is the **proximodistal** pattern, which refers to the development of motor abilities from the center outward to appendages.

In reference to motor skills, infants are able to use their core muscles to roll over before they can accurately grasp at items and before they have the digital dexterity to pick up small items like Cheerios.

These two patterns of development are consistent across all stages of development, except the adolescent period. In the adolescent period of physical development, bodies grow opposite to the proximodistal pattern resulting in teenagers with large feet and hands in comparison to the rest of their bodies. Growing opposite to the proximodistal pattern leads to teens appearing out of proportion with small trunks and long arms and legs.

Cognitive Development

The domain of cognitive development is the study of the changes in the way our brains make sense of the world around us. Children are not only different from adults in the amount of knowledge they have but also in the way they think. Children rely on different strategies than adults to organize information they encounter in the world. Children often think and learn in different ways across their development. Young children are limited in their logic and rationalizations but as they develop into adolescents, their skills in logic and rational thinking increase.

Jean Piaget is thought to have completely changed the study of children's thinking (Flavell, Miller, & Miller, 2002). Piaget's theory of cognitive development has influenced many areas such as school curricula and teaching styles. Researchers over the years have criticized and extended Piaget's initial work by adding to his theory and empirically supporting his claims. Current theorists and researchers still use Piaget's ideas to guide their thinking and scientific studies.

© Alexey Losevich, 2014. Used under license from Shutterstock, Inc.

Piaget's theory is so widely accepted because it conveys the general abilities and limitations of children at stages across their lives and because of its breadth and applicability to a variety of contexts. Central to Piaget's theory is the concept that children are active mentally and physically in their own cognitive development (Piaget, 1969, 1973). Children are fundamentally motivated to organize and understand their world. Therefore, children do not simply sit by while their cognitive abilities change; instead, children are like "little scientists" creating experiments to test out their ideas and drawing conclusions. From actively manipulating their world, children learn many important lessons without the assistance of others.

Information is organized into cognitive schemas, or frameworks placing information into classifications and groups (Piaget, 1963). For example, we all have a general understanding of what a cookie is, giving us a cookie schema. We know that cookies are often brown, sweet, and delicious food. We organize our experiences with cookies using this general schema for cookies. When experiences and information match the current structure of the schemas, children are in a state of equilibrium, or balance. They are satisfied with their current schemas, with no discrepancies between the categories and groups of their schemas and the outside world. However, when discrepancies do arise, inadequacies in the structure of their schemas become problematic leading to a state of disequilibrium, or unbalance. Children in a state of disequilibrium must resolve these discrepancies to reestablish cognitive balance.

Children use two basic processes, assimilation and **accommodation**, to help organize experiences into cognitive schemas (Piaget, 1999). Assimilation is the process of taking in new information in a form to match the current schemas. For example, children may have a schema for goats. They understand goats are furry, brown, medium-sized farm animals that produce milk. If children are exposed to goats that are black and white, this new experience does not match their current schema of goat. Children can assimilate this information into their schema for goat to now include that goats come in different colors.

© NikkiHoff, 2014. Used under license from Shutterstock, Inc.

The second process of organizing schemas is accommodation, which is adapting the current schemas to match the new information or experience. Using the above example, children exposed to llamas, which may have characteristics similar to goats, will need to accommodate their goat schema because the new information cannot be easily included in the goat schema. Children must develop an entirely new schema to describe llamas. The llama schema would describe llamas as furry, brown, larger farm animals with long necks. Children have accommodated the new information by developing new schemas.

© KarSol, 2014. Used under license from Shutterstock, Inc.

Piaget's theory of cognitive development suggested that children progress through their cognitive development in a series of stages (Piaget, 1969, 1973). Like all stage theories, children must progress through the stages in the same order and each new stage marks qualitatively different skills and abilities than the previous stages. According to Piaget, from birth through adolescence, children's cognitive skills are changed and altered across four stages of cognitive development: sensorimotor, preoperational, concrete operational, and formal operational.

Accommodation: The process of adapting the current schemas to match the new information or experiences.

Stages and Ages

During the sensorimotor stage, from birth to about 2 years of age, infants rely on their senses and their motor abilities to help them understand their world. Infants will place items in their mouths, grasp objects, throw items, and shake things to help them better understand their characteristics. When given a set of car keys, infants will place them in their mouths, shake them, and drop them on the floor. By manipulating the car keys, infants learn the keys' characteristics like shape, texture, temperature, and composition. Infants also learn what pleasant experiences are and what unpleasant experiences are.

Many parents have experienced their infants' "little experiments" when they are trying to learn about new objects. For example, children will bang their spoon on the table during dinner to hear the noise and understand the impact of the spoon on the plate. Once infants understand what noise the

© leungchopan, 2014. Used under license from Shutterstock, Inc.

STAGE OF COGNITIVE DEVELOPMENT	AGE RANGE
Sensorimotor	Birth to 2 years
Preoperational	2–7 years
Concrete Operational	7–12 years
Formal Operational	12+ years

spoon makes on the plate, they begin to bang the spoon on the table, and then the cup, and eventually drop the spoon on the floor. These "little experiments" provide infants with knowledge about sound, cause-and-effect, consequences of behaviors, and much more. Although this may be frustrating for the parents trying to enjoy a dinner at a restaurant, the infants are gaining and altering their cognitive schemas.

The major achievement of the sensorimotor stage of cognitive development is object permanence, the understanding that objects exist even when out of sight (Piaget, 1954). The development of object permanence occurs slowly over the first 2 years. At first, infants are only able to recognize or show interest in objects when they are in plain view. If that object is removed from view, infants, in the early parts of the sensorimotor stage, will not seek out the object. It is as if the object just disappears. At about 8 to 12 months of age, infants will begin to understand a hidden object has not disappeared completely but is just out of sight. Infants at this age will look for the hidden object. However, because of their lack of a complete understanding of object permanence, infants will commit the A-not-B error. Infants will search for the hidden object in the first location hidden. However, if the object is moved (even in their view), infants will not continue to search for the object in the second location.

The preoperational stage of cognitive development (ages 2–7 years) builds on the skills and schemas developed in the sensorimotor period. The preoperational stage is marked by grand increases in, and amazing limitations of, cognitive thought. Now that children have object permanence, they can start to expand their understanding and use objects but they still have limited cognitive ability. The greatest achievement of the preoperational stage is the development of symbolic thought. With symbolic thought, children are able to use one object to stand for another. Children can use a shoe to represent a telephone when playing, indicating their understanding of objects has moved beyond simple reality and location to creative and complex personal symbols.

Even with their new complex understanding of objects and schemas, children in the preoperational stage are severely limited in their thought processes. Children during this stage lack the ability to see the world from another person's point of view, termed **egocentrism**, which is pervasive across contexts and situations. Egocentrism can be demonstrated in both spatial abilities and speech. Children sitting on one side of a table with model of mountain scenery are unable to describe what another person may see from the opposite side of the table (Piaget & Inhelder, 1977). Additionally, children's conversations demonstrate this egocentric perspective. Children often are so focused on their own

Egocentrism: The inability to see the world from another person's point of view.

Watch the A-not-B Error Experiment

https://www.youtube.com/watch?v=4jW668F7HdA

To demonstrate object permanence and the A-not-B error, an example may be helpful. First, infants are shown an interesting toy, like a stuffed animal. After making sure the infant saw the stuffed animal and is interested in the toy, the stuffed animal is hidden under a blue blanket. Infants with no understanding of object permanence will not look for the stuffed animal under the blue blanket. Infants with some level of understanding of object permanence will remove the blue blanket to search for the toy. Once some level of object permanence is repeatedly established by hiding and seeking the stuffed animal under the blue blanket, the stuffed animal will be placed under the blue blanket but then moved (while the infant is watching) to under a pink blanket. Infants who commit the A-not-B error will search for the stuffed animal under the blue blanket but not under the pink blanket. Even with the repeated watching of the stuffed animal moved from under the blue blanket to under the pink blanket, infants who commit the A-not-B error will not search for the stuffed animal under the pink blanket. A complete understanding of object permanence will lead infants to search under the pink blanket because they understand the objects exist even when moved and not in sight.

side of the conversation they do not listen to the other side of the conversation. Consider the following conversation:

ELLIOT: "I like pizza . . ."

JAMES: "I have a TV in my room."

ELLIOT: "With pepperoni and cheese."

JAMES: "I like to watch cartoons on it."

The conversation between the two preschool boys above shows the egocentric focus on their own part of the conversation and the obliviousness to the other half of the conversation. As children progress through the preoperational stage, egocentric speech lessens.

During the concrete operational stage of cognitive development (ages 7–12 years), children overcome the limitations of the previous stage and develop logical thought. Around age 7 years, children begin to think about the world in a logical manner using reason to examine problems and situations. Children can now successfully complete the conservation task by reporting the short glass and the tall, skinny glass have the same amount of liquid because the contents of one glass was just poured into the tall, skinny glass. They are

Watch a Child Describing Mountain Scenery

https://www.youtube.com/watch?v=OinqFgsIbh0

Related to the limitations of egocentrism, children in the preoperational stage also become fixated on one characteristic of an object at the exclusion of other characteristics. This **centration** on the most noticeable characteristic of objects limits their ability to assess accurately changes in size, volume, mass, and distance. This limitation in cognitive ability is tested using the classic conservation task (Piaget, 1954). First, children are shown two identical short glasses of juice and are asked if the two glasses have the same amount of juice or a different amount of juice. Children demonstrate an understanding that the two glasses are identical and have the same amount of juice. Next, one glass of juice is poured from the short glass into a tall, skinny glass of juice and asked again if the tall, skinny glass and the short glass have the same amount of juice. Preoperational children will respond the tall, skinny glass of juice has more because it is taller, even though they just watched the liquid from the short glass being poured into the taller glass. Children are so focused on the height of the liquid in the glass they overlook the volume of juice has remained the same.

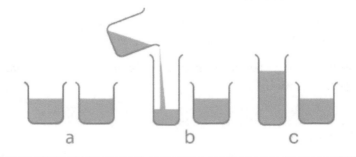

a   b   c

Centration: The fixation on one characteristic of an object at the exclusion of other characteristics.

no longer focused on the most obvious characteristics and can now consider multiple aspects of objects. However, this logical reasoning does not extend to hypothetical situations. Concrete-operational children still engage in trial-and-error when problem solving. Because they are unable to generate hypothetical scenarios, elementary school children will actually need to physically manipulate their world to test out their problem-solving skills. For example, when asked to mix paints to form a new color, children will not be able to think about hypothetical situations in which they have mixed colors and their outcomes, but instead children will need to mix real paints to test out their ideas.

In the final stage of Piaget's theory of cognitive development, the formal operational stage, the limitations in reasoning from the previous stage are overcome. For Piaget, the formal operational stage is the considered the final stage. Adolescents are now able to reason about situations and problems using hypothetical thought. When faced with new problem or situation, adolescents are able to generate possible outcomes and strategies without having to physically test them. In the above paint-mixing problem, adolescents are able to reason about what would happen if they mixed colors without actually having to mix the paints. Piaget believed that not all adolescents or adults will obtain hypothetical thought. However, for those who do, the wonders of the world open up to show the infinite possibilities and constructs. Cognitive skills obtained in the formal operational stage allow adolescents and adults to think about alternate realities and complex social constructs like justice and fairness.

Piaget's theory of cognitive development has many criticisms (Miller, 2011). First, the stage model of development implies thinking within the stage is consistently demonstrated across domains. Children's thinking is more variant than Piaget believed. For example, children's mastery of the liquid conservation task (mastering the concept of volume) does not mean children will be able to master changes in space or mass. Additionally, Piaget underestimated the cognitive abilities of infants and preschoolers. Piaget developed rather challenging tasks (like the conservation task) to test his concepts that were oftentimes overly complex for infant and preschoolers to understand and, therefore, master. Finally, Piaget understated the role of social interactions in cognitive development by focusing too much on the role of children actively manipulating their world. In addition to actively engaging their world, children also learn from their environment by observation and interactions with adults and peers (Bandura, 1977; Vygotsky 1962).

Social and Emotional Development

Humans spend quite of bit of time interacting with others in social settings, as we are, by nature, social beings. Social and emotional development addresses areas such as bonds between the caregiver and child, temperament, child rearing, morality, and social hurdles throughout the life span. Developmental psychologists who investigate social and emotional topics try to understand the type and strength of influence people and social constructs around us have on our developmental processes.

Attachment

One of the first big and influential relationships children have is with their first primary caregiver. This relationship is typically with the mother but can be with the father, grandmother, or others. However, most research has focused on the relationship between mother and child. Attachment is the bond that connects two people together.

Interest in attachment bonds began in the 1930s and 1940s after people noticed children who were orphaned or otherwise separated from their parents often struggled later socially with other relationships and parenting their own children (Spitz, 1949).

© Dmitri Mihhailov, 2014. Used under license from Shutterstock, Inc.

© Goodluz, 2014. Used under license from Shutterstock, Inc.

© Monkey Business Images, 2014. Used under license from Shutterstock, Inc.

These early observations led to some experimental research with rhesus monkeys (Harlow & Harlow, 1965; Harlow, Harlow, & Suomi, 1971; Harlow & Zimmerman, 1959). In a series of studies, Harry Harlow and colleagues were able to demonstrate the negative effects of being orphaned and isolated from birth. Baby rhesus monkeys were taken from their mothers and reared in isolation. The rhesus monkeys were well cared for and healthy but had not exposed to other rhesus monkeys during development. The developmental patterns of the rhesus monkeys raised in isolation were later compared to the developmental patterns of rhesus monkeys reared with their mothers.

Striking differences were observed. First, when the isolated monkeys were placed with other monkeys to socialize, the isolated monkeys' social skills were greatly lacking. The isolated monkeys appeared to be fearful of the other monkeys and spent time soothing themselves by rocking themselves. Second, the isolated monkeys showed little interest in relationships with other monkeys, including copulation. Last, when impregnated, the new isolated monkey mothers were poor mothers, often rejecting or ignoring their offspring. Some of the new isolated monkey mothers even attacked their offspring. Harlow's initial experimental research demonstrated the importance of early childhood exposure to parents and social interactions.

Additional studies by Harlow and colleagues examined the specific aspects of parental care that were most important for the development of attachment. Are the bonds between mother and child formed because mothers provide the food and care necessary for their children's survival, or was the parent–child bond formed because of the nurturing warmth and support mothers provide to their children? To investigate this question, Harlow and colleagues reared rhesus monkeys with two "mothers": one a wire mother providing food and nourishment and one cloth mother providing warmth and support. The baby rhesus monkeys preferred the warm cloth monkey to the wire monkey that provided food. The baby rhesus monkeys would nurse from the wire mothers while clinging to the cloth mothers. Also, when frightened or in need of comfort, the baby rhesus monkeys relied on the cloth mothers for soothing. This research shows that although food and nourishment are important to survival, the bonds between mother and child are best facilitated by the warmth and support.

Using the shocking findings of Harlow, as well ideas from evolutionary theory and Konrad Lorenz (Lorenz, 1952), John Bowlby proposed attachment theory, which was later extended by Mary

Ainsworth. Bowlby postulated that infants were not simply dependent on their mothers for survival but were innately motivated to explore and learn from the world (Bowlby, 1953; 1969). Infants need to have, what Bowlby termed, a **secure base** from which to explore their world. The secure base is a safe, supportive relationship infants can use to understand their world that provides infants with comfort and support when stressed and the encouragement to try things on their own and manipulate their world. The quality and process of the development of attachment shapes how infants and children view their world. If the initial attachment to caregivers is nurturing and supportive and the developmental process is smooth, infants and children will view the world positively. However, if the initial attachment to caregivers is unreliable and harsh and the developmental process is difficult, infants and children will have a negative view of the world.

Secure base: A safe, supportive relationship that infants use to explore and understand their world.

© Iakov Filimonov, 2014. Used under license from Shutterstock, Inc.

The process of developing initial attachments, as proposed by Bowlby, occurs through a series of four phases. In the first phase (birth to about 6 weeks), infants use their innate skills and reflexes (crying and kicking) to signal to caregivers their needs for food and comfort. In this phase, preattachment, infants are seeking out any caregiver to provide basic interactions and comfort. In the next phase (6 weeks to 6 months), termed attachment-in-the-making, infants begin to show preference for one caregiver over other people. Infants will begin to smile and coo at their preferred caregiver more than others, as well as be more easily soothed by the preferred caregiver. It is also at this phase infants start to use theses interactions with their preferred caregiver to develop expectations about the trustworthiness of the world. Between 6 months and 18 months in the clear-cut attachment phase, infants will actively seek out their preferred caregiver and begin to use this caregiver as their secure base. Because of the comfort the preferred caregiver provides, infants may become wary of strangers, possibly displaying distress or anxiety around new people. Finally, around 18 to 24 months, children will develop reciprocal relationships with their preferred caregiver, meaning the interactions are more mutually supportive. In addition, the anxiety and distress demonstrated in the previous phase decrease.

The attachments that infants develop with their primary caregiver do not develop separately. While infants are developing their preferred attachment, typically the mother, infants are also developing attachments to other caregivers, like fathers, grandparents, and siblings. These attachments to caregivers help infants and children develop **internal working models** setting the foundation for future relationships, as well as the development of self-identity, emotions, and self-worth. Internal working models are shaped by the dependability and quality of care received. Infants and children who receive reliable, quality care tend to develop a positive view of the world, themselves, and relationships. Infants who receive unreliable and/or lower quality care tend to develop a negative view of the world, themselves, and relationships.

Internal working model: The expectations and understanding of the world formulated by the first attachment with caregivers.

Strange situation: The procedure developed by Ainsworth to assess different attachment styles.

Ainsworth further developed the ideas of Bowlby by providing empirical support describing the different types of attachments infants and children can have with caregivers (Ainsworth, 1973). Based on her **strange situation** technique (Ainsworth, Blehar, Waters, & Wall, 1978), Ainsworth developed descriptions for secure and insecure attachments. During the strange situation procedure, securely attached infants will use their caregivers as a secure base to explore the room, will play with the available toys, will often bring toys to the caregivers, will show some distress when the caregiver leaves the room, and will be comforted by their caregiver's return. Most middle-class infants, about 60% to 65%, will be securely attached to at least one caregiver (Thompson, 1998; van IJzendoorn, Schuengel, & Bakermans,-Kranenburg, 1999). However, the rate is lower, about 50%, for infants who live below the poverty line.

Events During the Strange Situation Procedure

- Mother and infant enter research room with stranger. Stranger leaves.
- Infant plays with available toys and mother responds naturally.
- Stranger enters and after a few minutes mother leaves.
- Infant is alone in room with stranger. The two may interact naturally.
- Mother returns and stranger leaves. After a few minutes, mother leaves.
- Infant is alone in room for a few minutes.
- Stranger enters and interacts with infant.
- Mother returns.

Insecurely attached infants will show a variety of less positive reactions to the strange situation procedure. Infants labeled insecure/resistant are typically very clingy during the procedure. They will not explore the room or play with toys and will become very upset when the caregiver leaves the room. However, upon the caregiver's return, insecure/resistant infants will seek out their caregiver but will resist their caregiver's attempt at comfort. For middle-class infants, this category accounts for roughly 10% of attachments (van IJzendoorn et al., 1999). Infants determined to be insecure/avoidant typically avoid their caregiver during the strange situation and upon the caregiver's return do not acknowledge his or her presence. About 15% of middle-class infants will be classified as insecure/avoidant (van IJzendoorn et al., 1999).

That leaves about 10% to 15% of infants unclassified by Ainsworth's system because either the infants' behavior did not clearly match one category or their behavior was too disorganized for classification. Some of these infants are labeled disorganized/disoriented, whereas others are unclassifiable. Disorganized/disoriented infants typically want the support and attention of their caregivers but are often unsure or fearful of that attention (Main & Solomon, 1990). These infants may lack the skills to properly signal their needs, may be fearful of their caregiver, or may lack the social skills to properly interact with their caregiver.

Overall, children who were securely attached as infants tend to have better social skills (Lucas-Thompson & Clarke-Stewart, 2007), better control over their emotions (Cassidy, 1994), are more well-adjusted (Brumariu & Kerns, 2010), and have better relations with peers in adolescence (Carlson, Sroufe, & Egeland, 2004) than children who were insecurely attached as infants. The positive outcomes associated with being securely attached

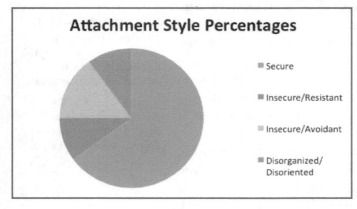

Attachment Style Percentages

- Secure
- Insecure/Resistant
- Insecure/Avoidant
- Disorganized/Disoriented

as infants could be due to the quality of parental care, the consistency of the environment, or both. Although children's attachments are relatively stable across time (Fraley, 2002), attachments can change with the environment (Lewis, Feiring, & Rosenthal, 2000). For example, children who are insecurely attached to their caregivers can become securely attached to a different caregiver in a different environment.

Parenting and Family

The quality, consistency, and type of parenting affect attachments and the long-term outcomes of those attachments. Parenting is a complex and ever-changing concept. As children age, the demands of caregiving change, which requires parents to adapt their parenting styles. To children, parents are instructors of manners, rules, cultures, relationships, social skills, activities, and events. Parents help teach children all about the world and help set up children's expectations for the future.

All parents have their own parenting style that sets the patterns of child–parent interactions. Four different parenting styles have been established by research (Baumrind, 1973): authoritative, authoritarian, permissive, and rejecting–neglecting. These parenting styles are based on the amount of parental responsiveness and the demands placed on children by their parents. Parental responsiveness relates to the amount of warmth and support parents provide their children. High responsiveness indicates parents are attentive to their children's needs and often respond in supportive, caring ways; whereas, low responsiveness indicates parents are less attentive or inconsistently attentive and attend to

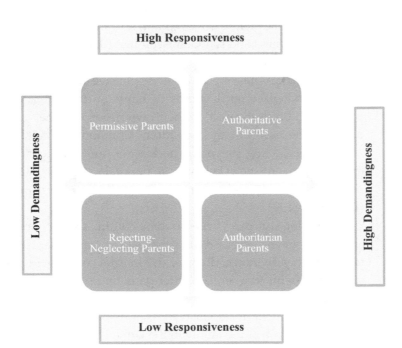

their children's needs in less caring, supportive ways or inconsistently in the level of warmth. Parental demandingness reflects the degree of control over and the amount of strict expectations parents have for their children. Parents who are high on demandingness are often controlling and expect their children to comply with their strict demands, whereas parents who are low on demandingness have no control over and place few demands on their children.

Authoritative parents are high in responsiveness and high in demandingness. They have clear, firm expectations and rules for their children and respond to their children's needs in attentive, supporting ways. Often children of authoritative parents are given some degree of autonomy and have the freedom to discuss and negotiate rules. However, the parents make the final decision. Punishment for breaking the rules is typically fair and matches in severity the degree of rule breaking. Children and adolescents of authoritative parents are socially competent, self-secure, and accepted by their peers, as well as show lower rates of drug use and negative behaviors (Baumrind, 1991a).

Authoritarian parents are low on responsiveness and high on demandingness. They can be overly controlling and can be cold when responding to their children's needs. Punishment is often harsh and intimidation tactics (e.g., threats and psychological manipulation) are a common way of trying to control their children. Children and adolescents of authoritarian parents have higher rates of depression and anxiety and lower self-esteem, as well as display more negative behaviors like aggression and delinquency (Baumrind, 1991b).

Permissive parents are highly responsive to but not demanding of their children. They are warm, attentive, and supportive of their children's needs but place no expectations on their children. Often permissive parents are too lenient with the rules and are unable to enforce the few rules they do have. Permissive parents do not lack rules because they do not care for their children. In fact, they are so warm and supportive of their children they do not want their children to be unhappy with or hindered by rules. Children of permissive parents tend to lack self-control, to have lower academic achievement, and more negative behaviors like impulsiveness and school misconduct (Baumrind, 1991).

Rejecting–neglecting parents are low on demandingness and responsiveness. They are often unresponsive to the needs of their children and place no demands or limits on their behavior. These parents can be so focused on their own needs that they can neglect or reject the needs of their children. Children and adolescents of rejecting–neglecting parents experience a range of negative consequences from antisocial behavior, to poor relationships, to high negative behaviors like delinquency, substance abuse, and promiscuity (Baumrind, 1991).

Parenting styles can vary based on culture, socioeconomic status, and environment. Stressful situations like economic hardship, parental mental health issues, divorce, and marital conflict can place pressures on parents that, in turn, alter parenting styles. Parents may be so focused on reducing the stressful event on their family that they do so at the detriment of responsiveness or demandingness.

The structure of the family in the United States has changed over the last 100 years. In the 1950s, the average age of marriage was about

Authoritative parenting style: Parenting characterized by low warmth and high demands.

Authoritarian parenting style: Parenting characterized by high warmth and high demands.

Permissive parenting style: Parenting characterized by high warmth and low demands.

Rejecting/neglectful parenting style: Parenting characterized by low warmth and low demand.

© dbdavidova, 2014. Used under license from Shutterstock, Inc.

20 years old; however, in 2008, the average age rose to about 25 to 26 years old (Cherlin, 2010). Also, women are more likely to delay child bearing. The number of women over 35 years old having their first baby rose from 1 in 100 in 1970 to 1 in 7 in 2010 (Martin, Hamilton, Ventura, Osterman, Wilson, & Mathews, 2012). In 2012, 6.7 million children lived with one divorced parent and several million more lived in stepparent families (U.S. Census Bureau, 2012). The stereotypical 1950s nuclear family is changing, resulting in more types of family arrangements.

© Golden Pixels LLC, 2014. Used under license from Shutterstock, Inc.

First-time parents over the age of 35 years tend to be more educated, make more money, and have higher-status jobs, as well as less likely to divorce or have more children overall (Bramlett & Mosher, 2002). Mothers and fathers who are first-time parents over the age of 35 years report more satisfaction with parenting, less harsh punishment, and more commitment to parenting than their younger counterparts (Cooney, Pederson, Indelicato, & Palkovitz, 1993; Ragozin, Basham, Crnic, Greenberg, & Robinson, 1982).

Parental divorce can have short-term and long-term negative consequences for children. In the short-term, children of divorced families can have slight drops in academic achievement, have higher rates of depression, be less socially competent with peers, and exhibit increased risk for substance abuse (Hetherington, Bridges, & Insabella, 1998). As adults, children from divorced families have higher rates of divorce and lower relationship satisfaction than children from intact families (Mustonen, Huaurre, Kiviruusu, Haukkala, & Aro, 2011). Despite the short-term and long-term risks of divorce on children, a majority of children only experience the short-term emotional upheaval of divorce with no real lasting negative consequences (Amato & Keith, 1991). When differences are found between children of divorced families and children of intact families, these differences are often quite small and better reflected by the coping styles and mental health stability of the family members prior to divorce (Emery & Forehand, 1996).

Temperament: Infants' and children's biological predisposition to respond to the world in predictable ways.

Temperament

Family dynamics and the influence of parenting can also be influenced by characteristics of the children called **temperament**. Temperament is defined as infant's and children's biological predisposition to respond to the world in a predictable way. Infant's and children's temperament is considered the foundation of later development of personality. For example, temperament dimensions associated with reactions to experiences and emotions can later develop into the personality dimensions of openness to new experiences and neuroticism (or emotional stability). Unlike personality, temperament dimensions do not include aspects of attitude and opinions but are innate, patterned, basic reactions to stimuli and experiences.

Several theories of temperament describe general trends in these patterned responses to the world and outside stimuli. Thomas and Chess

© Sergiy Bykhunenko, 2014. Used under license from Shutterstock, Inc.

(1977) suggested three general temperamental characteristics to describe most infants. Easy babies, as they are labeled, have easygoing temperament. They are quick to adjust to new experiences, establish predictable routines, are generally happy, and typically remain calm. In contrast, difficult babies tend to react negatively to new experiences, show high levels of fear and distress, and have irregular routines. Slow-to-warm-up babies start out somewhat difficult but over time become easier to manage. For example, when first exposed to a new person, they may be fearful but with repeated exposure, they become comfortable with the new person.

More contemporary researchers, like Mary Rothbart (2011), use empirically based dimensions. Although the names of the dimensions may vary, the six

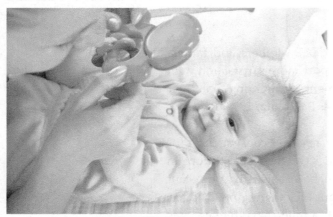

basic concepts included in the dimensions remain the same. The temperament dimension of fearful/distress/inhibition measures the amount and duration withdrawal and fear expressed when infants are presented with new stimuli. Infants high in this dimension are likely to cry and show distress to loud noises, large dogs, and changes in environment. Next, the dimension of irritable distress assesses infants' displays of fussiness, anger, or frustration when not allowed to do what they want. Infants high in this dimension will tend to be impatient when waiting for food or drink, throw temper tantrums to get what they want, and get mad when they cannot have their toy. Infants who are able to look at objects and events for prolonged periods of time are high in attention span and persistence. For example, infants who look at pictures or books for 5 minutes or longer or play with a toy for more than 10 minutes would score high on attention span and persistence. Positive affect and approach refers to the amount and intensity of positive emotions like laughing and smiling, as wells as seeking out new experiences and events. Infants high in this dimension smile and laugh often and approach new toys with positivity. How much infants move around is captured by the dimension of activity level. Infants high in activity level often squirm, kick, and wave their arms around. Finally, rhythmicity reflects infants' preferences for routines and predictability especially in bodily functions such as eating and

sleeping. Infants high in rhythmicity tend to go to sleep and get hungry at the same time every day and quickly establish regular patterns.

Temperament is relatively stable over time (Roberts & DelVecchio, 2000). Infants and children who are high on positive dimensions of temperament and low on negative dimensions of temperament show better social and emotional adjustment later in life (Coplan & Bullock, 2012). Temperament also affects parenting style and parent–child interactions. For example, children who are high in negative temperament dimensions tend to have parents that use strict punishment found in the authoritarian

parenting style (Eisenberg, Fabes, Shepard, Guthrie, Murphy, & Reiser, 1999). The complex relationship among parenting, attachment, and temperament has sparked many lines of research and even more questions.

Moral Development

Morality, according to Lawrence Kohlberg (1969, 1976, 1978), reflects people's sense of fairness and justice. Moral development, then, is the process of learning what is right/wrong, fair/unfair, or just/unjust. Kohlberg was most interested in the development of the thought processes behind moral decision making rather than the acquisition of "correct" moral choices. Children and adolescents move from self-centered reasoning to a social-based reasoning to a flexible reasoning style.

© Belinda Pretorius, 2014. Used under license from Shutterstock, Inc.

Using Piaget's work as a foundation, Kohlberg created a theory of moral development to examine the cognitive processes associated with moral decisions. To gain information about how people make moral decisions, Kohlberg developed an interview procedure using a series of ambiguous moral dilemmas. The Heinz Dilemma involves a man, Heinz, whose wife is dying of cancer. Heinz must choose to steal the lifesaving drugs from the local pharmacy or to allow his wife to die. Again, Kohlberg was not concerned with whether people felt Heinz should or should not steal the drugs; he was more concerned with their reasoning behind their decisions.

Based on the cognitive reasoning behind moral decisions, people can be classified into one of three general stages of moral development: preconventional,

Full Heinz Dilemma

A woman was near death from a special kind of cancer. There was one drug that the doctors thought might save her. It was a form of radium that a druggist in the same town had recently discovered. The drug was expensive to make, but the druggist was charging ten times what the drug cost him to produce. He paid $200 for the radium and charged $2,000 for a small dose of the drug. The sick woman's husband, Heinz, went to everyone he knew to borrow the money, but he could only get together about $1,000, which is half of what the drug cost. He told the druggist that his wife was dying and asked him to sell it cheaper or let him pay later. But the druggist said: "No, I discovered the drug and I'm going to make money from it." So Heinz got desperate and broke into the man's store to steal the drug for his wife. Should Heinz have broken into the laboratory to steal the drug for his wife? Why or why not? (Adapted from Kohlberg, 1981)

Preconventional moral reasoning: Kohlberg's first stage of moral development when children focus on receiving rewards or avoiding punishments.

conventional, and postconventional. Cognitive reasoning in the **preconventional** stage, typical during the preschool and early elementary school years, reflects thinking to seek reward or avoid punishment. In this stage, thinking is very self-focused, reflecting the egocentrism dominant during this level of cognitive development. Children will make moral decisions to gain positive outcomes (e.g., favor from others or tangible treats) or will make moral decisions to avoid negative outcomes (e.g., punishment or loss of admiration of others). For the Heinz dilemma, preconventional moral thinkers will answer affirmative that Heinz should steal the drug because his wife will love him for saving her life (reward) or because if she dies, Heinz will be lonely and sad (punishment). Conversely, examples of negative answers that Heinz should not steal the drug would be because Heinz would get sympathy from his friends if his wife died (reward) or because Heinz would get in trouble for stealing (punishment). Preconventional moral thinking is commonly overcome when egocentrism is replaced with logical thought.

Conventional moral reasoning: Kohlberg's second stage of moral development when people focus on maintaining social order.

Conventional moral reasoning is Kohlberg's next stage of moral development and is the most common level of moral thinking. Most adults reason using conventional moral thinking, which is focused on maintaining social order and laws. Now that adolescents and adults have logical thought and hypothetical reasoning, they are able to think about society and need to reduce chaos. Conventional moral thinkers consider the good of society and the value of applying rules fairly and justly to all members of the society. Examples of affirmative responses to the Heinz dilemma reflect reasoning about the need to maintain social order and include Heinz should steal the drug because the pharmacist is being unfair to cancer patients by charging so much for the drug or because by stealing the drug, Heinz is making the drug available for all cancer patients. Reasoning behind negative responses would be that Heinz should not steal the drug because you cannot have people just going around stealing things they want or because the pharmacist developed the drug and has the right to charge what he feels is a fair amount for his drug. Most adults reason using this type of thinking but this is not the final stage of Kohlberg's theory of moral development.

Postconventional moral reasoning: Kohlberg's third stage of moral development when people focus on equality and the greater good.

Postconventional moral reasoning, the final stage of Kohlberg's theory, is only achieved by a small group of adults. In fact, this stage is so rare Kohlberg never officially interviewed a person who could be classified at this level. However, examples of people who used this type of reasoning would be Martin Luther King, Jr., Mother Teresa, and Abraham Lincoln. Postconventional thinkers have a very flexible cognitive style allowing them to think about universal truths and the need to break the law occasionally for the greater good of universal truths. For example, Martin Luther King, Jr. used civil disobedience to break racial laws in the South to demonstrate all people deserve to be treated with respect and dignity. Possible responses indicating Heinz should steal the drug could be based on reasoning to show that all people should have access to life-saving treatment regardless of their ability to pay or that someone should not die simply because they cannot afford health care. In contrast, negative responses that Heinz should not steal the drug would be because Heinz would be impinging on the pharmacist's freedoms in an open society or because the needs of one person should not outweigh the needs of all people.

Kohlberg's theory has received much criticism. First, gender differences could exist in Kohlberg's stages. Carol Gilligan (1982) proposed women may score lower on Kohlberg's stages because they are less likely to reason based on fairness and justice. Instead, women are more likely to reason based on relationships, which would be more similar to Kohlberg's preconventional stage's focus on rewards and punishments from others. This relationship-focused reasoning is not indicative of lower moral reasoning but rather a different type of moral reasoning. However, research suggests few gender differences actually exist between males and females (Turiel, 1998).

Second, people who more often make life and death decisions such as doctors and lawyers tend to score higher on Kohlberg's stages (Miller, 2011). Most people do not have to decide whether to steal drugs to save a life but doctors and lawyers have more experience with these types of moral dilemmas, leading to deeper consideration of the moral situations. People with less experience with complex moral dilemmas may not be lower in moral reasoning but may have not had the time or the opportunity to reflect on the situation, causing their thinking to appear to be more self-focused or shallow.

Also, Kohlberg's theory has been criticized because the final stage, postconventional reasoning is unobtainable for most people (Miller, 2011). Even though people may be able to cognitively understand this level of reasoning, very few people are able to achieve this level of thinking as their dominant form of moral reasoning. By setting this as the highest level of thinking, Kohlberg may have been setting unrealistic expectations of people and series of stages that do not reflect the true complexity of moral reasoning.

Erikson's Theory of Psychosocial Development

Erik Erikson proposed a social development theory describing the different challenges faced across the life span (Erikson, 1950, 1959). In each of the eight stages of Erikson's theory, a crisis must be resolved. Each unique crisis must be resolved before the beginning of the next stage and crisis or people will struggle to resolve this issue across the life span. The crises are specific to the challenges and hurdles of development within that age range. The first five stages cover birth through the end of adolescence, with the final three stages covering adulthood.

Erikson's first stage, basic trust versus mistrust, should be successfully resolved by the end of the first year of life. The critical issue or crisis that must be resolved is infants' trust in caregiver support and their ability to cope with the world versus the general sense of mistrust of the world and the infants' abilities. If successfully resolved, infants will learn that the world (mainly their parents) is nurturing and supportive and can be relied on in times of need. With this trust in others comes infants' confidence in their abilities to appropriately interact with others and cope with changes. When not successfully resolved, infants develop a sense of skepticism about the world and doubt their abilities to cope with life's changes. Consistent and warm caregiving should lead to the successful resolutions of trust, whereas cold and/or inconsistent caregiving should lead the unsuccessful resolution of mistrust.

From ages 1 to 3-1/2 years, toddlers must learn a sense of independence and self-control to successfully resolve Erikson's next stage, autonomy versus shame and doubt. Toddlers now have increased motor skills, language abilities, and

Erikson's Stages, Age Range, and Crisis Information

STAGE	CRISIS TO RESOLVE	AGE RANGE
Basic Trust vs. Mistrust	Trusting in caregiver and own ability to cope with challenges	Infancy
Autonomy vs. Shame and Doubt	Making appropriate choices and having confidence in skills	Toddlerhood
Initiative vs. Guilt	Setting and attaining goals	Preschool
Industry vs. Inferiority	Learning the rules and customs of the culture	Childhood
Identity vs. Role Confusion	Developing a coherent identity	Adolescence–Early Adulthood
Intimacy vs. Isolation	Forming close, intimate relationship bonds	Early Adulthood
Generativity vs. Stagnation	Considering the legacy left behind	Middle Adulthood
Ego Integrity vs. Despair	Reflecting back on life	Late Adulthood

social interactions. With their new skills come the challenges that require toddlers to make appropriate choices and have confidence in their abilities to enact those choices. Toddlers are going to want to start doing things on their own like pouring their own juice and dressing themselves. Supportive caregiving allowing toddlers to learn these important skills without fear of reprisal helps to successfully resolve this crisis leading to autonomous, confident toddlers. In contrast, harsh or unsupportive caregiving during this crisis leads to toddlers who have high levels of shame and doubt their abilities to independently act on their world.

The crisis of the next stage in Erikson's theory is initiative versus guilt (ages 4–6 years). Erikson believed during the preschool years children must learn to set goals and how to achieve these goals. Setting and attaining goals require the ability to take action and have self-control. Caregivers teach their children these skills through behavioral examples and setting rules and standards for behaviors. Parents who are able to help their children set and attain reasonable goals lead to children who successfully resolve the stage and who develop solid internal motivators and abilities. However, parents who are overly controlling or critical will have children who do not successfully resolve the crisis and lack self-control or become overly controlling.

Because children are exposed to more people within their culture, such as teachers and friends, the responsibility of successful resolution of future crises extends beyond the parents to all people with whom children have contact. Erikson's fourth stage—industry versus inferiority (6 years to puberty)—involves children successfully learning the rules and customs of their culture. To resolve this crisis, children must accept and enact the standards and ideas of their culture into their cognitive and social skills, which allow them to appropriately interact with peers. Also, these cultural skills help children to become productive members of their culture, or become industrious. Children who do not gain the appropriate cultural knowledge tend to have feelings of social and personal inadequacy, or inferiority.

Erikson's fifth stage of psychosocial development is identity versus role confusion (adolescence through early adulthood). After puberty, adolescents have new internal and external pressures to form romantic relationships and set career and educational goals. Adolescence is a time of transition in identity: from the children they were to the adults they wish to become. The crisis of this stage is the need to develop coherent, fully considered identity. If successfully resolved, adolescents will be secure in their identity and career choices, leading to complex adult identities. If not successfully resolved, adolescents may be confused about who they are and lack educational and career goals to become secure adults.

During early adulthood, people must resolve the crisis of intimacy versus isolation. Successfully overcoming this crisis requires people to form close, intimate relationship bonds with others by becoming spouses, parents, and friends. People who do not overcome this crisis typically have a fear of losing their identity in those relationships and think about themselves first, leading to isolation from others.

Erikson's seventh stage, generativity versus stagnation, spans middle adulthood. During this time, people begin to think about their legacy to the world and contribution to the next generation. People who are able to help support and guide the next generation through their experiences have successfully resolved this stage's crisis by contributing positively to society. People who are still focused on their own needs and who do not foster the next generation have not successfully resolved this crisis, or have become stagnant in their phase in life.

The eighth and final stage of Erikson's theory is ego integrity versus despair. In late adulthood, people have the ability to reflect back over their lives and take stock of their accomplishments. When people are able to achieve a sense of purpose and meaning in life and take pride in their accomplishment, they have successfully resolved the final crisis of life. They have a solid sense of integrity. People who fear death and who do not find a sense of meaning in life will face despair in the final stages of life.

Summary

Developmental psychology is a complex field that uses unique data-collection methods and research designs to study change across time in the physical, cognitive, and social/emotional domains. Within the biological domain of development, we learned that prenatal development occurs in three periods: germinal, embryonic, and fetal. The germinal period is the shortest period lasting from conception to implantation in the uterine lining. During the embryonic period, the major foundations of all organ structures are developed causing embryos to be especially vulnerable to teratogens. The fetal period is marked by the most growth. The fetus puts on weight and gains inches preparing for birth.

We also learned about the biological domain of development and that infants are born with important reflexes, like the sucking reflex, that promote survival in the first few months of life. These reflexes often disappear before the end of first year. The four of the five senses are fully developed at birth with the fifth sense, vision, being fully developed by 6 months to 1 year of age.

One theory of cognitive development outlined in the chapter was Piaget's theory of cognitive development, which explains development in a series of four stages: sensorimotor, preoperational, concrete operational, and formal operational. Each stage builds on the previous stage and is marked by unique achievements and limitations. Piaget's theory has spurred much research and application.

Several aspects of social/emotional development were addressed. Attachment is the bonds that tie two people together. The first attachments to develop are with caregivers and provide the foundation for infants' views of the world and relationships. Secure attachments have been linked to positive outcomes in childhood, adolescence, and adulthood.

Parenting styles are different from parent to parent but follow four general trends in warmth and strictness. The authoritative parenting style is associated with the most positive outcomes for children and adolescents. The other three parenting style, authoritarian, permissive, and rejecting/neglecting, are associated with some positive and negative outcomes for children and adolescents.

Temperament is the predictable way that infants and children respond to the world and it varies from infant to infant. Several theories of temperament have been developed to describe the characteristics of infants and patterns of response. Temperament, in infancy, has been linked to both positive and negative outcomes later in life.

Kohlberg's theory of moral development is a series of stages that explains the cognitive processes behind moral decisions. People move from a self-focused reasoning to a universal, truths-based reasoning. Kohlberg established his stage theory using interviews about ambiguous moral dilemmas.

Erikson's theory of psychosocial development was based on the work of Freud but emphasized the psychosocial influences on development. According to Erikson, people progress through a series of eight stages in which a central conflict must be resolved. If unsuccessfully resolved, people will continue to struggle with that conflict throughout life until the conflict is successfully resolved.

© Anna Maltseva, 2014. Used under license
from Shutterstock, Inc.

CHAPTER EIGHT

PERSONALITY

Brooke Mann
Fort Hays State University

LEARNING OBJECTIVES

- Define and describe personality.
- Know the trait-type approaches to personality and understand the difference between trait and type.
- Identify and describe the Big Five personality characteristics.
- Outline main beliefs of biological approaches to personality such as Sheldon's and Eysenck's.
- Understand how Freud describes normal and abnormal personality development.
- Define *self-actualization*.
- Recognize some common examples of *projective* personality measures.
- Know the uses of some common *nonprojective* personality tests.

Traits, Types, and Concepts of Personality.
© kentoh, 2014. Used under license from Shutterstock, Inc.

Personality can be defined in a number of ways; however, most would agree that, generally, personality is a set of characteristics that shape how an individual thinks, behaves, and reacts. Personality is complex and influenced by genetics, learning history, and social experiences. This chapter discusses the major approaches to personality theory as well as common ways to measure or assess personality.

Adapted from *Psychology: The Human Puzzle* by Guy R. Lefrancois. Copyright © 2012 Bridgepoint Education. Reprinted by permission.

Personality

The fact is, we are all different: We all have a **personality**—a collection of characteristics that define who we are. In a general sense, personality can be defined as stable characteristics, including abilities, talents, habits, preferences, weaknesses, moral attributes, and predominant moods that vary from one person to another.

We all make use of masks, personality theorists tell us: in different situations, we have different behaviors.
© ArtFamily, 2014. Used under license from Shutterstock, Inc.

The word *personality* comes from the Latin word *persona*, which referred to the masks worn by Roman actors. Using these masks, an actor could play many different roles in a single play. A persona was, in a very literal sense, a way of changing one's personality, a way of becoming somebody else.

In one sense we all make use of *personae* (masks or roles): We appear to become different people in different situations. The type of behavior expected of us in formal situations is often quite different from what we display in less formal circumstances.

Personality: The set of attributes that characterize an individual, including temperamental, emotional, mental, and behavioral tendencies, influenced by genetics, learning, and social experiences.

Personality and Self

Note the terms *self* and *personality* are very closely related. The self is essentially the person viewed from the inside; how a person sees him- or herself. Personality is the self, too, but from a different view; it is the self as other's see the person, from the outside. In other words, it includes those aspects *self-*presented to the world. The correspondence between the two may be very high (as in an "open" person) or quite low. Presumably, the more closely our personae resemble our true *selves,* the more similar our selves and our personalities will be.

THE REAL PERSON

When someone does some horrendous thing to a cat or a car, neighbors are often shocked: "I would never have guessed in a million years. I can't believe that's the *real* them." But, at least in one sense, it *is* the real them, because we cannot easily separate people from their actions. Striking as one person's violation of their neighbors' expectations might be, we should not overlook the other 40 people on their block whose behaviors surprise no one. The woman who is known to be friendly and outgoing can always be counted on to organize block parties; the man who is conscientious continues to be thoughtful and well organized; and it is expected that the person who is somewhat neurotic will sometimes be moody and anxious. All these people exhibit behaviors consistent with what psychologists would identify as their dominant personality characteristics.

The self is how an individual views him- or herself from the inside; whereas personality, a reflection of the self, is how others see an individual, much like a "selfie."
© tanjichica, 2014. Used under license from Shutterstock,

Understanding how to identify and measure the factors determining consistency in behavior is what personality theorists have struggled to contribute.

The Common-Sense Approach

Being effective in a social environment requires a basic understanding of others—of their likely and unlikely behaviors, their probable actions and reactions. Those unlucky individuals who are less skilled at understanding others often seem inept and tactless and maybe a little socially awkward.

Even those who pride themselves on their "social intelligence" tend to operate with highly global notions of what other people are like and of what they are like themselves. Stagner (1958) provides a striking demonstration of this fact. An unethical salesman (experimenter) approaches a number of personnel managers with a new personality test. The test is not reliable or valid but managers are told it is an excellent personality test. They are invited to take it themselves and to buy it only if they are impressed with reports of their own personalities. After taking the test, each of 68 personnel managers is presented with statements such as these:

> *You prefer a certain amount of change and variety and become dissatisfied when hemmed in by restrictions and limitations.*

> *While you have some personality weaknesses, you are generally able to compensate for them.*

> *You have a tendency to be critical of yourself. (Stagner, 1958, p. 348)*

In this study, 91% of the managers thought the first statement was "rather good" or "amazingly accurate"; 89% and 92% thought the same thing of the second and third statements, respectively. This phenomenon is labeled the **Barnum effect** (after the founder of the famous circus, who claimed he had something for everyone). A large number of studies have since reported corroborating findings (e.g., Claridge, Clark, Powney, & Hassan, 2008; Wyman & Vyse, 2008). Rogers and Soule (2009) also found the Barnum effect among both Western and Chinese participants who were asked to rate the accuracy of astrological predictions. They also found those who were better educated or who had some background in psychology were less likely to fall victim to the Barnum effect. What a great reason to take general psychology!

Barnum effect: The tendency to accept vague personality descriptions of oneself as accurate.

Other fields contributing to the Barnum effect include graphologists (handwriting analysts), phrenologists (those who interpret personality on the basis of head contours), astrologers (those who look to the alignment of stars, planets, and moons), and palmists (palm readers).

According to the Barnum-effect research, there are certain things most people believe about themselves. A common-sense approach to personality might accept these beliefs as descriptive of all people. In fact, the vague and general statements typically used in this research are not very revealing at all. Instead, the statements often convey information that all people believe about themselves such as "Most of the time I try to do the morally right thing."

The Barnum effect describes our tendency to believe vague but plausible generalities such as might be offered by a fortune teller or a palm reader.

Psychology offers a variety of approaches and theories to explain personality and individual differences, none of which is exclusively correct or categorically wrong. Each approach or theory simply represents a different orientation and a different emphasis.

Because personality is a function of many different forces, it is not surprising that various theories focus on distinct aspects. Much of what you are is a function of your genetic composition; biological factors are therefore important in determining manifested personality. Similarly, private experience, social situations, cognitive factors, and psychodynamic forces may all be involved in personality. This suggests at least six approaches to personality theory: common-sense, trait-type, biological, psychodynamic, learning-based, and humanistic (Table 8.1).

Note some of the theories and principles discussed in relation to each of these approaches include aspects of other approaches. The decision to categorize a single position as a trait-type approach rather than social, or biological rather than psychodynamic, is based on the main characteristics of the position, but not on all its characteristics; some approaches represent more than one orientation.

TABLE 8.1   Approaches to Understanding Personality

APPROACH	MAJOR POINTS	REPRESENTATIVE THEORISTS
Common-Sense	Why did she do that? Does he like me? What is she really like?	You
Trait-Type	Discovering and verifying the existence of related clusters of traits composing personality types	The Greeks Jung Costa and McCrae
Biological	Looking at genes (genomics) and at brain structures and functions (neuropsychology) to identify processes and structures underlying personality	Eysenck Sheldon Researchers in genomics and neuropsychology
Psychodynamic	Clarifying the interplay of unconscious forces; understanding the conflict between basic inclinations and social/environmental constraints	Freud Jung
Learning-Based	Personality as learned habits, predispositions, attitudes; also looks at rational contributions to behavior and emotions, decision making, attributions	Watson Skinner Bandura Rotter
Humanistic	The self; worth, dignity, individuality	Maslow Rogers

The Trait-Type Approach

The thousands of adjectives, nouns, and phrases used to describe people are all examples of trait names. A **trait** is any distinct, consistent quality in which one person can be different from another. There are physical traits (blonde, big, buxom), behavioral traits (quick, quiet, quarrelsome), moral traits (bad, base, benign), and many more, totaling to approximately 17,000 possible traits used to describe a person (Allport & Odbert, 1936).

One approach to personality has been to attempt to reduce the total number of possible traits to a few highly representative adjectives. The most useful would be those most often displayed in human behavior, most variable from one person to another, and most distinct. Typically, all synonyms or near-synonyms are excluded from such lists, and an effort is made to pair the words as opposites. Thus, a person can be emotional or stable, humble or assertive, outgoing or withdrawn.

Another way of looking at a trait is to say it implies a prediction about behavior. To say an individual is bold is to predict the person is more likely to act boldly than are less bold people in similar circumstances. This, however, is quite different from saying a bold individual will always act boldly. Psychology mostly deals with *average* behavior, and thus the knowledge of predominant personality traits simply allows for predictions of behavioral tendencies. Predictions made using this method are more likely to be accurate than those based solely on intuition.

Among the best known of the trait approaches is that proposed by Cattell (1946), who reduced Allport and Odbert's list of more than 17,000 adjectives by eliminating all synonyms, obscure and infrequent words, and apparently irrelevant terms. After extensive analysis of individuals who had been rated by close friends using Cattell's adjectives, he further reduced the list to 16 traits by combining separate but closely related traits using a statistical process called **factor analysis**. This statistical procedure analyzes correlations among variables and combines those found to be closely related. It is commonly used to reduce large numbers of related variables—such as traits—to a smaller number of meaningful categories. Some of the 16 personality traits resulted from Cattell's work are shown in Figure 8.1. The traits are based on popular adjectives used to describe people in meaningful ways. The traits are arranged in pairs of opposites.

Cattell is now widely recognized as the founder of current personality and trait measurement (Denis, 2009). His approach to identifying and measuring personality traits continues to be widely used.

Personality **type** is a more inclusive term than *trait*. Whereas a trait is inferred from a tendency to behave in a given way in certain

Trait: Any distinct, consistent characteristic that can vary from one person to another.

Factor analysis: A statistical procedure for reducing correlational data to a smaller number of dimensions by grouping closely related variables.

Type: A related grouping of personality traits.

Conservative	⟷	**Experimenting**
Emotional	⟷	**Stable**
Forthright	⟷	**Shrewd**
Expedient	⟷	**Conscientious**
Humble	⟷	**Assertive**
Placid	⟷	**Apprehensive**
Practical	⟷	**Imaginative**
Relaxed	⟷	**Tense**
Shy	⟷	**Venturesome**
Sober	⟷	**Happy-go-lucky**
Trusting	⟷	**Suspicious**

FIGURE 8.1   Some of Cattell's 16 personality traits.

situations, a type describes a group of related traits. For example, *Type A* personality defines individuals who are characterized by *traits* such as aggressiveness, competitiveness, high need for achievement, and perhaps other traits such as low frustration tolerance, impatience, and rudeness.

It is important to note traits and types are not the causes of behavior, but indicate certain identifiable consistencies in behavior. Thus, people do not fight because they are hostile; but because they fight, we may describe them as hostile. If causes can be identified, it may be due to as much the situation as the person.

Early Trait-Type Approaches

An ancient approach to personality types was suggested by Greek philosophers, who described four distinct types of individuals: the *sanguine* (optimistic and happy); the *melancholic* (unhappy, depressed); the *choleric* (of violent temper); and the *phlegmatic* (apathetic, not easily moved to excesses of emotion; see Figure 8.2). They thought each of these personality types depended on fluids in the body—then called "humors." The sanguine individual had a

(a) *Sanguine (positive)*

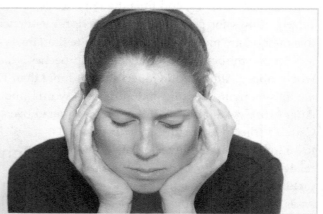
(b) *Melancholic (disheartened)*

(c) *Phlegmatic (indifferent)*

(d) *Choleric (angry)*

FIGURE 8.2   Personality types according to Greek philosophers.

preponderance of blood; the melancholic, of black bile; the choleric, of ordinary bile; and the phlegmatic, of phlegm. Unfortunately, science has revealed us not to be so simple; this information is now only of historical interest.

A widely accepted typology was originated by Carl Jung (1923), whose theory, like Sigmund Freud's, was a **psychodynamic theory**. Psychodynamic theories are based on the belief behavior is motivated by unconscious forces. These theories emphasize the interplay between unconscious and conscious motives. He believed many of our unconscious motives stem from **archetypes**. Archetypes are a sort of unconscious, shared historical memory—part of what he labeled the *collective unconscious*.

Among the most common archetypes, explains Jung, are the man/woman dichotomy (his labels are *anima/animus*). In a sense, these archetypes serve as motives impelling us to accept masculine and feminine characteristics. Similarly, there is an archetype relating to God, and this, he suggests, accounts for the existence of religions.

In his personality theory, Jung proposed two main *types*, which include great clusters of traits: **extraversion** (also spelled *extroversion*) and **introversion**. These represent the two possible attitudes with which all people approach life, Jung explained. On the one hand, there are extroverts—those who run toward life, are adventurous, bold, eager to live and to experience, are concerned with others, with sports, with all the external world. *Extroverts* are fun-loving, outgoing, friendly, and active.

Introverts, on the other hand, are those who turn inward and away from the world (*intro* meaning inward). They are concerned more with subjective than objective reality. *Introverts* are described as timid and quiet. According to Jung, they avoid social interaction and dislike adventure and physical risk.

Psychodynamic theory: The elaborate theory developed by Freud, based on his notion that behavior and personality are developed by unconscious urges and motivations.

Archetypes: Literally, the first or original model. In Jung's theory, a universal thought or shared historical memory which is largely unconscious.

Extraversion: This "Big Five" personality factor includes traits of outgoing, positivity, and energetic.

Introversion: The opposite of extraversion: withdrawn, shy, and reluctant to engage in social interaction.

Jung's typology describes *introverts*, who are more timid and quieter, and *extroverts*, who, like this woman, are bold, outgoing, and not averse to being the center of attention.
© Halfpoint, 2014. Used under license from Shutterstock, Inc.

The Big Five

Jung's ancient typology is a theory of personality that has withstood the test of time: today's personality theorists agree overwhelmingly that extraversion and introversion represent a consistent and important dimension of human personality. They also agree these two labels represent only one of five personality types—commonly labeled the **Big Five factors** (or the *Five Factor Model*).

The five factors were discovered independently by different researchers and have been extensively investigated over the years (Digman, 1990). Much of this research uses factor analysis to look at how different traits tend to co-occur. This has allowed personality theorists to reduce a very large number of traits to five *big* factors, each of which is one extreme of a pair of opposite types. Thus, *extraversion* is one of the five factors, but *introversion* is not: It is simply the opposite of extraversion.

The Big Five factors, which are thought to include most of the traits describing personality, are **c**onscientiousness, **a**greeableness, **n**euroticism, **o**penness,

Big Five factors: A widely accepted personality typology that includes extraversion, openness, conscientiousness, agreeableness, and neuroticism.

and **e**xtraversion. As a memory aid, note the first five letters spell the acronyms CANOE or OCEAN.

EXTRAVERSION

Those who have high levels of **extraversion** tend to be outgoing, to seek stimulation, and want to be in the company of others. They are engaged in the world, highly sociable, and energetic. At the other extreme are the introverts—those who shy away from social interaction. Whereas, extraverts tend to be gregarious, assertive, and bold, introverts tend to be solitary, withdrawn, and more timid. This does not mean introverts are necessarily shy and have no friends; however, research indicates they are likely to have fewer friends, and are more socially reserved (Selfhout et al., 2010).

OPENNESS

Openness is characterized by a high degree of inventiveness, adventurousness, and curiosity. Those who are highly open seek out new experiences; they want to know, to discover, to find out things. Openness implies an appreciation for different, unusual things, for art, and imagination. The opposite dimension is characterized by a more rigid, conventional, traditional approach to life. Those who are *closed* rather than open prefer things be straightforward and obvious rather than complex and ambiguous. Highly creative individuals tend to score high on the openness factor (Sung & Choi, 2009).

NEUROTICISM

Neuroticism is marked by fluctuating emotions, high anxiety, and a tendency toward negative moods such as anger and depression. Those who score high on this factor are sometimes described as *emotionally unstable*. They tend to be more vulnerable to the effects of stress and are more often in a bad mood. In contrast, those who score low on the neuroticism scale tend to be emotionally stable and calm when faced with stressful events. They are generally characterized by positive rather than negative moods.

Individuals scoring high in Openness exhibit characteristics of being adventurous, daring, and tend to try new things.

© Photobac, 2014. Used under license from Shutterstock, Inc.

CONSCIENTIOUSNESS

Those who are careful and highly responsible score high on the **conscientiousness** scale. They tend to exhibit a high degree of organization, self-discipline, thoroughness, and a need to achieve. Such individuals are often described as perfectionists or workaholics. They tend to be highly diligent, well-prepared workers (Woodman, Zourbanos, Hardy, Beattie, & McQuillan, 2010). In contrast, those who score low on conscientiousness display a lower need for achievement. They are more laid back, less disciplined, and less compulsive.

AGREEABLENESS

Agreeable people are those who are friendly and easygoing. They strive to be pleasant and cooperative. They are polite and compassionate, they value friendships, and they tend to have an optimistic view of people. In contrast, those low on the **agreeableness** factor are more suspicious of people, have a lower opinion of human nature, and are less likely to try to be accommodating and friendly. Research suggests anger and hostility may be associated with low agreeableness scores (Sanz, Garcia-Vera, & Magan, 2010). (See Figure 8.3 for a visual of the Big Five approach to personality types.)

Agreeableness: A "Big Five" personality factor comprised of the traits friendly, compassionate, and cooperative.

Stability of Personality

Some theorists believe personality changes dramatically depending on the situation. For example, Mischel (2004) showed scores on personality tests are not very useful in predicting a given individual's behavior in any specific situation. Behavior often seems to depend on the specific situation, taking into account the person's immediate emotions and goals.

On the other hand, there is strong evidence personality traits are relatively stable over much of the life span (Bolkan, Meierdiercks, & Hooker, 2009). There is considerable evidence that measures of the Big Five factors are highly useful in predicting typical patterns of behavior (McCrae & Costa, 1997). Although such measures do not lead to highly reliable predictions of what a person will do

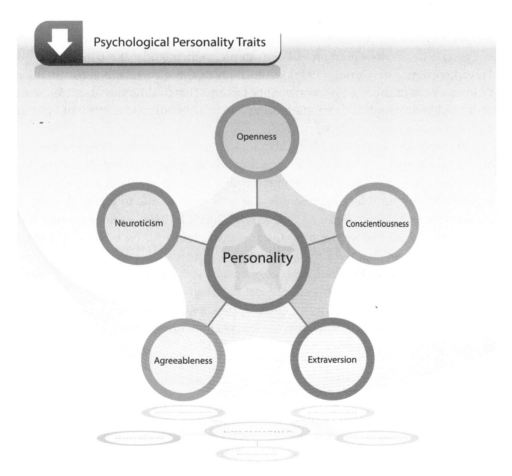

FIGURE 8.3   The Big Five factor model. A typology of human personality.

tonight, they allow us to make very useful *general* predictions about how a person is likely to behave in a wide variety of situations over a long period of time.

Although the Big Five factors are widely researched and widely accepted in personality theory, the approach has its critics. Some suggest there are other important factors not included in the model—factors such as honesty, sense of humor, masculinity–femininity, and conservativeness (Block, 1995). Others, such as Mischel (2004), argue the factors do not predict individual behaviors well. Still, others point out the five factors are based solely on statistical analyses of personality tests but lack a theoretical basis.

In closing, it is important to note the trait-type approaches to personality are primarily *descriptive;* their main concern is to describe and label the dimensions of personality rather than to explain how personality develops. In contrast, learning-based and biological approaches are more concerned with the *causes* of personality.

Biological Approaches

Genomics: The discipline studying genomes in an attempt to establish relationships between genes and characteristics.

Genome: The complete set of chromosomes of an organism. All of an organism's inheritable traits.

Biologically oriented theories of personality look at genetics as an important *cause* of our relatively stable behavioral tendencies, such as our tendency to seek or avoid social situations. **Genomics** is the discipline in genetics attempting to map the human **genome** and establish its relationship to human characteristics.

Whether genomics will find a demonstrable link between genes and personality has been widely debated. Research with identical and fraternal twins strongly suggests genetics does play a role. For example, in their study of 250 pairs of twins, Jang, Livesley, and Vernon (1996) found high positive correlations for identical twins on each of the Big Five personality factors. This finding has also been demonstrated in different cultures, suggesting that it is not only a side effect of Western culture (Yamagata et al., 2006).

Research in neuropsychology also looks for the biological bases of personality characteristics, and some personality-related psychological disorders. For example, some research indicates high impulsivity may be linked with deficits in frontal and temporal lobe functioning—deficits may be due to injury, disease, or genetics (Seres, Unoka, Bodi, Aspan, & Keri, 2009). In its extreme forms the trait of impulsivity may be an important characteristic of *borderline personality disorder* (discussed in later chapters).

Although the links among genes, neurological functioning, and personality are still not very clear, this should not be taken as an indictment of the field. Instead, the study of the genetic causes of personality is exciting and presents a fertile field for future scientific discoveries that may unlock some of the mysteries of why we behave the way we do.

Sheldon's Body Types

Among the first well-known systematic investigations of the relationship between biologically determined characteristics and personality traits was Sheldon's (1954) monumental study of body type. He began by looking at some of the common stereotypes people have about physical appearance and

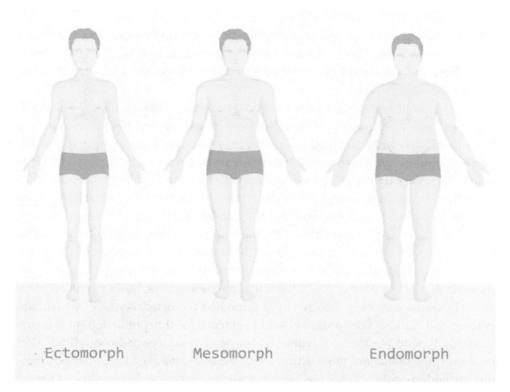

Ectomorph   Mesomorph   Endomorph

Sheldon's classification of body types; an interesting but controversial approach to personality receiving both support and criticism.

© eveleen, 2014. Used under license from Shutterstock, Inc.

personality. Is the robust person really happy and outgoing? Is the well-built person athletic and adventurous? Is the frail person intellectual and artistic?

Sheldon approached this problem by sorting 2,000 photographs of people into three categories based on general body types: *endomorph, mesomorph,* and *ectomorph.* **Endomorphs** are the larger individuals. **Mesomorphs** are muscular and strong and of medium weight. **Ectomorphs** are frail and slender.

After classifying body types into categories, Sheldon and his coworkers interviewed large groups of individuals to determine the relationship between body type and personality. They reported an extremely high correspondence between the two. Thus, Sheldon apparently confirmed endomorphs are complacent, tolerant, concerned with eating, and highly sociable; ectomorphs are withdrawn, secretive, and concerned with intellectual matters; and mesomorphs are adventurous, bold, and loud. However, Sheldon's results could be due to a confirmation bias, the predisposition to use methodology more likely to confirm one's own theories or hypotheses. One way researchers attempt to counteract confirmation bias is by using single- or double-blind experiments.

Sheldon cautioned, however, very few individuals fall solely into one category. Although many people tend to be more one type than another, most are actually a combination of all three body types. Thus, it is possible to identify the predominant temperament of an individual by analyzing body type, but personality characteristics pertaining to other body types may also be present.

Endomorphs: Sheldon's large somatotype, believed to love comfort, be relaxed, good natured, and sociable.

Mesomorphs: Sheldon's moderate somatotype, believed to love adventure, exercise, and activities that demand boldness and courage.

Ectomorphs: According to Sheldon, a frail, thin body type, described as withdrawn and concerned with intellectual matters.

RESEARCH ON SOMATOTYPES

Many investigations of the relationship between body type and personality have found very low relationships between the two (e.g., Hood, 1963). Still, there are a handful of studies reporting findings very similar to some of Sheldon's.

Why should body build be related to personality characteristics? Sheldon's argument was temperament is constitutional (hereditary) in the same way as is body build, and environmental influences are of minimal importance. It may be, as some genomics research with animals suggests, personality characteristics are, at least to some extent, determined by genetics (e.g., van Oers & Mueller, 2010).

Other explanations suggest it is the types of activities and interactions facilitated by body build most responsible for any relationship found between personality and physical characteristics. The mesomorph, whose body is better suited to robust physical activity, is more likely to be athletic. Not surprisingly, research provides corroboration: Athletes in many sports are more likely to be mesomorphs (Galaviz & de Leon Fierro, 2007). Similarly, a mesomorphic build may lead more easily to violence and aggression—as Sheldon had predicted. A study by Maddan, Walker, and Miller (2008) provided some evidence for this prediction by comparing body type to the kinds of crimes a sample of prisoners had committed. That mesomorphic builds are more attractive to the opposite sex than either ectomorphic or endomorphic builds has been confirmed in various studies (e.g. Dixson, Dixson, Bishop, & Parish, 2010). This, too, may explain some of the mesomorph's personality traits.

The frail ectomorph, by contrast, may experience more difficulty with physical activity. One of the consequences of this trait may be subsequent difficulty with social interaction, since much of the early learning important for effective socialization occurs in the physical activities of childhood. Consequently, the ectomorph turns inward, becomes withdrawn, and is more likely to develop solitary interests such as those exemplified by the arts. The endomorph may be seen as compensating for a tendency toward obesity by becoming gregarious and outgoing, by adopting a loving, good-willed, hedonistic approach to life.

There is another possible explanation based on the effects of social expectations. This argument maintains the frail person is expected to be interested in intellectual matters; the person who looks like an athlete is expected to be aggressive and active; and the larger person is expected to be friendly and relaxed. According to this explanation, the pressures of social expectations influence personality development.

Eysenck's Biological Theory

Social expectations, explains Hans Eysenck (1947, 1967), must be congruent with biological expectations and explainable at the biological level. One of Eysenck's basic premises is we are born with tendencies to behave in certain ways. He initially thought only two dimensions (types) were needed to describe human personality: extraversion and neuroticism (as opposed to introversion and emotional stability). Later, in collaboration with his wife, he added a third dimension: psychoticism (as opposed to self-control; Eysenck & Eysenck, 1976).

Eysenck uses the terms *extraversion* and *introversion* in much the same way as they are used in the Five Factor model. *Neuroticism* refers to a personality dimension ranging from emotional instability to stability. *Psychoticism* denotes high aggression, antisocial tendencies, and high egocentrism—contrasted with high self-control and respect for authority, rules, and laws.

Analysis of numerous personality tests led Eysenck to the conclusion that these dimensions of personality are essentially independent. An individual can be high on one without being high on the other, or can be high or low on all three. Although the tendency to be neurotic or extroverted (or their opposites) is largely genetically based, Eysenck does not rule out the influence of the environment. What he says, essentially, is individuals who score high on the neurotic factor have less stable (more labile) types of nervous systems and are more likely to acquire conditioned anxieties. This is principally because they react too strongly to situations evoking less intense emotional responses from individuals lower on a neuroticism scale (Figure 8.4).

RESEARCH EVIDENCE

Much of Eysenck's experimental work has been directed toward establishing the validity of these personality dimensions and their biological bases. A basic assumption underlying the theory is that the nervous systems of *extroverts* and introverts differ, as do those of neurotics or psychotics and so-called "normal" people. Accordingly, he predicted extroverts should have lower levels of cortical excitation (low arousal levels) than introverts. Pavlov had already demonstrated conditioning is closely related to the level of cortical activity with animals whose brains were most active. The high cortical–activity animals were conditioned more rapidly than others whose brains were typically at lower levels of arousal.

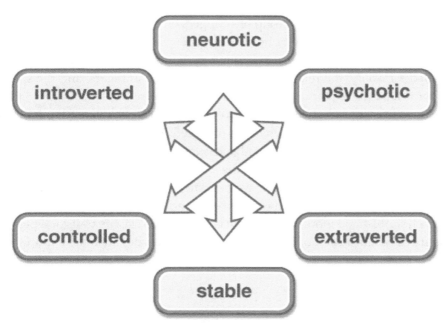

FIGURE 8.4   Eysenck's three dimensions of personality. Each dimension is independent of the others, so one individual might be high on two different factors and low on the third; another might be high on one and low on the other two.

To test his biological theory of personality, Eysenck used the research procedure of Pavlov. If Eysenck's theory was correct, then certain hypotheses derived from the theory should also be supported in an experiment. Specifically, if extroverts have more inhibited cortexes (lower arousal levels at resting states), they should condition more slowly than introverts. And, behold, this hypothesis was supported by research (Eysenck, 1967), which supported Eysenck's biological theory of personality.

Other indirect tests of Eysenck's theorizing come from studies of personality disorders and in countless practical applications of the personality test he developed (Revised Eysenck Personality Questionnaire). Using this test, researchers have found strong relationships between high introversion and suicide attempts (Li & Lei, 2010). Others have reported a relationship between happiness and low neuroticism (Robbins, Francis, & Edwards, 2010). The test has been found to be generally useful for identifying individuals at risk of mental disorders in a wide variety of different settings and cultures (Kokkinos, Panayiotou, Charalambous, Antoniadou, & Davazoglou, 2010).

EYSENCK'S ORGANIZATION OF PERSONALITY

Eysenck's view of the structure of personality may be summarized as follows: Our nervous systems differ in important ways from those of people who have fundamentally different personality characteristics than us. Basically, we inherit greater or lesser tendencies toward introversion–extroversion, neuroticism–stability, or psychoticism–self-control. These tendencies are evident in the functioning of our nervous systems. In sum, the tendencies give rise to behavioral predispositions, labeled traits. The traits themselves are translated into habits – consistent patterns of responding. Specific habits manifest themselves in our actual responses. Thus, personality is hierarchically structured.

As an example of the hierarchical nature of personality, consider Nathan, who finds himself telling jokes to a group of strangers on a commuter train out of New York. There is a high probability he would score near the top on an extroversion scale; hence his type is *high extrovert–low introvert*; the trait he is manifesting might be labeled *sociability*; the relevant habit is entertaining strangers; and the specific behavior is telling this story at this time, in this situation.

Had we known beforehand the extent of Nathan's extroversion, we might have predicted a behavior not unlike what was observed. Theorists who have been more concerned with the identification and measurement of specific traits, however, would point out, had we been aware of the extent of his trait of sociability, the same prediction could have been made. If we had known of his habit of telling jokes to strangers, our prediction would have been even more accurate. Consider, however, how much simpler and more economical it is to be able to classify traits or types than to classify habits. In addition, habits change; traits and types are more enduring.

A Psychodynamic Approach: Freud

Deep-seated psychological forces, sometimes instinctive, often unconscious, interacting with the environment produce personality and guide behavior, claimed Freud. This is a *psychodynamic* approach to personality—so called because it emphasizes the interaction of unconscious emotional and mental processes and their influence on personality and behavior.

Freud's Basic Ideas

Among the most basic of Freudian notions is the belief that powerful instinctual tendencies account for human behavior and development (Freud, 2003; Lear, 2005; Roazen, 1975). Most important among these are the urge to survive and to procreate (labeled eros after the Greek word for love). Because survival is not ordinarily threatened by reality, it is of secondary importance. Far more important in Freud's theory is the urge to procreate, which meets with considerable social resistance. Sexual urges are so important in this theory they warrant a separate label: **libido**.

A second important instinctual urge in Freud's system is the death wish (labeled **thanatos** after the Greek word for death). Freud thought this instinct is sometimes manifested in high-risk behaviors (such as car racing, skydiving, and related sports) and, more importantly, in aggressive behaviors. As a result, he gives sexuality and aggression a central position in his theory. These two forces are the main motivators of our behaviors, Freud explained, but their influence is largely unconscious: We are not ordinarily aware that many of our behaviors have sexual or aggressive significance.

THREE COMPONENTS OF PERSONALITY

There are three broad, sequential stages of personality development, says Freud. These are manifested in the development of id, ego, and superego.

- **Id** The Freudian infant is all primitive instincts, a bundle of unbridled psychic energy seeking almost desperately to satisfy urges based on the drive to survive and to procreate. These urges, labeled **id**, are a lifetime source of energy; they are the basic, underlying motives for all we do.

  Unlike older children and adults, the infant has no idea of what is possible or impossible, no sense of reality, no sense of right and wrong, no internal moral rules governing conduct. As a result, says Freud, the infant is driven by an almost overwhelming urge to obtain immediate satisfaction of impulses. An infant who is hungry does not wait; right now is the time for the nipple and the sucking!

- **Ego** But life is harsh, and almost from birth, there is an abrupt clash between these powerful libidinal urges and reality. Even hunger, the most powerful of the survival-linked drives, cannot always be satisfied immediately. The reality is the infant's satisfaction has to be delayed or denied. Even defecation cannot always occur at will. This constant conflict between id impulses and reality results in the development of the second aspect of personality, the **ego**.

  This rational component of human personality grows out of a realization of what is possible and what is not. It develops as a result of a child's experiences leading to the realization that delaying gratification is often a

Libido: A Freudian term for sexual urges.

Thanatos: A Freudian term denoting the death wish or death instinct.

Id: In Freudian theory, all the instinctual urges that humans inherit, including eros and thanatos.

The infant is all id, according to Freud—desperate to satisfy immediate urges, with no idea of what is possible or realistic. Feed me now! Or, of course, I'll cry.

© leungchopan, 2014. Used under license from Shutterstock, Inc.

Ego: In Freud's theory, the rational, reality-oriented level of human personality, developing as the child becomes aware of what the environment makes possible and impossible.

desirable thing, long-term goals sometimes require the denial of short-term goals. Although the id wants immediate gratification, the ego channels these desires in the most profitable direction.

Superego　The id and the ego work together. Both have the same goals: satisfying the needs and urges of the individual. But the third component of personality—the **superego**—has a different agenda.

The superego (or conscience) begins to develop in early childhood, says Freud, and results mainly from the child's identifying with parents. **Identification** involves attempting to become like others—adopting their values and beliefs as well as their behaviors. By identifying with their parents, children learn the religious and cultural rules governing their parents' behaviors; these rules become part of the superego. Because many religious, social, and cultural rules oppose the urges of the id, the superego and the id are often in conflict. Freud believed this conflict underlies many mental disorders and accounts for much deviant behavior (Figure 8.5).

Superego: The personality structure that defines the moral or ethical aspects of personality.

Identification: Refers to the process of assuming the goals, ambitions, mannerisms, and so on of another person.

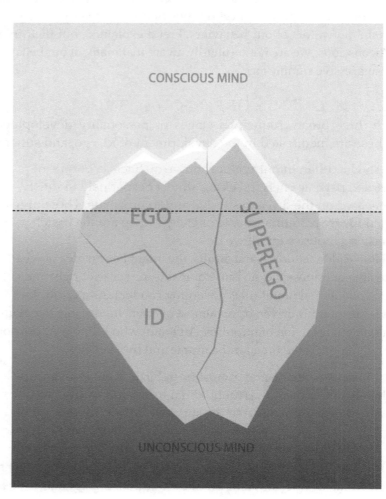

FIGURE 8.5　Freud's three components of personality.

© T and Z, 2014. Used under license from Shutterstock, Inc.

Psychosexual Stages

Parallel to the development of the three aspects of personality is the child's progression through what Freud labels the *psychosexual* stages. A psychosexual stage is a developmental stage characterized by identifiable sources of sexual gratification and by behaviors related to these sources of gratification. Through the course of development, these sources of gratification change; with each major change, a new developmental phase appears.

Fixation: A developmental delay due to unsuccessfully developing through a stage, sometimes manifested in personality characteristics and emotional disorders relating to the earlier stage.

To make matters simple, the stages are labeled according to the area or activity providing the greatest source of sexual gratification. In chronological order, they are oral, anal, phallic, latency, and genital. The ages corresponding to each of these stages, their major characteristics, and the dominant personality component are summarized in Table 8.2.

Regression: A Freudian expression for the phenomenon of reverting to some of the activities and preoccupations of earlier developmental stages.

Normal and Abnormal Personality

There are three main routes the individual may take in the course of development. One is shown in Table 8.2. It is the route presumably resulting in a normal personality. A second possibility is **fixation,** the cessation of development at a given stage, sometimes because of trauma (severe emotional shock) and sometimes because of excessive sexual gratification at the stage. The third possibility is **regression**, which involves reverting to a previous development stage, again sometimes because of trauma, or perhaps because of insufficient sexual gratification at a later stage.

The behavior of adults who are fixated at a certain stage, or who have regressed to that stage, is related to the forms of sexual gratification characteristic of the stage. Thus *oral characters* (fixated or regressed at the oral stage) are those who chew their nails, bite their lips, smoke, chew gum, and otherwise exercise their mouths. *Anal characters* are compulsive, orderly, stingy, and perhaps aggressive—these characteristics presumably being related to the pleasure (sexual gratification) associated with the retention and expulsion of feces during the anal stage. *Phallic characters* are concerned with the immediate satisfaction of their sexual urges without regard for the object of their satisfaction; they are sadists and rapists (according to Freudian theory).

According to Freud, oral characters are fixated at the oral stage and chew their nails, smoke, chew on pens, and so on. Unfortunately, our personalities have proven more difficult to classify than Freud's typology would imply.

© Jeanette Dietl, 2014. Used under license from

Defense Mechanisms

In both normal and abnormal development, explains Freud, the id constantly strives for gratification. Meanwhile, the superego battles against the id, raising moral and cultural objections to unbridled gratification. Through all this, the ego struggles to find some way of finding the gratification the id craves, but within the constraints imposed by the superego.

TABLE 8.2   Freud's Stages of Psychosexual Development

STAGE	APPROXIMATE AGE	CHARACTERISTICS	DOMINANT PERSONALITY COMPONENT
Oral	0–18 months	Sources of pleasure include sucking, biting, swallowing, playing with lips. Preoccupation with immediate gratification of impulses. Id is dominant.	Id
Anal	18 months–3 years	Sources of sexual gratification include expelling feces and urinating, as well as retaining feces.	Id and Ego
Phallic	3–6 years	Child becomes concerned with genitals. Source of sexual pleasure involves manipulating genitals. Period of **Oedipus complex** (where the father becomes the male child's rival—unconsciously) or **Electra complex** (a female version of the Oedipus complex).	Id, Ego, and Superego
Latency	6–11 years	Loss of interest in sexual gratification. Identification with like-sexed parent.	Id, Ego, and Superego
Genital	11+	Concern with adult modes of sexual pleasure, barring fixations or regressions.	Id, Ego, and Superego

Oedipus complex: A Freudian concept denoting the developmental stage (around 4 years) when a boy's increasing awareness of the sexual meaning of his genitals leads him to desire his mother and envy his father.

Electra complex: A Freudian stage (around 4 years) when a girl's awareness of her genital area leads her to desire her father and to become jealous of her mother.

Defense mechanisms: An unconscious mental strategy designed to avoid conflict and anxiety; examples include denial and repression.

In trying to compensate for not being able to satisfy all of the id's urges, the ego often resorts to **defense mechanisms**. Defense mechanisms are ways of channeling urges and of reinterpreting (and often distorting) reality. The ego is successful, explains Freud, when it eliminates or reduces the anxiety accompanying the continual struggle between the id and the superego. In a sense, these mechanisms are the ego's attempt to establish peace between the id and the superego so the personality can continue to operate in an apparently healthy manner. Thus, at one level, defense mechanisms are normal, healthy reactions to the world. What sometimes happens, however, is the individual comes to rely on them too much. The result may be a dramatically distorted view of self, of others, and of reality, and may be evident in various personality disturbances.

Several dozen distinct defense mechanisms have been described by Freud and his followers. The most common of these are summarized and illustrated in Table 8.3.

Review of Freudian Theory

Freud's theory is one of the most comprehensive and influential of all psychological theories. It continues to have an enormous impact on psychotherapy. Freudian theory has had a tremendous influence on our attitudes toward

TABLE 8.3   Some Freudian Defense Mechanisms

MECHANISM	EXAMPLE
Displacement: Undesirable emotions are directed toward a different object.	A man who is angry at his wife yells at his dog or drives his car unusually aggressively.
Reaction formation: Behavior is the opposite of the individual's actual feelings.	A woman loves an unobtainable man and behaves as though she dislikes him.
Intellectualization: Behavior motivated by anxiety-provoking emotions is stripped of its emotional meaning.	A football player who enjoys hurting opponents convinces himself he is moved by the desire to win and not by his desire to inflict pain.
Projection: Undesirable feelings or inclinations are attributed to others.	A student who is extremely jealous of another who has received a scholarship convinces himself it is the scholarship winner who is jealous of him.
Denial: Unpleasant, anxiety-provoking aspects of reality are distorted.	A heavy smoker, unable to give up the habit, concludes there is no substantial evidence linking nicotine with human diseases.
Repression: Unpleasant experiences are buried deep in the subconscious mind and become inaccessible to waking memory.	A person who was sexually abused as a child remembers nothing of the experience.

children and child rearing. More than anyone else, Freud was responsible for making parents realize how important early experiences can be.

Freudian theory has also had an enormous impact on the development of other theories. However, many of Freud's students and followers have rejected important aspects of the theory. For many, Freud paints too dark and cynical a picture of human nature: In his view, primitive forces over which we have no control drive us relentlessly toward the satisfaction of instinctual urges and bring us into repeated conflict with reality. In addition, the theory is clearly weak from a scientific point of view, based as it is on a limited number of observations collected by a single individual (Freud himself) and not subjected to any rigorous analysis.

In spite of these criticisms, Freud's work still stands as an immensely rich basis for thinking about and understanding human personality.

Learning-Based Approaches

Biological approaches to understanding personality focus on the relationship between inherited predispositions and manifested behavior; psychodynamic approaches are concerned with interactions among competing or cooperating psychic (mental) impulses; learning-based approaches are more concerned with the role of the environment, of social interaction, and of cognitive processes. The unifying theme of learning-based approaches to personality is primarily acquired through experiences rather than genetically determined or influenced.

Behaviorism

As we saw in previous chapters, behaviorism provides one explanation for how personality traits might be learned. Some early behaviorists such as John Watson were absolutely convinced that the metaphor of the mind as a *blank slate* (*tabula rasa* in Latin) was correct. "Give me the child and my world to bring it up in," he wrote, "and I'll make it crawl or walk; I'll make it climb and use its hands in constructing buildings of stone or wood; I'll make it a thief, a gunman, or a dope fiend. The possibility of shaping in any direction is almost endless" (Watson, 1928, p. 35).

The clear assumption of behavioristic approaches to personality is we are born with few genetically determined personality characteristics; what we become is a function of the experiences we have. In other words, personality characteristics are *learned*.

Skinner, another behaviorist who wholeheartedly accepted the *tabula rasa* doctrine, believed the consequences of our actions shape our behaviors and ultimately determine what we are most likely to do. Our environments, not our inherited natures, shape our traits. It is the experiences we have that make us brave or fearful, outgoing or shy, altruistic or selfish.

Few personality theorists now believe personality is entirely determined by environmental experiences. As Robins (2005) notes, about half of the variability in personality traits seems to be related to genetics, the other half is clearly shaped by environmental influences. Especially important among these are early social experiences.

Bandura's Social Cognitive Theory

Bandura's social cognitive theory, the details of which are included in previous chapters, is one of the best-known and most useful learning-based theories examining the effects of social experiences.

Manifested personality is highly influenced by context. We can't easily determine how naturally nurturing this mother is, by observing her interactions with her infant.

© Blend Images, 2014. Used under license from Shutterstock, Inc.

OBSERVATIONAL LEARNING

Much of our learning results from *observational learning,* explains Bandura—observing and imitating models. Learning to drive a car, for example, is not a question of classical conditioning, of trial and error, or of reinforcement of emitted behaviors. Instead, we instruct the learner in certain fundamentals, we show her the positions and purposes of various controls, we demonstrate their operation, and we allow her to attempt the task with verbal and sometimes physical guidance. In effect, what has happened is a number of models have been presented and imitated.

A model is not simply a person doing something that can then be imitated by a learner; it includes all the patterns for behavior complex societies present to their members, including books, verbal directions, film and cartoon characters, and a variety of other real or symbolic objects. Their prevalence is highly evident, as is their effectiveness.

Western societies present a preponderance of achievement-oriented, assertive, outgoing models for men. Not surprisingly, many males in these societies are achievement-oriented, assertive, and outgoing. In contrast, the Zuni culture presents models of cooperation and self-effacement, and these are the primary characteristics of its members (Roscoe, 1991).

It seems clear, manifested personality characteristics are highly influenced by social context. This does not mean theories based on the notion that there are inherited predispositions toward specific personality traits are incorrect. What it does indicate is biological predispositions will not necessarily be dominant over social influences.

RECIPROCAL DETERMINISM

A central belief of all learning-based approaches is that our behaviors are strongly influenced by their outcomes. Bandura explains what is most important is our understanding of the relationship between our behaviors and their consequences, and our ability to anticipate consequences. Because we can anticipate consequences, we not only direct our behaviors toward the most desirable ends, but we deliberately arrange our environments to maximize positive outcomes. So, in the end, we affect the environment and it affects us in what Bandura labels *triadic reciprocal determinism.* Our actions and the environment are two aspects of the triad; our personalities (what we know and feel; our wishes and desires; our inclinations) constitute the third.

PERSONAL AGENCY

Unlike Freud, who described human behavior as moved by instinctive and often unconscious forces and warring factions, Bandura insists we are agents of our own actions. Being agents, he explains, requires intentionality (being able to do what we intend), forethought (foreseeing the consequences of our actions), and self-efficacy (having a notion of our likelihood of success).

RELEVANCE OF BANDURA'S THEORY

The importance of Bandura's social learning theory of personality is not that it contributes to the identification of personality traits or to their measurement; nor is it particularly useful for understanding the structure of personality or the biological and dynamic forces at play. It does facilitate an understanding of the manifestation of personality.

Most of the personality traits identified are meaningful only in social interaction. Agreeableness, extroversion, sociability, dependency—these are all qualities of human interaction. They describe typical ways of relating to social realities. Furthermore, they are not characteristics individuals manifest regardless of their immediate social context. For example, highly aggressive individuals might well display their aggressive tendencies in athletics and other physical activities where aggression is socially approved; few are likely to display aggression in a church choir or university classroom.

In summary, social approaches to personality highlight the tremendous influence of social customs, traditions, expectations, and situations on the manifestation of personality characteristics. They argue that acceptable and unacceptable social behaviors are learned.

Rotter's Cognitive Approach

In the course of learning socially acceptable behaviors, we learn what to expect when we choose one behavior versus a different one. Expectations, Julian Rotter (1982) explains, guide our behaviors.

EXTERNALITY–INTERNALITY

In effect, expectations are beliefs about sources of reinforcement. Basically, claims Rotter, we can have one of two different attitudes toward our behaviors and their outcomes. We can be *externally oriented* or *internally oriented*—a notion later borrowed and elaborated by Weiner (2008) in his theory of motivation.

As we saw in a previous chapter, those who are internally oriented tend to take responsibility for the consequences of their actions. They see themselves as being in control; they attribute success or failure to internal factors (ability or effort). Those who are externally oriented believe they have little control over what happens to them. They attribute success or failure to external factors (luck and task difficulty). Expectations of reward, and behaviors, will be affected accordingly (Figure 8.6).

Various studies have uncovered a large number of situations where expectations based on *locus of control* affect behavior. Not surprisingly, those who think they are in control of outcomes (the internally oriented) are less likely to be obese (Adolfsson, Andersson, Elofsson, Rossner, & Unden, 2005); they are more likely to participate in and profit from treatments to counter various delinquent behaviors, including alcoholism (Cavaiola & Strohmetz, 2010); they are more likely to be successful at work and integrate more readily into new social environments (Vonthron & Lagabrielle, 2002); they are less likely to behave aggressively toward an intimate partner (Gallagher & Parrott, 2010); they are less likely to have eating disorders (Scoffier, Paquet, & d'Arripe-Longueville, 2010); and they tend to have generally more positive attitudes (Gianakos, 2002).

Personality theorists such as Bandura and Rotter look for regularities in individual decisions and beliefs, and they search for ways in which people can be identified on the basis of differences in their dominant modes of functioning. Their

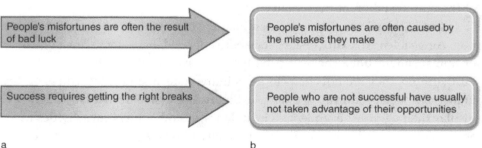

a   b

FIGURE 8.6   Items similar to those used by Rotter to assess a person's locus of control."

theories provide strong indications suggesting that important personality differences are evident in learned social interactions and they reflect our expectations.

Humanistic Approaches

But surely, the humanists protest, there is more to human behavior and personality than inherited predispositions, basic instincts, warring psychic forces, and learned expectations and beliefs. We need to take into consideration what it means to be human. We need to emphasize the worth and dignity of every individual.

Abraham Maslow's Self-Actualized Person

Like most humanistically oriented psychologists, Maslow's principal concerns have been with the development of the healthy person. Fundamental to his position is the notion we are moved by a hierarchy of needs, the lowest of which relate to physiological survival and the highest to the fullest and most desirable blossoming of the person. The process of growth is one of *self-actualization*—of *becoming* in the most abstract sense of the term. This involves a recognition of what one is, of what one can and should be, and a striving for fulfillment.

Maslow (1970) admits the concept of self-actualization is extremely difficult to define. It is characterized by the absence of "neurosis, psychopathic personality, psychosis, or strong tendencies in these directions" (p. 150). In addition, self-actualized people "may be loosely described as [making] full use and exploitation of talents, capacities, potentialities, etc." (p. 150).

Using these rather loose criteria, Maslow's search for self-actualized people among a group of 3,000 college students yielded only one actualized person and one or two dozen "potentials." Maslow concluded a fully actualized person is much more likely to be found among older people. He then selected a small number of cases (23) from among his contemporaries and historical figures. He interviewed them where possible (extremely informally), or read accounts of their lives. Maslow subsequently described some of their personality characteristics: autonomous and independent; highly accepting of themselves and others; tolerant; free of inhibitions; spontaneous and able to enjoy themselves; free of guilt.

Science might shudder to consider individuals were defined as being self-actualized by Maslow and were then interviewed by him to determine what self-actualized people were really like. The process is only slightly different from deciding authoritarian people are psychopaths, selecting a group of psychopathic authoritarian people, and interviewing them to determine whether authoritarian people are really psychopathic. The only surprises possible are those arising from errors in selection or in interviewer judgment.

Rogers's Phenomenology

Phenomenology is concerned with the world as it appears rather than as it actually might be. Humanistic positions are typically phenomenological; their main concern is with the individual at the center of realities, in essence,

Phenomenology: Concerned with the world of appearance—that is, the world as it appears to the individual.

self-created. The argument is no two people see the world in exactly the same way, and understanding people requires understanding their notions of the world.

Carl Rogers's theory of personality is well summarized by this abbreviated list of his theoretical beliefs (Rogers, 1951, Chap. 11):

1. Every individual exists in a continually changing world of which the person alone is the center. The person's world is thus private, unknown and unknowable by anyone else. As the existential philosophers have pointed out, existence is lonely; it is necessarily always alone.

2. My perception of the world is real. So is yours. We have our separate realities. If we are to understand each other, you must try to understand my world, and I yours.

3. We have one basic tendency—*actualization.* In short, we have an inner, directing need to develop ourselves in Maslow's sense of the word.

4. The structure of self—notions of I or me—develops as a result of interaction with the environment and, particularly, interaction with others.

5. Values attached to notions of self are obtained either as a result of direct experience or indirectly. Thus, I can learn I am good as a result of engaging in good behavior; or I can infer I am good as a result of having people tell me I am.

6. Most of our ways of behaving are consistent with our notions of self. We tend to engage in behaviors that do not violate our internalized conceptions of what we are like—our values and ideals.

Humanistic approaches do not present theories so much as a renewed emphasis on human worth and dignity. They look more to glorify the importance of the individual, the nature of being, and the sanctity of personal experience than to analyze and dissect in the sometimes impersonal laboratories of science. Their impact on approaches to mental health and counseling has been considerable. Carl Rogers's *person-centered therapy* continues to be widely applied in therapeutic settings (Cain, 2010).

Measuring Personality Variables

Say I want to hire somebody and I want to make sure he or she is cooperative, agreeable, not highly neurotic, and not afraid of the dark (the work is carried out in an unlit basement); how can I uncover somebody's personality?

I have four choices, Funder (2007) explains: I can look at *life outcomes* (whether candidates are married, have graduated, what work they have done, whether they sleep in the dark); *self-reports* (I can ask candidates about themselves, maybe give them questionnaires, ask them if they leave their lights on at night); *observer ratings* (I can ask their friends, families, former teachers, or expert judges what they are like and whether they willingly eat in dark places); or *objective tests* (instruments designed specifically to measure personality). Objective personality tests are typically described as being *projective* or *nonprojective.*

Projective Measures

I might also find out whether my candidates are afraid of the dark by asking them to respond to ambiguous descriptions, pictures, or sounds and trying to find evidence of fear or confidence projected into their descriptions. **Projective measures** of this kind have been used extensively in personality assessment. The assumption underlying the use of projective tests is that unconscious fears, desires, and other personality traits may be projected in descriptions of stimuli apparently unrelated to the underlying personality characteristics. Since these traits are unconscious, the argument goes, they would not ordinarily be revealed in conventional measures of personality.

Projective measures: Personality tests in which stimuli are ambiguous and testees' responses are interpreted as reflecting unconscious aspects of

THE RORSCHACH

Among the best known of the projective measures is the *Rorschach inkblot test,* so called because it presents the subject with ten stimulus cards with printed figures resembling elaborate inkblots (Figure 8.7). The scoring procedure is complicated, detailed, and not well validated, and interpretations of different experts vary a great deal. Furthermore, the relationships of scorer interpretations to the actual behavior of testees has been very difficult to establish, although there is evidence it can be used to discriminate between psychotic and nonpsychotic populations (Wood et al., 2010). It continues to be one of the most widely used personality measures in clinical practice (Sendin, 2010).

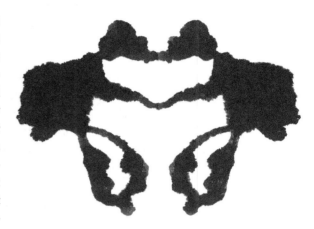

FIGURE 8.7   The Rorschach inkblot test.
© Kovalchuk Oleksandr, 2014. Used under license from Shutterstock, Inc.

THE THEMATIC APPERCEPTION TEST

Another well-known projective test is H. A. Murray's (1938, 1943) *thematic apperception test (TAT).* It consists of 30 black-and-white pictures showing people in various situations and asks subjects to tell a story suggested to them by the pictures. Clinicians often use the TAT as a way of gaining insight into the subject's fantasies. Although the test does not measure specific personality characteristics, it may be highly suggestive of preoccupations, fears, unconscious needs and desires, personal relationships, and related themes. It is widely used in clinical practice as well as in research (Teglasi, 2010). For example, it has been the basis of many investigations of need achievement, with scorers looking for achievement-related themes in subjects' descriptions of the pictures. It has also been used to look at the concerns and interests of highly creative children (Garces-Bacsal, 2010).

Nonprojective Measures

There are hundreds of paper-and-pencil or computer-based personality tests, usually referred to as *scales* or *inventories.* Scales measure specific dimensions of personality (sociability, neuroticism, and so on); inventories are more inclusive. Typically, inventories consist of a number of different scales and yield a profile of personality characteristics.

THE NEO-PI-R

The *Neuroticism Extraversion Openness Personality Inventory, Revised* (NEO-PI-R; Costa & McCrae, 1992) is an inventory designed specifically to assess the Big Five personality factors (**c**onscientiousness, **a**greeableness, **n**euroticism, **o**penness, and **e**xtraversion). It is available in a longer, 240-item format or in a shorter, 60-item inventory. Items are presented on what is called a Likert scale—a scale where the responder selects an option ranging from *strongly disagree* to *strongly agree.*

Research indicates this personality inventory has relatively high reliability (consistency) and validity in terms of its usefulness for predicting outcomes such as adjustment to career requirements. For example, scores on the NEO-PI-R correlate well with job success (Denis, Morin, & Guindon, 2010). It has been translated into many different languages and is reportedly useful across many cultures (Ortet et al., 2010; Plaisant, Courtois, Reveillere, Mendelsohn, & John, 2010).

THE MMPI-2

One of the best-known, most rigorously developed, and most widely used of the personality inventories is the *Minnesota Multiphasic Personality Inventory-2 (MMPI-2).* There are various forms of this test, which is normally computer scored. Ordinarily, it yields measures on a wide number of dimensions. Ten of the original scales are *clinical scales.* Closely related to these are newer *restructured clinical (RC) scales.* These clinical scales provide scores on dimensions such as depression, hypochondriasis, hysteria, paranoia, schizophrenia, and social introversion. Some scales are *validity scales:* They provide indications of the extent to which an individual's responses may be considered reliable and valid. In addition, there are various *supplementary scales* measuring things such as proneness to substance abuse and anxiety.

MMPI-2 items were first developed with groups of individuals who had been clearly diagnosed with disorders such as hypochondriasis, depression, or psychopathy. Scores obtained by these groups were then compared to scores obtained by a normal "control" group, and items were selected on the basis of how well they discriminated between groups. If, for example, hypochondriacs always responded in one way to ten items, and controls always responded differently, these ten items would then make up the hypochondriasis scale. It would then be possible to identify people who respond in the same way as hypochondriacs by looking at their scores on the scale.

In many ways, the MMPI-2 is a masterpiece of objective test construction. Evidence suggests it is useful in making discriminations among groups of people and in preliminary diagnosis of abnormal behavior—which is the purpose for which it was designed. It appears to have impressive validity when used for this purpose. However, it is also often used for personnel assessment or as a screening tool with presumably normal individuals—purposes for which it has questionable validity. Indications are it remains an extremely powerful tool for identifying emotional and mental disorders (Caldwell, 2006). Few instruments have been used more widely in psychological diagnosis, and few have stimulated more research.

Some Cautions

Although personality inventories and other assessment devices have proven useful in a number of situations, both practical and theoretical, it cannot yet be argued any specific personality trait can be measured with unquestioned validity and reliability. Results obtained from different inventories for the same individual are sometimes different, and not all predictions made on the basis of diagnostic instruments have been entirely reliable. For these reasons, interpretation of test scores requires both restraint and wisdom. Tests such as these can be dangerous in the hands of those who are not fully aware of their weaknesses. Users must constantly bear in mind that the stability of personality characteristics is still a matter of debate. A test revealing an individual to be tense does not establish anxiety is a pervasive and predominant personality characteristic in that person. Personality tests measure mood, fatigue, feelings of happiness or dejection, and a variety of other affective states. We know from our private experience that none of these is necessarily permanent.

Summary

Personality is defined as stable characteristics including habits, preferences, weaknesses, strengths, moral attributes, and ways of thinking, feeling, and behaving. The Barnum effect is the term applied to the tendency to believe vague generalities about personality. The major approaches to personality theory discussed in this chapter are types and traits, biological, psychodynamic, learning-based, and humanistic.

A personality trait is a specific quality that differentiates among different individuals (e.g., good-hearted or selfish); types are clusters of related traits. The Big Five personality factors are five independent personality dimensions, each of which can range from very high to very low: conscientiousness, agreeableness, neuroticism, openness, and extraversion.

Biological approaches emphasize the genetic underpinnings of personality. Historical biological approaches include Sheldon's suggestion that body type (ecto-, endo-, and mesomorph) is strongly associated with different temperaments. Eysenck's biological approach holds inherited differences in nervous system activity underlie the two main dimensions of personality, extraversion and introversion, as well as a third dimension, psychoticism. Recent approaches use genomics and neuropsychology to look for genetic and neurological structures and functioning underlying personality differences.

Psychodynamic approaches look at the interaction of basic inherited tendencies with physical and social reality to explain personality. In Freud's system, sexual and survival urges (id) often drive us in directions incompatible with social reality and conscience (superego). This leads to conflict that our conception of reality (ego) mediates and tries to resolve. Objects of sexual gratification progress from oral through anal, phallic, latent, and genital stages as we develop. Fixation and regression are two unhealthy possibilities, as is overreliance on defense mechanisms.

Learning-based approaches look at the role of the social and physical environment in determining personality. Behavioristic approaches describe how personality traits might be shaped and conditioned. Bandura's social cognitive theory describes personality development in terms of the effects of observation and the reciprocal determinism at play in person–behavior–environment interactions. It emphasizes the extent to which we are agents of our actions, anticipating and intending their outcomes, and estimating our likelihood of success in our endeavors (self-efficacy). Rotter's expectancy theory explains how locus of control (external and internal orientation) affects our personalities as reflected in our choice of behaviors.

Humanistic approaches focus on the development of self and the worth of the individual. Both Maslow and Rogers describe the development of human potential as the highest goal. They emphasize healthy human functioning and the uniqueness and worth of the individual.

Personality variables may be evident in life outcomes and observer ratings. They can also be measured with projective tests such as the Rorschach and TAT (where the individual reveals unconscious traits in responding to ambiguous stimuli), or with nonprojective written tests like the NEO-PI-R (which measures the Big Five personality types) and the MMPI-2 (which is designed mainly to measure personality disorders).

This chapter serves as an introduction into personality theory and approaches. Each approach emphasizes some part of personality theory and contains strengths and weaknesses. Personality can be influenced by many factors, including genetics, learning, and social experiences. It is important to have a basic understanding of these approaches as well as personality assessment measures.

© Alexander Sherstobitov, 2014. Used under license from Shutterstock, Inc.

CHAPTER NINE

PSYCHOLOGICAL DISORDERS AND THERAPIES

Dr. Leo Herrman and Gina Smith
Fort Hays State University

LEARNING OBJECTIVES

- Define mental illness.
- Differentiate between the terms *insanity* and *mental disorder*.
- Identify characteristics of the principal models used to understand mental disorders.
- List the neurodevelopmental disorders
- Recall the symptoms of the principal *anxiety disorders*.
- Identify characteristics of *disruptive, impulse-control,* and *conduct disorders* in childhood.
- Identify the most common mood disorders.
- Differentiate between bipolar disorder and schizophrenia.
- Name the main sexual and gender identity disorders.
- Describe the characteristics of different personality disorders.
- List the main approaches to therapies for mental disorders.

© mypokcik, 2014. Used under license from Shutterstock, Inc.

How, indeed, can we recognize madness (which, incidentally, is not a term commonly used in psychology; mental disorder or emotional disorder is more common)? And is it contagious? Is Alice justified in wanting to avoid mad people?

"'But I don't want to go among mad people,' Alice remarked. 'Oh, you can't help that,' said the Cat. 'We're all mad here. I'm mad. You're mad.' 'How do you know I'm mad?' said Alice. 'You must be,' said the Cat, 'or you wouldn't have come here.'"

—Lewis Carroll, Alice's Adventures in Wonderland

Adapted from *Psychology: The Human Puzzle* by Guy R. Lefrancois. Copyright © 2012 Bridgepoint Education. Reprinted by permission.

Current Definitions and Models

Mental disorder: Patterns of behavior or thought that are not reasonable or easily understood and are associated with "clinically significant" distress or impairment in coping with the environment.

In general, a **mental disorder** is a pattern of behavior or thought that is not reasonable or easily understood and that is associated with "clinically significant" distress or impairment in coping with the environment.

This definition is implicit in the descriptions and classifications of mental disorders provided by the American Psychiatric Association (not to be confused with the other APA, the American *Psychological* Association). There, each of the many different disorders is defined separately, mainly in terms of the nature, onset, and implications of characteristic symptoms.

© Stuart Miles, 2014. Used under license from Shutterstock, Inc.

Insanity: A legal term defined by law and determined by a court in consultation with mental health experts.

Models: Guides or ways of looking at whether a behavior is abnormal or not.

Intellectual disabilities: A significant departure from average intellectual and adaptive functioning.

Insanity is a legal term, defined by law and determined by a court in consultation with mental health experts. Hence it is a legal issue that might determine whether a convicted person is *responsible* for a crime. Individuals found not guilty by reason of insanity are frequently provided with treatment rather than punishment. Although innocent by reason of insanity is a very popular theme in today's media, in reality it is rarely used in criminal cases.

The term *insanity* is seldom used in medicine and psychology, although it has been retained by the courts. The terms *abnormality, mental illness, personality disorders, psychological disorders, emotional disorders, mental disorders,* or other more specific descriptions are preferred.

How we look at and define mental disorders depends greatly on the **models** we use. In one sense, models are guides, or ways of looking at things. Models tell us what to look for when we're trying to understand, explain, and define what we mean by mental disorders. Among the various models used for this purpose are the *statistical,* the *medical/biological,* the *behavioral,* the *cognitive,* and the *psychodynamic.*

The Statistical Model

One way of determining whether a behavior is abnormal is in relation to the prevalence of the behavior in the general population. According to this model, those whose behaviors or personality traits violate social norms and are therefore demonstrably different from the majority are abnormal in a statistical sense (Figure 9.1). Significant departure from normality with respect to emotional functioning, social behavior, perception, and so on may be directly related to mental health. Deviance is evident in behaviors and characteristics that have low frequency. To be afraid of red dirt is deviant because most people are not afraid of red dirt. But if you live where everybody knows red dirt is toxic, not being afraid of it might be abnormal.

The statistical model is useful in that it provides an objective method for identifying abnormal behavior. For example, **intellectual disabilities** are defined as a significant departure from average intellectual and adaptive functioning. Similarly,

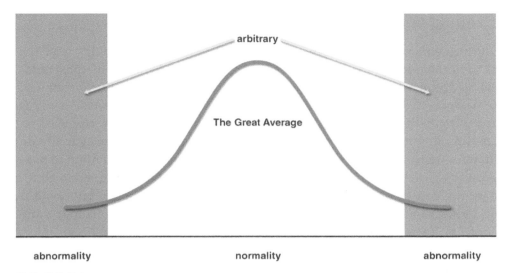

FIGURE 9.1 The statistical model of abnormality.

disorders such as **autism spectrum disorder** and **specific learning disabilities** are all defined in terms of behaviors that are not age-appropriate in a statistical sense.

Medical/Biological Models

Medicine deals with physical (organic) malfunctions due to injury, infection, chemical imbalances, genetics, or other causes, and can often be treated surgically or chemically. The medical view of psychological malfunction is analogous. Accordingly, a psychological abnormality is sometimes seen as a disease or illness caused by internal factors (infection, system malfunction, or genetics) and open to the same sorts of treatment that might be employed for organic malfunctions. The finding of the high heritability of disorders such as bipolar disorder and schizophrenia suggests, at least for these diseases, there may often be an underlying genetic cause (Walsh, McClellan, & McCarthy, 2008). For example, there is evidence that as much as one third of the risk of acquiring schizophrenia is due to identifiable genetic variations (Massachusetts General Hospital, 2009).

The most obvious advantage of the medical models is that they encourage the search for specific organic causes of various disorders and suggest means of dealing with them. They look not only at genes as a possible cause, but also at neurological functioning and especially at the role various neurotransmitters play. The development of highly effective drug therapies for disorders such as depression is related directly to information that neuroscience provides about the role of neurotransmitters in areas of the brain involved in emotion.

Autism spectrum disorder: A relatively early-appearing disorder; central features are persistent, pervasive, and sustained impairments in how an individual interacts with or communicates with others.

Specific learning disabilities: A developmental disorder marked by impairments in cognitive skills such as reading, writing, arithmetic, or mathematical skills.

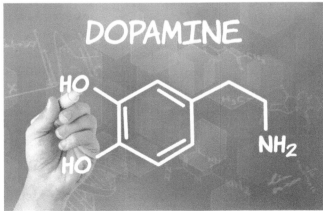

Behavioral Models

The principal difference between medical models of abnormality and the behavioral models lies in their explanations of causes. Whereas medical models ascribe abnormality to internal causes such as disease, injury, or chemical imbalances, behavioral models claim abnormal behavior is learned, just as is any other behavior (Watson, 1916). Most behavioral models are premised on conditioning theories, or variations thereof, and concentrate principally on manifestations of abnormal behavior without paying much attention to supposed causes. Whereas medical models lead to treatments designed to eliminate the causes of malfunctioning, behavioral models concentrate instead on "unlearning" unacceptable behavior and learning (or relearning) more "normal" forms of behavior.

Cognitive Models

The cognitive interpretation of psychological disorders revolves around the notion that these disorders involve cognitive problems that are often expressed in distortions of reality (Beck, 2008). Patients view themselves as worthless, unhealthy, and unhappy, have unrealistic appraisals of their future, and react inappropriately. Distorted views of reality are, in fact, one of the principal characteristics of the more serious mental disorders.

© Dima Groshev, 2014. Used under license from Shutterstock, Inc.

Contemporary cognitive models also take into account the interaction of genetic and neurological events with cognitive problems. For example, neuropsychological research provides a great deal of evidence indicating that an overactive amygdala may be associated with a higher risk of depression (Gaffrey et al., 2011). And genomics research (i.e., research on the contributions of genes) has discovered a variety of links between a genome (genetic complement) and a variety of disorders, including *bipolar* disorder (e.g., Choi et al., 2011).

Although the cognitive model considers these genetic and neurological causes, the emphasis is on the *cognitive* (intellectual) distortions underlying maladaptive behavior. For example, in this view, overreaction to stress may be genetically based, but it is mediated by cognitive distortions. Accordingly, therapies are directed toward altering individuals' perceptions of the world and of themselves—in other words, toward changing cognitions.

Psychodynamic Models

The *psychodynamic* model describes how our basic libidinal urges (*id*) are continually being impeded by our immediate circumstances (*ego*) as well as by the fact that society does not permit unbridled expression of sexuality or aggression (*superego*). The result of this conflict is anxiety, which we try to reduce in various ways including through defense mechanisms.

If the anxiety is sufficiently severe, or if there is an overreliance on defense mechanisms, the result may be mental disorders of various kinds. Also, if the individual stays stuck in a developmental stage or regresses back to an earlier stage, development is said to be abnormal.

Which Model?

These various models show how complicated human behavior and thought can be. It is not possible to say one of the models is correct and the others not; nor is it possible to state categorically that one is more useful than any other. Each leads to a different view of mental disorders, and each leads to different forms of intervention or treatment.

The statistical model is useful in providing a relatively objective means of identifying bizarre, unconventional behavior, although its value in increasing our understanding of abnormal behavior or our ability to deal with it is clearly limited. The statistical model is primarily useful as a descriptive tool, but does not help explain *why* an individual may display abnormal behavior.

Medical models are valuable in providing methods for identifying and describing malfunctions, and often in providing specific treatments for them, as is clear in the widespread use of medications that are often highly effective treatments for a variety of mental disorders.

The principal contribution of the behavioral and cognitive models has been the development of systematic learning-based therapies that have been highly effective in many situations.

Psychodynamic approaches, despite their historical influence, tend to be imprecise and speculative. The various models of mental disorders are summarized in Table 9.1.

Different models of mental disorders provide different explanations and different treatments. Most agree that mental disorders involve problems in coping with the world and, as in the case of the girl shown here, significant distress and unhappiness.

Classifications of Disorders

The ***Diagnostic and Statistical Manual of Mental Disorders***, 5th Edition (*DSM-5*), of the American Psychiatric Association (2013) presents classifications of mental disorders in terms of categories, severity, and distinguishing characteristics (specifiers) of each disorder. The *DSM* is used extensively in psychiatric diagnosis.

Diagnostic and Statistical Manual of Mental Disorders: A handbook used by health care professionals in the United States and much of the world as the authoritative guide to the diagnosis of mental disorders by classification in terms of categories, severity, and distinguishing characteristics of each disorder.

The *DSM* is the handbook used by health care professionals in the United States and much of the world as the authoritative guide to the diagnosis of mental disorders. The *DSM* contains descriptions, symptoms, and other criteria for diagnosing mental disorders. It provides a common language for clinicians to communicate about their patients and establishes consistent and reliable diagnoses that can be used in the research of mental disorders. It also provides a common language for researchers to study the criteria for potential future revisions and to aid in the development of medications and other interventions.

The *DSM-5* presents 22 separate major categories. Since its first edition, the *DSM* has been revised regularly, often adding new disorders and removing or combining others as new scientific evidence emerges about the nature of mental disorders. The most recent revision restructured the format, emphasizing a more dimensional approach to mental disorders adopting the premise that most mental disorders present themselves along a continuum of symptoms and severity.

TABLE 9.1   Models of Mental Disorders

MODEL	ABNORMALITY	WHAT THE THERAPIST LOOKS FOR	TREATMENT APPROACH
Statistical	A rare behavior	Uncommon behavior in a statistical sense	None. The statistical model identifies abnormal behavior but does not provide treatment.
Medical/ Biological	System malfunction	Organic, systemic, or genetic basis	Biological therapies treat abnormal behavior by looking for the biological cause of the behavior. A common example is drug therapy.
Behavioral	Learned behavior	Symptoms, not causes	Learning therapies that operate on the premise that bad behaviors can be eliminated and more appropriate and effective behaviors can be learned.
Cognitive	Inappropriate cognitions (beliefs, thoughts, perceptions)	Irrational or inappropriate beliefs about self or others	Cognitive therapies attempt to change how we think about and view our world, sometimes through learning more effective ways to view our problems.
Psychodynamic	Psychic conflicts, anxiety	History, relationships	Psychodynamic therapies may look for unconscious thoughts and urges and the resulting influence on behavior.

One of the important criteria for most *DSM-5* categories of mental disorders is the condition must present significant problems for the individual that cause a great deal of distress or impairment in their lives. The *DSM-5* classifications are summarized in Table 9.2.

The *DSM-5* presents well-defined criteria for diagnosing disorders. Clinicians do not need to rely on their interpretation of what is meant by a classification; they need only determine whether certain symptoms are present and apply relatively definite rules for making the diagnosis.

Today, the *DSM-5* is widely used by health care professionals. Such a detailed classification system is enormously useful in enabling researchers and clinicians to communicate and to understand what it is they are studying and treating. It provides a common language for describing mental disorders and a common set of criteria for identifying them.

TABLE 9.2 Major Categories of Mental Disorders According to the *DSM-5* of the American Psychiatric Association

MENTAL DISORDER	*DSM-5* DIAGNOSTIC CHARACTERISTICS	EXAMPLE
Neurodevelopmental Disorders	These disorders appear during childhood and are characterized by developmental problems that interfere with how we relate to others or perform in school or our jobs.	Intellectual Disabilities, Communication, Autism Spectrum, Attention-Deficit/Hyperactivity, Specific Learning Disorders and Motor Disorders
Schizophrenia Spectrum and Other Psychotic Disorders	These disorders are defined by problems in one or more of five areas: delusions, hallucinations, disorganized thinking, grossly disorganized or abnormal motor behaviors.	Delusional, Schizophrenia, Schizoaffective and Catatonic Disorders
Bipolar and Related Disorders	Disorders in this category are characterized by significant mood swings between periods of depressive and manic episodes.	Bipolar Disorders and Cyclothymic
Depressive Disorders	This disorder features long periods of sad, empty, or irritable mood, accompanied by changes in our feelings and thinking that significantly affect our ability to function.	Disruptive Mood Dysregulation, Depressive Disorders, and Premenstrual Dysphoric
Anxiety Disorders	These disorders center on long and very strong feelings of fear and dread. They go beyond normal reactions to danger or stress.	Anxiety Disorders, Phobias, Panic Disorders
Obsessive–Compulsive and Related Disorders	People with these disorders struggle with persistent thoughts, urges, or images that are experienced as intrusive and unwanted or repetitive behaviors or mental acts that an individual feels driven to perform.	Obsessive–Compulsive, Body Dysmorphic, Hoarding, Trichotillomania, and Excoriation
Trauma- and Stressor-Related Disorders	Individuals with this disorder experience abnormal amounts of distress following a traumatic or stressful event.	Posttraumatic Stress, Acute Stress, Adjustment and Reactive Attachment Disorders
Dissociative Disorder	Dissociative Disorders are characterized by a disruption of one's consciousness, memory, identity, emotion, perception, body representation, motor control, and behavior.	Dissociative Identity, Dissociative Amnesia, and Depersonalization/Derealizaton Disorders

TABLE 9.2 *(continued)*

MENTAL DISORDER	*DSM-5* DIAGNOSTIC CHARACTERISTICS	EXAMPLE
Somatic Symptoms and Related Disorders	The common feature of these disorders is the prominence of physical symptoms associated with a great deal of distress and impairment. Bodily symptoms are the major focus of these disorders for which there is no real medical reason.	Somatic Symptom, Illness Anxiety, Fictitious Disorder and Conversion Disorder
Feeding and Eating Disorders	Feeding and Eating Disorders involve serious problems of eating-related behaviors resulting in the significant impairment of one's physical health or psychosocial functioning.	Pica, Rumination Disorder, Anorexia Nervosa, Bulimia Nervosa, and Binge Eating
Elimination Disorders	Elimination Disorders involve the inappropriate elimination of urine or feces.	Enuresis and Encopresis
Sleep–Wake Disorders	Individuals with these disorders typically present with sleep–wake complaints regarding the quality, timing and amount of sleep resulting in problems with their daily functioning.	Insomnia, Narcolepsy, Apnea, Sleep Arousal or Behavior Disorders and Restless Legs Syndrome
Sexual Dysfunctions	This group of disorders is characterized by significant problems in a person's ability to respond sexually or to experience sexual pleasure, causing distress for the individual or problems in relationships.	Interest/Arousal Disorders, Orgasm Disorders, and Ejaculation Disorders
Gender Dysphoria	Gender Dysphoria is a condition where a person experiences discomfort or distress because there is a mismatch between their biological sex and gender identity. Individuals with this disorder feel that they are the wrong sex.	Gender Dysphoria
Disruptive, Impulse-Control, and Conduct Disorders	Disorders in this category involve problems in the self-control of emotions and behaviors. They show up in behaviors that violate the rights of others and/or bring the individual into significant conflict with social norms or authority figures.	Oppositional Defiant Disorder, Intermittent Explosive, Conduct Disorder, Pyromania, and Kleptomania

TABLE 9.2 *(continued)*

MENTAL DISORDER	*DSM-5* DIAGNOSTIC CHARACTERISTICS	EXAMPLE
Substance-Related and Addictive Disorders	Substance-Related Disorders encompass ten different classes of drugs plus one nonsubstance related disorder—gambling. The essential feature of this disorder is that the individual continues using a substance despite significant physical, psychological or social problems or, with gambling, continues that behavior despite significant economic or personal problems.	Substance Use Disorders and Substance-Induced Disorders plus Gambling Disorder
Neurocognitive Disorders	This category of disorders includes the group of disorders in which the primary problem is a big and dramatic decline in the ability to think, problem solve, and remember.	Delirium, Alzheimer's, Traumatic Brain Injury
Personality Disorders	These disorders represent a unique and long-lasting pattern of thoughts, feelings, and outward behaviors that are very different from what is usually expected from our culture.	Antisocial, Avoidant, Borderline, Narcissistic, Obsessive–Compulsive, Schizotypal
Paraphilic Disorders	These disorders involve strong and persistent sexual interests other than sexual interest in genital stimulation or what is considered normal sexual behavior between consenting adults.	Voyeurism, Exhibitionism, Sadism, Masochism, Pedophilic, Fetishism and Frotteurism

The Most Common Disorders

Mental disorders are common in all parts of the world. An estimated 26% to 30% of Americans ages 18 and older suffer from a diagnosable mental disorder in a given year (Kessler, Chiu, Dealer, & Walters, 2005; Lopez-Duran, 2011). When applied to the 2004 U.S. Census residential population estimate for ages 18 and older, this figure translates to 57.7 million people (2005). According to a 2011 Centers for Disease Control and Prevention (CDC) report, mental illnesses account for a larger proportion of disability in developed countries than any other group of illnesses, including cancer and heart disease. Twenty percent of children in the United States will be diagnosed with a mental illness in a given year.

Many people suffer from more than one mental disorder at a given time. Nearly half (45%) of those individuals with any mental disorder meet criteria for two or more disorders (Kessler, Chiu, Demler, & Walters, 2005). A survey of mental disorders in the United States reveals the most commonly diagnosed mental disorders are anxiety disorders, followed by impulse-control disorders, mood disorders, and substance-abuse disorders (Kessler et al., 2005; Figure 9.2). When nicotine dependence is included among substance-abuse disorders, it becomes the most frequently diagnosed disorder, at 35% (National Comorbidity Survey Replication [NCS-R], (2010).

Of these disorders, anxiety and the category of disorders defined as *disruptive, impulse-control* and *conduct disorders* appear earliest at a median age of 11; substance-use disorders, at age 20; and mood disorders are the latest to appear, at a median age of 30 (Kessler et al., 2005; Figure 9.3). We look at these most common classes of disorders before looking at related therapies.

Psychological Disorders

In our discussion of psychological disorders we focus on some of the more common major categories of disorders. They include neurodevelopmental disorders, psychotic disorders, mood disorders, anxiety and stress disorders, eating disorders, substance-related disorders, and personality disorders.

Neurodevelopmental Disorders

There are a number of disorders with onset in the developmental period, usually appearing early in childhood. The disorders are characterized by a range of developmental deficits in both specific and global areas of function. They produce impairments of personal, social, academic, or occupational functioning.

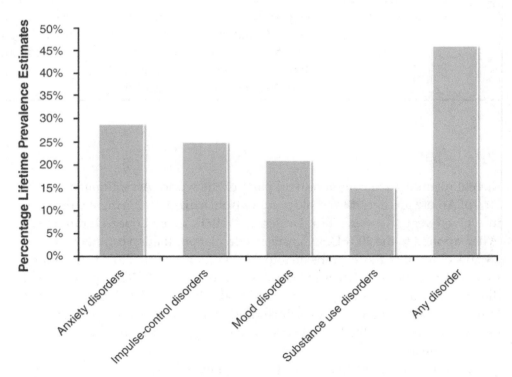

FIGURE 9.2   The four most commonly diagnosed mental disorders in America.

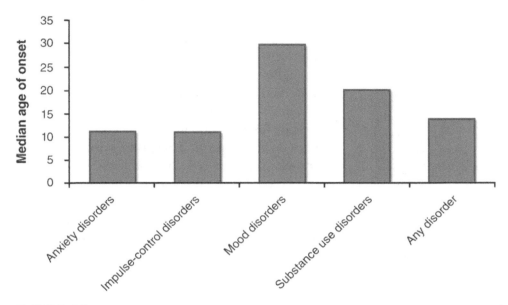

FIGURE 9.3 Median age of onset for the four most commonly diagnosed mental disorders in the United States.

Intellectual Developmental Disorder

The term intellectual developmental disorder (IDD) is used because it has less of a negative connotation or stigma than the old term—retardation. The essential features of this disorder are deficits in general mental abilities, and impairment in everyday adaptive functioning when compared to individuals of similar age. Deficit in intellectual functions involve such things as reasoning, problem solving, abstract thinking, judgment, academic learning, and learning from experience. Adaptive functioning refers to an inability to meet developmental and sociocultural standards for personal independence and social responsibility in activities of daily life such as communication, social participation, and independent living. The deficits of those with IDD can range from mild, moderate, severe, and profound.

There is no real cure for individuals with IDD. There is a wide variation of functioning and, depending on the degree of impairment, those individuals with mild IDD may be able to live independently with some help and supervision. Those individuals with profound IDD may have to be placed in special programs or institutions.

Autism Spectrum Disorder

The central features of *autism spectrum disorder (ASD)* are persistent, pervasive, and sustained impairments in how an individual interacts with or communicates with others. It usually appears very early during childhood. Studies have shown that parents of children with ASD notice a problem before their child's first birthday and differences in social, communication, and fine motor skills are evident from 6 months of age (Bolton et al., 2012). Individuals with ASD may display repetitive patterns of behavior, interest, or activity. The

© Ivelin Radkov, 2014. Used under license from Shutterstock, Inc.

problems in communication and interacting with others are big and lifelong. People with ASD just cannot get involved with others and share their thoughts and feelings. They make little eye contact, tend to look and listen less to people in their environment or fail to respond to other people, do not readily seek to share their enjoyment of toys or activities, and respond unusually when shown anger, distress, or affection.

According to recent estimates from the CDC (2014), the incidence of ASDs has increased dramatically in recent years and occurs in all racial, ethnic, and socioeconomic groups. Approximately 1 in 68 children has been identified with an ASD. ASDs are almost five times more common among boys (1 in 54) than among girls (1 in 252).

Researchers are unclear of the causes of ASD but there may be genetic and environmental factors. In identical twin studies, there is a 90% chance of having the disorder if a twin has it. If one sibling has ASD, the other siblings have 35 times the normal risk of also developing the disorder (National Institute of Mental Health, 2013).

Although there's no proven cure for ASD; treating ASD early, using school-based programs, and getting proper medical care can help the symptoms and increase the child's ability to function and learn. One type of widely accepted treatment is called *applied behavior analysis*. This form of intervention is designed to shape and establish new behaviors, such as learning to speak and play, and reduce undesirable ones. At this time, there are only a couple of antipsychotic medications approved by the Food and Drug Administration (FDA) to treat ASD. These medications can help reduce episodes of aggression, self-harm, or temper tantrums. Want to learn more about ASD? The following video from Webline Plus is very informative: http://www.nlm.nih.gov/medlineplus/videos/news/Symptoms_Autism_051514-1.html

Attention-Deficit/Hyperactivity Disorder

Attention deficit/ hyperactivity disorder. A persistent pattern of inattention and/or hyperactivity-impulsivity interfering with functioning or development.

The essential feature of **attention-deficit/hyperactivity disorder (ADHD)** is a persistent pattern of inattention and/or hyperactivity-impulsivity that interferes with functioning or development. Symptoms include difficulty staying focused and paying attention, difficulty controlling behavior, and hyperactivity (overactivity). This disorder must manifest itself in more than one setting, for example, in both the school and home. ADHD is one of the most common childhood disorders and can continue through adolescence and into adulthood. The disorder is common in most cultures in about 5% of children and about 2.5% adults (American Psychiatric Association, 2013).

Scientists are not sure what causes ADHD. It may be due to a combination of factors. Research suggests genes play a large role. Studies of twins show ADHD often runs in families. In addition to genetics, researchers are looking at possible environmental factors. For example, there may be a link between cigarette smoking and alcohol use during pregnancy and ADHD in children (Greenhill & Hechtman,

2009). Studies have also shown that preschoolers who are exposed to high levels of lead, sometimes found in the plumbing or paint of old buildings, may have a higher risk of developing ADHD (Froehlich et al., 2009). Some recent studies indicate there may be a link between food additives and hyperactivity. There is a popular belief that refined sugar may cause ADHD or make symptoms worse, but there is no real evidence to support this (National Institute of Mental Health, 2008).

ADHD is the most frequently diagnosed childhood mental disorder. In fact, many think it is grossly over diagnosed as a result of parents and teachers wanting explanations for child misbehaviors and pharmaceutical companies wanting to sell medication (Cohen, 2006). Another reason for over diagnosis may be as simple as the fact that many young boys are still relatively immature when they start kindergarten. As a result, their behaviors are marked by higher levels of activity and lower impulse control than is characteristic of older children. Following a study of some 12,000 kindergarten children, Elder (2010) reported younger children were 60% more likely than older children to be diagnosed with ADHD. By his estimates, as many as 1 million children in the United States may be wrongly diagnosed!.

Although there is no cure for ADHD, symptoms can be helped. Treatment typically involves medications and behavioral interventions. Early diagnosis and treatment can make a big difference in outcome.

Anxiety Disorders

Anxiety is among the most devastating and the most baffling of human emotions. It can range from mild trepidation to acute terror and can occur in response to a wide variety of situations, or sometimes without any apparent provocation. In many cases it is both natural and normal and can be an asset for survival in potentially dangerous situations; however, in many situations it is maladaptive and irrational, and is the basis of a number of disorders collectively known as the *anxiety disorders*, the most commonly diagnosed mental disorders.

Panic attacks: An episode occurring for no apparent reason involving intense fear and anxiety, often accompanied by physical symptoms such as shortness of breath and heart palpitations.

Panic disorder: A disorder characterized by recurrent and persistent panic attacks.

Panic Attacks Specifier and Panic Disorder

A relatively common anxiety disorder involves recurring episodes of intense fear and anxiety, often accompanied by physical symptoms such as shortness of breath and heart palpitations. These episodes, known as **panic attacks**, occur for no apparent reason. Victims often feel they are having a heart attack or that they're in danger of fainting or even dying. The person could also experience severe sweating, lightheadedness, and a feeling of terror about their physical and emotional well-being. In some individuals, attacks occur only once or twice in their lifetime. Those who suffer from recurrent and persistent panic attacks are diagnosed as suffering from **panic disorder**. It is not uncommon for patients suffering from

© Stuart Miles, 2014. Used under license from Shutterstock, Inc.

other mental disorders to also suffer from panic attacks (Ulas, Polat, Akdede, & Alptekin, 2010).

Causes of panic disorder are linked to both biological and psychological causes. Biologically, panic disorder has genetic implications as it tends to run in families. Psychologically, people with panic disorder tend to misinterpret physical symptoms and view physical symptoms as more problematic than they are.

Panic attacks are relatively common, affecting an estimated 10% of the population (Panic Disorder, 2010). Among well-known people who have reportedly suffered panic attacks are Sigmund Freud, Kim Basinger, Tom Cruise, Donny Osmond, Princess Diana, Johnny Depp, and many others (Famous People Affected by an Anxiety Disorder, 2011). If you are interested in how people who experience a panic attack would describe the event first-hand, watch the following video: http://www.youtube.com/watch?v=_qo4uPxhUzU

Generalized Anxiety Disorder

Generalized anxiety disorder: A disorder marked by excessive anxiety and worry, as a general state rather than episodic subjective sensation of anxiety, in the absence of specific situations or objects that might be associated with anxiety reactions.

The most commonly diagnosed mental disorders are anxiety disorders. **Generalized anxiety disorder** is marked by excessive anxiety and worry, as a general state rather than episodic subjective sensation of anxiety, in the absence of specific situations or objects that might be associated with anxiety reactions. The hallmark of this disorder is worry in the absence of specific triggers. Individuals suffering from generalized anxiety, sometimes termed free-floating anxiety, recognize themselves as being predominantly tense, nervous, and fearful, and cannot associate their anxiety with any specific stressor. Although unpleasant, generalized anxiety is not marked by the same degree of terror and sensation of impending doom that is the hallmark of a panic attack.

Generalized anxiety disorder is often a debilitating disease that is present in 3% to 5% of the population (Wittchen, 2002). It appears to be clearly linked to increased susceptibility to a variety of physical diseases, including autoimmune disorders such as rheumatoid arthritis, lupus, celiac disease, and many others (Vieira et al., 2010). It is also highly predictive of other anxiety disorders (Katja, Pine, Lieb, & Wittchen, 2010).

Phobic Disorders

Phobias: Intense, irrational fears, recognized by the person as unreasonable, and often leading to avoidance of certain objects or situations.

Phobias are intense, irrational fears, recognized by the person as unreasonable, and often leading to avoidance of certain objects or situations. These disorders are typically chronic and can be distinguished in terms of the objects or situations that bring them about and an individual goes to great lengths to avoid the feared object or situation. It is thought individuals can be conditioned to develop a phobia or that we are biologically wired to be fearful of potentially harmful objects or situations and some individuals are more susceptible to extreme responses to a trigger.

Agoraphobia

Literally, agoraphobia means fear of open or public places. This disorder manifests itself as severe anxiety related to places or situations from which departure or return home may be difficult, resulting in an active avoidance of such places. Individuals may experience anxiety at the thought of leaving home, or when traveling alone, being apart from friends, or being in strange places. Agoraphobia is often associated with serious personal distress. In extreme cases, individuals may become completely "housebound" for prolonged periods.

The prevalence of agoraphobia is uncertain, although some estimates suggest between 3% and 5% of the U.S. population may have the disorder (Kessler, Ruscio, Shear, & Wittchen, 2008). Many people who experience panic attacks also later develop agoraphobia. The disorder is seen more frequently in women than in men, and most often begins in adolescence or early adulthood, although it may occur considerably later.

Social Phobias

Social phobia involves a fear of social situations—that is, a fear of situations in which the individual is exposed to the judgment of others. The disorder's most common manifestations include avoidance of social situations and of public behaviors such as speaking formally to a group or giving a class presentation. Fear of using public rest rooms, washrooms, eating in public, appearing at certain social gatherings, and writing or performing in public are other manifestations of social phobia.

© Vereshchagin Dmitry, 2014. Used under license from Shutterstock, Inc.

Because social phobias often lead the individual to adopt a lifestyle and occupational role that don't demand a great deal of social contact, thus permitting adequate adjustment and functioning, relatively few people seek clinical help for this disorder.

Specific Phobias

Specific phobias include the variety of other specific fears that are not agoraphobic or social. Some of the most common phobias are listed in Figure 9.4. The criterion for a phobia is simply that the fear be irrational, completely out of proportion to the potential danger of the feared object or situation, and not shared by a significant number of other people. It is interesting to note, however, that human phobias tend to be limited to a number of common situations, most of which imply some sort of danger. Thus, although very few people have furniture or vegetable phobias, a much larger number are afraid of open spaces, heights, closed spaces, insects, snakes, and darkness.

Obsessive–Compulsive and Related Disorders

Have you ever seen or heard of the critically acclaimed television show *Monk?* The show featured the main character, retired homicide detective Adrian Monk, who cleverly solved crimes as a consultant for the San Francisco Police

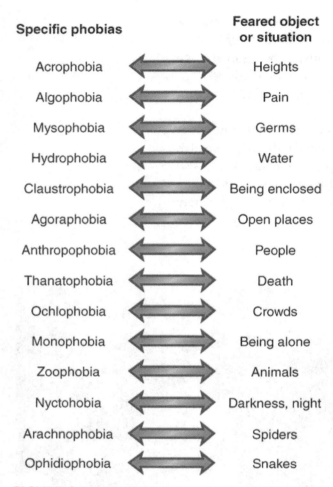

Specific phobias		Feared object or situation
Acrophobia	⟷	Heights
Algophobia	⟷	Pain
Mysophobia	⟷	Germs
Hydrophobia	⟷	Water
Claustrophobia	⟷	Being enclosed
Agoraphobia	⟷	Open places
Anthropophobia	⟷	People
Thanatophobia	⟷	Death
Ochlophobia	⟷	Crowds
Monophobia	⟷	Being alone
Zoophobia	⟷	Animals
Nyctohobia	⟷	Darkness, night
Arachnophobia	⟷	Spiders
Ophidiophobia	⟷	Snakes

FIGURE 9.4   Some common and uncommon specific phobias."

Obsessive-compulsive disorders: A disorder characterized by recurrent and unwanted thoughts and/or the need to perform repetitive physical or mental actions.

Posttraumatic stress disorder: A disorder that appears following exposure to an extremely traumatic event where fear is experienced long after the traumatic event.

Department. Aside from the compelling crime drama, the show was successful, in part, due to the obsessive–compulsive tendencies of Detective Monk, who took several minutes to write his name—"Mr. Monk"—on a chalkboard, and who carefully tried not to step on sidewalk cracks.

Obsessive-compulsive disorders (OCD) are defined by the presence of recurring thoughts or impulses that appear irrational to the person having them (obsessions) and/or behaviors that are not perceived as the result of the individual's wishes but that give rise to intense urges to engage in them and result in anxiety when they are resisted (compulsions). Thus, a compulsion is a behavior, and an obsession is a thought. Both obsessions and compulsions are perceived as incompatible with the individual's nature, but neither can easily be resisted. Other disorders in this category include body dysmorphic disorder, which is distress over perceived flaws or defects in one's physical appearance, causing significant impairment. Another example, hoarding disorder, is characterized by the abnormal and persistent difficulty discarding possessions. There is also trichotillomania (hair-pulling disorder) and excoriation (skin-picking disorder).

The most common obsessions revolve around cleanliness; some examples include a fear of germs and of dirt, and fear of thinking evil thoughts and feeling guilty. They also sometimes take the form of repetitive thoughts of violence, accompanied by considerable fear of engaging in some highly undesirable behavior. Alternatively, obsessions may be marked by perpetual indecision and doubting, which can be severe enough to prevent reaching any decision.

Compulsions typically involve a strong impulse to repeat some senseless and meaningless act over and over again (e.g., checking drawers and locks or touching certain objects repeatedly). They are also often centered on washing and cleansing rituals. Less commonly, they might take the form of hoarding—as in the case of the man who had more than 100 cats in his home and one paranoid dog (Gerson, 2010). Evidence suggests about 1% of the adult U.S. population can be classified as obsessive–compulsive (National Institute of Mental Health, 2011).

Treatment for OCD is similar to those treatments used for anxiety disorders. Some form of medication and psychotherapy is usually prescribed.

Posttraumatic Stress Disorder (Trauma- and Stressor-Related Disorders)

Psychological disorders that appear following exposure to an extremely traumatic event—such as war, rape, or a horrendous accident—sometimes take the form of **posttraumatic stress disorder** (PTSD). Symptoms may include flashbacks or nightmares during which the individual re-expe-riences the event. PTSD is often marked by sleep disturbances, anger and aggression, numbing/avoidance, hypervigilance, and significant impairment in social functioning. Compared with other military personnel, alcohol-related disorders are twice as likely for veterans who meet the criteria for PTSD (Jakupcak et al., 2010).

Estimates of the prevalence of PTSD vary widely. One study that looked at the results of 19 different investigations that had attempted to determine the prevalence of PTSD among veterans returning from Iraq found estimates ranging from a low of 1.4% to an astounding 31% (Sundin, Fear, Iversen, Rona, & Wessely, 2010).

Veterans are more educated in today's society about PTSD and are encouraged to seek treatment through their physicians and mental health providers as there are specific medications and therapies that can improve their quality of life and assist in the reintegration process.

In general, anxiety disorders are treated with medication, psy-chotherapy, or both. Treatment choices depend on the problem and the person's preference, although behavior therapy or cog-nitive–behaviorial therapy (CBT) appear to be the most widely accepted. With CBT, the cognitive part helps people change the thinking patterns supporting their fears, and the behavioral part helps people change the way they react to anxiety-provoking situa-tions. Medication will not cure anxiety disorders, but it can keep the

The most commonly diagnosed mental disorders are anxiety disorders. Drug therapy is currently the treatment of choice.

© Andrey_Popov, 2014. Used under license from Shutterstock, Inc.

symptoms under control. The most effective form of treatment tends to be a com-bination of medications and psychotherapy. Many people with anxiety disorders benefit from joining a self-help or support group; stress management techniques and meditation can also help.

Disruptive, Impulse-Control and Conduct Disorders

Despite being most common during childhood, disruptive, impulse-control, and conduct disorders are almost as prevalent as anxiety disorders, occurring in approximately one in four people. These disorders manifest at about the same age (see Figures 9.2 and 9.3). Disorders in this category are marked by failure to resist an impulse to engage in a behavior that is harmful either to the person or to others. They include a range of often aggressive behaviors. They are unique in that these problems are manifested in behaviors that violate the rights of others and/or bring the individual into significant conflict with soci-etal norms or authority figures.

Aggression-Based Impulse-Control Disorders

Intermittent explosive disorder is marked by the repeated failure to resist aggressive impulses. Children diagnosed with this disorder have typically engaged in a number of excessively violent acts against people or property, or both. As adults, they are at higher risk of aggression in their romantic relationships (Murray-Close, Ostrov, Nelson, Crick, & Coccaro, 2010).

Another aggression-based impulse-control disorder is oppositional defiant disorder. It is characterized by a pattern of hostile, disobedient, defiant behavior toward authority figures. The disorder is sometimes apparent in children given to violent temper tantrums and persistent negative moods. Bullying, stealing, and vandalism are other possible symptoms.

Conduct Disorder

Conduct disorder, which is often preceded by oppositional defiant disorder, is a disorder that begins in late childhood and often becomes more severe in adolescence. A related disorder among adults is antisocial personality disorder.

Conduct disorder is far more common among boys than girls, affecting between 6% and 16% of boys and between 2% and 9% of girls (Searight, Rottnek, & Abby, 2001). The disorder is marked by a persistent pattern of behaviors violating the rights of others or socially inappropriate for the child's age. Children with a conduct disorder are often selfish, relate poorly with others, and typically don't display a normal sense of guilt. They are frequently the school bullies, and demonstrate behaviors such as threatening, fighting, abusing animals, and vandalism.

Other Impulse-Control Disorders

There are a number of other impulse-control disorders, most of which are relatively uncommon. They include:

- **Kleptomania:** an irresistible urge to steal things even when they're not needed or particularly valuable
- **Pyromania:** a compulsion to set fires for personal pleasure and gratification
- **Trichotillomania:** marked by the recurrent pulling out of one's hair, resulting in noticeable hair loss and considerable tension if the individual tries to resist

Impulse control disorders are treated with medication and psychotherapy, usually some form of behavior therapy. These disorders often occur in conjunction with another condition, such as ADHD. Medication and therapy for that condition often helps alleviate the impulse-control disorder. Depression is often an underlying factor in some impulse-control disorders and consequently, treatment with antidepressants may be helpful.

Mood Disorders

The main feature of mood disorders is that they involve a significant disturbance in mood, typically expressed as depression or inappropriate euphoria (mania). Among serious mood disorders are major depressive disorder, bipolar disorder, and dysthymic disorder.

Major Depressive Disorder

Major depressive disorder is the most common of all mood disorders, affecting an estimated 6.7% of the adult U.S. population in a given year (National Institute of Mental Health, 2011). It is characterized by a conglomerate of symptoms, including apathy, listlessness, despair, loss of appetite, sleep disturbances, unwavering pessimism, and thoughts of suicide (although not all of these symptoms need be present in every case).

© travellight, 2014. Used under license from Shutterstock, Inc.

DSM-5 criteria for major depressive disorder stipulate there be at least one major depressive episode. A depressive episode is defined as a period of at least 2 weeks during which the individual suffers from a depressed mood and/or loss of interest and pleasure in normal life activities. The depressed mood typically characterizes most or all of every day.

There appears to be a clear relationship between suicide and depression. In fact, more than 90% of people who commit suicide suffer from depression or some other mental disorder (Suicide in the U.S., 2010).

Major depressive disorder: A disorder characterized by a conglomerate of symptoms, including apathy, listlessness, despair, loss of appetite, sleep disturbances, unwavering pessimism, and thoughts of suicide.

Bipolar disorder: A disorder characterized by mania and depression.

Bipolar Disorder

Bipolar disorder, previously labeled manic depression, is in a category called Bipolar and Related Disorders. It is approximately half as common as major depressive disorder, affecting an estimated 2.6% of the U.S. adult population (National Institute of Mental Health, 2011). It is marked by recurring episodes of mania or depression, although both are not always present. Occasionally the attacks are cyclical; that is, mania is followed by depression, which may then be followed by another period of mania, and so on. More frequently, individuals experience a single episode of mania and one of depression, not necessarily in that order, and may then be free of both for long periods—sometimes even decades. At other times, the condition is characterized principally by mania and is labeled bipolar disorder, Type I. Bipolar disorder Type II refers to a mood disorder where depression rather than mania dominates.

Mania contrasts sharply with periods of depression. It is characterized by periods of extreme and intense activity, irrepressible good humor, grandiose plans and involvements, and overwhelming displays of energy and joie de vivre.

Family and twin studies provide strong evidence of a genetic basis for bipolar disorder, where the heritability coefficient has been estimated at approximately 59% (Karege et al., 2010; Lichtenstein et al., 2009). In this context, heritability coefficient means the extent to which the variability in a characteristic is due to genetics. An example can be viewed at http://www.youtube.com/watch?v=fyJn_3LkE8w

Dysthymic Disorder Persistent Depressive Disorder (Dysthymic Disorder)

Whereas a major depressive episode lasts at least 2 weeks, dysthymic disorder (or dysthymia) describes a chronically depressed mood that lasts at least 2 years and is present most days during that period. Except for its longer duration, dysthymia is marked by much the same symptoms as a major depressive episode, but of lesser severity. In effect, it is a lower-grade, chronic, long-term depression.

Premenstrual Dysphoria Disorder

An additional category added in the *DSM-5* to the Mood disorders is premenstrual dysphoric disorder. Symptoms must be present in the week prior to menses and become minimal or absent in the weeks post menses. The symptoms include marked mood swings or depressed mood, marked irritability or anger, marked anxiety or feelings of being keyed up, difficulty concentrating, decreased interest in activities, a marked lack of energy, specific food cravings, changes in sleep patterns, and physical symptoms such as breast tenderness, joint pain or "bloating."

A person with depression can be treated in several ways. The most common treatments are medication and psychotherapy. For depressive symptoms, medications called antidepressants primarily work on brain chemicals called neurotransmitters, especially serotonin, norepinephrine, or dopamine. These chemicals are most involved in regulating our moods. Electroconvulsive shock therapy (ECT) is another very effective treatment for depression. This form of treatment creates seizures in the brain in a very brief and controlled situation. We are not sure how the ECT works but it seems to be just as effective as medications in many instances.

Although a mood disorder, bipolar disorder is very different from depression and cannot be cured, but it can be treated effectively over the long term. Proper treatment helps many people with bipolar disorder gain better control of their mood swings and related symptoms. Drugs called mood stabilizers are most effective.

When combined with medication, psychotherapy can be an effective treatment for depression or bipolar disorder.

Substance-Related and Addictive Disorders

The *DSM-5* provides criteria for diagnosis of substance use disorders, along with criteria for intoxication, withdrawal, substance/medication-induced disorders, and unspecified substance-induced disorders. There is a continuum between mild early use to more severe and serious addiction.

Drug intoxication: Recent use of a substance that induces a maladaptive and impairing state but is reversible.

Withdrawal symptoms: A state occurring when an individual who regularly uses a drug, stops or reduces drug use, and can have unpleasant and sometimes dangerous reactions.

There is evidence that some behaviors, such as gambling, activate the brain reward system with effects similar to those of drugs of abuse. The symptoms resemble substance use disorders to a certain extent; consequently, there is also a nonsubstance-related disorder—gambling disorder.

Substance Use Disorders

Substance use disorder is a continuum of drug use defined mainly in terms of **drug intoxication** and **withdrawal symptoms**. With increasing use, many drugs have diminishing effects. This is due primarily to the fact that most abused drugs are effective precisely because they increase the release of dopamine, the neurotransmitter associated with pleasure and reinforcement, or block its reuptake. One consequence is the brain produces *less* dopamine naturally as it becomes increasingly dependent on external sources. Hence the apparent increased tolerance and the need to use more of the drug.

Withdrawal, the physiological and psychological effects of stopping drug use, results from a sudden reduction in stimulation of those areas of the brain associated with pleasure and typically leads to feelings of dysphoria—the opposite of *euphoria*. Withdrawal symptoms vary depending on the drug, its manner of ingestion, and the individual. Withdrawal is often marked by depression and anxiety, as well as by a strong craving, this being the hallmark of addiction. Sudden and complete withdrawal from alcohol dependence can be fatal.

PREVALENCE AND TYPES OF DRUG USE

As Figure 9.5 indicates, nearly half (46%) of all Americans aged 12 and up have tried one or more drugs, although only 8% describe themselves as current users (those who have used the drug in the last 30 days). Nicotine and alcohol continue to be the most widely used drugs.

Drugs are typically classified in terms of their effects rather than their composition. There are **narcotics** such as morphine and opium, addictive drugs that produce sensations of well-being; **sedatives**, such as tranquilizers and barbiturates; **stimulants**, such as the amphetamines and cocaine; and **hallucinogens**, such as LSD, ecstasy, and Rohypnol. Marijuana is also ordinarily classified as a hallucinogenic drug, although its effects are seldom as dramatic as those of LSD or mescaline (see Table 9.3).

Narcotics: A drug type producing sensations of well-being.

Sedatives: A drug type causing drowsiness.

Stimulants: A drug classification causing excitement and joyfulness.

Hallucinogens: A drug type causing hallucinations.

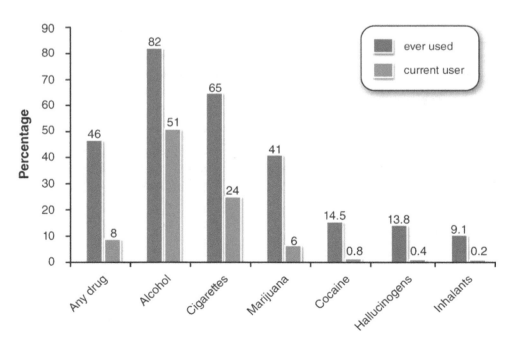

FIGURE 9.5   Drug use in the United States based on interviews of around 68,000 participants aged 12 or more.

TABLE 9.3 Symptoms of Drug Use and Their Effects on the Nervous System

DRUG	EARLY SYMPTOMS	LONG-TERM SYMPTOMS	EFFECTS ON NERVOUS SYSTEM
Narcotics (opium, morphine, heroin, codeine, methadone)	Medicinal breath Traces of white powder around nostrils (heroin is sometimes inhaled) Red or raw nostrils Needle marks or scars on arms Long sleeves (or other clothing) at inappropriate times Physical evidence may include cough syrup bottles, syringes, cotton swabs, and spoon or cap for heating heroin	Loss of appetite Constipation	Bind to painkilling sites to dull sensation of pain; block reuptake of neurotransmitters such as dopamine. Mimic endorphins (cause sensations of pleasure and well-being). With chronic use, the brain may stop producing endorphins so user develops tolerance and craves more drugs to feel good.
Sedatives (barbiturates, tranquilizers, alcohol, Rohypnol, and GHB [the "date-rape" drugs])	Symptoms of alcohol consumption with or without odor: —Poor coordination and speech —Drowsiness —Loss of interest in activity	Withdrawal symptoms when discontinued Possible convulsions	Activate GABA receptors (which are inhibitory and cause drowsiness). GHB increases dopamine levels in the brain (associated with sense of well-being).
Stimulants (cocaine, crack, amphetamines, caffeine, nicotine)	Excessive activity Irascibility Argumentativeness Nervousness Pupil dilation Dry mouth and nose with bad breath Chapped, dry lips Scratching or rubbing of nose Long periods without sleep Loss of appetite	Loss of appetite Possible hallucinations and psychotic reactions	Caffeine and amphetamines promote release of noradrenaline (causes excitement and wakefulness). Cocaine and crack promote release of dopamine and inhibit its reuptake (causes sense of euphoria); leads to tolerance and addiction.

TABLE 9.3 *(continued)*

DRUG	EARLY SYMPTOMS	LONG-TERM SYMPTOMS	EFFECTS ON NERVOUS SYSTEM
Hallucinogens (marijuana, LSD, PCP, mescaline, psilocybin)	Odor on breath and clothing Animated behavior or its opposite Bizarre behavior Panic Disorientation	None definite for marijuana Possible contribution to psychoses and possible recurrence of experiences later	Stimulate serotonin activity. Interfere with noradrenaline activity (produces hallucinations).
Inhalants (glue, paint thinner, aerosol sprays, solvents, other combustibles)	Odor of glue, solvent, or related substance Redness and watering of eyes Appearance of alcoholic intoxication Physical evidence of plastic bags, rags, aerosol glue or solvent containers	Disorientation Brain damage	Long-term use can break down myelin, leading to muscle spasms, tremors, and other physical problems.

Medication and behavioral therapy, especially when combined, are frequently used for treatment. The process often begins with detoxification, followed by treatment and relapse prevention. Treatment for addictive disorders is not simple, or brief. Addiction treatment must help the individual stop using drugs, maintain a drug-free lifestyle, and achieve productive functioning in the family, at work, and in society. Most substance abusers require long-term or repeated episodes of care to recover and stay drug free. And sometimes, as with other chronic conditions, episodes of relapse may require a return to prior treatment components.

Medications can be used to help with different aspects of the treatment process. Medications are used for withdrawal to suppress the withdrawal symptoms. After withdrawal, medications can also help to reestablish normal brain functioning to prevent relapse and reduce cravings.

Psychotherapy, especially behavioral therapy, helps patients engage in the treatment process, change their attitudes and behaviors related to drug abuse, and increase healthy life skills.

Other Disorders

The groupings of mental disorders we've considered so far are the most commonly diagnosed in the United States. The *DSM-5* lists a large number of additional categories, a few of which are summarized here.

Dissociative Disorders

Three principal dissociative disorders are described in the *DSM-5*. They are called dissociative because they involve the splitting or separating of aspects of personality and functioning. Dissociative symptoms are sometimes seen in patients with PTSD.

DISSOCIATIVE AMNESIA

Dissociative amnesia is defined by a sudden and temporary loss of memory not attributable to any organic cause. Typically the memory loss is for some unusually stressful or traumatic event. Some instances of dissociative amnesia involve loss of memory of violent outbursts or suicide attempts.

Dissociative amnesia may take different forms, distinguishable in terms of the type of material that cannot be remembered and the time period covered by the amnesia. In *localized* amnesia, the individual is unable to recall anything for a period of time following some event, such as a car accident. In *systematized* amnesia, some events may be recalled during the circumscribed period, but many others will have been completely forgotten.

Dissociative amnesia can include **dissociative fugue**, which involves a loss of memory. In addition, it involves wandering and sometimes assuming a new identity. People suffering from a fugue state undergo an episode during which they have forgotten who they are but are unaware of having been anyone else. During this time, they may leave their homes and even establish very different lives somewhere else. Both onset and recovery are usually rapid, but the individual may then be left with a feeling of disorientation and confusion.

Dissociative fugue: A loss of memory characterized by wandering and sometimes assuming a new identity.

Dissociative identity disorder: A complex type of dissociation in which individuals are from time to time dominated by distinctly different, complex, highly integrated personalities.

DISSOCIATIVE IDENTITY DISORDER

The dissociative aspects of amnesia and fugue states are obvious: In both cases, it is as though parts of the individual's personality and memory become separated from one another, some parts remaining temporarily inaccessible to the individual. **Dissociative identity disorder**, previously called *multiple-personality disorder*, involves a more complex type of dissociation in which individuals are from time-to-time dominated by distinctly different, complex, highly integrated personalities. Typically, domination by one personality is complete and does not involve any memory of other personalities, although it sometimes does. Shifts from one personality to another may be sudden and dramatic.

The Three Faces of Eve (Thigpen & Cleckley, 1954) presents a classic illustration of dissociative identity disorder. "Eve White," who had been in psychotherapy for a period of time following complaints of severe headaches and blackouts, was a quiet, demure, soft-spoken woman. The therapist had no reason to suspect a multiple personality, until one day:

> As if seized by sudden pain, she put both hands to her head. After a tense moment of silence, both hands dropped. There was a quick, reckless smile, and, in a bright voice that sparkled, she said, "Hi, there, Doc!" The demure and constrained posture of Eve White had melted into buoyant repose. (p. 137)

Multiple personality, a popular fiction theme, is a rare condition now labeled *dissociative identity disorder*. In a few classic cases, it manifests itself almost as clearly as this doctored photo indicates.

The "new" woman had no doubt that she was "Eve Black." Later, "Jane" emerged as a third personality.

The repeated shifts of personality that occur in a dissociative identity disorder do not occur in the fugue state. In addition, the two or more personalities that alternately dominate the individual diagnosed as having a dissociative identity disorder are complete personalities with well-integrated identities.

There is sometimes confusion between schizophrenia and "dissociative" or "multiple" identities, but the two are quite different. None of the schizophrenias involve dual (or triple) personalities in the sense of well-integrated, apparently normal, but separate manifestations of identity. In addition, the schizophrenias typically involve serious problems of perceptual or cognitive distortion.

Among well-known people who have spoken about their experiences with dissociative identity disorder are actress and comedian Roseanne Barr and retired football player Hershel Walker.

DEPERSONALIZATION/DEREALIZATION DISORDER

This is a disorder characterized by feelings of unreality. Those with depersonalization/derealizaton disorder often feel they are in a dreamlike state, and perhaps their body does not belong to them. Adam Duritz, front man for the rock group Counting Crows, says of his depersonalization disorder, "[It] makes the world seem like it's not real, as if things aren't taking place. It's hard to explain, but you feel untethered" (Celebrities with Dissociative Disorder, 2010). The disorder is uncommon and often disappears on its own.

Effective treatments for dissociative disorders include psychotherapy, medications, and hypnotherapy. Often the symptoms of dissociative disorders occur with other disorders, such as anxiety and depression, so the disorder may be treated using the same drugs prescribed for those disorders.

Schizophrenia Spectrum and Other Psychotic Disorders

This grouping includes a variety of disorders characterized by *psychotic* symptoms such as **hallucinations** (perceptions of experiences without corresponding external stimuli together with a compelling feeling that these are real) and **delusions** (false beliefs or opinions). These disorders are severe, debilitating conditions and are defined by abnormalities in one or more of the five domains: delusions, hallucinations, disorganized thinking (speech), grossly disorganized or abnormal motor behavior (catatonia), and negative symptoms Negative symptoms include diminished emotional expression, lack of motivation to do anything, and inability to experience pleasure and lack of interest in social interactions.

Delusional disorder involves the presence of delusions but no hallucinations. Other than delusional thinking, the person's behavior is not bizarre or odd.

SCHIZOPHRENIA

Among the most severe and the most common of the psychotic disorders, **schizophrenia** is characterized by emotional, cognitive, and perceptual confusion and a consequent breakdown of effective contact with others and with reality.

Hallucinations: Perceptions of experiences without corresponding external stimuli together with a compelling feeling that these are real.

Delusions: False beliefs or opinions.

Delusional disorder: A presence of delusions but no hallucinations.

Schizophrenia: A psychotic disorder characterized by emotional, cognitive, and perceptual confusion and a consequent breakdown of effective contact with others and with reality.

Schizophreniform disorder: Same symptoms as schizophrenia but the only differences are symptoms last only 1 to 6 months.

Brief psychotic disorder: Similar to schizophrenia; however, symptoms can last from 1 day to 1 month.

Schizoaffective disorder: Includes symptoms of schizophrenia in addition to a mood disorder such as depression or mania.

Shizophreniform disorder has the same kind of symptoms as schizophrenia but is different because it is brief and symptoms last only 1 to 6 months. **Brief psychotic disorder** is even shorter, lasting 1 day to 1 month. **Schizoaffective disorder** includes symptoms of schizophrenia in addition to a mood disorder such as depression or mania.

This classification of schizophrenias is not nearly as clear in practice as it might appear in theory. Numerous apparently schizophrenic patients cannot easily be classified within a single division, since symptoms often overlap or change over time

Various psychotic disorders appear to be related to malfunctions in the metabolic processes involved in the essential transformations that occur among synaptic neurotransmitters such as dopamine, serotonin, and epinephrine. The effectiveness of many psychotherapeutic drugs appears to result from their effects on neurotransmitters, providing added evidence that these are implicated in some mental disorders. In addition, research with animals has shown stressful environmental events may adversely affect essential metabolic processes in the brain.

Genomic research provides very strong evidence that schizophrenia in particular has a genetic component. Lichtenstein et al. (2009) summarized a large number of studies looking at incidence of schizophrenia among twins, full and half siblings, and parents and estimated the contribution of genetics to the disorder was approximately 64%. This finding is consistent with the belief that neurotransmitters are implicated in these mental disorders (Gray, Dean, Kronsbein, Robinson, & Scarr, 2010).

There is no cure for psychotic disorders so treatments focus on managing the symptoms of the disease. For the more serious forms such as schizophrenia, treatments include antipsychotic medications and various psychosocial treatments. Antipsychotic medications have been available since the mid-1950s. The older types are called conventional or "typical" antipsychotics and newer medications are called second generation, or "atypical" antipsychotics. The newer medications are much more effective and have fewer side effects. Psychosocial treatments can help people with psychotic disorders once stabilized on medication. Psychosocial treatments help these patients deal with the everyday challenges of the illness, such as difficulty with communication, self-care, work, and forming and keeping relationships.

Sexual and Gender Identity Dysphoria Disorders

GENDER DYSPHORIA DISORDERS

The *DSM-5* recognizes two major subgroups of disorders involving a marked incongruence between one's experienced/expressed gender and assigned gender. You can learn more at http://education-portal.com/academy/lesson/gender-identity-disorder-definition-and-social-perception-of-gender-dysphoria.html#lesson

GENDER DYSPHORIA IN CHILDREN AND GENDER DYSPHORIA IN ADOLESCENTS AND ADULTS

This disorder involves a strong desire to be of the other gender, a strong preference for wearing clothing consistent with the other gender, preference for toys and make-believe play involving the opposite gender, and a strong dislike of one's sexual anatomy, including secondary sex characteristics. Gender dysphoria in adolescents and adults share similar diagnostic criteria, with the exception of the reference toward toys and make-believe play seen in children.

Gender identity disorders are sometimes confused with *transvestism,* which is a different disorder. Transvestism refers to the act of *cross-dressing* (dressing in clothing that is culturally recognized as appropriate for the other sex) for sexual gratification.

Gender identity disorders sometimes lead individuals to undergo sex-change procedures, which typically include both surgery and hormone treatment—as did Chastity Bono, daughter (now son, Chaz) of Sonny Bono and Cher (Chaz Bono Granted Name, Gender Change, 2010).

PARAPHILIAS

Paraphilias are a variety of sexual deviations (*para:* deviation; *philia:* attraction or love). Among these are the fetishes, involving sexual attraction to nonliving objects such as women's undergarments, shoes, hats, and walnuts. Fetishism occurs primarily in males. Paraphilias eventually replace the person's desire for intimacy with another person.

> Paraphilias: Variety of sexual deviants such as exhibitionism, fetishism, and sadism.

Zoophilia denotes sexual attraction to animals and the exclusive or preferred use of animals for sexual arousal or release. It is apparently not as rare as once thought (Earls & Lalumiere, 2009).

Pedophilia describes a condition in which prepubertal children are employed as sexual partners or objects. Pedophilia is predominantly heterosexual rather than homosexual. It is the most commonly seen paraphilia in clinical practice (Fedoroff & Marshall, 2010). In particular, the use of children in pornographic books, films, and websites has increased dramatically.

Among the paraphilias are a number of other behaviors undertaken for sexual gratification. These include *exhibitionism* (flashing of private parts); *fetishism* (sexual arousal related to a physical object or situation); *frotteurism* (rubbing against a nonconsenting person); *masochism* and *sadism* (receiving or giving pain, respectively); *transvestic fetishism* (cross-dressing); and *voyeurism* (spying on people engaged in intimate behaviors).

There are no reliable statistics available on the prevalence of paraphilias, but they occur much more frequently in men than in women. One study found that 13.4% of adult male *psychiatric* inpatients admitted having one or more paraphilias—most commonly voyeurism and exhibitionism (Marsh et al., 2010).

SEXUAL DYSFUNCTIONS

The psychosexual dysfunctions include impediments to the enjoyment of normal sexual activity. Their principal psychological consequence is one of distress that may vary in severity depending on the individual concerned. Among sexual dysfunctions are inhibited sexual desire, inhibited sexual excitement (frigidity or impotence), inhibited female orgasm, inhibited male orgasm, premature ejaculation, dyspareunio (pain during coitus), and vaginismus (spasms of the vagina making coitus painful).

The various types of sexual and gender disorders all require different types of treatments. Medication is used less frequently than with other disorders and some form of psychotherapy or behavioral intervention is used. Treatment for gender dysphoria aims to help reduce or remove the distressing feelings of a mismatch between biological sex and gender identity, which might involve dressing and living as their preferred gender or taking hormones or having surgery to change their physical appearance.

With paraphilia, some form of behavioral therapy or behavior modification can be effective. Treatment depends on the nature of the paraphilia and may include medication, psychotherapy, and a sociocultural component (such as group or family therapy). Medications may be used to reduce or lower the sex drive, which decreases the sexual behavior.

Sexual dysfunctions are treated in a variety of ways depending on the particular problem. The focus is on restoring sexual functioning and pleasure. Physical causes are usually ruled out or managed before psychotherapy. Treatments for common conditions address such things as:

- **Lack of desire**—Treatment is a multistep process. Therapists begin by helping clients identify negative attitudes about sex, explore the origins of those ideas, and find new ways of thinking about sex. The focus then shifts to behavior: Therapists may ask clients to keep diaries of their sexual thoughts, watch erotic films, or develop fantasies. Therapists also address any relationship problems.
- **Erectile dysfunction**—Therapy focuses on reducing anxiety by taking the focus off intercourse. For men with physical problems, medication or devices can help.
- **Premature ejaculation**—Therapy focuses on behavioral training. With his partner's help, the man learns to withstand stimulation for longer and longer periods.
- **Painful intercourse**—The typical treatment focuses on relaxation training.

Somatic Symptom and Related Disorders

Somatic symptom disorders: A disorder in which the patient has symptoms suggestive of some medical problem but no such problem can be found.

Illness anxiety disorder: Extreme worry about having or acquiring a serious illness.

Conversion disorder: A disorder similar to somatic symptom disorder but individuals with this disorder have one or more symptoms of altered voluntary motor or sensory functioning such as paralysis, weakness, tremors, or problems with vision or hearing.

Another grouping of disorders included in the *DSM-5* is the **somatic symptom disorders**. These include a variety of conditions in which the patient has symptoms suggestive of some medical problem but no such problem can be found. People with this disorder are often very anxious about their health. The condition is not a result of consciously fabricating or exaggerating symptoms (called *malingering*) or what are called *factitious disorders* (where the patient deliberately produces or feigns symptoms). Those with somatic symptom disorders genuinely believe they are physically ill. Individuals with **illness anxiety disorder** have a preoccupation with having or acquiring a serious illness. They worry about their health and may perform excessive behaviors to avoid illness and focus on their health. **Conversion disorder** is similar to somatic symptom disorder but individuals with this disorder have one or more symptoms of altered voluntary motor or sensory functioning such as paralysis, weakness, tremors, or problems with vision or hearing.

Treatment for somatic symptom disorders usually involves some form of psychotherapy. If anxiety or stress is a factor, treatments for dealing with anxiety may also be used.

Personality Disorders

Personality disorders are evident in behaviors that are socially inappropriate, inflexible, and often antisocial. Most of these behaviors typically become apparent during childhood or adolescence and are manifested as relatively stable, although sometimes highly maladaptive, personality characteristics.

Unlike those with more serious mental disorders, persons suffering from personality disorders usually continue to function in society. Often, too, they experience little anxiety over their behaviors since they are ordinarily unaware of their maladaptive nature. Most are unlikely to seek help on their own. Many individuals diagnosed with other forms of mental disorder have a long-standing history of personality disorders.

The personality disorders identified in the *DSM-5* are the following:

- *Paranoid personality disorder* is marked by a profound, long-term, and unjustified conviction that other people are hostile, dangerous, and out to get them. It often leads to social isolation.
- *Schizoid personality disorder* is characterized by a disinterest in social relationships and a limited range of emotional reaction. It is sometimes evident in emotional coldness and a solitary lifestyle.
- *Histrionic personality disorder,* primarily a female disorder, is evident in excessive emotionality, attention seeking, and inappropriate flirtatiousness. People with histrionic personalities typically want to be the center of attention and are often egocentric and self-indulgent.
- *Narcissistic personality disorder,* primarily a male disorder, is evident in excessive self-love. Narcissus of the Greek legend loved himself above all else. Extreme arrogance, cavalier disregard for social convention and the rights of others, supreme confidence, and selfish exploitation of others are the principal characteristics of the narcissistic personality. Not surprisingly, such individuals appear only rarely in clinics.
- *Antisocial personality disorder* displays a pattern of pervasive disregard for, and violation of, the rights of others. Common characteristics might include lack of remorse for actions that hurt others, lack of empathy, cruelty to animals, poor and abusive relationships, and frequent problems with the law.
- *Borderline personality disorder* is evident in fluctuating and unpredictable moods that are often extreme. Those with borderline personality disorder tend to alternate between idealizing and devaluing, and they often have unstable and chaotic interpersonal relationships.
- *Schizotypal personality disorder* is marked by a need for social isolation, by what are often very different convictions and beliefs, and sometimes by odd or eccentric dress and behavior. Because the disorder is very similar to some forms of schizophrenia, its inclusion as a personality disorder is controversial.
- *Avoidant personality disorder* is characterized by an extreme and pervasive pattern of social inhibition evident in feelings of inadequacy and avoidance of social interaction.

Personality disorders: Behaviors that are socially inappropriate, inflexible, and often antisocial that typically become apparent during childhood or adolescence and are manifested as relatively stable.

- *Dependent personality disorder* describes a chronic and long-term condition in which the individual manifests excessive dependence on others for physical and emotional needs.
- *Obsessive–compulsive personality disorder (OCPD)* is different from obsessive–compulsive disorder (OCD) described earlier. Whereas OCD is an *anxiety disorder* marked by recurring obsessions (thoughts that won't go away) and compulsions (behaviors that must be carried out repeatedly), OCPD is a *personality disorder.* It is marked by a chronic and persistent maladaptive pattern of interacting with other people and with the environment. Among its manifestations are excessive preoccupation with orderliness, perfectionism, and details and a need to control all aspects of the environment.

There is a danger, when reading quick descriptions of disorders, to recognize clusters of symptoms among people we know and wonder whether they might have this or that disorder. For example, we all know people who are neat and orderly, but the fact is that probably none of them would come close to satisfying the criteria for OCPD. Nor are all people who are shy candidates for a diagnosis of *avoidant personality disorder.* Note that for all other personality disorders, diagnosis is made only on the basis of specific combinations of *persistent, prolonged,* and/or chronic beliefs and behaviors.

Personality disorders are commonly viewed as difficult, if not impossible, to treat. However, two interventions in particular—dialectical behavior therapy (DBT) and cognitive therapy (CT)—show promise, especial for one of the more common and most persistent, borderline personality disorder (Beck & Freedman, 1990; Leichsenring & Leibing, 2003). Psychotherapy is the main way to treat personality disorders. There are no medications specifically approved by the FDA to treat personality disorders. However, several types of psychiatric medications may help with various personality disorder symptoms.

Therapies

Therapy: Systematic processes for helping individuals overcome their psychological problems.

People decide to seek mental health treatment in the form of **therapy** for a variety of reasons. Some individuals are dissatisfied with their level of satisfaction in life and may seek assistance in evaluating goals in their life. This may be related to relationship issues, career or educational issues, or interpersonal struggles. Some individuals may be court ordered to seek services due to their involvement with the legal system, such as an arrest for domestic violence, a parenting evaluation due to being reported for abuse or neglect of a child, or because of an ongoing custody battle from a highly conflictual divorce. Others may seek treatment for a mental health disorder mentioned previously in the chapter. Some individuals are referred for services by their primary care physician, their pastor or priest, a friend or family member, or, in the case of a youth, school personnel may suggest services

Basically, there are three broad approaches to treating mental disorders. In many instances, these reflect the therapist's basic model, as summarized in Table 9.1. Thus, if the therapist views the disorder as being the result of a system malfunction (medical/biological model), drug therapy, electroconvulsive shock therapy, or, more rarely, surgery will be the therapies of choice. If the therapist thinks the disorder is a result of learning or inappropriate cognitions (behavioral and cognitive model), learning-based therapies may be employed. And if the therapist views disorders as resulting from psychic conflicts (psychodynamic model), some form of psychoanalysis may be used. It should be noted that traditional psychoanalysis is rarely used in today's society due to the emphasis on briefer types of treatment as a result of managed care issues in health care. In conclusion, most therapists use a variety of approaches in dealing with mental disorder. Only rarely are the nonmedical approaches used without also using some form of drug therapy (antidepressants, sedatives, antipsychotic drugs, and so on).

Medical Therapy

Science has provided practitioners with chemicals and surgical procedures that can sometimes rectify a condition before its more extreme results appear. Syphilis, for example, can, if unchecked, lead to neurological impairment and the manifestation of various mental disorders. Simple and highly effective treatment of syphilis with penicillin or related drugs in its early stages prevents their appearance. Similarly, thyroid problems, insulin problems, and a variety of metabolic and glandular problems can be controlled chemically.

DRUG THERAPY

Drug therapy for mental disorders involves psychiatric medications, sometimes called psychotropic or psychotherapeutic medications. These drugs have dramatically changed the face of mental health treatment and reduced the number of people who suffer serious and disabling symptoms and the severity of the symptoms. Medications treat the symptoms of mental disorders but they do not cure the disorder. They work differently for different people. Some people get great results from medications and only need them for a short time and other individuals have to take them for

© Kirill__M, 2014. Used under license from Shutterstock, Inc.

a long time or even a life time. As with all drugs, there are often side effects. Factors that can affect how medications work in people include:

- Type of mental disorder, such as depression, anxiety, bipolar disorder, and schizophrenia
- Age, sex, and body size
- Physical illnesses
- Habits like smoking and drinking
- Liver and kidney function
- Genetics
- Other medications and herbal/vitamin supplements
- Diet
- Whether medications are taken as prescribed (NIMH, 2014).

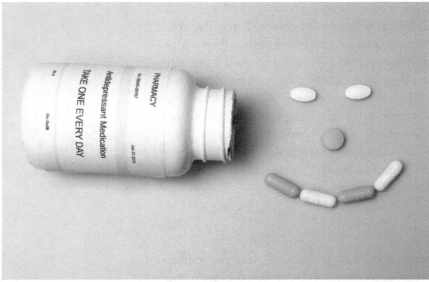

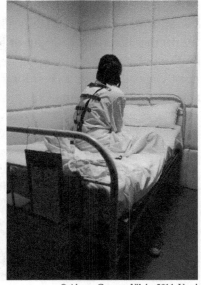

© Sherry Yates Young, 2014. Used under license from Shutterstock, Inc.

© Alvaro German Vilela, 2014. Used under license from Shutterstock, Inc.

Treatment of mental disorders has changed dramatically with drug therapy. Calming medications can now accomplish what required a straitjacket only a few decades ago.

Mild tranquilizers (Valium, Librium, Xanax, Ativan) reduce anxiety and are useful for phobias, panic disorders, PTSD, and so on. Drugs known as antidepressants (Celexa, Lexapro, Prozac) are widely used in the treatment of depression. Most are not effective for several weeks or even months after starting treatment. They work well for about a third of patients with major depression. Major tranquilizers (Haldol, Navane, Thorazine), called antipsychotic drugs, are used extensively with schizophrenic patients. Lithium and other drugs are widely used for bipolar disorder. Disulfiram (Antabuse) is sometimes used with alcohol addiction. There is some controversy over the effectiveness of these chemical substances. Most can have serious side effects; overdoses can sometimes be fatal. Their use frequently accompanies other forms of therapy where they might be employed simply to control anxiety or depression sufficiently so that the therapist can more effectively employ other treatments.

PSYCHOSURGERY

Another medical therapy involves surgical intervention. Among the most highly publicized of the surgical treatments is that of excising (removing) or making lesions (cuts) in the frontal lobes of the brain (**prefrontal lobotomy**), a procedure that is sometimes successful in reducing anxiety and alleviating depression. Among its frequent side effects, however, are a general dulling of emotional reaction, occasional epileptic seizures, listlessness, and sometimes stupor (Jones, 2009). The procedure is now seldom used and is, in fact, illegal in many states and countries (Mashour, Walker, & Martuza, 2005).

Prefrontal lobotomy: A surgical treatment that removes or makes lesions (cuts) in the frontal lobes of the brain to reduce anxiety and alleviate depression.

ELECTROCONVULSIVE THERAPY (ECT) TREATMENT

ECT or shock therapy involves the use of a brief burst of electric current aimed at inducing a seizure in the brain. ECT treatment is used most commonly in treating severe depression. This procedure is typically performed in a hospital setting and may involve a series of six to ten treatments spaced over a few months. Side effects can include short-term memory loss, confusion, and disorientation. Typically, these side effects subside in a short time period, but can linger and become problematic for the patient. ECT is rarely used and usually only in situations in which drug therapy is not effective.

Insight Therapy

The major insight therapy is *psychoanalysis,* which is based on Freudian theory. Its identifying characteristic is the belief that alleviating mental disorders depends upon achieving insight into the causes of present behavior. Freud believed mental disturbances result from conflict between basic impulses (id) and conscience (superego) that gives rise to anxiety. The ego's role is to find ways of reducing this anxiety. The psychoanalyst's main task is to uncover basic sources of conflict, many of which will have a sexual basis.

One of the techniques used in psychoanalysis is **free association**, where the patient is encouraged to say whatever comes to mind without evaluating or discarding material. The hope is these associated ideas will eventually lead therapist and patient back to a fundamental source of conflict or, failing that, the therapist will recognize where blocks to association occur. These **mental blocks** are assumed to be the ego's defenses against revealing sensitive issues. Through repeated verbal probing, the analyst may eventually be able to understand these blocks and perhaps even remove them.

The analysis of dreams is another technique employed in psychoanalysis. Freud believed that ego defenses are at their weakest during sleep, and that sources of intense psychodynamic conflict are therefore often revealed during dreams. He distinguished between the apparent (manifest) meaning of dreams (a baseball bat is a baseball bat, whether in a dream or in a batter's hand) and their symbolic meaning (for all you and I know, a baseball bat might be a symbol of penis envy in a dream).

In the course of repeated psychoanalytic sessions, the therapist pays particular attention to the relationship that develops between analyst and patient. According to Freud, this relationship often illustrates **transference**: the therapist becomes somebody of importance in the patient's life, perhaps embodying a source of historical conflict. Thus, patients react to their therapists as they would to a parent or a lover, displaying in their behavior many of the attitudes they might have had toward that important person, perhaps at a time when conflict was being born. In effect, attitudes and feelings that might be the basis of conflict are transferred to the analyst. Recognizing this, the analyst may then interpret this transference, along with information derived from analysis of dreams and of association, thereby arriving at some insight into the source of the patient's conflict.

Free association: A technique used in psychoanalysis where the patient is encouraged to say whatever comes to mind without evaluating or discarding material.

Mental blocks: The ego's defenses against revealing sensitive issues.

Transference: Redirection of feelings directed toward the therapist that are associated with important figures in the patient's life.

Learning-Based and Cognitive Therapy

Therapies based on learning theories stand in sharp contrast to psychoanalysis. The learning therapist is concerned mainly with the manifestations of disorders rather than with their causes, and assumes that these manifestations can be unlearned or that more acceptable forms of behavior can be learned in their stead. Accordingly, these therapies make extensive use of learning principles.

BEHAVIOR MODIFICATION

Behavior modification: The idea that people are influenced by the consequences of their behavior and their immediate environmental circumstances are more relevant than early experiences or psychic conflicts.

Although there are a variety of approaches to **behavior modification**, most are based on the general principle that people are influenced by the consequences of their behavior—that their immediate environmental circumstances are more relevant than early experiences or psychic conflicts.

Systematic desensitization: A type of therapy where the therapist tries to replace an undesirable response with another incompatible and more desirable response. The procedure is particularly effective for phobias.

In a procedure called **systematic desensitization** (or *counterconditioning*), the therapist tries to replace an undesirable response with another incompatible and more desirable response. The procedure is particularly effective for phobias (Head & Gross, 2009). When treating a severe bird phobia, for example, the therapist begins by training the patient in relaxation. Once she has learned to relax, she is presented with the least frightening item on an ordered list of fear-inducing situations that she has previously described—perhaps just an outdoor scene with no birds and no bird noises. She is asked to imagine this scene while relaxing, relaxation being incompatible with anxiety and fear. In successive sessions, the patient is encouraged to imagine other situations until she can imagine a bird without any anxiety. Eventually, she might be able to hold one in her hand.

Exposure therapy: When a therapist exposes a patient to fear- or anxiety-producing stimuli.

Closely related to systematic desensitization is **exposure therapy**, where the patient is simply exposed to fear- or anxiety-producing stimuli. The procedure is much faster than systematic desensitization because it is not based on the notion that the patient should feel no fear. Rather, it is based on the belief that simply exposing the patient repeatedly to the fear-related stimulus will lead to reduction and eventual elimination of fear reactions. Research indicates that exposure therapy, sometimes using computer-based *virtual reality* simulations, can be highly effective in treating anxiety disorders such as PTSD (Reger et al., 2011).

Aversive conditioning: When a therapist attempts to attach negative feelings and bring about avoidance behavior with respect to certain situations.

Aversive conditioning, another learning-based approach, attempts to attach negative feelings and bring about avoidance behavior with respect to certain situations. For example, patients might be subjected to a mild electric shock or other aversive stimulus when they engage in, or think about, some inappropriate behavior. Some sexual disorders such as fetishes can be effectively treated with this approach.

POSITIVE REINFORCEMENT

Another learning-based approach uses positive reinforcement for desirable behavior, sometimes combined with the withdrawal of reinforcement for undesirable behavior. For example, highly withdrawn patients might be given tokens, which can be exchanged for meaningful rewards, for social interaction. Instead of tokens, verbal reinforcement (praise) might be used.

RATIONAL EMOTIVE BEHAVIOR THERAPY

Rational emotive behavior therapy: Therapist has the patient focus on his or her immediate interpretation of the meanings of environmental events, rather than obscure historical causes.

Ellis's (1974; Ellis & MacLaren, 2005) **rational emotive behavior therapy (REBT)** is a *cognitive* therapy. It is premised on the assumption that our cognitive interpretations of events and situations are the root of emotional turmoil. Accordingly, therapy shouldn't focus on obscure historical causes but on the individual's immediate interpretation of the meanings of environmental events.

Ellis lists a number of erroneous assumptions that people make. When these assumptions are violated, the individual is anxious and unhappy. The goal of the therapist is to direct the patient's attention to these irrational ideas and to change them. The whole point is to replace irrational beliefs with more rational ones through cognitive and verbal means. Ellis lists many irrational beliefs, but he describes the following three as the main ones (Ellis, 2003):

1. I must always perform outstandingly well and win everybody's complete approval or I am bad, incompetent, and unworthy.

2. Other people must always treat me well and fairly; otherwise they are rotten and bad and don't deserve a good life.

3. My life must always be favorable, safe, hassle free, and enjoyable; if it isn't, I won't be able to bear it and it won't be worth living.

Ellis describes these irrational ideas as beliefs (B) in his A-B-C theory of disturbance. According to this theory, an emotional reaction or consequence (C) is usually ascribed to some specific experience (A, for activating event). In fact, however, the emotional consequence (C) is not a function of the event (A), but of the beliefs (B) the individual has. Since the majority of these beliefs are irrational (if they were rational, the emotional consequences would not ordinarily be disturbing), the goal of therapy is to replace irrational with rational beliefs (Figure 9.6).

COGNITIVE-BEHAVIORAL THERAPY

CBT is a combination of behavior therapy and cognitive therapy and is a common mode of therapy used today. The premise behind this treatment modality is for a therapist to help the client identify distorted or unhealthy thinking patterns and work toward changing these patterns. The belief is as you change your thoughts, then a change in behavior often ensues.

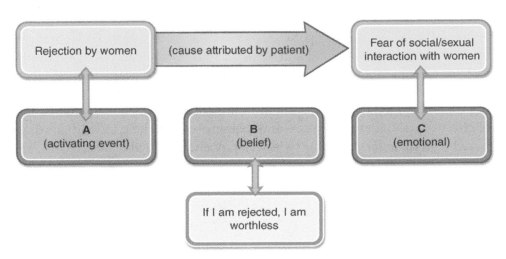

FIGURE 9.6   Ellis's A-B-C theory of disturbance.

The Effectiveness of Therapies

A large number of outcome studies have been conducted to look at the effectiveness of different therapies. Some look at improvements in morale—in the individual's sense of well-being and happiness. Others look at symptom reduction or at the reduction of impairment and at improvements in level of functioning. Many use highly objective measures, such as time spent doing compulsive behaviors, duration of abstinence from alcohol or drugs, incidence of gambling, or number of panic attacks.

Studies suggest some form of therapy is more helpful than no treatment (Smith, Glass, & Miller, 1980). Sharff (2012) and Bickmann (2005) also found people in treatment improved more quickly than those people who did not seek treatment. Although it is argued that no particular form of treatment is better than the other, research has shown that each major form of therapy is superior to no form of treatment or placebo (Prochaska & Norcross, 2010).

Outcome studies indicate clearly that therapies are often remarkably effective for pretty well all mental disorders, including substance abuse (Sledge & Hutchinson, 2010), borderline personality disorder (Waldinger, 2010), depression (Richards & Perri, 2010), and many other disorders. The move today is toward evidence-based treatment approaches, which have clear research support for best practices. Some therapies are clearly more effective than others for specific purposes. For example, *exposure therapy* has been shown to be highly effective in treating or preventing PTSD (Reger et al., 2011). Similarly, there is evidence that rational emotive behavior therapy is effective for depression—as are drug treatments (Sava, Yates, Lupu, Szentagotai, & David, 2009). And drug therapies are effective for an enormous number of mental disorders, including bipolar disorders, anxiety disorders, personality disorders, and psychotic disorders. A few additional types of therapy include: light therapy, Eye Movement Desensitization Reprocessing (EMDR), art therapy, play therapy, and animal-assisted therapy.

Summary

A mental disorder includes patterns of behavior or thought that are not reasonable or easily understood and are associated with "clinically significant" distress or impairment in coping with the environment. Many individuals in the United States are impacted by a mental disorder every year. Psychologists use the *DSM-5* to help diagnosis a multitude of disorders and a wide variety of effective treatment approaches and therapies exist to help individuals diagnosed with disorders continue to lead happy and productive lives.

© nenetus, 2014. Used under license
from Shutterstock, Inc.

CHAPTER TEN

SOCIAL PSYCHOLOGY

Darin Challacombe
Fort Hays State University

LEARNING OBJECTIVES

- Define social psychology.
- Differentiate among the terms *compliance* and *conformity*.
- Differentiate among the terms *attitudes, beliefs, opinions,* and *stereotypes*.
- Recall key forces related to attitude change.
- Define aggression.
- Describe the causes and manifestations of antisocial and prosocial behavior.
- Describe the concept of love.

> *You is smart. You is kind. You is important.*
>
> —Aibileen Clark to Mae Mobley in *The Help* (Stockett, 2009)

The 1960s were the stage for many changes in the United States, including the civil rights movement. As a recent college graduate, Eugenia "Skeeter" Phelan returns home to her high-society life in Jackson, Mississippi, with the desire to become a writer. Skeeter obtains a job with a local newspaper writing a column on household tips. Skeeter requests help on tips for the column from Aibileen Clark—a Black maid who works for a White family, the Holbrooks. Seeing the disparity between these families and their loyal maids, Skeeter decides to write about the maids, starting with Aibileen who has spent her entire life caring for others' children. Through persuasion and with great reluctance, Aibileen agrees to provide her story to Skeeter. The fact that a White person is interacting on a personal level with a Black person violates the Jim Crow laws, which were still very much in effect in Mississippi during the first part of the 1960s. At the same time, Hilly Holbrook, Aibileen's employer and Skeeter's best friend, attempts to renew the community's waning respect for these laws. After several prominent civil rights workers are killed, more maids join Aibileen and tell their stories to Skeeter, who is finally able to publish her book using a pseudonym.

The book and subsequent movie under the same name, *The Help*, provides a story of friendship and respect that transcends the (then) present societal status quos. This book also illustrates two of **social psychology's** most important concerns: human relationships—as illustrated in the friendship formed between Skeeter and Aibileen—and how stereotypes can be pervasive through communities—evident in how others in Mississippi respond to the changes brought on by the civil rights movement.

Social psychology: Studies the relationships among individuals or between individuals and groups.

What Is Social Psychology?

Social psychology is concerned with relationships among individuals or between individuals and groups. In Allport's (1968) terms, "Social psychologists regard their discipline as an attempt to understand how the *thought, feeling,* and *behavior* of individuals are influenced by the *actual, imagined,* or *implied* presence of others" (p. 3). Thus, social psychology says something about the opinions and stereotypes illustrated by Hilly and the Jim Crow laws, and also on how the relationship between Skeeter and Aibileen impacted the community's attempts to create positive civil rights changes (Stockett, 2009).

Social psychology's subject matter spans almost all facets of human behavior minus those that are clearly individual and not affected by the presence of others. Most of what we learn, think, feel, and do is influenced by others. Very few people have lives totally devoid of human relationships, and complete social isolation would require almost geographic remoteness or some form of mental disorder. Social psychology, however, tries to understand the socially influenced aspects of attitudes, relationships, and behaviors.

Attitudes and Attitude Change

Understanding social influence is paramount to understanding the formation and changing of attitudes, opinions, stereotypes, and prejudices.

Attitude: Prevailing and consistent tendency to react in a given way.

Opinion: Evaluations, which lack the strong motivational consequences of attitudes.

Stereotypes: Widely held beliefs about groups based on illogical reasoning or faulty generalization.

An **attitude** is a prevailing and consistent tendency to react in a given way based on individual beliefs. Attitudes have important emotional connotations, as well as behavioral and cognitive components. Attitudes are either positive or negative; neutral reactions do not qualify as attitudes. Attitudes have strong motivational consequences, distinguishing them from **opinions**. Although opinions are also evaluations, they do not drive people to action like attitudes do (Figure 10.1).

Stereotypes are widely held attitudes and opinions concerning identifiable groups. Stereotypes usually include value-laden beliefs and are often based on emotional reaction, illogical reasoning, and faulty generalization.

Although stereotypes are often assumed to be negative, they can also be positive. Negative stereotypes have been shown to have detrimental effects on many kinds of interactions, including, for example, the perception of older drivers as more prone to accidents (Joanisse, Gagnon, & Voloaca, 2013). In the Joanisse et al. study, older adults that were told about the negative stereotype of being more prone to accidents actually had more accidents than older adults not provided the stereotype. Current research also suggests that even positive stereotypes may have unintended negative effects (Markham, 2013).

FIGURE 10.1   The three components of attitudes and how emotions motivate behavior.
Photo © Ollyy, 2014. Used under license from Shutterstock, Inc.

As generalized beliefs about groups, stereotypes are virtually indispensable in daily interaction. They're like cognitive shortcuts telling us how to react without having to wait to see how other people are going to behave. For example, we may have a stereotype telling us panhandlers become aggressive if we look them in the eye but throw nothing in their hats. So either we don't look them in the eye or we toss a coin into their hats.

Not surprisingly, there is considerable research that some stereotypes agree remarkably well with more objective evaluations (Lee, Jussim, & McCauley, 1995). This doesn't mean stereotypes are invariably accurate and useful; many are bigoted, inappropriate, and plain unjust.

Unlike stereotypes, which are widely held beliefs about groups, **prejudices** are personal rather than shared prejudgments. To be prejudiced implies having arrived at an opinion prior to obtaining relevant facts. Even today, many people still hold prejudices against others who they see as different.

Prejudices: Personal beliefs about groups based on illogical reasoning or faulty generalization.

How attitudes, opinions, stereotypes, and prejudices are different is evident in a sample of most people's behaviors and beliefs. For example, a person's strong feeling that involvement in war is immoral and their attempt to persuade others they should protest illustrates an *attitude*—a personal, emotional, and clearly motivating belief. If this person were convinced military personnel are highly immoral even though he or she has had little exposure to them, that conviction would be a *prejudice*—a preconceived judgment. The individual's personal belief that seatbelt legislation is unnecessary and uneconomical is an opinion—a personal belief not necessarily shared by others and not directed toward an identifiable group. And their assumption that Americans are sufficiently resourceful and industrious that they will easily cope with global warming and other crises illustrates a *stereotype*— a belief about a specific group shared by a significant number of people.

Compliance and Conformity

Attitudes are powerful motives for behavior. Although attitudes tend to be stable and long lasting, they can change in response to various factors, including new information we acquire, social pressure, tendencies we have to obey or disobey, and the effects of persuasion. When we change our attitude, we usually also change our behavior by conforming or complying with the force or forces that changed our attitude.

The urge to conform is a powerful social motive, and this urge does much to ensure that societies function smoothly.

© bikeriderlondon, 2014. Used under license from Shutterstock, Inc.

Conformity: Long-term changes in behavior where attitudes have been affected, opinions modified, or stereotypes altered.

Compliance: Short-term changes in behavior, not altering beliefs.

We define **conformity** as long-term changes in behavior where attitudes have been affected, opinions modified, or stereotypes and prejudices altered. **Compliance**, on the other hand, usually indicates short-term changes in behavior that don't significantly alter any of these types of beliefs.

The distinction between conformity and compliance is subtler in practice than in theory. My son hates vegetables. If my son must eat all his vegetables before I allow him to leave the dinner table, he is only complying, assuming he still does not like vegetables. In order for my son to conform, he must learn to enjoy eating vegetables, and, subsequently, eat all of his vegetables off his plate by choice. If you came into my house and saw my son eating all his vegetables, you would not know if he was complying or conforming.

To bring the illustration closer to home, you may be said to conform to social norms to the extent that you approve of them and therefore act accordingly. Complying with the same social norms might involve exactly the same behavior but would be based on motives other than your approval of the norms.

Social Pressure and Compliance

Solomon Asch (1955) conducted one of the most classic studies of compliance. In a typical experiment, "participants" were placed in a semicircle facing an easel on which the experimenter placed two large cards. One of these cards had a single vertical line on it (the standard); the other had three vertical lines of different lengths, one of which is clearly equal in length to the standard (Figure 10.2). In a "test of perceptual accuracy," the "participants" were required to determine which of the three lines was equal to the standard.

The test was not of perceptual accuracy but of social pressure and its effects on compliance. Only one of the "participants" was actually a participant; the other "participants" were confederates. The confederates had been instructed to answer correctly for the first few trials and then to answer incorrectly but to agree on the incorrect answer. The actual participant had no reason to suspect the other individuals were not also participants. The true participant was the second to last to provide an answer.

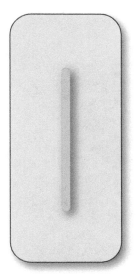 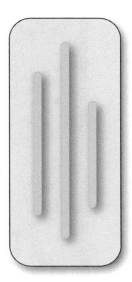

FIGURE 10.2 Asch (1955) used a simple visual perception test to determine the effects of social pressure. Both participants and the experimenter's confederates were asked which comparison line is the same length as the standard line. The confederates all chose an obviously incorrect line, but the confederate's solidarity pressured the participants to also choose an incorrect line.

In a series of studies carried out in three different institutions, over 120 participants answered incorrectly 36.8% of the time. A control group not exposed to social pressure answered correctly more than 99% of the time. Typically, participants were confronted with the conflicting opinions of as many as eight confederates. However, varying the number of confederates revealed that a majority of three was equally effective in eliciting compliance with the group (Asch, 1955). This observation is strikingly similar to the ancient Chinese proverb, *three men make a tiger* (which is interpreted to mean that people will believe the most absurd things as long as enough other people seem to believe them; see Figure 10.3).

When researchers questioned participants in the Asch experiment later, the participants indicated they knew all along their responses and those of the confederates were in error. But they still complied—later explaining their behavior in a variety of ways, such as "poor eyesight" or "misjudgment." Interestingly, not all the participants were

Are you part of the crowd or do you try to be unique?
© iQoncept, 2014. Used under license from Shutterstock, Inc.

equally susceptible to the effects of group pressure: one fourth of the participants continued to answer completely independently, never agreeing with the incorrect majority. In contrast, others nearly always agreed with the majority.

An individual's willingness to conform in social settings has since been studied outside of the lab setting and even by the TV industry for entertainment purposes. Another example of how our behaviors might be changed by those around

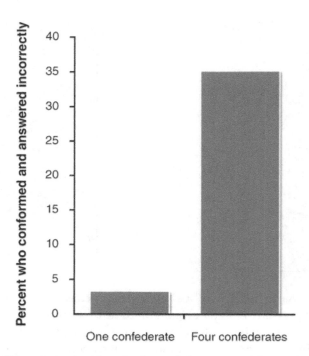

FIGURE 10.3   When paired with a single confederate, participants in the Asch (1955) study were about as accurate as if they had been alone. But when paired with four, they complied with the majority more than one third of the time. Adding more confederates did not increase compliance significantly.

us in everyday life is depicted in the following video. Think about what you would do in the same situation: https://www.youtube.com/watch?v=uuvGh_n3I_M

Many people interpret these experimental results as evidence of the gullibility of individuals and their susceptibility to group pressure. The implication is that these are undesirable qualities. However, it is precisely because we are susceptible to group pressures that complex social institutions such as governments, schools, and churches work. It is also because we are sensitive to the opinions and attitudes of others that we are able to interact effectively with them.

This should not be taken to mean compliance and conformity are always good; however, it does mean they are not always bad, in the same way that stereotypes aren't always totally wrong and useless.

Obedience

Let's say your superior orders you to do something like hurt some innocent person: How likely are you to contradict the order? Or will you just do as you are told?

THE MILGRAM STUDIES

Milgram (1963, 1965), in a remarkable series of controversial experiments, provided an answer to these questions. In Milgrim's studies, participants were duped into believing they were confederates of an experimenter studying the effects of punishment on learning. An alleged participant (actually a confederate, termed a *stooge* in this experiment) was to be presented with a series of learning tasks while attached to electrodes so he could be shocked whenever he made an error. The real participant's task was to depress the switch that would deliver the shock. Participants were first connected to the electrodes and administered a mild shock so they would have no reason to think that the shocks would not be real. They were then seated in front of an instrument panel containing a series of switches labeled from 15 to 450 volts, in 15-volt increments. Verbal descriptions above the switches ranged from "Slight shock" to "Danger: severe shock" at 390 volts and "XXX" at 435 volts.

In Milgram's (1963) first experiment, "victims" (stooges who did not actually receive any shocks) were placed in a separate room and were instructed to make a predetermined number of errors. The participants controlling the switches were instructed to administer a shock for every error the victim made, beginning with the first switch and progressing as high as necessary, in one-step increments. If a participant hesitated or indicated any unwillingness to continue, the experimenter would employ a predetermined verbal "prod"; that prod failing, a second would be employed, then a third, and finally a fourth. In all cases, the prods were given in sequence:

- **Prod 1.** *Please continue, or please go on.*
- **Prod 2.** *The experiment requires that you continue.*
- **Prod 3.** *It is absolutely essential that you continue.*
- **Prod 4.** *You have no other choice. You must go on. (p. 374)*

Amazingly, none of the participants categorically refused to obey from the outset. In fact, of the 40 original participants, 26 obeyed the experimenter's instructions right to the very end ("victims" committed sufficient errors to ensure that participants would have an opportunity to administer the most severe shock—450 volts). The remaining 14 all obeyed until at least the 300-volt level (Figure 10.4).

In related studies, Milgram (1965) looked at the effect of the distance between participant and victim using four different experimental conditions. In one, the participant could see, hear, and touch the victim, since both were in the same room. In a second, the participant could hear and see the stooge (typical a male confederate), but could not touch him. In a third condition, the participant could hear the stooge, but not see him, a curtain having been drawn between the two. In a final experimental condition, the participant could neither see nor hear the victim.

Again, participants complied with the experimenter's requests. But now, average intensity of shocks increased in direct proportion with the distance between the participant and the victim, with the highest shocks being administered when the participant could not see or hear the victim.

One finding that is sometimes overlooked when reporting the more sensational results of the Milgram obedience studies is that most participants, whether or not they obeyed, were disturbed by the procedure. Milgram (1963) writes:

> In a large number of cases the degree of tension reached extremes that are rarely seen in socio-psychological laboratory studies. [Participants] were observed to sweat, tremble, stutter, bite their lips, groan, and dig their fingernails into their flesh. These were characteristic rather than exceptional responses to the experiment. . . . On one occasion we observed a seizure so violently convulsive that it was necessary to call a halt to the experiment. (p. 375)

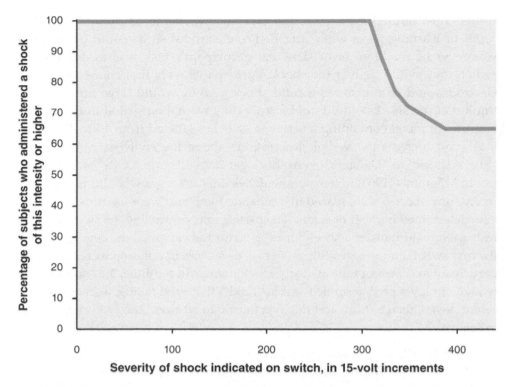

FIGURE 10.4   All participants in the Milgram study "obeyed" and administered shocks beginning at 15 volts and going to at least 300 volts. The next switch was labeled "extreme intensity shock." Five of 40 participants refused to go any further; 26 went all the way to 450 volts.

Studies such as these are disturbing for a number of reasons. They reveal aggressive aspects of humanity that many would prefer not to admit; they underline the power of authority and compliance in contrast to individual choice and freedom; and they present some serious moral issues with respect to deceiving participants into engaging in behaviors that potentially are psychologically damaging.

Given the fact that psychological investigations now typically require approval by an ethics committee and strict adherence to ethical guidelines, the Milgram studies have not often been replicated. Burger (2009) did replicate these studies with one significant variation: When participants reached the level of 150 volts (the point at which the "stooge" has been instructed to moan and protest), the experiment was discontinued.

Strikingly, Burger (2009) found obedience rates were only slightly lower 45 years after the original Milgram studies. Burger also found obedience rates for men and women did not differ significantly. Although, as Twenge (2009) noted, there has apparently been an increase in personality traits reflecting nonconformity (higher assertiveness and self-esteem), there continues to be a strong urge to comply with authority and to conform to the majority.

THE PRISON EXPERIMENT

Unquestioning compliance with authority has been dramatically demonstrated in concentration-camp atrocities performed under direct orders from powerful, potentially highly punitive or highly reinforcing superiors. More recently, it has been evident in the wanton acts of abuse and torture of prisoners at Abu Ghraib in Iraq (Bartone, 2010). Between 2003 and 2004, American personnel stationed at Abu Ghraib prison in Iraq tortured and abused enemy detainees. There may, however, be more to these atrocities than simple compliance with authority.

There is a culture among prisoners and guards, Zimbardo (2007) explains, that is the key to understanding how abuse and torture can occur under these circumstances. In the classic 1971 experiment carried out at Stanford, 12 young men, who were among 75 who had answered an advertisement asking for volunteers for an experiment on prison life, were abruptly arrested by police, handcuffed, and brought into a prison (actually, a converted basement space in a Stanford building). There they were stripped, searched, deloused, fingerprinted, and in every way treated like real prisoners. Their guards were 12 other student volunteers instructed to do whatever was required to maintain order and command respect.

The Stanford prison experiment suggests that we can quickly and easily adopt roles even when they run counter to our values. The Milgram studies further underscored our willingness to obey those in authority.
© sakhorn, 2014. Used under license from Shutterstock, Inc.

The results were sobering: Almost immediately, guards developed coercive, aggressive tactics, humiliating and dehumanizing prisoners. The guards forced the prisoners to do things like clean out toilet bowls with their bare hands, count aloud to reinforce their new numerical identities, and do physical exercise as "punishment" when they made errors. The conditions were so severe that 5 of the 12 prisoners had to be "released" before the experiment ended. The experiment was slated to run for 14 days, but it was abruptly terminated on the 6th day when one of the more than 50 outsiders who had seen the prison was shocked at what she saw and raised objections about the ethics of the experiment (Zimbardo, 2007).

The effects of the Stanford prison experiment were far greater than anticipated. Both the prisoners and the guards carried their roles to an unforeseen extreme. Fully one third of the guards exhibited what Zimbardo describes as genuinely sadistic tendencies. What the study illustrated was the power of institutions and of institutionalized roles. In contrast, the Milgram experiments were more about the power of individual authority.

The entire Stanford prison study was photographed and filmed and is available online (Stanford Prison Experiment, 2011).

Persuasion

Social influence is a powerful and pervasive force. We know people are influenced by norms expressed in the behaviors and attitudes of others, and we also know they respond to authority and to the roles they're called on to play. Research and common sense also suggest there are many subtle forms of social influence to which we are responsive. **Persuasion** is a global term for some of these influences. It refers to deliberate, usually verbal, attempts to alter beliefs or behavior. Television commercials, religious and political

Persuasion: Deliberate attempts to alter behavior or beliefs.

Persuading someone to do something can be hard. Wouldn't it be nice if we all had this key on our computers?
© iQoncept, 2014. Used under license from Shutterstock, Inc.

propaganda, newspaper and magazine advertising, and political campaigning all represent attempts at persuasion.

The most powerful forms of persuasion are those that succeed in changing attitudes rather than simply behavior. Attitudes may change as a result of events within the person, a typically slow process. This change may result from rational decisions and occur very rapidly. Attitudes may also change as a result of external events that are accidental rather than deliberately persuasive. Thus, an individual who is rescued from death by a member of a minority group toward which they held highly negative attitudes may quite suddenly develop positive attitudes toward the group. Attitudes may also change as a result of persuasion.

Three characteristics of persuasion are important in determining its effectiveness: the nature of the message, its source, and some of the characteristics of the person being persuaded.

IMPORTANCE OF MESSAGE CHARACTERISTICS

The nature of the message is important: It is much easier to persuade someone of something fitting with previous beliefs or with the individual's goals and wishes. For example, it is easier to believe a house is haunted if you already believe in ghosts or spirits. Conversely, it is difficult to change attitudes when the message runs counter to strongly entrenched prejudices and stereotypes.

IMPORTANCE OF MESSAGE SOURCE

Belief in the importance of the *source* of persuasion is evident in the advertising media's use of powerful models in their attempts to persuade. Research in social psychology suggests the belief is warranted. Persuasion coming from a source marked by qualities such as expertise, liking, and high trust is most effective (Feng & MacGeorge, 2010). Similarly, people are more easily persuaded by opinions apparently shared by many, rather than by few. Horcajo, Petty, and Brinol (2010) presented participants with strong or weak persuasive arguments, ascribing these either to a "majority" or to a "minority." Not surprisingly, whether they were strong or weak arguments, those arguments attributed to a majority source were more persuasive than those arguments thought to come from a minority.

The most powerful forms of persuasion are those that succeed in changing attitudes. That this will then result in a change in behavior is the hope of all politicians as they, like this man, try to persuade us.
© Halfpoint, 2014. Used under license from Shutterstock, Inc.

The persuader's motives also play an important role (Ranganath, Spellman, & Joy-Gaba, 2010). When persuaders were arguing in their own best interests, the persuasion was not nearly as effective as when the argument was opposed to the persuader's self-interest. When petroleum-linked interests suggest water and air contamination are not increasing as a result of oilfield activity, you are unlikely to believe them. The same argument presented by a radical "green" group is much more convincing.

IMPORTANCE OF AUDIENCE CHARACTERISTICS

Finally, certain characteristics of the person being persuaded, such as intelligence and independence, are also important. In one study, Cacioppo, Petty, Kao, and Rodriguez (1986) had participants read either a high-quality or a low-quality essay relating to why a university should institute comprehensive examinations. The more intelligent participants were more convinced by the high-quality essay. In contrast, other participants seemed less sensitive to the quality of the argument and were as easily convinced by the low-quality as by the high-quality essay.

In spite of these studies, attitudes are, by definition, pervasive predispositions to respond in given ways; as such, they resist change. Although it may be relatively simple for a skilled social psychologist to persuade individuals to vote for her, she may experience considerably more difficulty in getting them to love members of minority groups against whom they have highly negative prejudices. Persuasion is not likely to be at all effective in such endeavors, but prolonged face-to-face contact in a cooperative situation might be.

Cognitive Dissonance

In Chapter 6, we saw another source of attitude change: **cognitive dissonance**. Cognitive dissonance describes a situation where there is conflict among behavior, beliefs, or attitudes. The dissonance model predicts people will change their attitudes to conform to their behaviors when there is a conflict between the two, but only when there is insufficient justification for the behavior and when the behavior has been engaged in willingly. Experimentally, participants who were paid significant amounts for dissonant behavior, or who were forced to comply, showed little attitude change later.

In Shakespeare's *Romeo and Juliet*, the two youth brave the rejection of their families for their love.
© Nando Machado, 2014. Used under license from Shutterstock, Inc.

Cognitive dissonance is a theme in many movies and books. In Romeo and Juliet, the two Verona families, the Capulets and Montagues, are enemies. Yet, the movie is about the love between Juliet, a Capulet, and Romeo, a Montague. The cognitive dissonance is that Juliet and Romeo should be enemies, but fall madly in love with each other instead.

Researchers have studied the effects of forcing participants to engage in dissonant behavior, theorizing that participants exposed to the most severe threats for engaging (or not engaging) in some dissonance-inducing behavior will experience the least amount of dissonance. In other words, the participants would be

Cognitive dissonance: A situation where conflict exists among behavior, beliefs, or attitudes.

expected to change their attitudes—and their behaviors—less than those exposed to milder threats.

To study this prediction, Wan and Chiou (2010) selected 218 college students identified as having a strong inclination toward online gaming addiction. They had these students play a new and highly engaging online game and then asked them, individually, to convince a younger adolescent the game was not fun. They were instructed to continue until they had succeeded in convincing the "participant." In the "severe threat" manipulation, participants were told if they were unsuccessful in convincing the adolescent to agree with them, their parents would be informed of their addiction inclination. In the "mild threat" manipulation, participants were told their academic advisors would be notified if they gave up the persuasion task before completing it.

As expected, participants in the severe threat condition were far less likely to have changed their positive attitudes toward the online game. Because of the severity of the threat, their dissonant behavior was justified. In contrast, those exposed to mild threats would be expected to experience more dissonance because their behavior would not be so easily justified. As predicted, they were more likely to change their attitudes.

The bottom line is that if you resort to severe threats to coerce someone to do or not do something, you are less likely to get them to change their attitudes and subsequent behavior than if you can bring about the same behavior with less coercion—whether it be a reward or the threat of punishment.

In Wan and Chiou's 2010 study, participants were threatened into convincing younger adolescents that a video game was not fun. As predicted, participants in the severe threat condition were less likely to have changed their positive attitudes toward the online game at the end of the experiment.

© Elena Elisseeva, 2014. Used under license from Shutterstock, Inc.

Attribution and Attitude Change

Attributions: Inferences regarding the causes of behavior.

Dispositional attributions: Causes of behavior related to characteristics of an individual.

Situational attributions: Causes of behavior related to characteristics of the situation.

As we saw in Chapter 6, one explanation for attitude change in dissonance situations has to do with the **attributions** we make for our behaviors and feelings and for the behavior and feelings of others (the reasons we ascribe to them). We are constantly observing our behavior, the behavior of others, and the circumstances surrounding behavior. As we observe, we make inferences about ourselves and others, attributing causes to the behaviors we observe. In some cases our attributions are **dispositional attributions** (they involve characteristics of the actor); in others they are **situational attributions** (they involve characteristics of the situation); and perhaps in many cases we arrive at mixed attributions.

We can further explain an attribution-based attitude change following dissonant behavior with the following: If I willingly do A without compulsion or reward and am then asked to express my attitudes about doing A, I will most likely attribute my behavior to the fact that I believe that doing A is right, good, and consistent with my attitudes. If, however, I am compelled to do A against my inclinations, I can attribute my behavior to causes within myself or to the situation. If the situation justifies my behavior (the reward is sufficient or the threat is compelling enough), I will likely invoke a situational attribution and I won't change my attitude. If the situation doesn't justify my behavior, I need to attribute it to a personal characteristic (a disposition). The result is that I may change my attitude toward the activity.

OVERJUSTIFICATION

As described, attribution theories of attitude change in situations of forced compliance (dissonance-creating situations) maintain when there is low justification for engaging in dissonant behavior, people infer they did so because they wanted to. In contrast, when there is high justification, they attribute their behavior to external circumstances (e.g., compulsion or reward).

Lepper and Greene (1975, 1978) and others have also investigated the effects of justification on *consonant* behavior. These authors have proposed an **overjustification** hypothesis that says, in effect, large external rewards for behavior that are initially intrinsically motivated may undermine our attitudes toward the behavior. For example, if you whistle because you like whistling (intrinsic motivation: positive attitudes toward whistling), and later someone promises you a high reward for whistling, you might in the end come to like whistling much less.

Overjustification: Large external rewards reduce the intrinsic value of a behavior.

How does this hypothesis follow from attribution theory? Bright and Penrod (2009) describe the process as follows: Given our tendency to attribute our behaviors to intrinsic or extrinsic factors, following a behavior for which external justification is very salient (a behavior is externally *overjustified*), we are likely to attribute that behavior more to external causes than to internal causes. Having done so, we modify our attitudes (internal causes of behavior) and become less positively disposed toward the behavior.

This analysis might seem to contradict common sense. We have long assumed people like to do things that are highly rewarded, and have perhaps naively assumed if we increase rewards associated with a behavior, positive attitudes toward that behavior should also increase. But research on the overjustification hypothesis indicates these beliefs are wrong at least some of the time.

Antisocial Behaviors

How do we justify our antisocial behaviors like aggression and violence? Do external rewards serve to *justify* and explain these behaviors? Is there something in our dispositions that explains them?

Aggression and Violence

A popular stereotype of North American males is that they are assertive, intrusive, domineering individuals bent on achieving their goals even at the expense of others. People base this view on the observation of **aggression** in males. Aggression is defined as an action deliberately intended to do harm or undertaken with no consideration for the harm it might cause others. Aggressive behavior is basic to organized competitive sports such as football and hockey, is a key to success in the business and academic worlds, is one of the main themes of the entertainment media, and is characteristic of much human interaction.

Aggression: Actions with the intent to harm others.

FIGURE 10.5   An aggression continuum. Aggression is defined as actions intended to harm others or to achieve one's goals without consideration of others. Thus, in a strict sense, assertive, competitive, intrusive, domineering, and even violent behaviors (such as might be evident in sports) are not examples of aggression unless they are intended to do harm. Terrorism, a form of violence perpetrated against civilian groups, is an extreme form of aggression.

Photo © ArtFamily, 2014. Used under license from Shutterstock, Inc.

THEORIES OF AGGRESSION

It is important to note at the outset that strong assertiveness and competitiveness are not instances of aggression when they are not intended to inflict harm on others; nor are they undesirable in all circumstances. Although aggression may involve violence—actual physical damage to persons or property—it might also be passive (Figure 10.5).

Frustration–Aggression   A number of beliefs have dominated social psychology's attempts to understand and explain aggression. Among them is Dollard and Miller's **frustration–aggression hypothesis**—the contention that aggression is the result of anger and the most important cause of anger is **frustration** (Dollard, Miller, Doob, Mowrer, & Sears, 1939). To be frustrated is to be prevented from reaching a goal. The Dollard and Miller hypothesis argues that, following frustration, anger is experienced; but anger will result in aggression only if a suitable object or person releases the aggression (Figure 10.6).

This explanation of aggression has often been used to explain terrorism. Terrorism, an extreme form of aggression, may be linked to the frustration accompanying poverty, lack of opportunity, and repression (e.g., Zinchenko, 2009). In support of the frustration–aggression hypothesis, Hakulinen et al. (2013) report that higher unemployment is associated with higher hostility than among those employed.

Territoriality   Another explanation, attributed to ethologists, is based on the assumption that we are aggressive by nature. Ethologists base this explanation on observations of aggression among nonhuman animals, and the assumption is that since aggression appears to be common among other animals, it must have a biological basis.

Frustration–aggression hypothesis: Hypothesis that frustration leads to anger, which will result in aggression if a suitable object or person releases the aggression.

Frustration: Occurs when someone is prevented from achieving a goal.

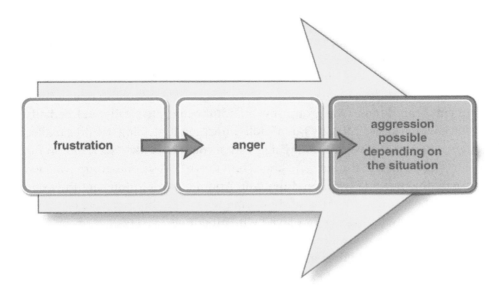

FIGURE 10.6 According to the Dollard and Miller frustration–aggression hypothesis, frustration leads to different degrees of anger, ranging from mild irritation to blind fury. Depending on the situation and the depth of emotion, frustration can also lead to aggressive behavior.

According to this theory, certain stimuli in the environment serve as releasers for aggression. In some cases, the stimuli are highly specific and have clear survival or reproductive significance, as when bighorn sheep fight for the right to mate. In other cases, the stimuli are less specific, as in the case of **territoriality**. For example, male chimpanzees patrol defined geographic areas, intent on aggressively repelling any encroachment by males from other communities. Those who violate their boundaries risk death (Amsler, 2010). The survival value of many aggressive behaviors in nonhuman animals and their frequent instinct such as specificity (i.e., the fact that aggression usually occurs only in response to specific conditions) provide strong evidence that aggression in animals is at least partly genetically based.

© Kitch Bain, 2014. Used under license from Shutterstock, Inc.

The situation with humans, however, is not as clear. Although there is a possibility that we have (or had) instinctual tendencies toward aggressiveness, learning and environment affect so much of our behavior that "instinctual" tendencies like territoriality are difficult to isolate. For example, some argue wars reflect territoriality (Fields, 2010) and others have suggested gang conflict might also be associated with territoriality (Deuchar & Holligan, 2010).

Territoriality: Example of an innate or biological aggressive tendency.

Still, the fact is that there are human societies where aggressive behavior is at an extreme minimum (e.g., the Zuni, the Hutterites, and the Amish); and there are others where it is at the opposite extreme (e.g., the Ik of Uganda, the Mundugumor of New Guinea, the Yanomamo of the Amazon). Although the existence of peaceloving societies does not prove we have no genetic tendencies toward aggression, it does indicate environmental and social factors are important.

Social learning theory:
Argues aggression is a result of learning from models in our environment.

Social Learning   **Social learning theory** (see Chapter 4) is a widely supported theory, which argues that aggressive behavior is often learned as a result of observing aggressive models.

In a classic study looking at the effects of aggressive models on children, Bandura, Ross, and Ross (1961) exposed 3- to 6-year-old children to one of three experimental conditions. One group saw an adult being physically and verbally aggressive with a large, inflated "Bobo" doll (punching it, striking it with a mallet, kicking it, sitting on it, while making aggressive comments like "sock him in the nose...," "throw him in the air...," "knock him down"). A second group watched as the experimenter totally ignored the doll. And a control group saw the Bobo doll only in the testing part of the study, during which the children were observed as they interacted with the doll or played with other toys.

The results of this study clearly illustrate the effect of aggressive models. When left alone with the doll, children exposed to the aggressive model were significantly more aggressive than children exposed to nonaggressive models. And often, their aggression was precisely imitative: If the model punched the doll, that is what these children did; if the model kicked the doll instead, then that, too, is what they did. And, strikingly, those exposed to nonaggressive models engaged in far less aggressive behavior than those not exposed to any models at all (Figure 10.7).

This study provides strong support for a social learning theory of aggression. And, in fact, many predictions based on social learning theory have been supported by research. For example, we would expect children who observe violence and aggression would themselves be more aggressive. In fact, that is often the case: Children who witness parental violence and abuse are more likely to be aggressive as adolescents (Ferguson, Miguel, & Hartley, 2009). And there is evidence, as well, that violence in children's television programs tends to increase aggression among viewers (Linder & Gentile, 2009; Strasburger, 2009).

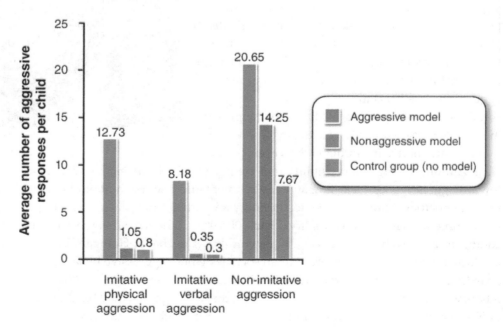

FIGURE 10.7   In the Bandura, Ross, and Ross (1961) study, children exposed to violent models consistently behaved more aggressively with the Bobo doll.

Physiology   We know that aggression, like all emotions, also has a physiological basis. For example, it appears aggression may be associated with hormones (injections of testosterone increase aggressiveness in monkeys); with olfaction (certain strains of mice respond aggressively to other mice who've been smeared with urine from mice that would ordinarily be aggressed upon); with brain damage or dysfunction or with stimulation of appropriate areas of the thalamus (rage can be produced in cats as a result of electrical stimulation); and with certain drugs (alcohol disinhibits aggression and is involved in a large number of violent crimes).

Research suggests at least five neurotransmitters and two hormones—the most important of which is testosterone—may be implicated in serious violent crimes (Beaver, 2010). But the fact that aggression has a physiological basis is not an adequate explanation for aggressive behavior because all aspects of human behavior have physiological bases. Nevertheless, knowledge of the physiological underpinnings of aggression, and of how these interact with the environment to produce aggression and violence, may prove useful in controlling extremes of violence (e.g., using psychosurgery and drugs; Figure 10.8).

VIOLENCE IN SOCIETY

The most obvious instances of aggression in society are those involving overt acts of violence: rape, homicide, assault, and destruction of property. Interpersonal violence, which includes the first three of these, is committed primarily by males. The extent to which these acts can be attributed to frustration, deprivation, pain, or sex-related factors, and the extent to which character and personality disorders or other factors are involved, is not clear. There is little doubt, however, that each of these factors can play a significant role.

The incidence of violent crimes in Western industrialized societies appears to have declined somewhat during the last decades. Still, the incidence of violence is high, with a total of 429 violent crimes per 100,000 U.S. population in 2009 (U.S. Census Bureau, 2012; Figure 10.9).

Violence in society is reflected not only in crime, but in international aggression as well. In the last century alone, well over half of all nations have been involved in war. Violence in the home is another example and one which is not always obvious. Child abuse presents one inexact index; the fact that 25% or more of all homicides and assaults involve members of the same family provides a second

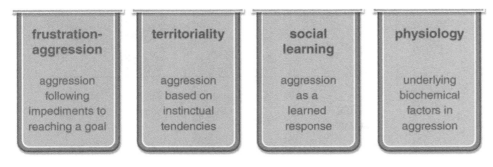

FIGURE 10.8   Four explanations for aggression. These aren't mutually exclusive, as aggression is often a function of several underlying factors.

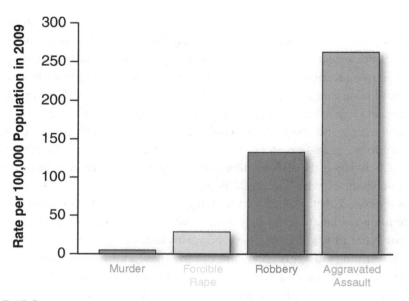

FIGURE 10.9   Number of violent crimes per 100,000 population in the United States in 2009. U.S. Census Bureau (2012). *Statistical Abstract, Table 307.*

index. In fact, violence among intimate partners, surely a prime source of aggressive models for children, is alarmingly high: 2,600 acts of rape, robbery, assault, and homicide per 100,000 population in 2008, with almost 85% of these acts carried out against women (U.S. Census Bureau, 2012). In 2007, 1,185 women and 346 men in the United States were killed by their partners (Figure 10.10); over half a million women and nearly as many men were victims of reported physical assault (U.S. Census Bureau, 2010).

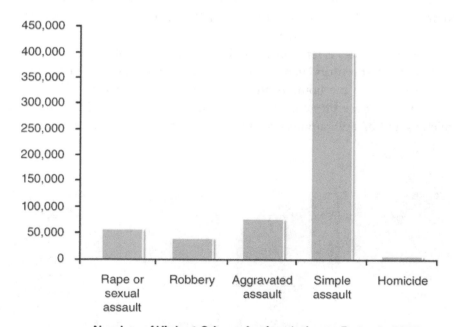

Number of Violent Crimes Against Intimate Partners 2007

FIGURE 10.10   Number of violent crimes committed against intimate partners in the United States in 2007. U.S. Census Bureau (2010). *Statistical Abstract, Table 307.*

Bystander Apathy

In the late 1970s' Monty Python movie *The Life of Brian*, the protagonist Brian unintentionally inspires a group of rabid followers who think he is a messiah and who devotedly follow him around, convinced that every little thing that happens around him is a miracle. Increasingly frantic to be rid of this mob, he yells at them, "Look. You've got it all wrong. You don't need to follow me. You don't need to follow anybody! You've got to think for yourselves. You're all individuals!"

"Yes, we are all individuals!" they respond in chorus.

"You're all different," says Brian.

"Yes, we are all different!" they respond. Except for one small voice from somewhere in the crowd. "I'm not," it says.

"Shh! Shhhh! Shhh!" Brian's followers respond.

Was this just another movie? Or, was this an accurate reflection of mob psychology and the effects of social pressure? How much of what we think and do is determined by the groups of which we are part?

The classic relevant case in social psychology literature is the story of Kitty Genovese, who was brutally attacked as she returned home from work at 3 o'clock one morning (Latané & Darley, 1968). What made her story remarkable was that 38 of her neighbors in Kew Gardens in New York supposedly came to their windows when she cried out in terror; none came to her assistance, even though her stalker took over half an hour to murder her, even leaving once and returning later to continue his attack. Initial reports are that no one even so much as called the police. She died.

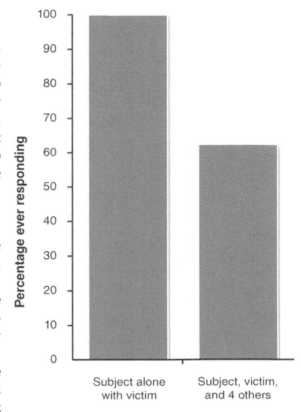

FIGURE 10.11 Effect of group size on the likelihood of responding in an emergency, based on Latané and Darley (1970).

THE BYSTANDER EFFECT

This episode has been widely reported and has served as the basis for the conclusion that being part of a large group witnessing an act that requires intervention often serves to inhibit helping behavior. And although this appears to be true under some circumstances, unfortunately the Kitty Genovese case has often been exaggerated. Later investigation uncovered that there were considerably fewer than 38 eyewitnesses to the murder (some only heard the attack), that Kitty Genovese had been involved in loud altercations on other occasions, and that one witness did, in fact, call the police (Manning, Levine, & Collins, 2007). Although this does not excuse the bystanders for not taking action, it is an explanation on why they didn't take action.

Still, there are other examples of what social psychologists call the **bystander effect**. Most of us would prefer to believe that the more people who witness an event where someone desperately needs assistance, the more likely it is that one of them will help. Sadly, in some circumstances, the more witnesses there are, the less likely it is that someone will intervene. For instance, how many times have you just driven by a stalled car on the side of the road, thinking that someone else will provide assistance?

Bystander effect: The more people who witness an event, the less likely they are to get help.

Latané and Darley (1970) conducted a series of experiments investigating the alleged apathy of bystanders. In one series of studies, participants alone in a room overheard an epileptic seizure apparently suffered by another "participant" (in fact, a tape-recorded "seizure"). Experimental conditions were such that participants either thought they're the only ones listening to the person having a seizure, or they believed there are other witnesses in different rooms. The dependent variable was whether or not the participant reported the seizure or otherwise tried to assist, and how long it took before helping behavior occurs.

As Figure 10.11 shows, all participants who thought they were alone with the victim responded by going to get help; in contrast, when participants thought there were four others besides the victim, only 62% responded.

In another experiment, participants were left in a room supposedly to wait for an interviewer (Latané & Darley, 1968). They were asked to fill out a questionnaire while waiting. Shortly thereafter, artificial smoke was blown into the room through a wall vent, continuing in irregular gusts, eventually filling the room, irritating the eyes, and making breathing difficult. If participants had not reported the smoke after 6 minutes, the experiment was discontinued and participants were debriefed. In one experimental condition, participants waited alone; in another, they waited with two other participants; and in a third, they were paired with two experimenter's confederates who had been instructed not to react to the smoke but to continue to fill out their questionnaires.

The results of these experiments were as expected: Participants alone reported the smoke 75% of the time; participants paired with two other participants reported it only 38% of the time and took longer before doing so. Most striking, only 1 of 10 participants paired with the confederates reported the smoke (Figure 10.12).

AN EXPLANATION

These studies indicate that individuals who have reason to believe themselves the only witnesses and hence the only immediate sources of intervention are more likely to involve themselves, either by reporting a potentially dangerous situation or by offering direct assistance. But when there are a number of

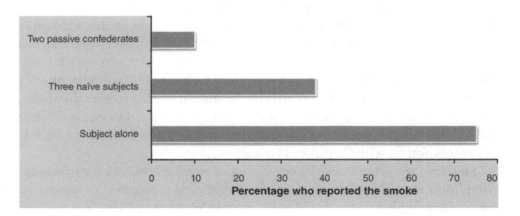

FIGURE 10.12   This is an illustration of the effect of group membership in emergency situations. In the Latané and Darley (1968) study, only 1 out of 10 participants reported the smoke when paired with two unalarmed confederates. Seventy-five percent reported it when left alone.

apparent witnesses, people are more reluctant to become involved. However, this doesn't necessarily mean witnesses remain apathetic. In fact, there is considerable evidence they do care. Participants who did not report the "epileptic seizure" were often visibly shaken, their hands trembling, their faces pale and drawn.

A number of factors may be responsible for the greater reluctance of people to become involved when others could also be involved. They may not see themselves as the most competent; perhaps they simply assume someone else has already intervened; perhaps, too, there is a fear of making a wrong judgment and of appearing foolish.

Darley and Latané (1968) attribute the bystander effect to one of three sources (or a combination of these): (a) a process of diffusion of responsibility, where the presence of others reduces the cost of nonintervention; (b) a process of social influence, where the nonintervention of others leads the participant to misinterpret the seriousness of the situation; and, (c) a process of audience inhibition, where the presence of others brings about fear of making a wrong decision and acting unwisely.

In the example of the stalled car on the side of the road, we potentially have many reasons why we just drive by without calling for assistance. For example, we think that nearly every person has a mobile phone, and, therefore, we believe that if the person needed help, the person would call for help him- or herself. Or, perhaps we are misinterpreting the situation – the driver is taking a rest from driving. Finally, we worry about acting unwisely and if we put ourselves in danger by offering help.

HOW COMMON IS THE BYSTANDER EFFECT?

It is perhaps reassuring that many recent studies have not found a bystander effect, or have found a considerably less dramatic one than might have been expected. For example, McMahon and Farmer (2009) found a majority of student athletes would be willing to intervene in a case involving sexual violence. Reluctance to do so was often related to lack of skills required to intervene. Whether a person becomes a rescuer or remains a bystander may depend on level of moral development (DeZalia, 2009).

A person's willingness to help is often related to the seriousness of the situation. In their 2011 meta-analysis, Fischer et al. found reduced bystander inhibition (or increased helping behavior) in situations deemed as dangerous. There is one possible explanation for this phenomenon: Dangerous situations are often readily identified as such and contain less or no ambiguity.

As Latané and Darley (1970) noted, before bystanders intervene, they must notice an event, interpret it as an emergency, make a decision as to their personal responsibility, select a form of assistance, and implement that assistance. When Kitty Genovese was murdered, not all of the witnesses interpreted the situation as an emergency. Manning, Levine, and Collins (2007) reported three of the five

Bystanders often ignore the plights of those who need help, especially if there are others around and if the cost of intervention is potentially high. Reassuringly, there are those, like this man, who gladly help.

witnesses who testified at the murder trial of the assailant reported they didn't immediately conclude a murder was taking place. And none of the court witnesses actually saw the stabbing. Nor is it likely that all who saw the situation as an emergency would then decide to take personal responsibility for bringing assistance—but one actually shouted and apparently frightened the attacker away, although he returned later. Others might have thought that someone else must have called the police—and apparently someone had! In the end, the incident, shocking though it might be given our implicit beliefs in the goodness of human nature, is not entirely surprising.

Choosing a form of assistance, other than calling on someone else (the police) for assistance, also presents a real problem. The man who was killing Kitty Genovese might not have hesitated to attack anyone else who might try to come to her assistance directly.

In summary, the Kitty Genovese case presents an extreme in which the possibility of intervening and the desirability of doing so are difficult and costly. It is not surprising that the likelihood of intervention is lessened by the presence of others who might also intervene.

Prosocial Behaviors

There is considerable evidence that real or imagined bystanders can have a powerful effect on prosocial behaviors such as helping and giving. For example, Potter, Moynihan, Stapleton, and Banyard (2009) found that exposing students to models engaging in prosocial behavior—in this case, having to do with intervening in cases of sexual violence—increased the likelihood the students would later try to help if they witnessed similar episodes.

Altruism

The apathy and nonintervention sometimes characteristic of situations in which a number of bystanders are involved are directly opposite to **altruistic behaviors** (self-sacrificing, helpful behaviors).

Altruistic behaviors:
Self-sacrificing and helpful behaviors.

Altruism is not uncommon among animal species. When a honeybee stings an intruder, it sacrifices its life for the hive; in a similar fashion, a bird that noisily signals an approaching hawk may save other birds. Although these behaviors might seem contrary to the basic biological law of *survival of the fittest,* they really aren't. That's because this law applies not to individuals but to species. Or, more specifically, to the genetic material that defines a species. This form of self-sacrificing altruism among animals actually increases the likelihood of survival of the species' genetic material. The death of a single individual is a small price to pay for the survival of a swarm or a flock.

Altruism among animals has led to a *sociobiological* theory of altruism championed by Richard Dawkins (1976/2006). According to this theory, altruism is nothing more than *genetic selfishness:* Genes can be thought of as having a selfish desire to become immortal through reproduction and survival. As a result, they push organisms toward behaviors designed to ensure the survival of the genetic material of that species, though not necessarily of the individual that carries the genes.

Thus, if an altruistic act increases the probability of reproduction of genes carried by the species, the survival needs of the species have been served. So, according to Dawkins's theory, an individual might take a risk in trying to save another if there is a chance that *both* will survive; however, there would be no net genetic advantage in being altruistic if one or the other will surely die.

Biology clearly doesn't explain all altruism. Nor does it explain the fact that some people willingly help those in distress while others don't. In addition to this **biological altruism**, there is what is labeled **reciprocal altruism**, in which an individual behaves altruistically with the expectation that others will reciprocate. For example, a monkey will willingly pick parasites off another's back—on the surface, a selfless, altruistic act. But later, the parasite-picking monkey will turn its back and expect the other to reciprocate.

We are sometimes a little like monkeys: We sacrifice and do good things for others in the expectation we might one day need them to reciprocate. Some donate blood at least partly for that reason. As Buchanan and Bardi (2010) show, we are sometimes altruistic because it makes us feel good—in which case, our altruism is not entirely selfless. They had participants perform altruistic acts (acts of kindness) at random over a 10-day period. Measures taken before and after this period indicated their life-satisfaction scores had improved significantly during this period.

Other studies of altruism indicate our altruistic behavior often depends on how altruistic we perceive others to be (Ellers & van der Pool, 2010). We are more likely to be altruistic if we think others are, or would be, under the same circumstances—a sort of positive bystander effect. These studies also reveal altruism is often related to the status of the actor, with higher-status individuals engaging in more altruistic behaviors (Liebe & Tutic, 2010).

Biological altruism: An explanation for altruistic behavior that asserts organisms are helpful to others to ensure survival of the species.

Reciprocal altruism: An explanation for altruistic behavior that asserts individuals are helpful to others because of the expectation this will be reciprocated.

Interpersonal Relationships

By definition, altruism goes beyond simple acts of warmth and kindness: It implies behavior where there is significant disadvantage to the doer or giver and clear potential advantage to the receiver.

Positive social behaviors are not always altruistic because they do not present us with a significant disadvantage. We may be kind and selfless out of a desire to establish and maintain a relationship with others. Sometimes we are nice simply because we want other people to like us: We are attracted to them and we want them to be attracted to us.

Interpersonal attraction: Positive thoughts of another person that are strongly influenced by proximity, similarity, and physical attraction.

The Rules of Attraction

Interpersonal attraction is generally considered "positive emotional evaluation of another person" (Montoya & Horton, 2014, p. 59). Interpersonal attraction can be thought of as the spectrum between liking and loving, and it appears to be strongly influenced by three things: proximity, similarity, and physical attraction.

Interpersonal attraction is strongly influenced by propinquity, similarity, and physical attraction.
© Syda Productions, 2014. Used under license from Shutterstock, Inc.

PROPINQUITY

Propinquity: Physical proximity; factor related to physical attraction.

People in closer physical proximity (often referred to as **propinquity**) tend to have more in common and have much stronger ties than among those more physically distant (Hipp & Perrin, 2009). Propinquity, which is closely related to *similarity,* can describe stronger connection between people who attend the same churches, colleges, and clubs and go to the same beaches, bars, and bingos.

SIMILARITY

Do opposites attract? Some early research speculated people are attracted to each other on the basis of their differences. Submissive people might be attracted to dominant people. Each might fulfill certain needs the other has. It is, however, not as logical to assume a highly aggressive individual will be attracted to a highly pacific individual or an extrovert will naturally gravitate toward an introvert, or, to carry the argument to its illogical extreme, the more dissimilar two individuals are, the more they will love each other.

In fact, research has found that similarity between people is associated with attraction. Newcomb (1961) provided a house for 17 male university students so he could study friendship patterns among them. Not surprisingly, roommates, regardless of similarity of interests and beliefs, tended to be attracted at the beginning. But as time passed and students got to know each other better, similarity gradually emerged as the most important factor in determining friendships.

Montoya and Horton (2013) conducted a meta-analytic review of 240 studies on similarity and attraction. The studies showed that attitude-similarity was important in interpersonal attraction, especially as it related to the degree of similarity and the awareness of attitude similarity. An older study of online attraction confirms these findings. Antheunis, Valkenburg, and Peter (2010) looked at interaction patterns and social attraction among 704 members of a social networking site very similar to Facebook, MySpace, and Friendster. They found participants used three different strategies to reduce uncertainty about other members' attitudes, emotions, and behavior: *passive strategies* such as simply observing how the target person interacts with others; *active strategies* such as asking other people about the target person; and, most effective, *interactive strategies* where the two people interact directly. Interactive strategies often involve self-disclosure, which tends to elicit self-disclosure in the other person.

Results of this study indicate that in an online situation, knowing important things about the other person (reduction of uncertainty) is closely related to social attraction. Furthermore, degree of attraction is closely related to how similar each person thinks the other is. Montoya and Horton (2013) also found this was a consistent theme through other attitude-similarity studies.

People who are similar in important ways tend to like each other more than those who are less similar. For this pair, the beads, the headband, and the dress are loud signals of similarity.

PHYSICAL ATTRACTIVENESS

Physical attractiveness is often an important variable. Walster, Aronson, Abrahams, and Rottman (1966) arranged for an elaborate "dating" experiment at the University of Minnesota involving 376 men and 376 women who were to attend a dance. Participants were unaware the dance had been arranged for experimental purposes. They were simply told they would be "computer matched" with a partner and were asked to fill out questionnaires for that purpose. Meanwhile, experimenters surreptitiously assigned them physical attractiveness ratings so as to divide them into three groups: ugly, average, and attractive. (In this age's more politically correct climate, it is unlikely that researchers would use the label *ugly* for those less physically attractive.)

Participants were then matched randomly except no woman was matched with a shorter partner. Of the 376 pairs thus formed, all but 40 actually attended the dance. During the intermission, some 2½ hours after the start of the dance, participants were asked to fill out an apparently anonymous questionnaire—which, of course, was not at all anonymous. It dealt with how much they liked their date, how attractive the date was, how comfortable the participant felt, how much the date seemed to like the participant, how similar the participant thought the date was in terms of attitudes and beliefs, how much effort each was putting into making sure that the other had a good time, and whether or not they were likely to date again. Actual frequency of subsequent dating was ascertained some 4 to 6 months later by contacting all participants directly.

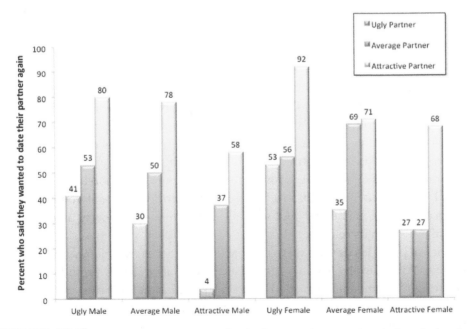

FIGURE 10.13 How important is physical attractiveness in dating behavior? Strikingly, the most attractive partners in a "random" dating study were those consistently more likely to be asked out again. Image courtesy of the author. Data from Walster, Aronson, Abrahams, & Rottman (1966). Importance of physical attractiveness in dating behavior. *Journal of Personality and Social Psychology, 4,* 508–516.

Graph courtesy of the author. Data Source: *Journal of Personality & Social Psychology.*

The most important finding from this study was that of all the measures employed (intelligence, self-acceptance, extroversion, and a number of other scores in student files based on standardized tests such as the MMPI), physical attractiveness was the only significant variable in determining degree of social attraction. More attractive males and females were much less attracted to those classified as "ugly" or "average." Although members of the least attractive group would, in general, date anybody, they too said they preferred those more attractive (Figure 10.13).

That physical attractiveness is perceived as exceptionally important in interpersonal attraction is underlined in a study by Toma and Hancock (2010), which found online daters exaggerate their physical attractiveness in their self-descriptions. And the least attractive tend to exaggerate more than the more attractive.

Seidman and Miller (2013) tracked eye movement across a Facebook page to determine what parts of the page participants focused on the most. Participants tended to pay more attention to personal information, such as likes or interests, on pages of males; conversely, participants focused more on the pictures and appearance of females' Facebook pages.

Physical attraction appears to be one of the most important factors at the beginning of a romantic relationship.
© pio3, 2014. Used under license from Shutterstock, Inc.

Liking and Loving

Freud (1914/1955) put it very simply: "[In] the last resort, we must begin to love in order not to fall ill, and we are bound to fall ill if, in consequence of frustration, we are unable to love" (p. 95).

Love: The province of poets rather than scientists. A strong, interpersonal attraction, says science: a combination of passion, intimacy, and commitment.

How likely is it that we will fall ill if we cannot **love**? Science does not answer this question as confidently as have the poets. But then love was the province of the poet long before science claimed it. And even now, poets may know more about love than does science. Of the wonder and joy and all-consuming nature of love, the poets have had little doubt; however, about love's practical value, the poets remain less certain. "True love," writes the poet Szymborska (1995), "Is it normal, is it serious, is it practical / What does the world get from two people who exist in a world of their own?" But we have little time for the poetry of love—here we deal only with its science.

Science provides us with ways of measuring, if not of completely understanding, love. For example, Rubin's (1970) *Loving and Liking Scales* provide a way of measuring interpersonal attraction. The scales are based on the assumption that those who like each other sense that they have things in common, evaluate each other positively, and appreciate each other's company. Items that indicate liking (but not loving) are items like *I think that _____ is unusually well adjusted,* or *I would highly recommend _____ for a responsible job.*

Loving implies deeper feelings, feelings of intense caring, strong attachment, and intimacy. Love brings with it a degree of emotional interdependence, a quality of exclusiveness and absorption. If you simply like someone, that person doesn't dominate your thoughts and your dreams; nor are you concerned that someone else might also like the same person. Love, on the other hand, often brings with it a measure of fierce possessiveness and the possibility of jealousy and pain—perhaps the possibility of ecstasy as well. Rubin (1970) measures love with items such as *I feel that I can confide in* _____ *about virtually everything,* or *If I could never be with* _____, *I would feel miserable.*

In *The Help,* Aibileen clearly has strong feelings for Hilly's daughter, Mae Mobley (Stockett, 2009). Did Aibileen love or like Mae Mobley?

A Model of Love

According to Sternberg (1986), interpersonal attraction is no simple thing. There are at least eight varieties of it: nonlove, romantic love, liking, fatuous love, infatuation, companionship, empty love, and consummate love. What differentiates these states from one another is the combination of intimacy, passion, and commitment involved in each. Accordingly, Sternberg has given us a **triangular theory of love**. But the triangle in this theory is not the classical male or male–female or female–female and male love triangle: It is the intimacy–passion–commitment triangle (Figure 10.14).

In this model, *intimacy* refers to emotions that bring people closer together—emotions such as respect, affection, and support. Feelings of intimacy are what lead two people to want to share things, perhaps to disclose personal, private experiences and feelings. The more intimate you are with someone, the more likely you will be closer to them or spend time with them.

Passion is a strong, sometimes almost overwhelming, desire to be with another person. Passion is often, although not always, sexual. Sternberg suggests that passion is a feeling that builds rapidly but then gradually subsides. Sumter,

Triangular theory of love: Sternberg's theory of loving involving commitment, passion, and intimacy.

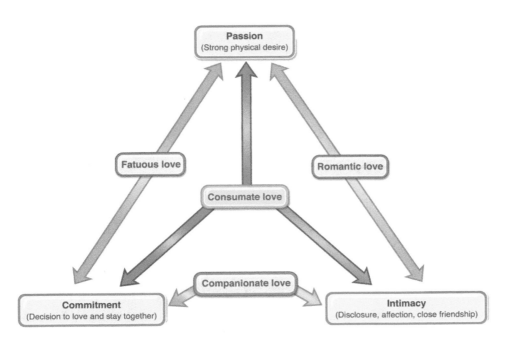

FIGURE 10.14 In Sternberg's triangle of love, different combinations of commitment, passion, and intimacy determine the nature of the love relationship.

Valkenburg, and Peter (2013) showed higher passion in adults than in adolescents, with only a slight decline in passion for older adults. These findings contradict common thought that older adults have significantly less passion than younger adults.

Commitment implies a decision-making process and may involve either a short-term or a long-term decision. On a short-term basis, commitment requires making the decision that one is in love. From a long-term point of view, commitment involves deciding to cultivate and maintain the loving relationship. In practice, this often implies a decision to share living arrangements and sometimes the raising of a family, either in marriage or otherwise. In the Sumter et al. (2013) study, commitment increased proportionally in adolescents with age; however, the adult participants did not indicate any change in commitment as the adults aged.

Sternberg's (1986) theory of love holds that it is the particular combination of these three components—intimacy, passion, and commitment—that determines the nature of the relationship. As Figure 10.15 shows, for example, empty love involves commitment but is devoid of passion or of intimacy ("Okay, we'll stay together until the children are gone. Then goodbye!"). **Consummate love,** on the other hand, has all three components.

According to Sternberg, there is a pattern to the development of many relationships. Two individuals might begin with nonlove—no passion, commitment, or intimacy. In time, nonlove might give way to infatuation, which has passion but no commitment or intimacy—or perhaps to romantic love, which now adds

Consummate love:
Love that has all three components from the triangular theory.

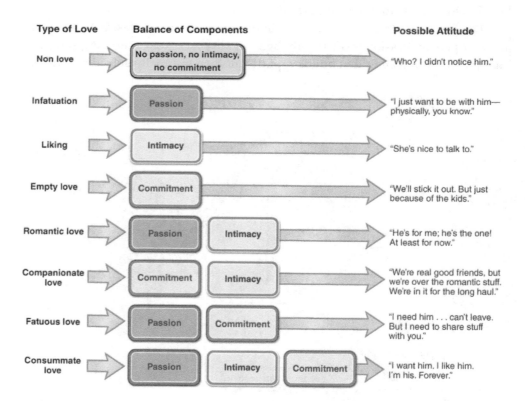

FIGURE 10.15   How can you tell whether you really are in love? One way is to analyze your relationship in terms of the Sternberg model, looking at the balance among passion (physical attraction and desire), intimacy (affection, mutual disclosure), and commitment (conscious decision to love, to share, to be together).

intimacy but is still short of commitment. Eventually, consummate love might evolve as commitment is brought into the relationship. And perhaps the end result will be marriage or some other long-term commitment. You should remember this when you are sitting next to someone in class—that person may eventually become your spouse.

Even consummate love is not a static, unchanging thing. Sternberg (1986) points out that passion is usually very high early in a consummate relationship. But with the passage of time, it diminishes; at the same time, commitment and intimacy might increase. Research suggests that intimacy and commitment may be more important for a lasting love relationship than is passion (Madey & Rodgers, 2009).

As Gibran says, the ways of love are hard and steep . . . love carries no guarantees.

© Natali Glado, 2014. Used under license from Shutterstock, Inc.

A Last Word to the Poets

As we noted at the outset, while it is nice to believe that science has a grasp of love, it is possible that poets and sages know love better than science.

So, if we are not to be three parts dead, perhaps we should all heed Kahlil Gibran's (1923) advice:

> When love beckons to you, follow him,
> Though his ways are hard and steep.

There is a good chance, if the philosophers and the poets are correct, that love will turn out to be the most important piece of the human puzzle.

Summary

The subject matter of social psychology deals with how thinking, feeling, and behavior are influenced by the real or imagined presence of others. In this chapter, we first looked at how attitudes form, change, and influence behavior. We discussed the tendency to obey authority demonstrated in the Milgram studies and to assume socially accepted roles in the Stanford prison study. Next, the chapter examined human interactions, including those that are anti-social (aggression), prosocial (helping), and friendly. We concluded our discussion of social psychological with the topic of love, including various types and factors, and the impact of physical attraction.

GLOSSARY

Absolute threshold A method used to study the limits of sensation; the smallest amount of a physical stimulus that can be correctly detected 50% of the time.

Accommodation The process of adapting the current schemas to match the new information or experiences.

Acetylcholine A neurotransmitter present in the peripheral as well as central nervous system, involved in voluntary activity as well as physiological functions (such as heart and respiration rates).

Action potential A pulse-like electrical discharge along a neuron. Sequences of linked action potentials are the basis for the transmission of neural messages.

Active Deception Active deception is deception by commission

Active vocabulary Words actually used in speech.

Adaptation In perception, refers to a change in sensitivity resulting from stimulus conditions.

Adrenal glands Endocrine glands situated at the top of the kidneys, involved in releasing hormones at times of stress.

Adrenaline Also called *epinephrine*. A substance produced by the adrenal glands, released in response to stress.

Afterimage A visual image that continues after the stimulus that caused it is no longer present.

Aggression Actions with the intent to harm others.

Agonists An agent or drug that enhances the activity of some naturally occurring substance. For example, cocaine is a dopamine agonist in that it appears to stimulate the activity of dopamine.

Agoraphobia Intense anxiety about, or avoidance of, unfamiliar places.

Agreeableness   A "Big Five" personality factor comprised of the traits friendly, compassionate, and cooperative.

Alleles   Each of two corresponding forms of a gene, one being inherited from each parent.

Alpha waves   Slower, deeper brain waves characteristic of deep relaxation, having a frequency of 8 to 13 cycles per second.

Altruistic behaviors   Self-sacrificing and helpful behaviors.

Amnesiacs   Those who experience partial or total loss of memory, sometimes resulting from head trauma.

Amok   A primarily male disorder common to Malaysia and other Southeast Asian countries, characterized by violent, homicidal episodes followed by amnesia.

Amplitude   With respect to sound waves, defined as the height of wave peaks, related to perceived loudness.

Amygdala   A small structure in the limbic system (part of the forebrain) that is involved in emotion and aggression and that plays an important role in the processing and storage of memories that have to do with emotion.

Androgens   Male sex hormone.

Animistic thinking   Attributing lifelike qualities to inanimate objects.

Anonymous Research   Research that has ensured no identifying information is gathered and participants cannot be identified once the study is concluded

Anorexia nervosa   Psychological disorder characterized by being significantly underweight.

Anosmia   Inability to detect odors.

Antagonists   A drug that blocks the effectiveness of a neurotransmitter. For example, *beta blockers* are antagonists that reduce blood pressure by impeding receptivity of adrenaline receptors.

APGAR scale   Assessment scale used right after birth to determine the condition of the baby.

Aphagia   Undereating.

Archetypes   Literally, the first or original model. In Jung's theory, a universal thought or shared historical memory which is largely unconscious.

Archival research   Describes research that relies on preexisting records such as census counts, birth records, and school achievement records.

Army Alpha   The test given to literate military personnel to determine rank.

Army Beta   The nonverbal test given to illiterate military personnel to determine rank.

Arousal theory   A theory stating that individuals behave in a way to maintain an optimal level of arousal.

Arousal   To excite.

Artificial insemination   The process of introducing sperm in a female's reproductive tract without sexual intercourse.

Asperger's syndrome   A developmental disorder characterized by impaired social interactions and repetitive behavior patterns. Now considered one of the *autism spectrum* disorders.

Assimilation   The process of taking in new information in a form to match the current schemas.

Association areas of the brain   Parts of the four cerebral lobes involved in higher mental processes like thinking, learning, and remembering.

Assumption   A belief that guides reasoning and research, accepted as fact, but often unprovable.

Attachment   The bond that ties two people together.

Attention deficit hyperactivity disorder (ADHD)   A disorder marked by excessive general activity for a child's age, attention problems, high impulsivity, and low frustration tolerance. Also termed hyperactivity.

Attention   A concentrated mental effort that functions as a filter to ignore unimportant events and focus on important events.

Attentiondeficit/Hyperactivity Disorder   A persistent pattern of inattention and/or *hyperactivity*-impulsivity interfering with functioning or development.

Attitude   Prevailing and consistent tendency to react in a given way.

Attribution theory   The attempt to attach meaning to ourselves or others.

Attributions   Inferences regarding the causes of behavior.

Auditory cortex   The part of our brain that is primarily responsible for processing the auditory information.

Authoritative parenting style   Parenting characterized by low warmth and high demands.

Autism spectrum disorder   A relatively early-appearing disorder; central features are persistent, pervasive, and sustained impairments in how an individual interacts with or communicates with others.

Autism   A complex developmental disability marked by impairments in social interaction and communication skills. Classified as a *pervasive mental disorder.*

Autobiographical memory   A type of declarative memory consisting of knowledge about personal experiences, tied to specific times and places.

Autonomic nervous system   That part of the peripheral nervous system that is not ordinarily under conscious control. It regulates physiological functions such as respiration, heart rate, temperature, and digestion and includes the sympathetic and parasympathetic systems.

Average   A mathematical indication of central tendency, obtained by summing the numbers that describe a characteristic and dividing by the number of cases involved. Although averages are often good descriptions of the characteristics of a group, they frequently do not describe individuals at all well.

Aversive conditioning   When a therapist attempts to attach negative feelings and bring about avoidance behavior with respect to certain situations.

Axon   The elongated part of a nerve cell. Axons ordinarily transmit impulses from the cell body to adjoining dendrites.

Barnum effect   The tendency to accept vague personality descriptions of oneself as accurate.

Basic orienting system   The perceptual system whose principal function is to provide the organism with information about position of the body, movement, and relation to the gravitational plane. Sometimes called the *vestibular sense.*

Behavior modification   systematic application of learning principles to change behavior

Behaviorism   The scientific study of the prediction and control of behavior

Behavioristic theories   Theories concerned with objective evidence of behavior rather than with consciousness and mind.

Beta waves   Typical shallow and rapid brain waves of person who is awake, having a frequency of 13 to 30 cycles per minute.

Big Five factors   A widely accepted personality typology that includes extraversion, openness, conscientiousness, agreeableness, and neuroticism.

Binge-eating disorder   Psychological disorder characterized by excessive binging, however, the individual does not engage in purging behaviors.

Biological altruism   An explanation for altruistic behavior that asserts organisms are helpful to others to ensure survival of the species.

Biological constraints   Limitations on learning that result from biological factors rather than from experience.

Bipolar disorder   A disorder characterized by mania and depression.

Birth of the placenta   The third stage of the process of delivery in which the placenta and other supporting structures detach from uterine wall and pass through the birth canal.

Blind spot   A gap in the retina due to the exit of the optic nerve where no photoreceptors are located; this causes a blind spot in the visual field during sensation.

Blocking   A phenomenon in classical conditioning in which conditioning to a specific stimulus becomes difficult or impossible because of prior conditioning to another stimulus.

Body senses   Sensory systems involved in perceptions of our body. Include the vestibular sense (balance and movement), skin senses (pain, temperature, and touch), and the kinesthetic sense (awareness of limb and body position and movement).

Bottom-up processing   An information-gathering process starting from each individual stimulus.

Brain fag   A form of study-induced mental exhaustion found primarily in West Africa, evident in depression, insomnia, anxiety, and learning problems.

Brain stem   Part of the brain that connects the spinal cord with the higher brain centers. Includes the hindbrain (medulla, pons, cerebellum) and the midbrain (reticular formation).

Brain   A complex clustering of nerve cells that is centrally involved in coordinating activities and events in various parts of an organism. The human brain is reputedly the most complex structure in the universe.

Brief psychotic disorder   Similar to schizophrenia; however, symptoms can last from 1 day to 1 month.

Bubba psychology   An expression for folk beliefs in psychology; also referred to as naive or implicit theories. *Bubba* (or sometimes *bubbe* or *bubbie*) means grandmother.

Bulimia nervosa   Psychological disorder characterized by binging and purging.

Bulimia   An eating disorder characterized by episodes of binge eating followed by severe dieting and sometimes purging or the use of laxatives and diuretics or extreme exercise.

Bystander effect   The more people who witness an event, the less likely they are to get help.

Case study   An in-depth observation of an individual, animal, event, or treatment method

Central executive system   In Baddeley's model of working memory, the system concerned with regulating the flow of information from sensory storage, processing it for long-term storage, and retrieving it from long-term storage.

Central executive   A part of Alan Baddeley's working memory model responsible for coordinating the input and output of information to working memory, as well as to integrate the separate pieces of information from the visuospatial sketchpad and phonological loop; the "CEO" of working memory.

Central nervous system   The human nervous system, which includes the brain and the spinal cord.

Centration   The fixation on one characteristic of an object at the exclusion of other characteristics.

Cephalocaudal   Pattern of development from head to toe.

Cerebellum   A major brain structure attached to the rear of the brain stem, the principal functions of which appear to be coordinating motor activity and maintaining balance.

Cerebral cortex   The convoluted outer covering of the cerebrum, the main functions of which have to do with higher mental processes like thinking and imagining. (See *cerebrum*.)

Cerebrum   The main part of the human brain, consisting of the two cerebral hemispheres and covered by the cerebral cortex.

CHC Theory of Intelligence   The most researched and widely supported theory of intelligence.

Chemical senses   Senses that respond to the chemical properties of substances and gases: namely, taste and olfaction.

Chromosomes   In the nucleus of all cells, the microscopic bodies that contain genes, which are the carriers of heredity.

Chunking   A memory process whereby related items are grouped together into more easily remembered "chunks" (for example, a prefix and four digits for a phone number, rather than seven unrelated digits).

Circadian rhythm   A biological/behavioral cycle that is approximately 1 day long. It describes our sleep/wake and temperature cycles.

Classical conditioning   Learning through stimulus substitution as a result of repeated pairings of an unconditioned stimulus with a conditioned stimulus

Clinical psychologists   Trained psychologists specializing in helping people with emotional and behavioral problems. (See *counseling psychologists.*)

Cochlea   The spiral structure in the inner ear that contains both fluid and the basilar membrane; the latter houses sensory receptors for audition.

Cocktail party phenomenon   The fleeting and unconscious availability for processing of stimuli to which the individual is not paying attention.

Cognitive apprenticeship   Novice learners are paired with older learners, teachers, or parents who serve as mentors and guides.

Cognitive dissonance   A situation where conflict exists among behavior, beliefs, or attitudes.

Cognitive theories   Theories that look at intellectual processes such as those involved in thinking, problem solving, imagining, and anticipating.

Cognitivism   An approach concerned mainly with intellectual events such as problem solving, information processing, thinking, and imagining.

Commitment   The decision-making aspect of Sternberg's theory of love; involves deciding that one is in love and resolving what to do about it.

Complexity   With respect to sound waves, defined in terms of the mixture of waves emanating from vibratory sources, giving rise to subjective impressions of timbre.

Compliance   Short-term changes in behavior, not altering beliefs.

Conception   When a sperm fertilizes an egg.

Concurrent schedule of reinforcement   A situation in which two or more different reinforcement schedules, each typically related to a different behavior, are presented at the same time.

Conditioned response   Previously the UR that is now given in response to the CS

Conditioned stimulus   A once neutral stimulus that becomes conditioned after repeated pairings with the US

Conduct disorder   A child and adolescent disorder marked by behaviors that violate the rights of others without apparent feelings of guilt, often evident in bullying, fighting, threatening, vandalism, theft, and so on.

Cones   A specific group of photoreceptors that are specialized to process color and are useful for daylight vision and high visual acuity.

Confederate   A participant in the study who is also part of the research team

Confidential Research   Research in which participants can be identified by information that is gathered. However, this information is kept in a manner that participant responses are not shared with others and the participants cannot be identified

Conformity   Long-term changes in behavior where attitudes have been affected, opinions modified, or stereotypes altered.

Conscientiousness   A "Big Five" personality trait, it includes awareness of one's personal identity and mental processes like thinking, imagining, and feeling.

Consciousness   Awareness of one's personal identity. Self-awareness. Awareness of mental processes like thinking, imagining, and feeling.

Conservation task   A technique used to display limitations in thinking during the preoperational stage.

Constructivism   A general term for student-centered approaches to teaching, such as discovery-oriented approaches, reciprocal learning, or cooperative instruction—so called because of their assumption that learners should build (construct) knowledge for themselves.

Consummate love   Love that has all three components from the triangular theory.

Contiguity   Closeness in time of the stimulus and response

Control group   Group of participants not exposed to the independent variable

Conventional moral reasoning   Kohlberg's second stage of moral development when people focus on maintaining social order.

Conversion disorder   A disorder similar to somatic symptom disorder but individuals with this disorder have one or more symptoms of altered voluntary motor or sensory functioning such as paralysis, weakness, tremors, or problems with vision or hearing.

Cornea   The transparent coating that covers the eyeball.

Correlation fallacy   The mistaken belief that if two variables are correlated, they must be causally related. Correlation is not proof of causation.

Correlation   A statistical relationship between variables. High positive correlation means that high scores on one variable are generally accompanied by high scores on the second. A high negative correlation means that high scores on one are typically associated with *low* scores on the second.

Correlational research methods   Provides information on the initial link between variables of interest

Correlational research   Research designed to uncover relationships between variables without determining cause and effect.

Counseling psychologists   Psychologists whose main function is to *counsel* individuals regarding issues relating to vocational or educational choices, learning problems, relationships, and mild emotional, physical, and mental disorders. (See *clinical psychologists.*)

Creationism   The belief that present life forms were created by a supreme being.

Criterion   (plural *criteria*) A standard, value, or goal by which something is judged; a necessary condition.

Cross-sectional design   Research design that collects information from different groups of people of different ages.

Cross-sectional study   Method of investigation that involves observing and comparing different subjects, usually at different age levels.

Culturally biased   A term used when an intelligence test gives an unfair advantage to White, affluent, male test takers.

Culturally loaded   A term used when many of the items on the intelligence test are derived from the mainstream culture.

Daydreaming   Engaging in waking dreams or reveries that are mainly under the dreamer's control.

Decibel   The scientific unit of measurement for loudness.

Declarative memory   Explicit, conscious long-term memory; may be either semantic or episodic.

Defense mechanisms   An unconscious mental strategy designed to avoid conflict and anxiety; examples include denial and repression.

Delivery   The second stage of the process of delivery in which the fetus passes through the birth canal.

Delta waves   Very slow brain waves (frequency of up to 4 per second) characteristic of deep sleep.

Delusional disorder   A presence of delusions but no hallucinations.

Delusions   False beliefs or opinions.

Demand characteristics   Hints and cues participants use to tell themselves how the researcher wants them to behave

Dendrites   Hair-like extensions emanating from the cell body of the neuron. Dendrites ordinarily receive impulses from adjoining axons.

Deoxyribonucleic acid (DNA)   A substance assumed to be the basis of all life, consisting of four chemical bases arranged in a mind-boggling number of combinations in the form of a double spiral (helix).

Dependent variable   Variable observed or measured

Depersonalization disorder   An Axis I DSM-IV-TR disorder marked by feelings of unreality, as though everything were a dream.

Depressant   A type of drug that slows down physiological functions. Alcohol is a commonly abused depressant and it slows down respiration.

Descriptive research   Describes the characteristics of an individual or of a group. Designed to answer one or more questions relating to who, what, where, when, and how (for example: What is the average age at which North American children say their first word?).

Deterministic   Having to do with the belief that every action has an identifiable cause that can be predicted given sufficient knowledge about prior events and their effects. Often contrasted with belief in free will.

Developmental psychologists   Study cognitive, physical, and emotional changes that occur between conception and death.

Developmental psychology   The study of change across the life span.

Diagnostic and Statistical Manual of Mental Disorders   A handbook used by health care professionals in the United States and much of the world as the authoritative guide to the diagnosis of mental disorders by classification in terms of categories, severity, and distinguishing characteristics of each disorder.

Difference threshold   A method used to study the sensitivity of sensation; the smallest difference between two stimuli that can be correctly detected 50% of the time; this is also called the just-noticeable difference.

Difficult infants   A type of temperament characterized by irregularity with respect to things like eating, sleeping, and toilet functions; withdrawal from unfamiliar situations; slow adaptation to change; and intense as well as negative moods.

Dilation and effacement   The first stage of the process of delivery in which the fetus turns head down and the cervix begins to expand.

Direct reinforcement   Results from the consequences of the act itself.

Discovery learning   A learner-centered approach to teaching in which the acquisition of new knowledge comes about largely through the learner's own efforts.

Discriminative stimulus (SD)   Skinner's term for the features of a situation that an organism can discriminate to distinguish between occasions that might be reinforced or not reinforced.

Disequilibrium   A state of cognitive imbalance, in which information does not match current cognitive schemas.

Dispositional attributions   Causes of behavior related to characteristics of an individual.

Dissociative disorders   Disorders that involve separating certain memories or thoughts from normal consciousness.

Dissociative fugue   A loss of memory characterized by wandering and sometimes assuming a new identity.

Dissociative identity disorder   A complex type of dissociation in which individuals are from time to time dominated by distinctly different, complex, highly integrated personalities.

Distortion theory   A theory of forgetting that recognizes that what is remembered is often changed or reconstructed.

Dizygotic twins   Twins that result from two separate eggs and that are therefore fraternal (nonidentical).

Dominant gene   A gene that takes precedence over other genes in determining a related trait.

Dopamine   A neurotransmitter centrally involved with pleasure and reinforcement and also implicated in some instances of drug addiction as well as in conditions such as Parkinson's disease.

Double blind study   Neither the participant nor the researcher knows to which group the participant has been assigned

Double-blind procedure   An experimental procedure in which neither the subjects nor the examiners know who is in the experimental group and who is in the control group.

Drive reduction   Behaviors that reduce an individual's drive.

Drive   Cause to move.

Drug intoxication   Recent use of a substance that induces a maladaptive and impairing state but is reversible.

Drug tolerance   Habituation to a drug. Evident in the observation that the effects of a drug often lessen with increasing use.

Dyadic interactions   Interactions involving two individuals.

Dysphoria   The opposite of euphoria; a common feature of drug withdrawal.

Dysthymic disorder   Marked by a serious, chronic depression lasting at least 2 years.

Eardrum   The thin membrane at the end of the ear canal that vibrates at a specific frequency when bombarded by sound waves.

Easy infants   A temperament type marked by high regularity in behaviors such as eating and sleeping; high interest in novel situations; high adaptability to change; and a preponderance of positive moods, as well as low or moderate intensity of reaction.

Echolocation   The use of sound to localize objects, based on the amount of time it takes an echo to return to the sound source.

Ectomorphs   According to Sheldon, a frail, thin body type, described as withdrawn and concerned with intellectual matters.

Educational psychologists   Are concerned with issues relating to understanding and improving teaching and learning in educational settings.

Effector   A specialized cell or organ that carries out a response to a nerve impulse.

Ego   In Freud's theory, the rational, reality-oriented level of human personality, developing as the child becomes aware of what the environment makes possible and impossible.

Egocentrism   The inability to see the world from another person's point of view.

Elaboration   A memory strategy that involves forming new associations, linking with other ideas or images.

Elaborative rehearsal   A type of rehearsal in which a person actively tries to tie new information to pre-existing information already in long-term memory. The net effect is to increase the likelihood that the new information is retained in long-term memory.

Electra complex   A Freudian stage (around 4 years) when a girl's awareness of her genital area leads her to desire her father and to become jealous of her mother.

Electrodermal response   Electrical conductivity of the skin.

Electroencephalogram (EEG)   An instrument used to measure electrical activity in the brain.

Eliciting effect   Imitative behavior in which the observer does not copy the model's responses but simply behaves in a related manner.

Embryo   The developing fetus, between 2 and 8 weeks after conception.

Embryonic period   Second period of prenatal development from implantation to 2 months.

Emotions   Motives.

Encoding   The process of transforming experienced information into a form that can be later stored and used by the brain.

Endocrine system   A system of glands that secrete hormones whose functioning affects things such as growth, maturation, behavior, and emotion. Includes the pituitary, the adrenal glands, and the gonads.

Endomorphs   Sheldon's large somatotype, believed to love comfort, be relaxed, good natured, and sociable.

Entity theory   The belief that intelligence is fixed and unchanging.

Episodic memory   A type of long-term memory (explicit memory, to be exact); conscious recollection of one's personal experiences that took place at a specific time in a certain place.

Equal loudness contours   Lines measuring the function of loudness and frequencies of sound waves.

Equilibrium   A state of cognitive balance, in which information matches current cognitive schemas.

Eros   A term employed by Freud to describe the life instinct, the urge for survival and procreation.

Estrogen   Female sex hormone.

Ethnic psychosis   A mental disorder such as Windigo that is specific to an ethnic group.

Ethologist   One who studies the behavior of animals in their natural habitats.

Event-related field (ERF)   A measure of magnetic fields at the scalp relating to neural activity typically associated with specific stimuli.

Event-related potential (ERP)   A measure of electrical activity in identifiable areas of the brain, corresponding to specific stimuli.

Evolution   A scientific theory that holds that present life forms have developed from preexisting species through a series of modifications governed by laws of natural selection and diversification of species.

Evolutionary psychology   An approach in psychology defined by its attention to biology and genetics as sources of explanation for human learning and behavior.

Ex post facto study   A study in which the experimenter does not assign subjects to experimental conditions or exercise control over these conditions; the experimenter simply studies participants on the basis of differences that already exist among them.

Expectancy-value theory   The belief that motivation is determined by the expectancy of success and the value of the reward.

Experimental group   Group exposed to the independent variable

Experimental psychologists   Psychologists involved in the use of experimental (scientifically controlled) research.

Experimental research   Involves the manipulation of a variable of interest and assignment of participants to treatment conditions

Experimenter bias   An unconscious phenomenon whereby experimenters' expectations influence their observations. Not to be confused with experimenter dishonesty.

Explicit memory   A type of long-term memory; conscious memory about facts or experiences.

Exposure therapy   When a therapist exposes a patient to fear- or anxiety-producing stimuli.

Extinction   Process by which classically conditioned responses are eliminated

Extraversion   This "Big Five" personality factor includes traits of outgoing, positivity, and energetic.

Extrinsic reinforcement   Reinforcement to increase a behavior in the future that comes from an external source (e.g., reading to earn a reward)

Factor analysis   A statistical procedure for reducing correlational data to a smaller number of dimensions by grouping closely related variables.

Fading theory   The belief that the inability to recall long-term memories increases with the passage of time as memory traces fade. Also termed *decay theory*.

Fallopian tube   One of two tubes that link the ovaries and the uterus, where conception ordinarily occurs.

False memory syndrome   Describes the possibility that a memory—especially of a highly traumatic event—may be a memory of something that has not actually occurred.

Fast mapping   The learning of a concept, like a word, in a single trial.

Fetal period   Third and final period of prenatal development from 2 months to birth.

Fetus   An immature child in the uterus.

Fixation   A developmental delay due to unsuccessfully developing through a stage, sometimes manifested in personality characteristics and emotional disorders relating to the earlier stage.

Flashbulb memories   A type of long-term memory. Memories formed by dramatic and surprising public or personal events; typically known to be immune from forgetting.

Flynn effect   The observation that there are gains in measured IQ over generations.

Forgetting   Loss from memory over time; contrasted with extinction, which occurs as a result of cessation of reinforcement.

Fovea   An area at the center of the retina that contains the highest density of cones; visual acuity is highest in this region.

Free association   A technique used in psychoanalysis where the patient is encouraged to say whatever comes to mind without evaluating or discarding material.

Frequency   With respect to sound waves, the number of waves per second in Hertz units, giving rise to the perception of pitch.

Frontal lobes   Frontal part of the cerebral cortex, centrally involved in higher thought processes.

Frustration   Occurs when someone is prevented from achieving a goal.

Frustration–aggression hypothesis   Hypothesis that frustration leads to anger, which will result in aggression if a suitable object or person releases the aggression.

Functional magnetic resonance imaging (fMRI)   A diagnostic imaging technique that detects extremely subtle changes in magnetic fields in the human body, allowing technicians to view real-time, computer-enhanced images of soft tissue. Used extensively to diagnose disease as well as to study neural activity in the brain.

Functionalism   The study of how the mind of an organism adapts to its current environment

Gender identity disorder   Persistent, overwhelming cross-gender identification and discomfort with one's anatomical gender.

Generalize To engage in a process whereby conclusions derived under one set of circumstances are extended to other similar circumstances. The objective of most scientific investigations is to arrive at conclusions that can be generalized.

Generalized anxiety disorder A disorder marked by excessive anxiety and worry, as a general state rather than episodic subjective sensation of anxiety, in the absence of specific situations or objects that might be associated with anxiety reactions.

Genes The carriers of heredity.

Genetic makeup The assortment of genes that compose the individual's genetic code.

Genome The complete set of chromosomes of an organism. All of an organism's inheritable traits.

Genomics The discipline studying genomes in an attempt to establish relationships between genes and characteristics.

Genotype Genetic makeup. The assortment of genes that compose the individuals genetic code.

Germinal period First period of prenatal development from conception to implantation

Glial cells Cells that support neural functioning. Among other functions, they clean out debris and form protective coatings around nerves. (See *myelin sheath.*)

Gonads Hormone-producing sex glands. Testes in the male; ovaries in the female.

Group test A type of test usually used to measure intelligence that may be given to large groups at one time.

Habituation A decrease in response to a stimulus following repeated or prolonged exposure. Also used to describe *drug tolerance.*

Hair cells Thin, hair-like structures that are the sensory receptors for audition; these are located on the basilar membrane inside the cochlea.

Hallucinations Perceptions of experiences without corresponding external stimuli together with a compelling feeling that these are real.

Hallucinogens A drug type causing hallucinations.

Hawthorne effect   Describes the observation that individuals who are aware that they are members of an experimental group sometimes perform better simply for that reason.

Hering's opponent process theory   A theory that suggests we perceive color in terms of paired opposing groups of colors: red-green, yellow-blue, and black-white.

Heritability coefficient   The proportion of the total variation in a trait that is due to heredity. *High heritability* means that a large proportion of the variation in a characteristic is caused by a variation in genes.

Hippocampus   A limbic system structure in the forebrain, which is primarily involved in learning and memory.

Holistic education   A label for educational approaches that attempt to remedy what is seen as the failure of traditional education to educate the whole brain—especially the right hemisphere, which is speculatively linked with music, art, and emotion.

Holophrase   A word the child uses to convey as much meaning as an adult would convey with a much longer phrase.

Hormones   Chemicals that have a pronounced effect on growth, maturation, behavior, and emotions and that are produced by endocrine glands and secreted directly into the bloodstream.

Humanism   A philosophical and psychological orientation primarily concerned with our worth as individuals and with those processes that are considered to make us more human.

Humanistic psychology   A branch of psychology whose primary concern is with the development of the self and with the uniqueness of the individual. Sometimes referred to as *third force* psychology; the other two forces are behaviorism and Freudian theory. (See *humanism*.)

Hyperphagia   Overeating.

Hypnosis   A state characterized by heightened suggestibility (willingness to do and to believe what is suggested by the hypnotist).

Hypothalamus   A small structure at the base of the brain involved in the functioning of the autonomic nervous system and in temperature regulation.

Hypothesis   An educated guess, often based on theory, which can be tested. A prediction based on partial evidence of some effect, process, or phenomenon, which must then be verified experimentally.

Hypothetical thought   The ability to think about possible solutions and outcomes to problems or abstract ideas.

Id   In Freudian theory, all the instinctual urges that humans inherit, including eros and thanatos.

Identification   Refers to the process of assuming the goals, ambitions, mannerisms, and so on of another person.

Identity   In Erikson's theory, a term closely related to *self*. To achieve identity is to arrive at a clear notion of who one is.

Illness anxiety disorder   Extreme worry about having or acquiring a serious illness.

Imaginary audience   An egocentric tendency to assume that we are the focus of other people's attention, that everyone is aware of and interested in our dress and behavior.

Imaginary playmate   My imaginary playmate is my best friend and goes everywhere with me and likes a lot of the same things I do and gets upset if I don't say hello and . . .

Imitation   Copying behavior. To imitate a person's behavior is simply to use that person's behavior as a pattern.

Implicit memory   A type of long-term memory; memory about how to perform a task (usually accessed unconsciously).

Impulse-control disorder   Marked by the repeated inability to refrain from a behavior that is harmful or seriously distressful.

In vitro fertilization   The fertilization of egg cells outside the womb—literally in glass (in *vitro*).

Inattentional blindness   Diverted attention resulting in failure of accurate scene detection as if we are blind to that event.

Incentive motivation   The notion that the greater the subjective value of an item or reward, the more someone is motivated to achieve the item or reward.

Incremental theory   The belief that intelligence is malleable and can be improved upon with effort.

Independent variable   Variable manipulated by the researcher

Individual test   A test, usually used to measure intelligence, that can be given to only one individual at a time.

Industrial/organizational psychologists Psychologists concerned with applying psychological principles to workplace-related issues.

Infancy The first 2 years of life.

Inhibitory/disinhibitory effect The type of imitative behavior that results either in the suppression (inhibition) or appearance (disinhibition) of previously acquired deviant behavior.

Insanity A legal term defined by law and determined by a court in consultation with mental health experts.

Insight The sudden recognition of relationships among elements of a problem.

Instinctive drift Refers to the tendency of organisms to revert to instinctual, unlearned behaviors.

Instincts Complex unlearned, behaviors

Institutional Review Board (IRB) A committee that reviews proposals of intended research and evaluates if the research is ethical and if the rights of the participants are being protected

Intellectual disability Commonly called *mental retardation,* a significant general depression in the ability to learn, usually accompanied by deficits in adaptive behavior.

Intelligence quotient The global score derived from standardized intelligence tests.

Intelligence The overall capacity to think and act logically and rationally within one's environment.

Intermittent explosive disorder An impulse-control disorder marked by recurring failure to resist aggressive impulses, leading to excessive violence against people or property.

Internal working model The expectations and understanding of the world formulated by the first attachment with caregivers.

Interpersonal attraction Positive thoughts of another person that are strongly influenced by proximity, similarity, and physical attraction.

Intimacy In Sternberg's theory of love, refers to emotions that lead two people to want to share things.

Intrinsic reinforcement   Reinforcement to increase a behavior in the future that comes from an internal source (e.g., reading because one loves to read)

Introspection   The examination of one's own mind to inspect and report on personal thoughts or feelings about conscious experiences

Introversion   The opposite of extraversion   withdrawn, shy, and reluctant to engage in social interaction.

Intuitive thinking   Thought based on immediate comprehension rather than logical processes.

Iris   The colored part of the eye; a muscle in the center of which is an opening that forms the pupil.

Kinesthetic sense   One of the body senses, often referred to as the "muscle and joint sense," consisting of receptors sensitive to movement of muscles, joints, and tendons.

Law of effect   Behaviors followed by reinforcement are more likely to be repeated and behaviors not followed by reinforcement are less likely to recur.

Learning   Relatively permanent changes in behavior that result from experience; not caused by fatigue, maturation, drugs, injury, or disease

Lens   The transparent structure behind the pupil, capable of changing its shape to focus light on the retina.

Libido   A Freudian term for sexual urges.

Limbic system   A grouping of brain structures located beneath the cerebral cortex, associated mainly with emotion, memory, and reinforcement and punishment.

Link system   A mnemonic system that requires forming linked visual images of what is to be recalled.

Loci system   A mnemonic system in which images of items to be recalled are "placed" in familiar locations.

Locus of control   Whether we internally or externally attribute our successes or failures.

Logical thought   The ability to rationally think about problems and situations.

Longitudinal design   Research design that collects information from the same group of people across time.

Longitudinal study   Psychological investigation in which the same subjects are examined over a period of time.

Long-term memory   One of the human memory systems that can store information for a long-period of time.

Love   The province of poets rather than scientists. A strong, interpersonal attraction, says science: a combination of passion, intimacy, and commitment.

Magical thinking   Thinking, often characteristic of preschoolers and young children, that is not entirely logical or scientifically valid, but rather inventive and surprising and sometimes bizarre—hence *magical*.

Magnetoencephalogram (MEG)   A recording of magnetic fields that correspond to electrical activity of the brain. MEG recordings are obtained at the scalp by means of a magnetoencephalograph to yield event-related fields (ERFs).

Magnocellular pathway   A visual pathway for peripheral vision and low spatial resolution images from the retina.

Major depressive disorder   A disorder characterized by a conglomerate of symptoms, including apathy, listlessness, despair, loss of appetite, sleep disturbances, unwavering pessimism, and thoughts of suicide.

Major depressive episode   At least 2 weeks of significantly depressed mood, loss of interest, and other symptoms of depression.

Medulla   The lowest part of the brain, found at the very top of the spinal cord and containing nerve centers involved in regulating physiological activity such as breathing, digestion, and heart functioning.

Melatonin   A natural hormone closely tied to sleep/wake cycles. Also called the *sleep hormone*.

Memory   The process of encoding, storage, and retrieval of any piece of information obtained through conscious experience; a memory can also be an individual instance of encoded, stored, and retrieved information.

Menarche   A girl's first menstrual period.

Mental age   The age given at which a child is currently performing intellectually.

Mental blocks   The ego's defenses against revealing sensitive issues.

Mental disorder   Patterns of behavior or thought that are not reasonable or easily understood and are associated with "clinically significant" distress or impairment in coping with the environment.

Mesomorphs Sheldon's moderate somatotype, believed to love adventure, exercise, and activities that demand boldness and courage.

Metaneeds Higher-level needs related to an organism's tendency toward growth.

Mind A term referring primarily to human consciousness. Often defined as originating from or resulting in processes of the brain associated with activities like thinking, imagining, and perceiving.

Mnemonic aids Systematic aids to remembering, like rhymes, acrostics, or visual imagery systems.

Mnemonist Professional memorizer.

Modal model of memory A widely accepted model of memory that describes three types of storage: sensory, short-term, and long-term.

Model A pattern for behavior that can be copied by someone. Also refers to descriptions of objects or phenomena. In science, models often serve as a sort of mental guide.

Modeling effect The type of imitative behavior that involves learning a novel response.

Models Guides or ways of looking at whether a behavior is abnormal or not.

Molecular genetics The branch of genetics that deals with hereditary transmission. Concerned with how genes are copied, how mutations come about, and how genes are expressed in species characteristics.

Monozygotic twins Twins resulting from the division of a single fertilized egg—hence *identical twins.*

Mood disorders Mental disorders involving mood disturbance—for example, bipolar disorder and major depressive disorder.

Motivation Conscious and unconscious forces that instigate, direct, and control our behavior.

Multiple intelligences A theory suggesting that intelligence is a product of a number of abilities rather than one ability.

Myelin sheath An insulating, protective coating that surrounds nerve fibers and facilitates neural transmission.

Naïve realism A philosophical idea that states the world should exist in only one form and therefore all the viewers should see the world as it exists.

Nanometer   One billionth of a meter.

Narcotics   A drug type producing sensations of well-being.

Naturalistic observation   Observe people or animals in their natural settings

Nature-nurture controversy   The debate over whether heredity or environment is most influential in determining developmental outcomes.

Need for achievement   A strong desire to excel, meet some inner standard of excellence, and do well.

Negative reinforcer   Unwanted or painful stimulus is removed and consequently, the probability that the behavior will be repeated is increased

Nerve   Bundles of fibers consisting of neurons, whose functions is the transmission of neural impulses.

Nervous system   All parts of the body composed of nerve cells, the function of which is to transmit messages. The major components of the human nervous system are the brain, the spinal cord, receptor systems associated with the major senses, and other nerve cells implicated in the functioning of muscles and glands.

Neurogenesis   The active production of new neurons. Most prevalent during the prenatal period but also occurs in adulthood.

Neurons   A single nerve cell, the smallest unit of the nervous system and its basic structural unit. The function of the neuron is to transmit impulses, which are basically electrical but are made possible through chemical changes.

Neuroscience   A biologically based science that looks at the nervous system—especially the brain—to understand consciousness and higher mental processes.

Neuroses   A once common label for a variety of milder mental disorders characterized by anxiety and fear.

Neuroticism   This "Big Five" personality factor includes the traits nervous, sensitive, and moody.

Neurotransmitters   Naturally produced chemicals that are released by nerve cells and that initiate or facilitate transmission of messages among nerve cells (e.g., serotonin, dopamine, norepinephrine, and acetylcholine).

Nominal fallacy   The assumption that naming something explains it.

Nondeclarative memory   Unconscious, nonverbalizable effects of experience such as might be manifested in acquired motor skills or in classical conditioning.

Nonexperimental research   Makes observations about how variables are related to one another and describes the findings

Nonnaturalistic observation   Observations that occur in a laboratory or in other circumstances where the investigator deliberately manipulates or otherwise affects the phenomena being observed.

Nonsense syllables   Meaningless combinations of vowels and consonants, like gar, lev, and kur, often used to study memory.

Norepinephrine   A neurotransmitter linked with arousal, memory, and learning. Anomalies in the functioning of the norepinephrine system may be linked to manifestations of depression. Also called *noradrenaline*.

Normal distribution   A probability distribution that takes the form of a symmetrical bell-shaped graph and that describes the expected distribution of many events and characteristics.

Obedience   Performance of a behavior in response to orders from an authority figure.

Obesity   Medical condition related to being overweight.

Object concept   Piaget's expression for a child's understanding that the world is composed of objects that continue to exist when they aren't being sensed.

Object permanence   The understanding that objects exist even when out of sight.

Observational learning   Bandura's theory involving learning through observing and imitating models

Obsessive-compulsive disorders   A disorder characterized by recurrent and unwanted thoughts and/or the need to perform repetitive physical or mental actions.

Occipital lobe   The part of our brain responsible for processing the visual information.

Occlusion   A phenomenon in which an object closer to a viewer appears to block another object that is farther away from the viewer.

Oedipus complex   A Freudian concept denoting the developmental stage (around 4 years) when a boy's increasing awareness of the sexual meaning of his genitals leads him to desire his mother and envy his father.

Olfaction   The sense of smell.

Olfactory epithelia   Thin mucus membranes located in each nostril, containing odor-sensitive cells.

Openness   A "Big Five" personality factor consisting of the traits inventive, curious, and unconventional.

Operant conditioning   (Skinner) describes changes in the probability of a response as a function of its consequences

Operant   An apparently voluntary response emitted by an organism.

Operation   Piaget's term for a thought process characterized by certain rules of logic.

Opinion   Evaluations, which lack the strong motivational consequences of attitudes.

Oppositional defiant disorder   A disorder marked by extremely disobedient, hostile, and defiant behavior in the face of authority.

Optic chiasm   The point in the brain at which the optic nerves from each eye meet and partly cross over to the other side of the brain.

Optic nerve   A large bundle of axons that leave the back of the eye and carries visual information to the visual cortex of the brain.

Organization   A memory strategy involving grouping items to be remembered in terms of similarities and differences.

Overjustification   Large external rewards reduce the intrinsic value of a behavior.

Ovum   The sex cell produced by a mature female, consisting of 23 chromosomes rather than 23 pairs of chromosomes.

Pacinean corpuscles   The sensory receptors for touch located under the skin; these sensory receptors respond to pressure applied to the surface of the skin.

Panic attacks   An episode occurring for no apparent reason involving intense fear and anxiety, often accompanied by physical symptoms such as shortness of breath and heart palpitations.

Panic disorder   A disorder characterized by recurrent and persistent panic attacks.

Paradoxical effect   Literally, a surprising or contradictory effect; used to describe the apparently sedating effect that some stimulants (such as Ritalin) have on children who suffer from excessive activity.

Paradoxical sleep   Another label for REM sleep, so called because during this stage of sleep physiological functions such as heart and respiration rate are very similar to those of a waking state.

Paraphillias   Variety of sexual deviants such as exhibitionism, fetishism, and sadism.

Parasympathetic nervous system   Part of the autonomic nervous system that regulates physiological reactions that accommodate emotional reactions.

Parietal lobes   Cerebral lobes located just above the temporal lobes, between the frontal and occipital lobes. The parietal lobes are involved in sensation.

Parkinson's disease   A central nervous system disease characterized by tremors, slow movement, and other symptoms; associated with low dopamine levels in the brain.

Parvocellular pathway   A visual pathway for central vision and high spatial resolution images.

Passion   In Sternberg's love theory, a strong, often sexual, and sometimes overwhelming desire to be with another person.

Passive Deception   Passive deception is deception by omission

Passive vocabulary   Words that are understood but that may not actually be used in speech.

Perception   The detailed process of interpreting and making sense of a combination of sensations.

Peripheral nervous system   The neural networks that fan out from the central nervous system to various parts of the body.

Permissive parenting style   Parenting characterized by high warmth and low demands.

Personal fable   An expression of adolescent egocentrism marked by the elaboration of fantasies, the hero of which is the adolescent.

Personality disorders   Behaviors that are socially inappropriate, inflexible, and often antisocial that typically become apparent during childhood or adolescence and are manifested as relatively stable.

Personality   The set of attributes that characterize an individual, including temperamental, emotional, mental, and behavioral tendencies, influenced by genetics, learning, and social experiences.

Persuasion   Deliberate attempts to alter behavior or beliefs.

Phenomenology   Concerned with the world of appearance—that is, the world as it appears to the individual.

Phenotype   A person's manifested characteristics, resulting from the interaction of genotype with the environment. (See *genotype.*)

Phi phenomenon   The illusion of motion created by presenting a rapid succession of slightly different static images.

Philosophy   The pursuit of wisdom; the study of reality in an attempt to arrive at an accurate and unified conception of the universe and its nature. Because people are part of the universe, philosophy originally included attempts to understand humans—which is now the discipline of psychology.

Phobias   Intense, irrational fears, recognized by the person as unreasonable, and often leading to avoidance of certain objects or situations.

Phonetic system   A powerful mnemonic system in which previously learned associations between numbers and mental images are used to recall large numbers of items forward, backward, or in any order.

Phonological loop   A part of Alan Baddeley's working memory model specialized to process verbal and auditory information.

Photons   A visible light particle. In *quantum physics,* an elementary particle that is the basic unit of light and other forms of radiation.

Photoreceptor   A type of sensory receptor specifically for vision, which is located on the retina at the back of the eye.

Physiological basis of aggression   Biological factors impacting aggression such as hormones.

Physiological needs   Basic needs to satisfy internal functions of an organism.

Pibloktoq   Arctic hysteria, a 19th-century form of madness found almost exclusively among the Inuit, marked by bouts of screaming and crying and sometimes shedding one's clothing.

Pinna   The outer funnel-shaped structure of the ear; normally, this is what people refer to as their ear.

Pituitary gland   A small endocrine gland found as a protrusion off the hypothalamus. The *master gland* involved in controlling functioning of other endocrine glands.

Placebo control group   Participants are exposed to a placebo

Placebo   An inert substance or object

Placenta   A flat, thick membrane attached to the inside of the uterus during pregnancy, connected to the fetus by means of the umbilical cord.

Play   Activities with no goal other than the enjoyment derived from them.

Pons   A small brain structure that appears as a bulge at the front of medulla. Part of the brain stem involved in breathing and arousal.

Population   In an experiment, the group to which results are to be generalized.

Positive reinforcer   Pleasing or positive stimulus is given and consequently, the probability that the behavior will be repeated is increased

Positron emission tomography (PET)   An imaging technique used extensively in medicine and in physiological and neurological research. Records changes in blood flow by detecting the distribution of radioactive particles injected in the bloodstream.

Postconventional moral reasoning   Kohlberg's third stage of moral development when people focus on equality and the greater good.

Posttraumatic stress disorder   A disorder that appears following exposure to an extremely traumatic event where fear is experienced long after the traumatic event.

Preconventional moral reasoning   Kohlberg's first stage of moral development when children focus on receiving rewards or avoiding punishments.

Prefrontal lobotomy   A surgical treatment that removes or makes lesions (cuts) in the frontal lobes of the brain to reduce anxiety and alleviate depression.

Prejudices   Personal beliefs about groups based on illogical reasoning or faulty generalization.

Prenatal development   Period of development from conception to birth.

Primary reinforcers   Stimuli that are naturally rewarding for an organism.

Proactive interference   When earlier learning interferes with the recall of subsequent learning.

Process of delivery   The three-stage process of giving birth.

Projective measures   Personality tests in which stimuli are ambiguous and testees' responses are interpreted as reflecting unconscious aspects of personality.

Propinquity   Physical proximity; factor related to physical attraction.

Proprioceptive sensation   Sensation relating to bodily position and movement arising from receptors within the body.

Protowords   The infant's first wordlike sounds used to signify a specific person or object.

Proximodistal   Pattern of development from core out to appendages.

Psychiatrists   Medical doctors with extensive additional training in the identification and treatment of mental and emotional disorders.

Psychoactive drug   A chemical substance that has the ability to alter perception, mood, behavior, and/or physiological function.

Psychoanalysis   A psychotherapeutic technique based on the belief that humans face psychological distress as a result of unconscious conflicts and desires (primarily sexual or aggressive) brought on during childhood

Psychodynamic theory   The elaborate theory developed by Freud, based on his notion that behavior and personality are developed by unconscious urges and motivations.

Psychodynamic   Relating to conscious and unconscious forces that influence behavior and personality.

Psychological hedonism   An approach to explaining human behavior suggesting that humans act in a way to achieve pleasure and avoid pain.

Psychological needs   The need for affection, belonging, achievement, independence, social recognition and self-esteem.

Psychology   Systematic investigation of human behavior and thought

Psychometric *g*   A term coined by Spearmen regarding a person's general or overall intelligence.

Psychosocial development   Erikson's phrase to describe human development as a sequence of stages involving the resolution of crises that are mainly social.

Puberty   Sexual maturity following pubescence.

Pubescence   Changes of adolescence leading to sexual maturity.

Pupil   The opening in the iris that allows light to pass through the lens and into the eyeball.

Random sampling   A sampling procedure in which each member of the population has an equal chance of being selected for the sample.

Rapid-eye-movement sleep (REM sleep)   Sometimes referred to as the stage 5 of sleep, the stage during which most of our dreaming occurs.

Rational emotive behavior therapy   Therapist has the patient focus on his or her immediate interpretation of the meanings of environmental events, rather than obscure historical causes.

Receptors   Specialized cells or groups of cells that respond to sensory stimulation.

Recessive gene   A gene whose characteristics are not manifested in offspring when paired with the corresponding dominant gene.

Reciprocal altruism   An explanation for altruistic behavior that asserts individuals are helpful to others because of the expectation this will be reciprocated.

reciprocal teaching   a method designed to improve reading comprehension

Reflex   A simple, unlearned behavior like blinking in response to something coming toward the eye.

Reflexes   Stimulus–response associations

Refractory period   A brief period after firing during which a neuron is "discharged" and is incapable of firing again.

Regression   A Freudian expression for the phenomenon of reverting to some of the activities and preoccupations of earlier developmental stages.

Rehearsal   The process of repeatedly introducing new information in order to retain the information in short-term memory, or to introduce into long-term memory.

Reinforcement   The effect of a reinforcer.

Reinforcer   any stimulus condition or consequence that increases the probability of a response

Rejecting/neglectful parenting style   Parenting characterized by low warmth and low demand.

Reliability   Consistency of your measure to produce similar results on different occasions

Repression   A Freudian term for the process by which intensely negative or frightening experiences are lost from conscious memory.

Respondent   A response elicited by a known, specific stimulus. An unconditioned response.

Response   A muscular, glandular, or mental reaction to a stimulus.

Reticular formation   (*Reticular activating system; RAS*) That portion of the brain stem assumed to be responsible for the physiological arousal of the cortex as well as for the control of sleeping and waking.

Retina   A light-sensitive membrane at the back of the eye that contains the sensory receptors for vision.

Retrieval cues   Stimuli like sounds, words, locations, smells, and so on that facilitate recall (that remind the individual of something).

Retrieval   The process of recognizing and then correctly recalling a piece of information from storage in long-term memory.

Retrieval-cue failure   Inability to remember due to the unavailability of appropriate cues.

Retroactive interference   When subsequently learned material interferes with the recall of previously learned material.

Reuptake   The process by which a nerve cell recaptures some of the neurotransmitters it has released. Some medications and drugs function to increase neurotransmitter effectiveness by blocking reuptake.

Rods   A specific group of photoreceptors that are specialized to process dim light and are useful for night vision and peripheral vision.

Sample   A subset of a population. A group with characteristics similar to those of the larger group from which they are selected.

Sapir-Whorf hypothesis   The belief that language is essential for and determines thought (strong form); or the belief that language limits but does not determine thought (weak form).

Schema (also scheme or schemata)   The label used by Piaget to describe a unit in cognitive structure. A scheme is, in one sense, an activity together with its structural connotations. In another sense, a scheme may be thought of as an idea or a concept. It usually labels a specific activity: the looking scheme, the grasping scheme, the sucking scheme.

Schemas   A cognitive framework placing information into classifications and groups.

Schizoaffective disorder   Includes symptoms of schizophrenia in addition to a mood disorder such as depression or mania.

Schizophrenia   A psychotic disorder characterized by emotional, cognitive, and perceptual confusion and a consequent breakdown of effective contact with others and with reality.

Schizophreniform disorder   Same symptoms as schizophrenia but the only differences are symptoms last only 1 to 6 months.

School psychologists   Psychologists who deal with behavioral and learning problems affecting schoolchildren and issues relating to testing and placement of gifted or challenged children.

Science   An approach and an attitude toward the search for knowledge that emphasize objectivity, precision, and replicability.

Scientific method   Framework for the systematic study of behavior and mental processes

Secondary reinforcers   stimuli that may not be reinforcing initially but that eventually become reinforcing as a function of having been associated with other reinforcers.

Secure base   A safe, supportive relationship that infants use to explore and understand their world.

Sedatives   A drug type causing drowsiness.

Self-actualization   An ongoing process in which an organism attempts to reach its potential.

Self-efficacy   Our belief of personal competence.

Semantic memory   A type of long-term memory (explicit memory, to be exact); it is one's general knowledge about the world and specific concepts.

Sensation   The detection of physical stimuli in the environment such as light waves, sound waves, pressure, or chemical molecules.

Senses   Specialized organs by means of which stimulation is received and felt (for example, organs related to sight, smell, touch, taste, and hearing.)

Sensitive period   Time when the major systems are being formed and are most vulnerable to damage.

Sensorimotor stage   Piaget's first stage of cognitive development.

Sensorimotor   First stage of Piaget's stages of cognitive development. It describes how infants understand their world. They understand their world mainly in terms of the activities they perform and the sensations that result.

Sensory adaption   A decline in a sensation's sensitivity resulting from the presence of a constant stimulus.

Sensory memory   A form of memory that holds large amounts of sensory information such as sights and sounds for a very brief amount of time, normally only a few seconds.

Serotonin   A neurotransmitter, the bulk of which is found in the gut, where it regulates intestinal activity. Too low levels of serotonin may be associated with depression.

Seven deadly sins of memory   A term coined by Schacter to illustrate the forgetful nature of human memory systems.

Sex chromosome   A chromosome in sperm and egg cells responsible for determining the sex of the offspring.

Sex-linked defects   Defects due to the action of a gene located on the sex chromosome, most often on the X chromosome, and most often manifested in males.

Sexual dysfunctions   Problems relating to sexual desire or response.

Shaping   Reinforcing small sequential steps in a chain of behaviors, leading to the desired final behavior

Short-term memory   A type of temporary memory used to hold information long enough for an individual to process it, and make sense of it; also called working memory.

Significant   In research, refers to findings that would not be expected to occur by chance alone more than a small percentage (for example, 5 or 1 percent) of the time.

Single blind study   Only the researcher knows to which group the participant has been assigned

Single-blind procedure   An experimental procedure in which either the investigators or the participants are not aware of who are members of the experimental group and who are members of the control group.

Situational attributions   Causes of behavior related to characteristics of the situation.

Skin senses   Also called the cutaneous senses, the body senses consisting of skin receptors sensitive to touch, temperature, and pain.

Skinner box   an experimental chamber used in operant conditioning experiments

Slow-to-warm-up infants   An infant temperament type marked by low activity level; high initial withdrawal from the unfamiliar; slow adaptation to change; and a somewhat negative mood, with moderate or low intensity of reaction.

Social cognitive theory   An explanation of learning and behavior that emphasizes the role of social reinforcement and imitation as well as the importance of the cognitive processes that allow people to imagine and to anticipate.

Social learning theory   Argues aggression is a result of learning from models in our environment.

Social phobia   Excessive fear of embarrassment in social situations, often leading to avoidance.

Social psychology   Studies the relationships among individuals or between individuals and groups.

Socialization   The process of learning behaviors that are appropriate and inappropriate for a given culture.

Solipsism   A philosophical idea that states the world exists by the viewer's conscious state and may be different from the objective state of this world.

Somatic symptom disorders   A disorder in which the patient has symptoms suggestive of some medical problem but no such problem can be found.

Somatic system   Part of the peripheral nervous system concerned with bodily sensations and muscular movement.

Somatoform disorders   A grouping of mental disorders characterized by physical complaints that appear to be medical in nature but cannot be explained by injury, disease, drug abuse, or other mental disorders.

Sound waves   Displacements of molecules caused by vibratory events whose subjective effect is the perception of sound.

Specific learning disabilities   A developmental disorder marked by impairments in cognitive skills such as reading, writing, arithmetic, or mathematical skills.

Specific phobia   Excessive and unreasonable fear brought about by a specific stimulus.

Sperm cell   The sex cell produced by a mature male, consisting of 23 chromosomes rather than 23 pairs of chromosomes.

Spinal cord   Main link between the brain and sensory and motor systems, closely involved in reflexes such as the knee-jerk reflex.

Statistical procedure   A way of analyzing data (observations). Typically used in scientific investigations to determine whether a set of observations might have been expected to occur by chance.

Stereotypes   Widely held beliefs about groups based on illogical reasoning or faulty generalization.

Stimulant   A type of drug that speeds up physiological functions. Cocaine is an abused stimulant and it speeds up the heart rate.

Stimulus (*pl.* stimuli)   A physical stimulus is any change in the physical environment capable of exciting a sense organ. Stimuli can also be internal events such as glandular secretions or even thoughts.

Stimulus discrimination   Involves making different responses to highly similar stimuli

Stimulus generalization   Involves making the same responses to different but related stimuli

Storage   The process of storing.

Strange situation   The procedure developed by Ainsworth to assess different attachment styles.

Stratified sampling   A sampling procedure that takes steps to ensure that subgroups of the population are represented proportionally in the final sample.

Structuralism   The study of breaking down conscious experience into its fundamental elements: sensations, feelings, and images

Subject variable   Characteristic or attribute of a participant that can impact the participant's behavior or thoughts

Substance-related disorders   Disorders related to drug abuse or to the effects of various chemical or gaseous substances, including medications.

Suggestibility   A characteristic of a hypnotic state wherein subjects become exceedingly ready to believe whatever is *suggested by* the hypnotist and willing to perform whatever activities are asked of them.

Superego   The personality structure that defines the moral or ethical aspects of personality.

Survey research   A questionnaire is designed to obtain information regarding individuals' behaviors, attitudes, or opinions

Survey   A research method that involves sampling a large group of individuals.

Susto   A Latino disorder marked by listlessness, muscle tics, and anxiety and attributed to the loss of one's soul following some trauma.

Symbolic model   A model other than a real-life person. For example, books, television, and written instructions are important symbolic models.

Symbolic thought   The ability to mentally use one object to stand for another.

Sympathetic nervous system   Part of the autonomic nervous system that instigates the physiological responses that accompany emotional behavior.

Synapse   A microscopic gap between the end of an axon and an adjacent dendrite, axon, or other cell across which neural impulses (neurotransmitters) travel.

Synaptic knob   Slight enlargements on the wispy branches at the ends of axons.

Synesthesia   A condition in which different sensations overlap and are processed simultaneously. A person with synesthesia might see a musical note or *hear* a color.

Systematic desensitization   A type of therapy where the therapist tries to replace an undesirable response with another incompatible and more desirable response. The procedure is particularly effective for phobias.

Taste buds   The sensory receptors for gustation that are located deep within porous structures on the tongue; there are five basic types of taste buds.

Temperament   Infants' and children's biological predisposition to respond to the world in predictable ways.

Temporal lobes   Cerebral structure located on either side of the cerebrum, associated primarily with speech, language, and hearing.

Teratogens   Substances that can cross the placental barrier and damage the developing organism during pregnancy.

Territoriality   Example of an innate or biological aggressive tendency.

Thalamus   A small brain structure that serves as a major relay center for incoming sensory signals.

Thanatos   A Freudian term denoting the death wish or death instinct.

Therapy   Systematic processes for helping individuals overcome their psychological problems.

Theta waves   Slow brain waves (4 to 7 per second) characteristic of the early stages of sleep.

Third force psychology   Maslow's term for the humanistic movement in psychology—so labeled to differentiate it from the *first force* (behaviorism) and the *second force* (Freudian psychodynamic theory).

Top-down processing   An information-gathering process starting from an individual's knowledge, expectations, and prior experiences.

Trait   Any distinct, consistent characteristic that can vary from one person to another.

Transduction   The process of converting a physical stimulus into a meaningful and useful neural signal capable of being interpreted by the brain.

Transference   Redirection of feelings directed toward the therapist that are associated with important figures in the patient's life.

Transitive inference   A type of logical thinking in which an inference is made about the relationship of two objects or events by comparing them with a third rather than by comparing them directly.

Triadic reciprocal determinism   Describes the three principal features of our social cognitive realities our personal factors (our personalities, our intentions, what we know and feel); our actions (our actual behaviors); and our environments (both the social and physical aspects of our world).

Triangular theory of love   Sternberg's theory of loving involving commitment, passion, and intimacy.

Triarchic theory of successful intelligence   Sternberg's view that intelligence involves analytical, creative, and practical abilities, as well as skill in selecting and shaping environments to maximize adaptation.

Type   A related grouping of personality traits.

Umami   One of the five distinct tastes humans can distinguish, variously described as *savory* or *meaty*.

Umbilical cord   A long, thick cord attached to the placenta at one end and to what will be the child's navel at the other.

Unconditioned response (UR)   The automatic, unlearned response an organism gives when the US is presented.

Unconditioned stimulus (US)   A stimulus that elicits an automatic, unlearned response from an organism.

Uterus   The womb, where the infant develops prenatally.

Validity   Ability of your measurement to accurately measure what it is supposed to measure.

Variable   An event or characteristic with at least two possible values.

Vestibular organ   The part of the inner ear, consisting of the semicircular canals, involved in balance, body orientation, and movement.

Vestibular sense   The sense, highly dependent on the semicircular canals in the inner ear, that provides us with information about balance and movement.

Vicarious reinforcement   When you see someone doing something repeatedly, you unconsciously assume that the behavior must be reinforcing for that person.

Visual constancies   Properties of visual perception that enable us to perceive color, size, and shape as being constant under a variety of different conditions.

Visual-spatial sketch pad   One of the slave systems in Baddeley's model of working memory, concerned with the processing of material that is primarily visual or spatial.

Visuospatial sketchpad   A part of Alan Baddeley's working memory model specialized to process visual and spatial information.

Wavelength   In vision, a property of light waves measured in nanometers (billionths of a meter) and related to the perception of color.

Weber's law   A principle in sensation that suggests that the size of the difference threshold is relative to the strength of the original stimulus.

"What" pathway   A visual pathway projected into the temporal lobe that responds to and integrates information about the size, color, and/or the identity of an object.

"Where" pathway   A visual pathway projected into the parietal lobe that integrates information about the location of an object.

Windigo   A primarily male disorder found among some Native American tribes in which the victim becomes convinced that he will become a *Windigo*—a person-eating creature.

Withdrawal symptoms   A state occurring when an individual who regularly uses a drug, stops or reduces drug use, and can have unpleasant and sometimes dangerous reactions.

Working memory   The Baddeley model describing how information is processed in short-term memory by means of a control system (central executive system) and systems that maintain verbal material (phonological loop) and visual material (visual-spatial sketch pad).

Yerkes–Dodson Law   A law stating that there is an optimal level of arousal and performance.

Young-Helmholtz trichromatic theory   A theory that recognizes the existence of three cone systems whose different responses to light waves determine perception of color.

Zygote   The fertilized egg that starts to divide.

REFERENCES

Adolfsson, B., Andersson, I., Elofsson, S., Rossner, S., & Unden, A. L. (2005). Locus of control and weight reduction. *Patient Education and Counseling, 56*(1), 55–61.

Ainsworth, M. D. S. (1973). The development of infant-mother attachment. In B. M. Caldwell and H. N. Ricciuti (Eds.), *Review of child development research* (Vol. 3, pp. 1–94). Chicago, IL: University of Chicago Press.

Ainsworth, M. D. S., Blehar, M. C., Waters, E., & Wall, S. (1978). *Patterns of attachment: A psychological study of the strange situation.* Hillsdale, NJ: Erlbaum.

Allport, G. W. (1968). The historical background of modern social psychology. In G. Lindzey & E. Aronson (Eds.), *Handbook of social psychology* (Vol. 1, 2nd ed.). Cambridge, MA: Addison-Wesley.

Allport, G. W., & Odbert, H. S. (1936). Trait names: A psycho-lexical study. *Psychological Monographs, 47*, 2–11. doi:10.1037/h0093360

Almas, E., & Landmark, B. (2010). Non-pharmacological treatment of sexual problems—A review of research literature 1970-2008. *European Journal of Sexology and Sexual Health/Revue europeene de sexology et de santé sexuelle, 19*(4), 202–211.

Amato, P. R., & Keith, B. (1991). Parental divorce and the well-being of children: A meta-analysis. *Psychological Bulletin, 110,* 26–6.

American Academy of Neurology. (2009, March 17). Shrinking in hippocampus area of brain precedes Alzheimer's disease. *Science Daily.* Retrieved July 22, 2010, from http://www.sciencedaily.com/releases/2009/03/090316173214.htm

American Psychiatric Association. (2013). *Diagnostic and statistical manual of mental disorders* (5th ed.). Arlington, VA: American Psychiatric Publishing.

American Psychiatric Association. (2000). *Diagnostic and statistical manual of mental disorders* (4th ed., text revision). Washington, DC: Author.

Amsler, S. J. (2010). Energetic costs of territorial boundary patrols by wild chimpanzees. *American Journal of Primatology, 72*(2), 93–103.

Anderson, J. R. (1990). *Cognitive psychology and its implications* (3rd ed.). New York, NY: W. H. Freeman and Company.

Antheunis, M. L., Valkenburg, P. M., & Peter, J. (2010). Getting acquainted through social network sites: Testing a model of online uncertainty reduction and social attraction. *Computers in Human Behavior, 26*(1), 100–109.

Anton, S. D., Martin, C. K., Han, H., Coulon, S., Cefalu, W. T., Geiselman, P., & Williamson, D. A. (2010). Effects of stevia, aspartame, and sucrose on food intake, satiety, and postprandial glucose and insulin levels. *Appetite, 55*(1), 37–43.

APA Directory Survey 2005, compiled by APA Research Office. Retrieved July 13, 2010, from http://www.apa.org/workforce/publications/05–member/table–3.pdf

APA. (2010). Divisions. Retrieved July 13, 2010, from http://www.apa.org/about/division/index.aspx

Arim, R. G., & Shapka, J. D. (2008). The impact of pubertal timing and parental control on adolescent problem behaviors. *Journal of Youth and Adolescence, 37*(4), 445–455.

Arnone, D., Horder, J., Cowen, P. J., & Harmer, C. J. (2009). Early effects of mirtazapine on emotional processing. *Psychopharmacology, 203*(4), 685–691.

Arnulf, I., & Leu-Semenescu, S. (2009). Sleepiness in Parkinson's disease. *Parkinsonism & Related Disorders, 15*(Suppl. 3), S101–S104.

Asch, S. E. (1955). Opinions and social pressure. *Scientific American, 193*(5), 31–35.

Asch, S.E. (1951). Effects of group pressure upon the modification and distortion of judgment. In H. Guetzkow (Ed.) *Groups, leadership, and men*. Pittsburgh, PA: Carnegie Press.

Asensio, S., Romero, M. J., Romero, F. J., Wong, C., Alia-Klein, N., Tomasi, D., Wang, G. J., Telang, F., Volkow, N. D., & Goldstein, R. Z. (2010). Striatal dopamine D2 receptor availability predicts the thalamic and medial prefrontal responses to reward in cocaine abusers three years later. *Synapse, 64*(5), 397–402.

Ashcraft, M. H., & Radvansky, C. A. (2010). *Cognition* (5th ed.). Upper Saddle River, NJ: Prentice Hall.

Atkinson, R. C., & Shiffrin, R. M. (1968). Human memory: A proposed system and its control processes. In K. W. Spence & J. T. Spence (Eds.), *The psychology of learning and motivation, 2*. London: Academic Press.

Aubrey, C. (1993). An investigation of the mathematical knowledge and competencies which young children bring into school. *British Educational Research Journal, 19,* 27–41.

Azevedo, F. A. C., Carvalho, L. R. B., Grinberg, L. T., Farfel, J. M., Ferretti, R. E. L., Leite, R. E. P., Filho, W. J., Lent, R., & Herculano-Houzel, S. (2009). Equal numbers of neuronal and nonneuronal cells make the human brain an isometrically scaled-up primate brain. *Journal of Comparative Neurology, 513*(5), 532–541.

Baddeley, A. D. (2007). *Working memory, thought, and action.* New York: Oxford University Press.

Baddeley, A. D., & Hitch, G. J. (1974). Working memory. In G. Bower (Ed.), *The psychology of learning and motivation.* New York: Academic Press.

Balaban, M. T., & Reisenauer, C. D. (2005). Sensory development. In N. J. Salkind (Ed.), *Encyclopedia of human development.* Thousand Oaks, CA: Sage. Retrieved from http://www.sage-ereference.com/human development

Bandura, A. (2001). Social cognitive theory: An agentic perspective. *Annual Review of Psychology, 52,* 1–26.

Bandura, A. (1997). *Self-efficacy: The exercise of control.* New York: W. H. Freeman.

Bandura, A. (1977). *Social learning theory.* Englewood Cliffs, NJ: Prentice Hall.

Bandura, A., & Walters, R. (1963). *Social learning and personality development.* New York: Holt, Rinehart & Winston.

Bandura, A., Ross, D., & Ross, S. A. (1961). Transmission of aggression through imitation of aggressive models. *Journal of Abnormal and Social Psychology, 63,* 575–582.

Banks, M. S., & Ginsburg, A. P. (1985). Early visual preferences: A review and new theoretical treatment. In H. W. Reese (Ed.), *Advances in child development and behavior* (Vol. 19, pp. 207–246). New York, NY: Academic Press.

Barber, L. K., Bagsby, P. G., & Munz, D. C. (2010). Affect regulation strategies for promoting (or preventing) flourishing emotional health. *Personality and Individual Differences, 9*(6), 663–666.

Barber, T. X., & Westland, S. (2011). *Thinking therapeutically: Hypnotic skills and strategies explored.* Norwalk, CT: Crown House Publishing.

Bartels, M., Rietveld, M. J., Van Baal, G. C., & Boomsma, D. I. (2002). Genetic and environmental influences on the development of intelligence. *Behavior Genetics, 32*(4), 237–249. doi: 10.1023/A:1019772628912

Bartone, P. T. (2010). Preventing prisoner abuse: Leadership lessons of Abu Ghraib. *Ethics and Behavior, 20*(2), 161–173.

Batista, J., & Freitas-Magalhaes, A. (2009). The recognition of basic emotions in temporal lobe epilepsy. In A. Freitas-Magalhaes (Ed.), *Emotional expression: The brain and the face* (pp. 24–56). Porto, Portugal: Edicoes Universidade Fernando Pessoa.

Baumrind, D. (1973). The development of instrumental competence through socialization. In A. D. Pick (Ed.), *Minnesota Symposia on Child Psychology* (Vol. 7, pp. 3–46). Minneapolis, MN: University of Minnesota Press.

Baumrind, D. (1991a). The influence of parenting style on adolescent competence and substance use. *Journal of Early Adolescence, 11*, 56–95. doi: 10.1177/0272431691111004

Baumrind, D. (1991b). Parenting styles and adolescent development. In R. M. Lerner, A. C. Petersen, & J. Brooks-Gunn (Eds.), *Encyclopedia of adolescence* (pp. 746–758). New York, NY: Garland.

Beaver, K. M. (2010). The biochemistry of violent crime. In C. J. Ferguson (Ed.), *Violent crime: Clinical and social implications* (pp. 75–98). Thousand Oaks, CA: Sage Publications.

Beck, A. T. (2008). The evolution of the cognitive model of depression and its neurobiological correlates. *American Journal of Psychiatry, 165*(8), 967–977.

Beck, A.T., & Freedman, A. (1990). Cognitive therapy of personality disorders. New York: Guilford..

Belin, P., Zatorre, R. J., Lafaille, P., Ahad, P., & Pike, B. (2000). Voice-selective areas in human auditory cortex. *Nature, 403*, 309–312. doi: 10.1038/35002078

Bell, J. H., & Bromnick, R. D. (2003). The social reality of the imaginary audience: A grounded theory approach. *Adolescence, 38*(150), 205–219.

Bender, J. A., Pollack, A. J., & Ritzmann, R. E. (2010). Neural activity in the central complex of the insect brain is linked to locomotor changes. *Current Biology, 20*(10), 921–926.

Benjamin, Jr., L.T. (2008). Psychology before 1900. In S. F. Davis & W. Buskist (Eds.) *21st century psychology: A reference handbook* (pp. 2–11). Thousand Oaks, CA: Sage Publications.

Benjamin, L. T. Jr. (2008). The Pulfrich pendulum effect: When to and fro is roundabout. In L. T. Benjamin Jr. (Ed.), *Favorite activities for the teaching of psychology* (pp. 79–82). Washington, DC: American Psychological Association.

Berger, C., Donnadieu, S., Meary, D., Kandel, S., & Mazens, K. (2010). Feature perception of speaking faces in newborn infants. *Psychologie Francaise, 55*(1), 49–58.

Berlyne, D. E. (1960). *Conflict, arousal, and curiosity.* New York: McGraw-Hill.

Bermudez-Silva, F. J., Viveros, M. P., McPartland, J. M., & de Fonseca, F. R. (2010). The endocannabinoid system, eating behavior and energy homeostasis: The end or a new beginning? *Pharmacology, Biochemistry and Behavior, 95*(4), 375–382.

Bernard, L. L. (1924). *Instinct: A study in social psychology.* New York: Holt, Rinehart & Winston.

Bhaduri, N. P., Sarkar, K., Sinha, S., Chattopadhyay, A., & Mukhopadhyay, K. (2010). Study on DBH genetic polymorphisms and plasma activity in attention deficit hyperactivity disorder patients from Eastern India. *Cellular and Molecular Neurobiology, 30*(2), 265–274.

Bickman, L. (2005). A common factors approach to improving mental health services. *Mental Health Services Research, 7*(1), 1–4. doi: 10.1007/s11020-005-1961-7

Billock, V. A., & Tsou, B. H. (2010, February). "Impossible" colors: See hues that can't exist. *Scientific American,* 72–77.

Blake, R., & Sekuler, R. (2005). *Perception* (5th ed.). New York, NY: McGraw-Hill.

Blakemore, C. (1977). *Mechanics of the mind.* Cambridge, MA: Cambridge University Press.

Block, J. (1995). A contrarian view of the five-factor approach to personality description. *Psychology Bulletin, 117*(2), 187–215. doi:10.1037/0033-2909.117.2.187

Boake, C. (2002). From the Binet–Simon to the Wechsler–Bellevue: Tracing the history of intelligence testing. *Journal of Clinical and Experimental Neuropsychology, 24*(3), 383–405. doi: 10.1076/jcen.24.3.383.981

Bolkan, C. R., Meierdiercks, P., & Hooker, K. (2009). Addressing stability and change in the six-foci model of personality: Personality development in midlife and beyond. In M. C. Smith & N. DeFrates-Densch (Eds.), *Handbook of research on adult learning and development* (pp. 220–240). New York, NY: Routledge/Taylor & Francis Group.

Bolles, R. C. (1970). Species-specific defense reactions and avoidance learning. *Psychological Review, 77,* 32–48.

Bolton, P.F., Golding, J., Emond, A., & Steer, C.D. (2012) Autism spectrum disorder and autistic traits in the Avon Longitudinal Study of Parents and Children: Precursors and early signs. *Journal of American Academy of Child and Adolescent Psychiatry, 51*(3), 249–260. doi: 10.1016/j.jaac.2011.12.oo9

Boroditsky, L. (2003). Linguistic relativity. In L. Nadel (Ed.), *Encyclopedia of cognitive science* (pp. 917–922). London: Macmillan.

Borrero, J. C., Frank, M. A., & Hausman, N. L. (2009). Applications of the matching law. In W. T. O'Donohue & J. E. Fisher (Eds.), *General principles and empirically supported techniques of cognitive behavior therapy* (pp. 415–424). Hoboken, NJ: John Wiley & Sons.

Bowlby, J. (1953). *Child care and the growth of love.* London, England: Penguin Books.

Bowlby, J. (1969). *Attachment and loss: Vol 1. Attachment.* New York, NY: Basic Books.

Bradshaw, G. L., & Anderson, J. R. (1982). Elaborative encoding as an explanation of levels of processing. *Journal of Verbal Learning and Verbal Behavior, 21,* 165–174.

Bramlett, M. D., & Mosher, W. D. (2002). *Vital and health statistics: Series 22. Cohabitation, marriage, divorce, and remarriage in the United States.* Hyattsville, MD: National Center for Health Statistics

Bransford, J. D., & Stein, B. S. (1993). *The IDEAL problem solver* (2nd ed.). New York: W. H. Freeman.

Bregman, J. (2005). Apgar score. In N. J. Salkind (Ed.), *Encyclopedia of human development.* Thousand Oaks, CA: Sage. Retrieved from http://www.sage-ereference.com/humandevelopment

Breland, K., & Breland, M. (1961). The misbehavior of organisms. *American Psychologist, 16,* 681–684.

Breland, K., & Breland, M. (1966). *Animal behavior.* New York: Macmillan.

Bright, C. N., & Penrod, B. (2009). An evaluation of the overjustification effect across multiple contingency arrangements. *Behavioral Interventions, 24*(3), 185–194.

Brightman, R. A. (1988). The Windigo in the material world. *Ethnohistory, 35*(4), 337–379.

Brody, B. A. (2001). Defending animal research: An international perspective. In E. F. Paul & J. Paul (Eds.), *Why animal experimentation matters: The use of animals in medical research. New studies in social policy* (pp. 131–147). New Brunswick, NJ: Transaction.

Brown, D. C. (Ed.). (2009). *Advances in the use of hypnosis for medicine, dentistry and pain prevention/management.* Norwalk, CT: Crown House Publishing.

Brown, J. L. (1964). States in newborn infants. *Merrill-Palmer Quarterly, 10,* 313–327.

Brown, R., & Kulik, J. (1977). Flashbulb memories. *Cognition, 5,* 73–99. doi: 10.1016/0010-0277(77)90018-X

Bruer, J. T. (2006). Points of view: On the implications of neuroscience research for science teaching and learning: Are there any? *CBE Life Science Education, 5*(2), 104–110.

Brumariu, L. E., & Kerns, K. A. (2010). Parent–child attachment and internalizing symptoms in childhood and adolescence: A review of empirical findings and future directions. *Development and Psychopathology, 22,* 177–203. doi:10.1017/S0954579409990344

Brungart, D. S., & Simpson, B. D. (2007). Cocktail party listening in a dynamic multitalker environment. *Perception and Psychophysics, 69*(1), 79–91.

Buchanan, K. I., & Bardi, A. (2010). Acts of kindness and acts of novelty affect life satisfaction. *Journal of Social Psychology, 150*(3), 235–237.

Bullock, M. (1985). Animism in childhood thinking: A new look at an old question. *Developmental Psychology, 21,* 217–255.

Burger, J. M. (2009). Replicating Milgram: Would people still obey today? *American Psychologist, 64*(1), 1–11.

Bush, D. E. A., Schafe, G. E., & LeDoux, J. E. (2009). Neural basis of fear conditioning. In G. G. Berntson & J. T. Cacioppo (Eds.), *Handbook of neuroscience for the behavioral sciences* (Vol. 2, pp. 762–764). Hoboken, NJ: John Wiley & Sons.

Bussing, R., Mason, D. M., Bell, L., Porter, P., & Garvan, C. (2010). Adolescent outcomes of childhood attention-deficit/hyperactivity disorder in a diverse community sample. *Journal of the American Academy of Child and Adolescent Psychiatry, 49*(6), 595–605.

Butler, T., Schofield, P. W., Greenberg, D., Allnutt, S. H., Indig, D. C., Vaughan, D'Este C., Mitchell, P. B., Knight, L., & Ellis, A. (2010). Reducing impulsivity in repeat violent offenders: An open label trial of a selective serotonin reuptake inhibitor. *Australian and New Zealand Journal of Psychiatry, 44*(12), 1137–1143.

Buysse, D. J., Strollo, P. J. Jr., Black, J. E., Zee, P. G., & Winkelman, J. W. (2008). Sleep disorders. In R. E. Hales, S. C. Yudofsky, & G. O. Gabbard (Eds.), *The American Psychiatric Publishing textbook of psychiatry* (5th ed., pp. 921–969). Arlington, VA: American Psychiatric Publishing.

Cacioppo, J. T., Petty, R. E., Kao, C. F., & Rodriguez, R. (1986). Central and peripheral routes to persuasion: An individual difference perspective. *Journal of Personality and Social Psychology, 31*, 1032–1043.

Cain, D. J. (2010). *Person-centered psychotherapies.* Washington, DC: American Psychological Association.

Caldwell, A. B. (2006). Maximal measurement or meaningful measurement: The interpretive challenges of the MMPI-2 Restructured Clinical (RC) Scales. *Journal of Personality Assessment, 87*, 193–201. doi:10.1207/s15327752jpa8702_09

Canivez, G. L., Konold, T. R., Collins, J. M., & Wilson, G. (2009). Construct validity of the Wechsler Abbreviated Scale of Intelligence and Wide Range Intelligence Test: Convergent and structural validity. *School Psychology Quarterly, 24*(4), 252–265.

Cannon, W. B. (1929). *Bodily changes in pain, hunger, fear, and rage* (2nd ed.). New York: Appleton Century Crofts.

Cannon, W. B. (1939). *The wisdom of the body.* New York: Norton.

Cannon, W. B., & Washburn, A. L. (1912). An explanation of hunger. *American Journal of Physiology, 29*, 441–454.

Carlson, B. M. (2007). *Principles of regenerative biology.* Burlington, MA: Academic Press.

Carlson, E. A., Sroufe, L. A., & Egeland, B. (2004). The construction of experience: A longitudinal study of representation and behavior. *Child Development, 75,* 66–83. doi: 10.1111/j.1467-8624.2004.00654.x

Cartwright, Rosalind D. (2010). *The twenty-four hour mind: The role of sleep and dreaming in our emotional lives.* New York: Oxford University Press.

Cassia, V. M., Turati, C., & Simion, F. (2004). Can a nonspecific bias toward top-heavy patterns explain newborns' face preferences? *Psychological Science, 15,* 379–383. doi: 10.1111/j.0956-7976.2004.00688.x

Cassidy, J. (1994). Emotion regulation: Influences of attachment relationships. *Monographs of the Society for Research in Child Development, 59* (2–3 Serial No. 240), 228–249.

Cattell, R. B. (1946). *Description and measurement of personality.* New York: Harcourt Brace & World.

Cavaiola, A. A., & Strohmetz, D. B. (2010). Perception of risk for subsequent drinking and driving related offenses and locus of control among first-time DUI offenders. *Alcoholism Treatment Quarterly, 28,* 52–62. doi:10.1080/07347320903436169

Celebrities with dissociative disorders. (2010). Retrieved April 15, 2011, from http://www.associatedcontent.com/article/5734796/celebrities_with_dissociative_disorders.html?cat70

Centers for Disease Control and Prevention (2011). Mental illness surveillance among U.S. adults. Retrieved from http://www.cdc.gov/mental healthsurveillance

Centers for Disease Control and Prevention (2014). Autism spectrum disorder. Retrieved from http://www.cdc.gov/ncbddd/autism/data.html

Charles, E. P., & Rivera, S. M. (2009). Object permanence and method of disappearance: Looking measures further contradict reaching measures. *Developmental Science, 12*(6), 991–1006.

Chaudhuri, A. (2011). *Fundamentals of sensory perception.* New York, NY: Oxford University Press.

Chaz Bono granted name, gender change. (2010). Associated Press. Retrieved April 15, 2011, from http://today.msnbc.msn.com/id/36997743/ns/today–entertainment/

Chen, W. C. (2009). Test anxiety and under-performance: An analysis examination process. *Bulletin of Educational Psychology, 40*(4), 597–618.

Cherlin, A. J. (2010). Demographic trends in the United States: A review of research in the 2000s. *Journal of Marriage and Family, 72,* 403–419. doi: 10.1111/j.1741-3737.2010.00710.x

Cherry, E. C. (1953). Some experiments on the recognition of speech with one and two ears. *Journal of the Acoustical Society of America, 25,* 975–979.

Chiesa, M., & Hobbs, S. (2008). Making sense of social research: How useful is the Hawthorne Effect? *European Journal of Social Psychology, 38*(1), 67–74.

Choi, K. H., Higgs, B. W., Wendland, J. R., Song, J., McMahon, F. J., & Webster, M. J. (2011). Gene expression and genetic variation data implicate PCLO in bipolar disorder. *Biological Psychiatry, 69*(4), 353–359.

Ciribassi, J. (2009). Understanding behavior: Feline hyperesthesia syndrome. *Compendium: Continuing Education For Veterinarians, 31*(3), E10.

Claridge, G., Clark, K., Powney, E., & Hassan, E. (2008). Schizotypy and the Barnum effect. *Personality and Individual differences, 44,* 436–444. doi:10.1016/j.paid.2007.09.006

Clump, M. A. (2006). An active learning classroom activity for the "cocktail party phenomenon." *Teaching of Psychology, 33*(1), 51–53.

Cohen, D. (2006). Critiques of the "ADHD" enterprise. In G. Lloyd, J. Stead, & D. Cohen (Eds.), *Critical new perspectives on ADHD* (pp. 12–33). New York: Routledge.

Cohen-Yavin, I., Yoran-Hegesh, R., Strous, R. D., Kotler, M., Weizman, A., & Spivak, B. (2009). Efficacy of reboxetine in the treatment of attention-deficit/hyperactivity disorder in boys with intolerance to methylphenidate: An open-label, 8-week, methylphenidate-controlled trial. *Clinical Neuropharmacology, 32*(4), 179–182.

Collings, V. B. (1974). Human taste response as a function of locus of stimulation on the tongue and soft palate. *Perception & Psychophysics, 16,* 169–174.

Colvin, S. S. (1905). Is subjective idealism a necessary point of view for psychology? *The Journal of Philosophy, Psychology and Scientific Methods, 2*(9), 225–231. doi: 10.2307/2011704

Comer, R.J. (2013). *Abnormal psychology* (8th ed.). New York, NY: Worth Publishers.

Connor, D. F., Steeber, J., & McBurnett, K. (2010). A review of attention-deficit/hyperactivity disorder complicated by symptoms of oppositional defiant disorder or conduct disorder. *Journal of Developmental and Behavioral Pediatrics, 31*(5), 427–440.

Conrad, P., & Schneider, J. W. (1992). *Deviance and medicalization: From badness to sickness.* Philadelphia: Temple University Press.

Conway, M. A., Anderson, S. J., Larsen, S. F., Donnelly, C. M., McDaniel, M. A., McClelland, A. G. R., Rawles, R. E., & Logie, R. H. (1994). The formation of flashbulb memories. *Memory & Cognition, 22,* 326–343. doi: 10.3758/BF03200860

Cooney, T. M., Pedersen, F. A., Indelicato, S., & Palkovitz, R. (1993). Timing of fatherhood: Is "on-time" optimal? *Journal of Marriage and the Family, 55,* 205–215.

Copeland, W., Shanahan, L., Miller, S., Costello, E. J., Angold, A., & Maughan, B. (2010, May 17). Outcomes of early pubertal timing in young women: A prospective population-based study. *American Journal of Psychiatry (doi: 10.1176/appi.ajp.2010.09081190).* Retrieved August 24, 2010, from http://ajp.psychiatryonline.org/cgi/reprint/appi.ajp.2010.09081190v1

Coplan, R. J., & Bullock, A. (2012). Temperament and peer relationships. In M. R. Zentner & R. L. Shiner (Eds.), *Handbook of temperament* (pp. 442–461). New York, NY: Guilford Press.

Coren, S., Ward, L. M., & Enns, J. T. (2004). *Sensation and perception* (6th ed.). New York, NY: Wiley.

Corkin, S. (1984). Lasting consequences of bilateral medial temporal lobectomy: Clinical course and experimental findings in HM. *Seminars in Neurology, 4,* 249–259. doi: 10.1055/s-2008-1041556

Costa, P. T. Jr., & McCrae, R. R. (1992). *Revised NEO Personality Inventory (NEO-PL-R) and NEO Five-Factor Inventory (NEO-FFI manual).* Odessa, FL: Psychological Assessment Resources.

Costanzo, R. M. (2005). Regeneration and rewiring the olfactory bulb. *Chemical Senses, 30*(Suppl. 1), 33–34.

Cowan, N. (2001). The magical number four in short-term memory: A reconsideration of mental storage capacity. *Behavioral and Brain Sciences, 24,* 87–185. doi: 10.1017/s0140525x01003922

Cowan, N. (2010). The magical mystery four: How is working memory capacity limited, and why? *Current Directions in Psychological Science, 19,* 51–57. doi: 10.1177/0963721409359277

Craig, C. R. (2006). *Modern pharmacology with clinical applications* (6th ed.). Philadelphia: Lippincott.

Craik, F. I. M., & Lockhart, R. S. (1972). Levels of processing: A framework memory research. *Journal of Verbal Learning and Verbal Behavior, 11,* 671–684. doi: 10.1016/S0022-5371(72)80001-X

Da Cunha, C., Wietzikoski, E. C., Dombrowski, P., Bortolanza, M., Santos, L. M., Boschen, S. L., & Miyoshi, E. (2009). Learning processing in the basal ganglia: A mosaic of broken mirrors. *Behavioural Brain Research, 199*(1), 157–170.

Darley, J. M., & Latané, B. (1968). Bystander intervention in emergencies: Diffusion of responsibility. *Personality and Social Psychology, 8,* 377–383.

Darwin, C. (1859). *On the origin of species by means of natural selection, or the preservation of favoured races in the struggle for life.* London: John Murray.

Davis, O. S. P., Arden, R., & Plomin, R. (2008). g in middle childhood: Moderate genetic and shared environmental influence using diverse measures of general cognitive ability at 7, 9, and 10 years in a large population sample of twins. *Intelligence, 36,* 68–80.

Dawkins, R. (1976/2006). *The selfish gene.* New York: Oxford University Press.

Deary, I. J., Strand, S., Smith P., & Fernandes, C. (2007). Intelligence and educational achievement. *Intelligence, 35*(1), 13–21.

DeCasper, A., & Fifer, W. P. (1987). Of human bonding: Newborns prefer their mothers' voices. In J. Oates & S. Sheldon (Eds.), *Cognitive development in infancy* (pp. 111–118). Hillsdale, NJ: Erlbaum.

Delgado, J. M. R. (1969). *Physical control of the mind.* New York: Harper & Row.

DeLisi, M., Umphress, Z. R., & Vaughn, M. G. (2009). The criminology of the amygdala. *Criminal Justice and Behavior, 36*(11), 1241–1252.

Denis, P. L., Morin, D., & Guindon, C. (2010). Exploring the capacity of NEO PI–R facets to predict job performance in two French-Canadian samples. *International Journal of Selection and Assessment, 18*(2), 201–207. doi:10.1111/j.1468-2389.2010.00501.x

Dennis, D. J. (2009). Review of the Cattell controversy: Race, science, and ideology. *Journal of the History of the Behavioral Sciences, 45,* 390–392. doi:10.1002/jhbs.20399

Dethier, V. G. (1976). *The hungry fly: A physiological study of the behavior associated with feeding.* Cambridge, MA: Harvard University Press.

Deuchar, R., & Holligan, C. (2010). Gangs, sectarianism and social capital: A qualitative study of young people in Scotland. *Sociology, 44*(1), 13–30.

DeZalia, R. P. (2009). A sociocultural perspective on genocide: A review of the psychology of genocide: Perpetrators, bystanders, and rescuers by Steven Baum. *Culture Psychology, 15*(3), 349–362.

DiFranza, J. R. (2008, May). Hooked from the first cigarette. *Scientific American,* 82–87.

Digman, J. M. (1990). Personality structure: Emergence of the five-factor model. *Annual Review of Psychology, 41,* 417–440. doi:10.1146/annurev. ps.41.020190.002221

Dijkgraaf, S. (1960). Spallanzani's unpublished experiments on the sensory basis of object perception in bats. *Isis, 51*(1), 9–20.

Dixson, B. J., Dixson, A. F., Bishop, P. J., & Parish, A. (2010). Human physique and sexual attractiveness in men and women: A New Zealand-U.S. Comparative Study. *Archives of Sexual Behavior, 39,* 798–806. doi:10.1007/s10508-008-9441-y

Dollard, J., Miller, N. E., Doob, L. W., Mowrer, O. H., & Sears, R. R. (1939). *Frustration and aggression.* New Haven, CT: Yale University Press.

Dweck, C. S. (2006). *Mindset: The new psychology of success.* New York: Random House.

Dweck, C. S., & Grant, H. (2008). Self-theories, goals, and meaning. In J. Y. Shah & W. I. Gardner (Eds.), *Handbook of motivation science* (pp. 408–416). New York: Guilford Press.

Earls, C. M., & Lalumiere, M. L. (2009). A case study of preferential bestiality. *Archives of Sexual Behavior, 38*(4), 605–609.

Ebbinghaus, H. (1885/1964). *Memory* (H. A. Ruger & C. E. Busenius, Trans.). New York: Dover.

Eccles, J. S., & Wigfield, A. (2002). Motivational beliefs, values, and goals. *Annual Review of Psychology, 53,* 109–132.

Ego-Stengel, V., & Wilson, M. A. (2010). Disruption of ripple-associated hippocampal activity during rest impairs spatial learning in the rat. *Hippocampus, 20*(1), 1–10.

Eisenberg, N., Fabes, R. A., Shepard, S. A., Guthrie, I. K., Murphy, B. C., & Reiser, M. (1999). Parental reactions to children's negative emotions:

Longitudinal relations to quality of children's social functioning. *Child Development, 70,* 513–534.

Ekman, P. (2005). Conclusion: What we have learned by measuring facial behavior: Further comments and clarifications. In P. Ekman & E. L. Rosenberg (Eds.), *What the face reveals: Basic and applied studies of spontaneous expression using the facial action coding system (FACS)* (2nd ed., pp. 605–626). New York: Oxford University Press.

Elder, T. E. (2010, June 17). The importance of relative standards in ADHD diagnoses: Evidence based on exact birth dates. *Journal of Health Economics.* Online version retrieved August 30, 2010, from http://www.ncbi.nlm.nih.gov/pubmed/20638739

Elert, G. (Ed.). (1997). *Age of Homo sapiens: The physics factbook.* Retrieved July 19, 2010, from http://hypertextbook.com/facts/1997/TroyHolder.shtml

Elkind, D. (1967). Egocentrism in adolescence. *Child Development, 38,* 1025–1034.

Ellers, J., & van der Pool, N. C. E. (2010). Altruistic behavior and cooperation: The role of intrinsic expectation when reputational information is incomplete. *Evolutionary Psychology, 8*(1), 37–48.

Ellis, A. (1974). *Humanistic psychotherapy: The rational-emotive approach.* New York: Julian Press.

Ellis, A. (2003). Early theories and practices of rational emotive behavior therapy and how they have been augmented and revised during the last three decades. *Journal of Rational-Emotive & Cognitive-Behavior Therapy, 21*(3/4), 219–243.

Ellis, A., & MacLaren, C. (2005). *Rational emotive behavior therapy.* Atascadero, CA: Impact Publishers.

Emery, R. E., & Forehand, R. (1996). Parental divorce and children's well-being: A focus on resilience. In R. J. Haggerty, L. R. Sherrod, N. Garmezy, & M. Rutter (Eds.), *Stress, risk, and resilience in children and adolescents: Processes, mechanisms, and interventions* (pp. 64–99). Cambridge, England: Cambridge University Press.

Engels, R. (2009). Early pubertal maturation and drug use: Underlying mechanisms. *Addiction, 104*(1), 67–68.

Erikson, E. H. (1959). *Identity and the life cycle: Selected papers.* New York: International Universities Press.

Erikson, E. H. (1963). *Childhood and society*. New York: W. W. Norton.

Erikson, E. H. (1968). *Identity, youth and crisis*. New York: W. W. Norton.

Eriksson, S., Palsdottir, V., Garemo, M., Mellstrom, D., & Strandvik, B. (2010). Metabolic profiles of fat and glucose differ by gender in healthy 8-year-olds. *Acta Paediatrica, 99*(1), 78–82.

Estrada, A., Keeley, J. A., & Leduc, P. A. (2007). Facilitating aviation emergency procedure recall using a pictorial mnemonic system. *International Journal of Applied Aviation Studies, 7*(1), 11–27.

Ethical principles of psychologists and code of conduct. (2011). American Psychological Association. Retrieved on April 7, 2011, from http://www.apa.org/ethics/code/index.aspx

Eysenck, H. J. (1947). *Dimensions of personality*. London, Eng.; Routledge & Kegan Paul.

Eysenck, H. J. (1967). *The biological basis of personality*. Springfield, IL: Charles C. Thomas.

Eysenck, H. J. , & Eysenck, S. B. G. (1976). *Psychoticism as a dimension of personality*. London, Eng.: Hodder and Stoughton.

Eysenck, M. W., & Keane, M. T. (2005). *Cognitive psychology: A student's handbook* (5th ed.). New York, NY: Psychology Press.

Fagan, T. K., & Wise, P. S. (2007). *School psychology: Past, present, and future* (3rd ed.). Bethesda, MD: NASP Publications.

Famous people affected by an anxiety disorder. (2011). Retrieved April 25, 2011, from http://www.anxietycentre.com/anxiety-famous-people.shtml

Farina, A. (1976). *Abnormal psychology*. Englewood Cliffs, NJ: Prentice-Hall.

Farooqi, S. (2010). Genes and obesity. In P. G. Kopelman, I. D. Caterson, & W. H. Dietz (Eds.), *Clinical obesity in adults and children* (3rd ed., pp. 82–91). Hoboken, NJ: Wiley-Blackwell.

Faye, C., & Sharpe, D. (2008). Academic motivation in university: The role of basic psychological needs and identity formation. *Canadian Journal of Behavioural Science, 40*(4), 189–199.

Fedoroff, J. P., & Marshall, W. L. (2010). Paraphilias. In D. McKay, J. S. Abramowitz, & S. Taylor (Eds.), *Cognitive-behavioral therapy for refractory cases: Turning failure into success* (pp. 369–384). Washington, DC: American Psychological Association.

Feldman, B. (2001). *The Nobel prize: A history of genius, controversy, and prestige.* New York: Arcade Publishing.

Feng, B., & MacGeorge, E. L. (2010). The influences of message and source factors on advice outcomes. *Communication Research, 37*(4), 553–575.

Ferguson, C. J., Miguel, C. S., & Hartley, R. D. (2009). A multivariate analysis of youth violence and aggression: The influence of family, peers, depression, and media violence. *Journal of Pediatrics, 155*(6), 904–908.

Ferrari, P. F., Paukner, A., Ruggiero, A., Darcey, L., Unbehagen, S., & Suomi, S. J. (2009). Interindividual differences in neonatal imitation and the development of action chains in rhesus macaques. *Child Development, 80*(4), 1057–1068.

Festinger, L. A. (1957). *A theory of cognitive dissonance.* Stanford, CA: Stanford University Press.

Festinger, L., & Carlsmith, J. M. (1959). Cognitive consequences of forced compliance. *Journal of Abnormal and Social Psychology, 58*, 203–210.

Fevzi, U., Ergin, E., Rivers, D. B., & Gençer, N. (2006). Age and diet influence the composition of venom from the endoparasitic wasp *Pimpla turionellae* L. (Hymenoptera: Ichneumonidae). *Archives of Insect Biochemistry and Physiology, 63(4),* 177–187.

Fields, G. (2010). Enclosure: Palestinian landscape in a "not-too-distant mirror." *Journal of Historical Sociology, 23*(2), 216–250.

Fields, R. D. (2008, March). White matter. *Scientific American,* 54–61.

Fischer, P., Greitemeyer, T., & Frey, D. (2008). Unemployment and aggression: The moderating role of self-awareness on the effect of unemployment on aggression. *Aggressive Behavior, 34*(1), 34–45.

Fischer, P., Krueger, J. I., Greltemeyer, T., Vogrincic, C., Kastenmuller, A., Frey, D., . . . Kainbacher, M. (2011). The bystander-effect: A meta-analytic review on bystander intervention in dangerous and non-dangerous emergencies. *Psychological Bulletin, 137*(4), p. 517-537. doi:10.1037/a0023304

Five perspectives on the association between marital transitions and children's adjustment. *American Psychologist, 53,* 167–184. doi:10.1037/0003-066X53.2.167

Flavell, J. H. (1985). *Cognitive development* (2nd ed.). Englewood Cliffs, NJ: Prentice-Hall.

Fletcher, H., & Munson, W. A. (1933). Loudness, its definition, measurement and calculation. *Journal of the Acoustical Society of America, 5*, 82–108. doi: 10.1121/1.1915637

Flynn, J. P. (1967). The neural basis of aggression in cats. In D. C. Glass (Ed.), *Neurophysiology and emotion*. New York: Rockefeller University Press.

Flynn, J. R. (1994). IQ gains over time. In R. J. Sternberg (Ed.), *Encyclopedia of human intelligence* (pp. 617–623). New York: Macmillan.

Flynn, J. R., & Weiss, L. G. (2007). American IQ gains from 1932 to 2002: The WISC subtests and educational progress. *International Journal of Testing, 7*(2), 209–224.Foo, P., Warren, W. H., Duchon, A., & Tarr, M. J. (2005). Do humans integrate routes into a cognitive map? Map- versus landmark-based navigation of novel shortcuts. *Journal of Experimental Psychology: Learning Memory and Cognition, 3*(2), 195–215.

Foschi, R., & Cicciola, E. (2006). Politics and naturalism in the 20th century psychology of Alfred Binet. *History of Psychology, 9*(4), 267–289. doi: 10.1037/1093-4510.9.4.267

Fraley, R. C. (2002). Attachment stability form infancy to adulthood: Meta-analysis and dynamic modeling of developmental mechanisms. *Personality and Social Psychology Review, 6*, 123–151. doi: 10.1207/s15327957pspr0602_03

Freese, J., & Meland, S. (2002). Seven tenths incorrect: Heterogeneity and change in the waist-to-hip ratios of Playboy centerfold models and Miss America pageant winners. *Journal of Sex Research, 39*(2), 133–138.

Freud, S. (1914/1955). On narcissism: An introduction. In J. Strachey (Ed. and Trans.), *The standard edition of the complete psychological works of Sigmund Freud* (Vol. 14, pp. 67–103). London: Hogarth.

Freud, S. (2003). *An outline of psychoanalysis* (H. Ragg-Kirby, Trans.). New York, NY: Penguin Books.

Friedman, D. (2003). Cognition and aging: A highly selective overview of event–related potential (ERP) data. *Journal of Clinical and Experimental Neuropsychology, 25*, 702–720.

Froehlich TE, Lanphear BP, Auinger P, Hornung R, Epstein JN, Braun J, Kahn RS. Association of tobacco and lead exposures with attention-deficit/hyperactivity disorder. *Pediatrics.* 2009 Dec;*124*(6):e1054–63. Epub 2009 Nov 23. PubMed PMID: 19933729; PubMed Central PMCID: PMC2853804

Funder, D. C. (2007). *The personality puzzle* (4th ed.). New York, NY: Norton.

Fuson, K. C. (2009). Avoiding misinterpretations of Piaget and Vygotsky: Mathematical teaching without learning, learning without teaching, or helpful learning-path teaching? *Cognitive Development, 24*(4), 343–361.

Gaffrey, M. S., Luby, J. L., Belden, A. C., Hirshberg, J. S., Volsch, J., & Barch, D. M. (2011). Association between depression severity and amygdala reactivity during sad face viewing in depressed preschoolers: An fMRI study. *Journal of Affective Disorders, 129*(1–3), 364–370.

Gafner, G. (2010). *Techniques of hypnotic induction.* Norwalk, CT: Crown House Publishing.

Galaviz, U. Z., & de Leon Fierro, L. G. (2007). Somatotype of semiprofessional soccer players classified by their position in the game. [Spanish]. *RICYDE. Revista internacional de Ciencias del Deporte/The International Journal of Sport Science, 3*(9), 29–36.

Galaviz, U. Z., & de Leon Fierro, L. G. (2007). Somatotype of semiprofessional soccer players classified by their position in the game. *The International Journal of Sport Science, 3*(9), 29-36.

Gallagher, K. E., & Parrott, D. J. (2010). Influence of heavy episodic drinking on the relation between men's locus of control and aggression toward intimate partners. *Journal of Studies on Alcohol and Drugs, 71*(2), 299–306.

Garces-Bacsal, R. M. (2010). Tales gifted children tell: Exploring PTAT responses as path-ways to socio-affective concerns. *Gifted Child Quarterly, 54*(2), 138–151. doi:10.1177/0016986209358616

Gardner, H. (2006). *Multiple intelligences: New horizons* (rev. ed.). New York: Basic Books.

Garnham, A. (2009). Cognitivism. In J. Symons & P. Calvo (Eds.), *The Routledge companion to philosophy of psychology* (pp. 99–110). New York: Routledge/ Taylor & Francis Group.

Gerressu, M., Mercer, C. H., Graham, C. A., Wellings, K., & Johnson, A. M. (2008). Prevalence of masturbation and associated factors in a British national probability survey. *Archives of Sexual Behavior, 37*(2), 266–278. Retrieved July 15, 2010, from http://www.ncbi.nlm.nih.gov/sites/ent rez?Dbpubmed&CmdShowDetailView&TermToSearch17333329

Gerson, J. (2010, September 1). Animal hoarding a mental disorder. *Edmonton Journal*, A9.

Gianakos, I. (2002). Predictors of coping with work stress: The influences of sex, gender role, social desirability, and locus of control. *Sex Roles, 46*, 149–158. doi:10.1023/A:1019675218338

Gibbons, F. X., Eggleston, T. J., & Benthin, A. C. (1997). Cognitive reactions to smoking relapse: The reciprocal relation between dissonance and self-esteem. *Journal of Personality and Social Psychology, 72,* 184–195.

Gibran, K. (1923). *The prophet.* New York: A. A. Knopf.

Gibson, J. J. (1966). *The senses considered as perceptual systems.* Boston: Houghton Mifflin.

Gilad, Y., Wiebe, V., Przeworski, M., Lancet, D., & Pääbo, S. (2004). Loss of olfactory receptor genes coincides with the acquisition of full trichromatic vision in primates. *PLoS Biology, 2,* 0120–0125. doi: 10.1371/journal.pbio.0020005

Giles, J. (2008). Sex hormones and sexual desire. *Journal for the Theory of Social Behaviour, 38*(1), 45–66.

Gilestro, G. F., Tononi, G., & Cirelli, C. (2009). Widespread changes in synaptic markers as a function of sleep and wakefulness in *Drosophilia. Science, 324,* 109–112.

Gilligan, C. (1982). *In a different voice: Psychological theory and women's development.* Cambridge, MA: Harvard University Press.

Gleitman, L., & Papafragou, A. (2005). Language and thought. In K. J. Holyoak & R. G. Morrison (Eds.), *The Cambridge handbook of thinking and reasoning* (pp. 633–662). London: Cambridge University Press.

Goldman, W. P., & Seamon, J. G. (1992). Very long-term memory for odors: Retention of odor-name associations. *American Journal of Psychology, 105,* 549–563.

Gomez, S., & Queiroz, L. S. (1982). The effects of black widow spider venom on the innervations of muscles paralysed by botulinum toxin. *Quarterly Journal of Experimental Physiology, 67*(3), 495–506.

Goodwin, C. J. (2008). Psychology in the 20th century. In S. F. Davis & W. Buskist (Eds.) *21st century psychology: A reference handbook* (pp.12–20). Thousand Oaks, CA: Sage Publications.

Gottfredson, L., & Saklofske, D. H. (2009). Intelligence: Foundations and issues in assessment. *Canadian Psychology, 50*(3), 183–195. doi: 10.1037/a0016641

Gottfried, J. (2010). Central mechanisms of odour object perception. *Nature Reviews Neuroscience, 11,* 628–641. doi: 10.1038/nrn2883

Graf, P., & Schacter, D. L. (1985). Implicit and explicit memory for new associations in normal and amnesic subjects. *Journal of Experimental*

Psychology: Learning, Memory, & Cognition, 11, 501–518. doi: 10.1037/0278-7393.11.3.501

Granzier, J. J. M., Brenner, E., & Smeets, J. B. J. (2009). Reliable identification by color under natural conditions. *Journal of Vision, 9*(1), Art ID 39.

Gray, L. J., Dean, B., Kronsbein, H. C., Robinson, P. J., & Scarr, E. (2010). Region and diagnosis-specific changes in synaptic proteins in schizophrenia and bipolar I disorder. *Psychiatry Research, 78*(2), 374–380.

Gray, L., Watt, L., & Blass, E. M. (2000). Skin-to-skin contact is analgesic in healthy newborns. *Pediatrics, 105*, e14.

Greenhill LL, Hechtman LI (2009). Attention-deficit/hyperactivity disorder. In B.J. Sadock et al., (Eds.). *Kaplan and Sadock's Comprehensive textbook of psychiatry*, 9th ed., vol. 2, pp. 3560–3572. Philadelphia: Lippincott Williams and Wilkins

Gregory, R. L. (1997). *Eye and brain: The psychology of seeing* (5th ed.). Princeton, NJ: Princeton University Press.

Griffin, A. S., & Galef, B. G. Jr. (2005). Social learning about predators: Does timing matter? *Animal Behaviour, 69*(3), 669–678.

Gronfier, C., Wright, K. P. Jr., Kronauer, R. E., & Czeisler, C. A. (2007). Entrainment of the human circadian pacemaker to longer-than-24-h days. *The National Academy of Sciences of the USA, 104*(21), 9081–9086. Retrieved April 4, 2011, from http://www.pnas.org/content/104/21/9081.full.pdf

Guidelines for ethical conduct in the care and use of animals. American Psychological Association. Retrieved April 7, 2011, from http://www.apa.org/science/leadership/care/guidelines.aspx

Gulick, W. L., Gescheider, G. A., & Frisina, R. D. (1989). *Hearing: Physiological acoustics, neural coding, and psychoacoustics.* New York, NY: Oxford University Press.

Guthrie, E. R. (1935). *The psychology of learning.* New York: Harper & Brothers.

Hakulinena, C., Jokelaa, M., Hintsanenb, M. Pulkki-Råbacka, L., Elovainioc, M., Hintsaa, T., Hutri-Kähönend, N., Viikarie, J., & Raitakarif, O. T. (2013). Hostility and unemployment: A two-way relationship? *Journal of Vocational Behavior, 83*(2), 153–160. doi: 10.1016/j.jvb.2013.04.003

Harlow, H. F. (1953). Mice, monkeys, men, and motives. *Psychological Review, 60*, 23–32.

Harlow, H. F., & Harlow, M. K. (1965). The affectional systems. In A. M. Schrier, H. F. Harlow, & F. Stollnitz (Eds.), *Behavior of nonhuman primates* (Vol. 2, pp. 287–334). New York, NY: Academic Press.

Harlow, H. F., & Zimmerman, R. R. (1959). Affectional responses in the infant monkey. *Science, 130,* 421–432.

Harlow, H. F., Harlow, M. K., & Suomi, S. J. (1971). From thought to therapy: Lessons from aprimate laboratory. *American Scientist, 59,* 538–549.

Harper, F. D., & Guilbault, M. (2008). Maslow's hierarchy of basic needs. In N. J. Salkind (Ed.), *Encyclopedia of educational psychology* (Vol. 2, pp. 633–639). Thousand Oaks, CA: Sage Publications.

Harris, B. D. (1963). *Children's drawings as measures of intellectual maturity.* New York: Harcourt, Brace & World.

Hartmann, E. (2007). The nature and functions of dreaming. In D. Barrett & P. McNamara (Eds.), *The science of dreams* (Vol. 3, pp. 171–192). Westport, CT: Praeger.

Hay, D. F., Munday, L., Roberts, S., Carta, R., Water, C. S., Perra, O., . . . van Goozen, S. (2011). Known risk factors for violence predict 12-mounth-old infants' aggressiveness with peers. *Psychological Science, 22,* 1205–1211. doi:10.1177/0956797611419303

Head, L. S., & Gross, A. M. (2009). Systematic desensitization. In W. T. O'Donohue & J. E. Fisher (Eds.), *General principles and empirically supported techniques of cognitive behavior therapy* (pp. 640-647). Hoboken, NJ: John Wiley.

Hebb, D. O. (1972). *A textbook of psychology* (3rd ed.). Philadelphia: Saunders.

Hergenhahn, B.R., & Henley, T. (2014). *An introduction to the history of psychology* (7th Ed.) Belmont, CA: Wadsworth.

Herman-Giddens, M. E., Slora, E. J., Wasserman, R. C., Bourdony, C. J., Bhapkar, M. V., Koch, G. G., & Hasemeir, C. M. (1997). Secondary sexual characteristics and menses in young girls seen in office practice: A study from the pediatric research in office settings network. *Pediatrics 99*(4), 505–512.

Heron, W. (1957, January). The pathology of boredom. *Scientific American, 196,* 52–56.

Herrnstein, R. J. (1997). *The matching law: Papers in psychology and economics* (H. Rachlin & D. I. Laibson, Eds.). New York: Russell Sage.

Herrnstein, R. J., & Murray, C. (1994). *The bell curve: Intelligence and class structure in American life*. New York: Free Press.

Hetherington, E. M., Bridges, M., & Insabella, G. M. (1998). What matters? What does not?

Higbee, K. L. (1977). *Your memory: How it works and how too improve it*. Englewood Cliffs, NJ: Prentice-Hall.

Hipp, J. R., & Perrin, A. J. (2009). The simultaneous effect of social distance and physical distance on the formation of neighborhood ties. *City & Community, 8*(1), 5–25.

Hoefling, A., & Strack, F. (2010). Hunger induced changes in food choice. When beggars cannot be choosers even if they are allowed to choose. *Appetite, 54*(3), 603–606.

Holland, S. K., Vannest, J., Mecoli, M., Jacola, L. M., Tillema, J. M., Karunanayaka, P. R., Schmithorst, V. J., Yuan, W., Plante, E., & Byars, A. W. (2007). Functional MRI of language lateralization during development in children. *International Journal of Audiology, 46*, 533–551.

Holliman, C. (2009). *The mnemonics book: Easy ways to remember hard things*. Chapel Hill, NC: Professional Press.

Homa, D. (2008). Long-term memory. In N. J. Salkind (Ed.), *Encyclopedia of educational psychology* (Vol. 2, pp. 620–624). Thousand Oaks, CA: Sage Publications.

Hood, A. B. (1963). A study of the relationship between physique and personality variables measured by the MMPI. *Journal of Personality, 31*, 97–107.

Hood, A. B. (1963). A study of the relationship between physique and personality variables measured by the MMPI. *Journal of Personality, 31*, 97–107. doi:10.1111/j.1467-6494.1963.tb01843.x

Horcajo, J., Petty, R. E., & Brinol, P. (2010). The effects of majority versus minority source status on persuasion: A self-validation analysis. *Journal of Personality and Social Psychology, 99*(3), 498–512.

Horn, J. L., & Blankson, A. N. (2012). Foundations for better understanding of cognitive abilities. In D. P. Flanagan & P. L. Harrison (Eds.), *Contemporary intellectual assessment: Theories, tests, and issues* (pp. 73–98). New York, NY: The Guilford Press.

Husain, M., & Jackson, S. R. (2001). Vision: Visual space is not what it appears to be. *Current Biology, 11*, 753–755. doi: 10.1016/S0960-9822(01)00439-0

Hussaini, S. A., Komischke, B., Menzel, R., & Lachnit, H. (2007). Forward and backward second-order Pavlovian conditioning in honeybees. *Learning and Memory, 14,* 678–683.

Hutchinson, S., Hui-Lin Lee, L., Gaab, N., & Schlaug, G. (2003). Cerebellar volume of musicians. *Cerebral Cortex, 13*(9), 943–949.

Hyman, I. E. Jr., Husband, T. H., & Billings, F. J. (1995). False memories of childhood experiences. *Applied Cognitive Psychology, 9*(3), 181–197.

Insurance Institute for Highway Safety (IIHS). (2009). *Fatality facts: Teenagers 2008.* Arlington, VA: The Institute. Retrieved August 24, 2010, from http://www.iihs.org/research/fatality_facts_2008/teenagers.html

Izard, C. E. (2009). Emotion theory and research: Highlights, unanswered questions, and emerging issues. *Annual Review of Psychology, 60,* 1–25.

Jacobs, N., & Harvey, D. (2010). The extent to which teacher attitudes and expectations predict academic achievement of final year students. *Educational Studies, 36*(2), 195–206.

Jacoby, L. L., Toth, J. P., & Yonelinas, A. P. (1993). Separating conscious and unconscious influences of memory: Measuring recollection. *Journal of Experimental Psychology: General, 122,* 139–154. doi: 10.1037/0096-3445.122.2.139

Jaffke, F. (1996). *Work and play in early childhood.* Edinburgh: Floris Books.

Jakupcak, M., Tull, M. T., McDermott, M. J., Kaysen, D., Hunt, S., & Simpson, T. (2010). PTSD symptom clusters in relationship to alcohol misuse among Iraq and Afghanistan war veterans seeking post-deployment VA health care. *Addictive Behaviors, 35*(9), 840–843.

James, W. (1890/1950). *Principles of psychology* (Vol. 1). New York: Holt.

Jang, K. L., & Livesley, W. J. (2006). Heritability of the Big Five personality dimensions and their facets: A twin study. *Journal of Personality, 64*(3), 577–591.

Jang, K. L., Livesley, W. J., & Vernon, P. A. (1996). Heritability of the Big Five personality dimensions and their facets: A twin study. *Journal of Personality, 64,* 577–591. doi:10.1111/j.1467-6494.1996.tb00522.x

Jaszyna–Gasior, M., Schroeder, J. R., Thorner, E. D., Heishman, S. J., Collins, C. C., Lo, S., & Moolchan, E. T. (2009). Age at menarche and weight concerns in relation to smoking trajectory and dependence among adolescent girls enrolled in a smoking cessation trial. *Addictive Behaviors, 34*(1), 92–95.

Joanisse, M., Gagnon, S., & Voloaca, M. (2013). The impact of stereotype threat on the simulated driving performance of older drivers. *Accident Analysis and Prevention, 50*, 530–538. doi:10.1016/j.aap.2012.05.032

Johnson, M. K., Bransford, J. D., & Solomon, S. (1973). Memory for tacit implications of sentences. *Journal of Experimental Psychology, 98*, 203–205.

Jokela, M. (2010). Characteristics of the first child predict the parents' probability of having another child. *Developmental Psychology, 46*(4), 915–926.

Jones, E. (2009). Review of madness to mental illness: A history of the Royal College of Psychiatrists. *Psychological Medicine: A Journal of Research in Psychiatry and the Allied Sciences, 39*(4), 695.

Jung, C. G. (1923). *Psychological types*. New York, NY: Harcourt Brace and World.

Jung, C. G. (1923). *Psychological types*. New York: Harcourt Brace and World.

Kagan, J. (1997). Temperament and the reactions to unfamiliarity. *Child Development, 68*, 139–143.

Kalat, J. W. (2009). *Biological psychology* (10th ed.). Belmont, CA: Cengage/Thomson/Wadsworth.

Kamin, L. J. (1969). Predictability, surprise, attention and conditioning. In B. A. Campbell & R. M. Church (Eds.), *Punishment and aversive behavior*. New York: Appleton-Century-Crofts.

Kapornai, K., Gentzler, A. L., Tepper, P., Kiss, E., Mayer, L., Tamas, Z., Kovacs, M., & Vetro, A. (2007). Early developmental characteristics and features of major depressive disorder among child psychiatric patients in Hungary. *Journal of Affective Disorders, 100*(1–3), 91–101.

Karege, F., Perroud, N., Schurhoff, F., Meary, A., Marillier, G., Burkhardt, S., Ballmann, E., Fernandez, R., Jamain, S., Leboyer, M., La Harpe, R., & Malafosse, A. (2010). Association of AKT1 gene variants and protein expression in both schizophrenia and bipolar disorder. *Genes, Brain and Behavior, 9*(5), 503–511.

Katja, B. K., Pine, D. S., Lieb, R., & Wittchen, H. U. (2010). Incidence and risk patterns of anxiety and depressive disorders and categorization of generalized anxiety disorder. *Archives of General Psychiatry, 67*(1), 47–57.

Katona, C., & Robertson, M. (2005). *Psychiatry at a glance* (3rd ed.). Oxford: Blackwell Publishing.

Keane, M. M., Gabrieli, J. D., Monti, L., Fleischman, D. A., Cantor, J. M., & Noland, J. S. (1997). Intact and impaired conceptual memory processes in amnesia. *Neuropsychology, 11*, 59–69.

Keefe, B. D., & Watt, S. J. (2009). The role of binocular vision in grasping: A small stimulus-set distorts results. *Experimental Brain Research, 194*,(3), 435–444.

Keel, P. K., Eddy, K. T., Thomas, J. J., & Schwartz, M. B. (2010). Vulnerability to eating disorders across the lifespan. In R. E. Ingram & J. M. Price (Eds.), *Vulnerability to psychopathology: Risk across the lifespan* (2nd ed., pp. 489–494). New York: Guilford Press.

Keith-Lucas, T., & Guttman, N. (1975). Robust single-trial delayed backward conditioning. *Journal of Comparative and Physiological Psychology, 88*, 468–476.

Kessler, R., Chiu, W., Demler, O., & Walters, E. (2005). Prevalence, severity, and comorbidity of twelve-month DSM-IV disorders in the National Comorbidity Survey Replication (NCS-R). *Archives of General Psychiatry. 62*(6), 617–627. doi: 10.1001/archpsyc.62.6.617

Kessler, R. C., Patricia, P., Demler, O., Jin, R., Merikangas, K. R., & Walters, E. E. (2005). Lifetime prevalence and age-of-onset distributions of DSM-IV disorders in the National Comorbidity Survey Replication. *Archives of General Psychiatry, 62*, 593–602.

Kessler, R. C., Ruscio, A. M., Shear, K., & Wittchen, H. U. (2009). Epidemiology of anxiety disorders. In M. M. Anthony & M. B. Stein (Eds.), *Oxford handbook of anxiety and related disorders* (pp. 19–33). London: Oxford University Press.

Kidd, R. (2004, November). The canine sense of smell. *Whole Dog Journal.* Retrieved August 5, 2010, from http://www.whole-dog-journal.com/issues/7_11/features/Canine-Sense-of-Smell_15668-1.html

Kim, K., & Smith, P. K. (1999). Family relations in early childhood and reproductive development. *Journal of Reproductive and Infant Psychology, 17*, 133–148.

Klein, S. B., Robertson, T. E., & Delton, A. W. (2010). Facing the future: Memory as an evolved system for planning future acts. *Memory & Cognition, 38*, 13–22. doi: 10.3758/mc.38.1.13

Klineberg, O., (1938). Emotional expression in Chinese literature. *Journal of Abnormal and Social Psychology, 33*, 517–520.

Knight, A. (2008). The beginning of the end for chimpanzee experiments? *Philosophy, Ethics, and Humanities in Medicine, 3*, Art ID 16.

Knight, D. C., Waters, N. S., & Bandettini, P. A. (2009). Neural substrates of explicit and implicit fear memory. *NeuroImage, 45*(1), 208–214.

Koelsch, S. (2010). Towards a neural basis of music-evoked emotions. *Trends in Cognitive Sciences, 14*(3), 131–137.

Koerner, E. F. K. (2000).Towards a "full pedigree" of the "Sapir–Whorf hypothesis." From Locke to Lucy. In M. Pütz & M. H. Verspoor (Eds.), *Explorations in linguistic relativity* (pp. 1–24). Amsterdam, Netherlands: H. John Benjamins.

Kohlberg, L. (1969). Stage and sequence: The cognitive-developmental approach to socialization. In D. A. Goslin (Ed.), *Handbook of socialization theory and research* (pp. 347–480). New York, NY: Rand McNally.

Kohlberg, L. (1976). Moral stages and moralization: The cognitive-developmental approach. In T. Lickona (Ed.), *Moral development and behavior: Theory, research, and social issues* (pp. 31–53). New York, NY: Holt, Rinehart, and Winston.

Kohlberg, L. (1978). Revisions in the theory and practice of moral development. In W. Damon (Ed.), *New directions for children and adolescent development: No. 2. Moral development* (Vol. 1978, pp. 83–87). San Francisco, CA: Jossey-Bass

Kohlberg, L. (1981). *Essays on moral development, Vol. I: The philosophy of moral development*. San Francisco, CA: Harper & Row.

Köhler, W. (1927). *The mentality of apes*. New York: Harcourt, Brace, & World.

Kokkinos, C. M., Panayiotou, G., Charalambous, K., Antoniadou, N., & Davazoglou, A. (2010). Greek EPQ-J: Further support for a three-factor model of personality in children and adolescents. *Journal of Psychoeducational Assessment, 28*(3), 259–269. doi:10.1177/0734282909351023

Koriat, A., Melkman, R., Averill, J. R., & Lazarus, R. S. (1972). Self control of emotional reactions to a stressful film. *Journal of Personality, 40,* 601–619.

Kroger, C., Schweiger, U., Sipos, V., Kliem, S., Arnold, R., Schunert, R., & Reinecker, H. (2010). Dialectical behaviour therapy and an added cognitive behavioural treatment module for eating disorders in women with borderline personality disorder and anorexia nervosa or bulimia nervosa who failed to respond to previous treatments. An open trial with a 15-month follow-up. *Journal of Behavior Therapy and Experimental Psychiatry, 41*(4), 381–388.

Kuncel, N. R., Ones, D. S., & Sackett, P. R. (2010). Individual differences as predictors of work, educational, and broad life outcomes. *Personality and Individual Differences, 49*(4), 331–336.

Kwong See, S. T., & Nicoladis, E. (2010). Impact of contact on the development of children's positive stereotyping about aging language competence. *Educational Gerontology, 36*, 52–66.

Laczo, J., Vlcek, K., Vyhnalek, M., Vajnerova, O., Ort, M., Holmerova, I., Tolar, M., Andel, R., Bojar, M., & Hort, J. (2009). Spatial navigation testing discriminates two types of amnestic mild cognitive impairment. *Behavioural Brain Research, 202*(2), 252–259.

Lajtha, A., & Sershen, H. (2010). Nicotine-alcohol reward interactions. *Neurochemical Research, 35*(8), 1248–1258.

Landers, D. M. (2007). The arousal-performance relationship revisited. In M. BarEli (Ed.), *Essential readings in sport and exercise psychology.* Champaign, IL: Human Kinetics.

Laney, C., & Loftus, E. F. (2010). Truth in emotional memories. In B. H. Bornstein & R. L. Wiener (Eds.), *Emotion and the law: Psychological perspectives* (pp. 157–183). New York: Springer Publishing.

Lashley, K. S. (1924). Studies of cerebral function in learning. *Archives of Neurological Psychiatry, 12*, 249–276.

Latané, B., & Darley, J. M. (1968). Group inhibition of bystander intervention. *Journal of Personality and Social Psychology, 10*(3), 215–221.

Latané, B., & Darley, J. M. (1970). *The unresponsive bystander: Why doesn't he help?* New York: Appleton-Century-Crofts.

Lazar, R. M., Minzer, B., Antoniello, D., Festa, J. R., Krakauer, J. W., & Marshall, R. S. (2010). Improvement in aphasia scores after stroke is well predicted by initial severity. *Stroke, 41*, 1485–1488.

Lazarus, R. S. (1974). Cognitive and coping processes in emotion. In B. Weiner (Ed.), *Cognitive views of human motivation.* New York: Academic Press.

Lazarus, R. S. (1999). *Stress and emotion: A new synthesis.* New York: Springer.

Lear, J. (2005). *Freud.* New York: Routledge.

Leclair-Visonneau, L., Oudiette, D., Gaymard, B., Leu-Semenescu, S., & Arnulf, I. (2010). Do the eyes scan dream images during rapid eye movement sleep? Evidence from the rapid eye movement sleep behaviour disorder model. *Brain: A Journal of Neurology, 133*(6), 1737–1746.

LeDoux, J. (2010). From the integrated mind to the emotional brain. In P. A. Reuter-Lorenz, K. Baynes, G. R. Mangun, & E. A. Phelps (Eds.), *The cognitive neuroscience of mind: A tribute to Michael S. Gazzaniga* (pp. 89–98). Cambridge, MA: MIT Press.

Lee, Y. T., Jussim, L. J., & McCauley, C. R. (Eds.). (1995). *Stereotype accuracy: Toward appreciating group differences.* Washington, DC: American Psychological Association.

Leichsenring, F., & Leibing, E. (2003). The effectiveness of psychodynamic therapy and cognitive behavior therapy in the treatment of personality disorders: A meta-analysis. *American Journal of Psychiatry*, 160(7), 1223–1232

Lepper, M. R., & Greene, D. (1975). Turning play into work; Effects of adult surveillance and extrinsic rewards on children's intrinsic motivation. *Journal of Personality and Social Psychology, 31*, 479–486.

Lepper, M. R., & Greene, D. (1978). Overjustification research and beyond: Toward a means-ends analysis of intrinsic and extrinsic motivation. In D. Greene & M. R. Lepper (Eds.), *The hidden costs of reward* (pp. 109–148). Hillsdale, NJ: Lawrence Erlbaum Associates.

Levack, B. P. (2006). *The witch hunt in early modern Europe* (3rd ed.). London and New York: Longman.

Levran, O., Londono, D., O'Hara, K., Randesi, M., Rotrosen, J., Casadonte, P., Linzy, S., Ott, J., Adelson, M., & Kreek, M. J. (2009). Heroin addiction in African Americans: A hypothesis-driven association study. *Genes, Brain and Behavior, 8*(5), 531–540.

Lewis, M. D. (2005). Bridging emotion theory and neurobiology through dynamic system modeling. *Behavioral and Brain Sciences, 28*, 169–194.

Lewis, M., Feiring, C., & Rosenthal, S. (2000). Attachment over time. *Child Development, 71*, 707–720. doi: 10.111/1476-8624.00180

Li, Y., & Lei, X. (2010). Social support and personality of patients with suicide attempt without mental illness. *Chinese Journal of Clinical Psychology, 18*(2), 194–195.

Lichtenstein, P., Yip, B. H., Björk, C., Pawitan, Y., Cannon, T. D., Sullivan, P. F., & Hultman, C. M. (2009). Common genetic determinants of schizophrenia and bipolar disorder in Swedish families: A population-based study. *Lancet 373*(9659), 234–239.

Liebe, U., & Tutic, A. (2010). Status groups and altruistic behaviour in dictator games. *Rationality and Society, 22*(3), 353–380.

Lilienfeld, S. O., Lynn, S. J., Ruscio, J., & Beyerstein, B. L. (2010). *50 great myths of popular psychology: Shattering widespread misconceptions about human behavior.* Malden, MA: Wiley-Blackwell.

Linder, J. R., & Gentile, D. A. (2009). Is the television rating system valid? Indirect, verbal, and physical aggression in programs viewed by fifth grade girls and associations with behavior. *Journal of Applied Developmental Psychology, 30*(3), 286–297.

Ling, L., Clark, R. F., Erikson, T., & Trestrail, J. H. (2001). *Toxicology secrets.* Philadelphia: Hanley & Belfus.

Lipsitt, L. P. (1971, December). Babies: They're a lot smarter than they look. *Psychology Today*, 70–72, 88–89.

Loftus, E. F. (1975). Leading questions and the eyewitness report. *Cognitive Psychology, 7*, 560–572. doi: 10.1016/0010-0285(75)90023-7

Loftus, E. F. (1979). *Eyewitness testimony.* Cambridge, MA: Harvard University Press.

Loftus, E. F. (1997). Creating false memories. *Scientific American, 227*(3), 70–75.

Loftus, E. F. (2007). Memory distortions: Problems solved and unsolved. In M. Garry & H. Hayne (Eds.), *Do justice and let the sky fall: Elizabeth Loftus and her contribvutions to science, law, and academic freedom* (pp. 1–14). Mahwah, NJ: Lawrence Erlbaum.

Loftus, E. F., & Palmer, J. C. (1974). Reconstruction of automobile destruction: An example of the interaction between language and memory. *Journal of Verbal Learning &Verbal Behavior, 13*, 585–589. doi: 10.1016/S0022-5371(74)80011-3

Lopez-Duran, N. (2011, October 18) Fifty percent (50%) of teens have experienced a psychiatric condition by their 18th birthday. *Child Psychology Research.* Retrieved May 2013, from http://www.child-psych.org/2010/10/fifty-percent-50-of-teens-have-experienced-a-psychiatric-condition-by-their-18th-birthday.html

Lorayne, H., & Lucas, J. (1997). *The memory book: The classic guide to improving your memory at work, at school, and at play.* New York: Random House.

Lorenz, K. (1952). *King Solomon's ring: New light on animal ways.* New York, NY: Crowell.

Lucas-Thompson, R., & Clarke-Stewart, K. A. (2007). Forecasting friendship: How marital quality, maternal mood, and attachment security are linked to children's peer relationships. *Journal of Applied Developmental Psychology, 28,* 499–514. doi:10.1016/j.appdev.2007.06.004

Lustig, C., & Hasher, L. (2001). Implicit memory is not immune to interference. *Psychological Bulletin, 127,* 629–650. doi: 10.1037/0033-2909.127.5.618

Lynn, R. (2008). *The global bell curve: Race, IQ, and inequality worldwide.* Augusta, GA: Washington Summit Publishers.

Lynn, S. J., Boycheva, E., Deming, A., Lilienfeld, S. O., & Hallquist, M. N. (2009). Forensic hypnosis: The state of the science. In L. Jennifer , K. S. Douglas, & S. O. Lilienfeld (Eds.), *Psychological science in the courtroom: Consensus and controversy* (pp. 80–99). New York: Guilford Press.

Macfarlane, A. (2008). Olfaction in the development of social preferences in the human neonate. In R. Porter & M. O'Connor (Eds.), *Ciba Foundation Symposium 33—Paren—Infant Interaction.* Chichester, UK: John Wiley & Sons. doi: 10.1002/9780470720158.ch7

Mack, A., & Rock, I. (1998). *Inattentional blindness: Perception without attention.* Cambridge, MA: MIT Press.

Macmillan, M. (2008). Phineas Gage–Unravelling the myth. *The Psychologist, 21*(9), 828–831.

Macmillan, M. (Ed.). (2000). *An odd kind of fame: Stories of Phineas Gage.* Cambridge, MA: MIT Press.

Maddan, S., Walker, J. T., & Miller, J. M. (2008). Does size really matter? A reexamination of Sheldon's somatotypes and criminal behavior. *The Social Science Journal, 45,* 330–344. doi:10.1016/j.soscij.2008.03.009

Madey, S. F., & Rodgers, L. (2009). The effect of attachment and Sternberg's Triangular Theory of Love on relationship satisfaction. *Individual Differences Research, 7*(2), 76–84.

Magnussen, S., Greenlee, M. W., Aslaken, P. M., & Kildebo, O. O. (2003). High-fidelity perceptual long-term memory revisited—and confirmed. *Psychological Science, 14,* 74–76.

Main, M., & Solomon, J. (1990). Procedures for identifying infants as disorganized/disoriented during the Ainsworth Strange Situation. In M. T. Greenberg, D. Cicchetti, & E. M. Cummings (Eds.), *Attachment in the preschool years: Theory research and intervention* (pp. 121–160). Chicago, IL: University of Chicago Press.

Manning, R., Levine, M., & Collins, A. (2007). The Kitty Genovese murder and the social psychology of helping. *American Psychologist, 62*(6), 555–562.

Maranon, G. (1924). Contribution à l'étude de l'action émotive de l'adrénaline. *Revue Française Endocrinologique, 2,* 301–325.

Marcia, J. E. (1966). Development and validation of ego-identity status. *Journal of Personality and Social Psychology, 3,* 551–558.

Marcia, J. E. (1980). Identity in adolescence. In J. Adelson (Ed.), *Handbook of adolescent psychology* (pp. 159–187). New York: Wiley.

Marinkovic, K., Oscar-Berman, M., Urban, T., O'Reilly, C. E., Howard, J. A., Sawyer, K., & Harris, G. J. (2009). Alcoholism and dampened temporal limbic activation to emotional faces. *Alcoholism: Clinical and Experimental Research, 33*(11), 1880–1892.

Markham, A. (2013, February 15). The pain of positive stereotypes. *Psychology Today.* Retrieved from http://www.psychologytoday.com/blog/ulterior-motives/201302/the-pain-positive-stereotypes

Marsh, P. J., Odlaug, B. L., Thomarios, N., Davis, A. A., Buchanan, S. N., Meyer, C. S., & Grant, J. E. (2010). Paraphilias in adult psychiatric inpatients. *Annals of Clinical Psychiatry, 22*(2), 129–134.

Martin, J. A., Hamilton, B. E., Ventura, S. A., Osterman, M. J. K., Wilson, E. C., & Mathews, T. J. (2012, August 28). Birth: Final data for 2010. *National Vital Statistics Reports, 61*(1).

Martin, L. E., Holsen, L. M., Chambers, R. J., Bruce, A. S., Brooks, W. M., Zarcone, J. R., Butler, M. G., & Savage, C. R. (2010). Neural mechanism associated with food motivation in obese and healthy weight adults. *Obesity, 18*(2), 254–260.

Marx, D. M. (2009). On the role of group membership in stereotype-based performance effects. *Social and Personality Psychology Compass, 3*(1), 77–93.

Mashour, G. A., Walker, E. E., & Martuza, R. L. (2005). Psychosurgery: Past, present, and future. *Brain Research Reviews, 48*(3), 409–419.

Maslow, A. H. (1970). *Motivation and personality* (2nd ed.). New York: Harper & Row.

Mason, O. J., & Brady, F. (2009). The psychotomimetic effects of short-term sensory deprivation. *Journal of Nervous and Mental Disease, 197*(10), 783–785.

Massachusetts General Hospital. (2009, July 2). Many genetic contributions to schizophrenia, bipolar disorder discovered. *ScienceDaily.* Retrieved April 14, 2011, from http://www.sciencedaily.com/releases/2009/07/090701131303.htm

McClelland, D. C. (1958). Risk taking in children with high and low need for achievement. In J. W. Atkinson (Ed.), *Motives in fantasy, action, and society*. New York: Van Nostrand Reinhold.

McClelland, D. C., Atkinson, J. W., Clark, R. A., & Lowell, E. L. (1953). *The achievement motive*. New York: Appleton-Century-Crofts.

McCrae, R. R., & Costa, P. T. (1997). Personality trait and structure as a human universal. *American Psychologist, 52*, 509–516. doi:10.1037/0003-066X. 52.5.509

McMahon, S., & Farmer, G. L. (2009). The bystander approach: Strengths-based sexual assault prevention with at-risk groups. *Journal of Human Behavior in the Social Environment, 19*(8), 1042–1065.

Mead, H. K., Beauchaine, T. P., & Shannon, K. E. (2010). Neurobiological adaptations to violence across development. *Development and Psychopathology, 22*(1), 1–22.

Meletis, C. D., & Wood, S. G. (2009). *His change of life: Male menopause and healthy aging with testosterone*. Westport, CT: Praeger Publishers/ Greenwood Publishing Group.

Mennella, J. A., Griffin, C. E., & Beauchamp, G. K. (2004). Flavor programing during infancy. *Pediatrics, 113*, 840–845.

Mennella, J. A., Jagnow, C. J., & Beauchamp, G. K. (2001). Prenatal and postnatal flavor learning by human infants. *Pediatrics, 107*(6), e88. Retrieved August 22, 2010, from www.pediatrics.org/cgi/content/full/107/6/ e88

Milgram, S. (1963). Behavioral study of obedience and disobedience to authority. *Journal of Abnormal and Social Psychology, 67*, 371–378.

Milgram, S. (1965). Some conditions of obedience and disobedience to authority. *Human Relations, 18*, 67–76.

Millar, G. (2001). *The Torrance kids at midlife: Selected case studies of creative behavior*. Westport, CT: Ablex Publishing.

Millar, G. (2010). *The power of creativity: Results of the 50-year follow-up to the Torrance longitudinal study of creative behavior*. Bensenville, IL: Scholastic Testing Service.

Miller, G. A. (1956). The magical number seven, plus or minus two: Some limits on our capacity for processing information. *Psychological Review, 63*(2), 81–97. doi: 10.1037/h0043158

Miller, H. C., Rayburn-Reeves, R., & Zentall, T. R. (2009). Imitation and emulation by dogs using a bidirectional control procedure. *Behavioural Processes, 80*(2), 109–114.

Miller, P. H. (2011). *Theories of developmental psychology* (5th ed.). New York, NY: Worth.

Milner, B. (1970). *Memory and the medial temporal regions of the brain. Biology of memory.* New York, NY: Academic Press.

Minnier, E., Misanin, J. R., & Hinderliter, C. F. (2007). Age and interstimulus interval in forward and backward long-trace taste-aversion conditioning. *Perceptual and Motor Skills, 105*(3, Pt 2), 1223–1226.

Mischel, W. (2004). Toward an integrative science of the person. *Annual Review of Psychology, 55,* 1–22. doi:10.1146/annurev.psych.55.042902.130709

Modgil, S., & Modgil, C. (Eds.). (1982). *Jean Piaget: Consensus and controversy.* London: Praeger.

Montoya, R. M., & Horton, R. S. (2013). A meta-analytic investigation of the processes underlying the similarity-attraction effect. *Journal of Social and Personal Relationships, 30*(1), 64–96. doi:10.1177/ 0265407512452989.

Montoya, R. M., & Horton, R. S. (2014). A two-dimensional model for the study of interpersonal attraction. *Personality and Social Psychology Review, 18*(1), 59–86. doi:10.1177/108886831351887

Moore, J. (2010). Philosophy of science, with special consideration given to behaviorism as the philosophy of the science of behavior. *The Psychological Record, 60*(1), 137–150.

Moors, A. (2009). Theories of emotion causation: A review. *Cognition & Emotion, 23*(4), 625–662.

Moray, N. (1959). Attention in dichotic listening: Effective cues and the influence of instruction. *Quarterly Journal of Experimental Psychology, 11,* 56–60.

Morcom, A. M., Bullmore, E. T., Huppert, F. A., Lennox, B., Praseedom, A., Linnington, H., & Fletcher, P. C. (2010). Memory encoding and dopamine in the aging brain: A psychopharmacological neuroimaging study. *Cerebral Cortex, 20*(3), 743–757.

Moulton, S. T., & Kosslyn, S. M. (2008). Using neuroimaging to resolve the psi debate. *Journal of Cognitive Neuroscience, 20,* 182–192. doi: 10.1162/ jocn.2008.20.1.182

Mozzachiodi, R., & Byrne, J. H. (2010). More than synaptic plasticity: Role of nonsynaptic plasticity in learning and memory. *Trends in Neurosciences, 33*(1), 17–26.

Mulvaney, M. K., & Mebert, C. J. (2007). Parental corporal punishment predicts behavior problems in early childhood. *Journal of Family Psychology, 21*(3), 389–397.

Murphy, R., Straebler, S., Cooper, Z., & Fairburn, C. G. (2010). Cognitive behavioral therapy for eating disorders. *Psychiatric Clinics of North America, 33*(3), 611–627.

Murray, H. A. (1938). *Explorations in Personality*. New York: Oxford University Press.

Murray, H. A. (1943). *Thematic Apperception Test Manual*. Cambridge, MA: Harvard University Press.

Murray-Close, D., Ostrov, J. M., Nelson, D. A., Crick, N. R., & Coccaro, E. F. (2010). Proactive, reactive, and romantic relational aggression in adulthood: Measurement, predictive validity, gender differences, and association with intermittent explosive disorder. *Journal of Psychiatric Research, 44*(6), 393–404.

Must, A., & Anderson, S. E. (2010). Childhood obesity: Definition, classification and assessment. In P. G. Kopelman, I. D. Caterson, & W. H. Dietz (Eds.), *Clinical obesity in adults and children* (3rd ed., pp. 375–391). Hoboken, NJ: Wiley-Blackwell.

Mustonen, W. Huurre, T., Kiviruusu, O., Haukkala, A., & Aro, H. (2011). Long-term impact of parental divorce on intimate relationship quality in adulthood and the mediating role of psychosocial resources. *Journal of Family Psychology, 25*, 615–619. doi:10.1037/a0023996

Naglieri, J. A. (1988). *DAP: draw a person: A quantitive scoring system*. New York: Harcourt Brace Jovanovich.

Nairne, J. S., Pandeirada, J. N.S., Gregory, K. J., & Van Arsdall, J. E. (2008). Adaptive memory: Fitness relevance and the hunter-gatherer mind. *Psychological Science, 20*, 740–746. doi: 10.1111/j.1467-9280.2009.02356.x

Naish, P. L. N. (2010). Hypnosis and hemispheric asymmetry. *Consciousness and Cognition: An International Journal, 19*(1), 230–234.

Narayan, V., & Haddad, P. M. (2011). Antidepressant discontinuation manic states: A critical review of the literature and suggested diagnostic criteria. *Journal of Psychopharmacology, 25*(3), 306–313.

National Comorbidity Survey Replication (NCS–R). (2010). Retrieved August 30, 2010, from http://www.hcp.med.harvard.edu/ncs/ftpdir/NCS–R_Lifetime_Prevalence_Estimates.pdf

National Institute of Mental Health (2008). *Attention Deficit Hyperactivity Disorder* (NIH Publication No. 08-3572). Available online: http://www.nimh.nih.gov/health/publications/attention-deficit-hyperactivity-disorder/adhd_booklet.pdf

National Institute of Mental Health. (2011). *Obsessive compulsive disorder among adults*. Retrieved April 14, 2011, from http://www.nimh.nih.gov/statistics/1OCD_ADULT.shtml

National Institute of Mental Health. (2014). *Autism spectrum disorder.* Retrieved from http://www.nimh.nih.gov/health/topics/autism-spectrum-disorders-asd/index.shtml

Neisser, U. (1976). *Cognition and reality: Principles and implications of cognitive psychology.* San Francisco: Freeman.

Neubauer, D. N. (2009). Asleep: Inside and out. *Primary Psychiatry, 16*(5), 17–18.

Newcomb, T. M. (1961). *The acquaintanceship process.* New York: Holt, Rinehart & Winston.

Newell, A. (1990). *Unified theories of cognition.* Cambridge, MA: Harvard University Press.

Newman, S. M., Paletz, E. M., Obermeyer, W. H., & Benca, R. M. (2009). Sleep deprivation in pigeons and rats using motion detection. *Sleep: Journal of Sleep and Sleep Disorders Research, 32*(10), 1299–1312.

Nickerson, R. S., & Adams, M. J. (1979). Long-term memory for a common object. *Cognitive Psychology, 11*, 287–307. doi: 10.1016/0010-0285(79)90013-6

Nicolas, S., & Levine, Z. (2012). Beyond intelligence testing: Remembering Alfred Binet after a century. *European Psychologists, 17*(4), 320–325. doi: 10.1027/1016-9040/a000117

Nishitani, S., Miyamura, T., Tagawa, M., Sumi, M., Takase, R., Doi, H., Moriuchi, H., & Shinohara, K. (2009). The calming effect of a maternal breast milk odor on the human newborn infant. *Neuroscience Research, 63*(1), 66–71.

Norton, A. (2014, April 22). New drug may help prevent migraines. *WebMD.com.* Retrieved from http://www.webmd.com

Nowak, R. (1994). Nicotine scrutinized as FDA seeks to regulate cigarettes. *Science, 263*, 1555–1556.

Oakland, T., & Dowling, L. (1983). The "Draw-A-Person Test": Validity properties for nonbiased assessment. *Learning Disability Quarterly, 6*(4), 526–534.

Oakley, D. A., & Halligan, P. W. (2010). Psychophysiological foundations of hypnosis and suggestion. In S. J. Lynn, J. W. Rhue, & I. Kirsch (Eds.), *Handbook of clinical hypnosis* (2nd ed., pp. 79–117). Washington, DC: American Psychological Association.

Obesity rates continue to climb in the United States. (2007). Johns Hopkins Bloomberg School of Public Health. Retrieved August 20, 2010, from http://www.jhsph.edu/publichealthnews/press_releases/2007/wang_adult_obesity.html

Öhman, A., Carlsson, K., Lundqvist, D., & Ingvar, M. (2007). On the unconscious subcortical origin of human fear. *Physiology & Behavior, 92*(1–2), 180–185.

Okado, Y., & Stark, C. E. L. (2005). Neural activity during encoding predicts false memories created by misinformation. *Learning & Memory, 12(1),* 3–11.

Olds, J. (1956). Pleasure centers in the brain. *Scientific American, 195,* 105–116.

Olds, J. (1958). Self-stimulation of the brain. *Science, 127,* 315–324.

Orne, M. T. (2009). On the simulating subject as a quasi-control group in hypnosis research: What, why, and how. In E. Fromm & R. E. Shor (Eds.), *Hypnosis: Developments in research and new perspectives* (2nd ed., pp. 519–566). Piscataway, NJ: Transaction Publishers.

Ortet, G., Escriva, P., Ibanez, M. I., Moya, J., Villa, H., Mezquita, L., & Ruiperez, M. A. (2010). The short version of the Junior Spanish NEO-PI-R (JS NEO-S). *International Journal of Clinical and Health Psychology, 10*(2), 327–344.

Osborn, L. (2010). Number of species identified on earth. *Current Results Nexus.* Retrieved July 19, 2010, from http://www.currentresults.com/Environment-Facts/Plants-Animals/number-species.php

Palmer, S. E. (1999). *Vision science: Photons to phenomenology.* Cambridge, MA: MIT Press.

Panic disorder. (2010). *NHS choices: Your health.* Retrieved April 14, 2011, from http://www.nhs.uk/conditions/panic–disorder/Pages/Introduction.aspx

Panksepp, J. (2010). Evolutionary substrates of addiction: The neurochemistries of pleasure seeking and social bonding in the mammalian brain. In J. D. Kassel (Ed.), *Substance abuse and emotion* (pp. 137–167). Washington, DC: American Psychological Association.

Parke, R. D., & Slaby, R. G. (1983). The development of aggression. In P. H. Mussen (Series Ed.) & E. M. Hetherington (Vol. Ed), *Handbook of child psychology: Vol. 4. Socialization, personality and social development* (pp. 547–641). New York, NY: Wiley.

Parker, S. (1962). Eskimo psychopathology in the context of Eskimo personality and culture. *American Anthropologist, 64*, 76–96.

Parrott, W. G. (2004). The nature of emotion. In M. B. Brewer & M. Hewstone (Eds.), *Emotion and motivation* (pp. 5–20). Malden: Blackwell Publishing.

Pavlov, I. P. (1927). *Conditioned reflexes* (G. V. Anrep, Trans.). London: Oxford University Press.

Pearce, J. C. (1977). *Magical child: Rediscovering nature's plan for our children.* New York: Bantam Books.

Peterson, L. R., & Peterson, N. J. (1959). Short-term retention of individual verbal items. *Journal of Experimental Psychology, 58*, 193–198.

Piaget, J. (1951). *Play, dreams and imitation in childhood.* New York: W. W. Norton.

Piaget, J. (1954). *The construction of reality in the child* (M. Cook, Trans.) New York, NY: Basic Books.

Piaget, J. (1960). *The child's conception of the world.* London: Routledge.

Piaget, J. (1963). *The origins of intelligence in children.* New York, NY: W. W. Norton.

Piaget, J. (1969). *The child's conception of the world.* Totowa, NJ: Littlefield Adams.

Piaget, J. (1973). *The language and though of the child.* New York, NY: Meridian World.

Piaget, J. (1999). The stages of intellectual development of the child. In A. Slater & D. Muir (Eds.), *Blackwell reader in developmental psychology* (pp. 35–42). Malden, MA: Blackwell.

Piech, R. M, Pastorino, M. T., & Zald, D. H. (2010). All I saw was the cake. Hunger effects on attentional capture by visual food cues. *Appetite, 54*(3), 579–582.

Pinker, S. (1997). *How the mind works.* New York: W. W. Norton & Company.

Pizlo, Z., Sawada, T., Li, Y., Kropatsch, W. G., & Steinman, R. M. (2010). New approach to the perception of 3D shape based on veridicality, complexity, symmetry and volume. *Vision Research, 50*(1), 1–11.

Plaisant, O., Courtois, R., Reveillere, C., Mendelsohn, G. A., & John, O. P. (2010). Factor structure and internal reliability of the French Big Five Inventory (BFI-Fr). *Convergent and discriminant validation with the NEO-PI-R. Annales Medico Psychologiques, 168*(2), 97–106. doi:10.1016/j.amp.2009.09.003

Plomin, R., Fulker, D. W., Corley, R., & DeVries, J. C. (1997). Nature, nurture, and cognitive development from 1 to 16 years: A parent-offspring study. *Psychological Science, 8,* 442–447.

Plucker, J. A. (1999). Is the proof in the pudding? Reanalyses of Torrance's (1958 to present) longitudinal data. *Creativity Research Journal, 12*(2), 103–114.

Poncelet, J., Rinck, F., Bourgeat, F., Schaal, B., Rouby, C., Bensafi, M., & Hummel, T. (2010). The effect of early experience on odor perception in humans: Psychological and physiological correlates. *Behavioural Brain Research, 208*(2), 458–465.

Porter, J., Craven, B., Khan, R. M., Chang, S.-J., Kang, I., Judkewicz, B., … Sobel, N. (2007). Mechanisms of scent-tracking in humans. *Nature Neuroscience, 10,* 27–29. doi: 10.1038/nn1819

Porter, R. H., & Rieser, J. J. (2005). Retention of olfactory memories by newborn infants. In R. T. Mason, M. P. LeMaster, and D. Muller-Schwarze (Eds.), *Chemical signals in vertebrates 10* (pp. 300–307). New York: Springer.

Posner, M. I. (1980). Orienting of attention. *Quarterly Journal of Experimental Psychology, 32,* 3–25. doi: 10.1080/00335558008248231

Pothakos, K., Robinson, J. K., Gravanis, I., Marsteller, D. A., Dewey, S. L., & Tsirka, S. E. (2010). Decreased serotonin levels associated with behavioral disinhibition in tissue plasminogen activator deficient (tpa-/-) mice. *Brain Research, 1326,* 135–142.

Potter, S. J., Moynihan, M. M., Stapleton, J. G., & Banyard, V. L. (2009). Empowering bystanders to prevent campus violence against women: A preliminary evaluation of a poster campaign. *Violence against Women, 15*(1), 106–121.

Pouliot, S. (2010). Recognition memory for emotionally arousing odors: A neuropsychological investigation. *Dissertation Abstracts International: Section B: The Sciences and Engineering, 70*(8–B), 5214.

Presley, C. A., Meilman, P. W., & Lyerla, R. (1997). *Alcohol and drugs on American college campuses: Issues of violence and harassment*. Carbondale: Core Institute, Southern Illinois University.

Primate gallery: Living primate species. Retrieved July 19, 2010, from http:// homepage.mac.com/wildlifeweb/primate/photos/species.html

Prochaska, J. O., & Norcross, J. C. (2010). *Systems of psychotherapy: A transtheoretical analysis* (7th ed.). Pacific Grove, CA: Brookes/Cole.

Prokop, P., & Vaclav, R. (2008). Seasonal aspects of sexual cannibalism in the praying mantis (*Mantis religiosa*). *Journal of Ethology, 26*(2), 213–218.

Pullum, G. K. (1991). *The great Eskimo vocabulary hoax and other irreverent essays on the study of language*. Chicago: University of Chicago Press.

Ragozin, A. S., Basham, R. B., Crnic, K. A., Greenberg, M. T., & Robinson, N. M. (1982). Effects of maternal age on parenting role. *Developmental Psychology, 18*, 627–634. doi: 10.1037/0012-1649.18.4.627

Ranganath, K. A., Spellman, B. A., & Joy-Gaba, J. A. (2010). Cognitive "category-based induction" research and social "persuasion" research are each about what makes arguments believable: A tale of two literatures. *Perspectives on Psychological Science, 5*(2), 115–122.

Rauschecker, J. P., & Tian, B. (2000). Mechanisms and streams for processing of "what" and "where" in auditory cortex. *Proceedings of the National Academy of Science, 97*, 11800–11806. doi: 10.1073/pnas.97.22.11800

Ray, O., & Ksir, C. (1990). *Drugs, society, and human behavior* (5th ed). St. Louis: Times Mirror/Mosby.

Reder, L. M., Park, H., & Kieffaber, P. D. (2009, January). *Psychological Bulletin, 135*(1), 23–49.

Reger, G. M., Holloway, K. M., Candy, C., Rothbaum, B. O., Difede, J. A., Rizzo, A. A., & Gahm, G. A. (2011). Effectiveness of virtual reality exposure therapy for active duty soldiers in a military mental health clinic. *Journal of Traumatic Stress, 24*(1), 93–96.

Revonsuo, A. (2000). The reinterpretation of dreams: An evolutionary hypothesis of the function of dreaming. *Behavioral and Brain Sciences, 23*(6), 1016–1017.

Revonsuo, A., Kallio, S., & Sikka, P. (2009). What is an altered state of consciousness? *Philosophical Psychology, 22*(2), 187–204.

Reynolds, B. A., & Weiss, S. (1992, March). Generation of neurons and astrocytes from isolated cells of the adult mammalian central nervous system. *Science, 255*(5052), 1707–1710.

Ribases, M., Ramos-Quiroga, J. A., Sanchez-Mora, C., Bosch, R., Richarte, V., Palomar, G., Gastaminza, X., Bielsa, A., Arcos–Burgos, M., Muenke, M., Castellanos, F. X., Cormand, B., Bayes, M., & Casas, M. (2011). Contribution of LPHN3 to the genetic susceptibility to ADHD in adulthood: A replication study. *Genes, Brain and Behavior, 10*(2), 149–157.

Richards, C. S., & Perri, M. G. (Eds.). (2010). *Relapse prevention for depression.* Washington, DC: American Psychological Association.

Richman, J. E., McAndrew, K. G., Decker, D., & Mullaney, S. C. (2004). An evaluation of pupil size standards used by police officers for detecting drug impairment. *Optometry: Journal of the American Optometric Association, 75,* 1–8. doi: 10.1016/s1529-1839(04)70037-8

Riediger, M., Schmiedek, F., Wagner, G. G., & Lindenberger, U. (2009). Seeking pleasure and seeking pain: Differences in prohedonic and contra-hedonic motivation from adolescence to old age. *Psychological Science, 20*(12), 1529–1535.

Roazen, P. (1975). *Freud and his followers.* New York: Knopf.

Robbins, M., Francis, L. J., & Edwards, B. (2010). Happiness as stable extraversion: Internal consistency reliability and construct validity of the Oxford Happiness Questionnaire among undergraduate students. *Current Psychology: Research Reviews, 29*(2), 89–94. doi:10.1007/s12144-010-9076-8

Roberts, B. W., & DelVecchio, W. F. (2000). The rank-order consistency of personality traits from childhood to old age: A qualitative review of longitudinal studies. *Psychological Bulletin, 126,* 3-25.

Robins, R. W. (2005). The nature of personality: Genes, culture, and national character. *Science, 310*(5745), 62–63.

Rodieck R. W. (1998). *The first steps in seeing.* Sunderland, MA: Sinauer Associates.

Roethlisberger, S. J., & Dickson, W. J. (1939). *Management and the worker.* Cambridge, MA: Harvard University Press.

Rogers, C. R. (1951). *Client-centered therapy: Its current practice.* Boston: Houghton Mifflin.

Rogers, P., & Soule, J. (2009). Cross-cultural differences in the acceptance of Barnum profiles supposedly derived from Western versus Chinese astrology. *Journal of Cross-Cultural Psychology, 40* (3), 381–399. doi:10.1177/0022022109332843

Roscoe, W. (1991). *The Zuni man-woman.* Albuquerque: University of New Mexico Press.

Rosenthal, R., & Fode, K. L. (1963). Psychology of the scientist: V. Three experiments in experimenter bias. *Psychological Reports, 12,* 491–511.

Rosenthal, R., & Jacobson, L. (1968). *Pygmalion in the classroom: Teacher expectations and pupils' intellectual development.* New York: Holt, Rinehart & Winston.

Rosenzweig, M. R., Leiman, A. L., & Breedlove, S. M. (1999). *Biological psychology.* Sunderland, MA: Sinauer Associates.

Rothbart, M. K. (2011). *Becoming who we are: Temperament and personality in development.* New York, NY: Guilford Press.

Rotter, J. R. (1982). *The development and application of social learning theory.* New York: Praeger.

Rowan, J. (1998). Maslow amended. *Journal of Humanistic Psychology, 38,* 81–92.

Rowell, A. M., & Faruqui, R. A. (2010). Persistent hyperphagia in acquired brain injury; an observational case study of patients receiving inpatient rehabilitation. *Brain Injury, 24*(7–8), 1044–1049.

Rubel, A. J. (1964). The epidemiology of a folk illness: Susto in Hispanic America, *Ethnology, 3* (3), 268–283.

Rubie-Davies, Christine M. (2010). Teacher expectations and perceptions of student attributes: Is there a relationship? *British Journal of Educational Psychology, 80*(1), 121–135.

Rubin, Z. (1970). Measurement of romantic love. *Journal of Personality and Social Psychology, 16,* 265–271.

Russell, B. (1927). *Philosophy.* New York: Norton.

Russell, B. (1929/1970). *Marriage and morals.* New York: Liveright.

Saguy, A. C., & Gruys, K. (2010). Morality and health: News media constructions of overweight and eating disorders. *Social Problems, 57*(2), 231–250.

Salerni, N., Assanelli, A., D'Odorico, L., & Rossi, G. (2007). Qualitative aspects of productive vocabulary at the 200- and 500-word stages: A comparison between spontaneous speech and parental report data. *First Language, 27*(1), 75–87.

Sanz, J., Garcia-Vera, M. P., & Magan, I. (2010). Anger and hostility from the perspective of the Big Five personality model. *Scandinavian Journal of Psychology, 51* (3), 262–270. doi:10.1111/j.1467-9450.2009.00771.x

Sattler, J. M. (2008). *Assessment of children: Cognitive foundations* (5th ed.). San Diego, CA: Jerome M. Sattler Publisher, Inc.

Sava, F. A., Yates, B. T., Lupu, V., Szentagotai, A., & David, D. (2009). Cost-effectiveness and cost-utility of cognitive therapy, rational emotive behavioral therapy, and fluoxetine (Prozac) in treating clinical depression: A randomized clinical trial. *Journal of Clinical Psychology, 65*(1), 36–52.

Schachter, S. (1971). Some extraordinary facts about obese humans and rats. *American Psychologist, 26,* 129–144.

Schachter, S., & Singer, J. E. (1962). Cognitive, social, and physiological determinants of emotional state. *Psychological Review, 69,* 379–399.

Schacter, D. L. (1999).The seven sins of memory: Insights from psychology and cognitive neuroscience. *American Psychologist, 54,* 182–203. doi: 10.1037/0003-066X.54.3.182

Schacter, D. L., & Tulving, E. (1994). What are the memory systems of 1994? In D. L. Schacter & E. Tulving (Eds.), *Memory systems.* Cambridge, MA: MIT Press.

Schacter, D. L., Wagner, A. D., & Buckner, R. L. (2000). Memory systems of 1999. In E. Tulving & F. I. M. Craik (Eds.), *The Oxford handbook of memory.* New York, NY: Oxford University Press.

Scherer, K. R. (2005). What are emotions? And how can they be measured? *Social Science Information, 44,* 695–729.

Schneider, W. J., & McGrew, K. S. (2012). The Cattell-Horn-Carroll model of intelligence. In D.P. Flanagan & P. L. Harrison (Eds.), *Contemporary intellectual assessment: Theories, tests, and issues* (pp. 99–144). New York, NY: The Guilford Press.

Schredl, M. (2010). Explaining the gender difference in dream recall frequency. *Dreaming, 20*(2), 96–106.

Schredl, M., Atanasova, D., Hormann, K., Maurer, J. T., Hummel, T., & Stuck, B. A. (2009). Information processing during sleep: The effect of olfactory stimuli on dream content and dream emotions. *Journal of Sleep Research, 18*(3), 285–290.

Scoffier, S., Paquet, Y., & d'Arripe-Longueville, F. (2010). Effect of locus of control on disordered eating in athletes: The mediational role of self-regulation of eating attitudes. *Eating Behaviors, 11*(3), 164–169. doi:10.1016/j.eatbeh.2010.02.002

Scoville, W. B., & Milner, B. (1957). Loss of recent memory after bilateral hippocampal lesions. *Journal of Neurology, Neurosurgery & Psychiatry, 20*, 11–21. doi: 10.1136/jnnp.20.1.11

Searight, H. R., Rottnek, F., & Abby, S.L. (2001). Conduct disorder: Diagnosis and treatment in primary care. *American Family Physician, 63*(8), 1579–1589.

Seidman, G., & Miller, O. S. (2013). Effects of gender and physical attractiveness on visual attention to Facebook profiles. *Cyberpsychology, Behavior, and Social Networking, 16*(1), 20–24. doi:10.1089/cyber.2012.0305

Sekuler, R., & Blake, R. (2002). *Perception* (4th ed.). New York, NY: McGraw-Hill.

Sela, L., & Sobel, N. (2010). Human olfaction: a constant state of change-blindness. *Experimental Brain Research, 205*, 13–29. doi: 10.1007/s00221-010-2348-6

Self, D. W., & Staley, J. K. (Eds.). (2010). *Behavioral neuroscience of drug addiction.* New York: Springer.

Selfhout, M., Burk, W., Branje, S., Denissen, J., van Aken, M., & Meeus, W. (2010). Emerging late adolescent friendship networks and Big Five personality traits: A social network approach. *Journal of Personality, 78*(2), 509–538. doi:10.1111/j.1467-6494.2010.00625.x

Sendin, M. C. (2010). Rorschach usefulness in treatment planning. *Rorschachiana, 31*(1), 70–89.

Seres, I., Unoka, Z., Bodi, N., Aspan, N., & Keri, S. (2009). The neuropsychology of borderline personality disorder: Relationship with clinical dimensions and comparisons with other personality disorders. *Journal of Personality Disorders, 23*(6), 555–562. doi:10.1521/pedi.2009.23.6.555

Sharf, R. S. (2012). *Theories of psychotherapy and counseling: Concepts and cases* (5th ed.). Pacific Grove, CA: Brookes/Cole.

Shavinina, L. V. (2009). A new approach to the identification of intellectually gifted individuals. In L. K. Silverman (Ed.), *The measurement of giftedness: International Handbook on Giftedness* (pp. 1017–1031). New York: SpringerLink.

Sheldon, W. H. (1954). *Atlas of men: A guide to somatotyping the adult male of all ages*. New York: Harper.

Shepherd, G. M. (2006). Smell images and the flavor system in the human brain. *Nature, 444,* 316–321. doi: 10.1038/nature05405

Shevell, S. K., & Krantz, D. H. (2010). Leo M. Hurvich (1910–2009). *American Psychologist, 65*(4), 292.

Siegel, J. M. (2003). Why we sleep: The reasons that we sleep are gradually becoming less enigmatic. *Scientific American, 5,* 92–97.

Siegel, S. (2001). Pavlovian conditioning and drug overdose: When tolerance fails. *Addiction Research & Theory, 9*(5), 503–513.

Simons, D. J., & Chabris, C. F. (1999). Gorillas in our midst: Sustained inattentional blindness for dynamic events. *Perception, 28,* 1059–1074. doi: 10.1068/p2952

Singer, J. L. (2009). Researching imaginative play and adult consciousness: Implications for daily and literary creativity. *Psychology of Aesthetics, Creativity, and the Arts, 3*(4), 190–199.

Skinner, B. F. (1953). *Science and human behavior*. New York: Macmillan.

Skinner, B. F. (1969). *Contingencies of reinforcement: A theoretical analysis*. New York: Appleton-Century-Crofts.

Skinner, B. F. (1971). *Beyond freedom and dignity*. New York: Knopf.

Skinner, B. F. (1989). *Recent issues in the analysis of behavior*. Columbus, OH: Merrill.

Slanger, E., & Rudestam, K. E. (1997). Motivation and disinhibition in high risk sports: Sensation seeking and self-efficacy. *Journal of Research in Personality, 31,* 355–374.

Slater, A., Field, T., & Hernandez-Reif, M. (2007). The development of the senses. In A. Slater & M. Lewis (Eds.), *Introduction to infant development*. New York, NY: Oxford University Press.

Sledge, W. H., & Hutchinson, J. (2010). Psychotherapy and psychosocial interventions in the treatment of substance abuse. In S. G. Lazar (Ed.),

The Committee on Psychotherapy. (2010). Psychotherapy is worth it: A comprehensive review of its cost-effectiveness (pp. 175–226). Arlington, VA: American Psychiatric Publishing.

Slomski, A. (2006). The addicted brain. *Proto: Massachusetts General Hospital dispatches from the frontiers of medicine.* Retrieved June 1, 2010, from http://protomag.com/assets/the–addicted–brain

Smeets, P. M., Lancioni, G. E., Ball, T. S., & Oliva, D. S. (1985). Shaping self-initiated toileting in infants. *Journal of Applied Behavior Analysis, 18*(4), 303–308.

Smith, M. L., Glass, G. V., & Miller, T. I. (1980). *The benefits of psychotherapy.* Baltimore, MD: Johns Hopkins University Press.

Smith-Machin, A. L. (2009). Reducing the risk of disordered eating among female college students: A test of alternative interventions. *Dissertation Abstracts International: Section B: The Sciences and Engineering, 70*(4-B), 2588.

Sokol, R. J., Delaney-Black, V., & Nordstrom, B. (2003). Fetal alcohol spectrum disorder. *Journal of the American Medical Association, 290,* 2996–2999. doi:10.1001/jama.290.22.2996

Spelke, E. S., & Hermer, L. (1996). Early cognitive development: Objects and space. In R. Gelman & T. K. Au (Eds.), *Perceptual and cognitive development* (pp. 71–114). San Diego, CA: Academic Press.

Sperling, G. (1960). The information available in brief visual presentations. *Psychological Monographs, 74*(Whole No. 498), 1–29. doi: 10.1037/h0093759

Spinath, F. M., Ronald, A., Harlaar, N. , Price, T. S. , & Plomin, R. (2003). Phenotypic *g* early in life: On the etiology of general cognitive ability in a large population sample of twin children aged 2–4 years. *Intelligence, 31,* 195–210.

Spitz, R. A. (1949). The role of ecological factors in emotional development in infancy. *Child Development, 20,*145–155.

Spoor, F., Leakey, M., Gathogo, P., Brown, F., Antón, S., McDougall, I., Kiarie, C., Manthi, F., & Leakey, L. (2007, August 9). Implications of new early Homo fossils from Ileret, east of Lake Turkana (Kenya). *Nature, 448,* 688–691. Retrieved from http://www.nature.com/nature/journal/v448/n7154/full/nature05986.html

Stagner, R. (1958). The gullibility of personnel managers. *Personnel Psychology, 11,* 347–352. doi:10.1111/j.1744-6570.1958.tb00022.x

Standing, L. (1973). Learning 10,000 pictures. *Quarterly Journal of Experimental Psychology, 25*, 207–222.

Stanford prison experiment: A simulation study of the psychology of imprisonment conducted at Stanford University. Retrieved February 19, 2014, from http://www.prisonexp.org/

Stern, C. (1956). Hereditary factors affecting adoption. In *A Study of Adoption Practices* (Vol. 2). New York: Child Welfare League of America.

Sternberg, R. (2005). The triarchic theory of successful intelligence. In D. P. Flanagan & P. L. Harrison (Eds.), *Contemporary intellectual assessment* (2nd ed., pp. 103–119). New York: Guilford Press.

Sternberg, R. (2006). *Cognitive psychology* (4th ed.). Belmont, CA: Wadsworth Publishing.

Sternberg, R. J. (1986). A triangular theory of love. *Psychological Review, 93*, 119–135.

Sternberg, R. J., & Kaufman, J. C. (1998). Human abilities. *Annual Review of Psychology, 49*, 479–502.

Stockett, K. (2009). *The help.* New York, NY: Amy Einhorn Books/Putnam.

Strasburger, V. C. (2009). Media and children: What needs to happen now? *JAMA: Journal of the American Medical Association, 301*(21), 2265–2266.

Suicide in the U.S.: Statistics and prevention. (2010). National Institute of Mental Health. Retrieved August 30, 2010, from http://www.nimh.nih.gov/health/publications/suicide-in-the-us-statistics-and-prevention/index.shtml#factors

Sumter, S. R., Valkenburg, P. M., & Peter, J. (2013). Perceptions of love across the lifespan: Differences in passion, intimacy, and commitment. *International Journal of Behavioral Development, 37*(5), 417–427. doi: 10.1177/0165025413492486

Sundet, J. M., Erikson, W., & Tambs, K. (2008). Intelligence correlations between brothers decrease with increasing age difference: Evidence for shared environmental effects in young adults. *Association for Psychological Science, 19*(9), 843–847. doi: 10.1111/j.1467-9280.2008.02166.x

Sundin, J., Fear, N. T., Iversen, A., Rona, R. J., & Wessely, S. (2010). PTSD after deployment to Iraq: Conflicting rates, conflicting claims. *Psychological Medicine: A Journal of Research in Psychiatry and the Allied Sciences, 40*(3), 367–382.

Sung, S. Y., & Choi, J. N. (2009). Do Big Five personality factors affect individual creativity? The moderating role of extrinsic motivation. *Social Behavior and Personality, 37*(7), 941–956.

Super, C. M., & Harkness, S. (1998). The development of affect in infancy and early childhood. In M. Woodhead, D. Faulkner, & K. Littleton (Eds.), *Cultural worlds of early childhood.* New York: Routledge.

Szymborska, W. (1995). *View with a grain of sand: Selected poems.* New York: Harcourt Brace.

Tailby, C., Majaj, N. J., & Movshon, J. A. (2010). Binocular integration of pattern motion signals by MT neurons and by human observers. *Journal of Neuroscience, 30*(21), 7344–7349.

Teglasi, H. (2010). *Essentials of TAT and other storytelling assessments* (2nd ed.). Hoboken, NJ: John Wiley & Sons.

The official division 30 definition and description of hypnosis. (2010). The Society of Psychological Hypnosis: Division 30 of the American Psychological Association. Retrieved July 27, 2010, from http://psychologicalhypnosis.com/info/the-official-division-30-definition-and-description-of-hypnosis/

The Rolling Stone Interview: John Lennon, Part I. (1971). Retrieved April 13, 2011, from http://www.jannswenner.com/Archives/John_Lennon_Part1.aspx

The science of sleep. (2010). *Science & Nature: Human Body & Mind.* BBC. Retrieved July 27, 2010, from http://www.bbc.co.uk/science/humanbody/sleep/articles/whatissleep.shtml

Thigpen, C. H., & Cleckley, H. (1954). *The three faces of Eve.* Kingsport, TN: Kingsport Press.

Thomas, A., & Chess, S. (1977). *Temperament and development.* New York: Brunner/Mazel.

Thompson, R. A. (1998). Early sociopersonality development. In W. Damon (Series Ed.) & N. Eisenberg (Vol. Ed.), *Handbook of child psychology: Vol. 3. Social, emotional and personality development* (5th ed., pp. 25–104). Hoboken, NJ: Wiley

Thomsen, M., Fink-Jensen, A., Woldbye, D. P. D., Wortwein, G., Sager, T. N., Holm, R., Pepe, L. M., & Caine, S. B. (2008). Effects of acute and chronic aripiprazole treatment on choice between cocaine self-administration and food under a concurrent schedule of reinforcement in rats. *Psychopharmacology, 201*(1), 43–53.

Thorndike, E. L. (1898). Animal intelligence: An experimental study of the associative processes in animals. *Psychological Review Monograph Supplement, 2*(8).

Thorndike, R. L., & Hagen, E. (1977). *Measurement and evaluation in psychology and education* (4th ed.). New York: Wiley.

Tolman, E. C., & Honzik, C. H. (1930). Insight in rats. *University of California Publications in Psychology, 4*, 215–232.

Toma, C. L., & Hancock, J. T. (2010). Looks and lies: The role of physical attractiveness in online dating self-presentation and deception. *Communication Research, 37*(3), 335–351.

Total isolation. (2008). BBC, *Science and Nature*. Retrieved April 11, 2011, from http://www.bbc.co.uk/sn/tvradio/programmes/horizon/broadband/tx/isolation/

Tulving, E. (1972). Episodic and semantic memory. In E. Tulving & W. Donaldson (Eds.), *Organization of memory*. London: Academic Press.

Tulving, E. (1989). Remembering and knowing the past. *American Scientist, 77*, 361–367.

Tulving, E. (2002). Episodic memory: From mind to brain. *Annual Review of Psychology, 53*, 1–25. doi: 10.1146/annurev.psych.53.100901.135114

Tulving, E., Schacter, D. L., McLachlan, D. R., & Moscovitch, M. (1988). Priming of semantic autobiographical memory: A case study of retrograde amnesia. *Brain and Cognition, 8*, 3–20.

Turiel, E. (1998). Moral development. In W. Damon (Series Ed.) and R. M. Lerner and N. Eisenberg (Vol. Ed.), *Handbook of child psychology: Vol 3. Social, emotional, and personality development* (pp. 863–932). New York, NY: Wiley.

Turner, J. E., & Goodin, J. B. (2008). Motivation and emotion. In N. J. Salkind (Ed.), *Encyclopedia of educational psychology* (Vol. 2, pp. 692–696). Thousand Oaks, CA: Sage Publications.

Twenge, J. M. (2009). Change over time in obedience: The jury's still out, but it might be decreasing. *American Psychologist, 64*(1), 28–31.

Twitmyer, E. B. (1905). Knee jerks without stimulation of the patellar tendon. *Psychological Bulletin, 2*, 43.

U. S. Census Bureau. (2012). Living arrangements of children: Tables CH-5, CH-6. Retrieved from http://www.census.gov/hhes/families/data/children.html

U.S. Census Bureau Population Estimates by Demographic Characteristics (2005). *Table 2: Annual Estimates of the Population by Selected Age Groups and Sex for the United States: April 1, 2000 to July 1, 2004* (NC-EST2004-02). Retrieved from http://www.census.gov/popest/national/asrh/./.

U.S. Census Bureau. (2010). *The 2010 statistical abstract: The national data book.* Washington, DC: U.S. Government Printing Office.

U.S. Census Bureau. (2010a). *International data base, June 2010 update.* Retrieved June 20, 2010, from http://www.census.gov/ipc/www/idb/world popgraph.php

U.S. Census Bureau. (2010b). *The 2010 statistical abstract: The national data book: Table 202.* Washington, DC: U.S. Government Printing Office.

U.S. Census Bureau. (2010c). *The 2010 statistical abstract: The national data book.* Washington, DC: U.S. Government Printing Office.

U.S. Census Bureau. (2012). *The 2012 statistical abstract: The national data book.* Washington, DC: U.S. Government Printing Office.

Ulas, H., Polat, S., Akdede, B. B., & Alptekin, K. (2010). Impact of panic attacks on quality of life among patients with schizophrenia. *Progress in Neuro-Psychopharmacology & Biological Psychiatry, 34*(7), 1300–1305.

van Honk, J., Harmon-Jones, E., Morgan, B. E., & Schutter, D. J. L. G. (2010). Socially explosive minds: The triple imbalance hypothesis of reactive aggression. *Journal of Personality, 78*(1), 67–94.

van Ijzendoorn, M. H., Schuengel, C., & Bakermans-Kranenburg, M. J. (1999). Disorganized attachment in early childhood: Meta-analysis of precursors, concomitants and sequelae. *Development and Psychopathology, 11,* 225–249.

van Oers, K., & Mueller, J. C. (2010). Evolutionary genomics of animal personality. *Philosophical transactions of the Royal Society: Biological Sciences, 365*(1560), 3991–4000.

Vargha-Khadem, F., Gadian, D. G., Watkins, K. E., Connelly, A., Van Paesschen, W., & Mishkin, M. (1997). Differential effects of early hippocampal pathology on episodic and semantic memory. *Science, 277,* 376–380. doi: 10.1126/science.277.5324.376

Verkoeijen, P. P. J. L., & Delaney, P. F. (2008). Rote rehearsal and spacing effects in the free recall of pure and mixed lists. *Journal of Memory and Language, 58*(1), 35–47.

Vernon, D. (2009). *Human potential: Exploring techniques used to enhance human performance.* New York: Routledge/Taylor & Francis Group.

Vieira, M. M., Ferreira, T. B., Pacheco, P. A. F., Barros, P. O., Almeida, C. R. M., Araujo-Lima, C. F., Silva-Filho, R. G., Hygino, J., Andrade, R. M., Linhares, U. C., Andrade, A. F. B., & Bento, C. A. M. (2010). Enhanced th17 phenotype in individuals with generalized anxiety disorder. *Journal of Neuroimmunology, 229*(1-2), 212–218.

Volpe, J. J. (2008). *Neurology of the newborn.* Philadelphia: Saunders.

Vonthron, A. M., & Lagabrielle, C. (2002). The influence of locus of control orientation and internal versus external causal attributions on obstacles during work, in professional integration strategies. *Psykhe: Revista de la Escuela de Psicologia, 11*(2), 197–205.

Vyazovskiy, V. V., Cirelli, C., Pfister-Genskow, M., Faraguna, U., & Tononi, G. (2008). Molecular and electrophysiological evidence for net synaptic potentiation in wake and depression in sleep. *Nature Neuroscience, 11,* 200–208.

Vygotsky, L. S. (1962). *Thought and language* (E. Hanfmann & G. Vaker, Trans.). Cambridge, MA: MIT Press.

Waldinger, R. J. (2010). Psychotherapy in the treatment of borderline personality disorder. In S. G. Lazar (Ed.), *The Committee on Psychotherapy. (2010). Psychotherapy is worth it: A comprehensive review of its cost-effectiveness* (pp. 61–86). Arlington, VA: American Psychiatric Publishing.

Walker, J., Halliday, D., & Resnick, R. (2008). *Fundamentals of physics* (8th ed.). Hoboken, NJ: Wiley.

Walsh, T., McClellan, J. M., McCarthy, S. E., et al. (2008). Rare structural variants disrupt multiple genes in neurodevelopmental pathways in schizophrenia. *Science, 320*(5875), 539–543.

Walster, E., Aronson, V., Abrahams, O., & Rottman, L. (1966). Importance of physical attractiveness in dating behavior. *Journal of Personality and Social Psychology, 4,* 508–516.

Wan, Chin-Sheng, & Chiou, Wen-Bin. (2010). Inducing attitude change toward online gaming among adolescent players based on dissonance theory: The role of threats and justification of effort. *Computers & Education, 54*(1), 162–168.

Wasserman, J. D. (2012). A history of intelligence assessment: The unfinished tapestry. In D. P. Flanagan & P. L. Harrison (Eds.), *Contemporary intellectual assessment: Theories, tests, and issues* (pp. 3–55). New York, NY: The Guilford Press.

Watanabe, S. (2010). Pigeons can discriminate "good" and "bad" paintings by children. *Animal Cognition, 13*(1), 75–85.

Watson, J. B. (1916). Behavior and the concept of mental disease. *Journal of Philosophy, Psychology, and Scientific Methods, 13*, 589–597. doi: 10.2307/2012555

Watson, J. B. (1928). *The ways of behaviorism*. New York: Harper.

Watson, J. B. (1930). *Behaviorism* (2nd ed.). Chicago: University of Chicago Press.

Weiner, B. (2008). Reflections on the history of attribution theory and research: People, personalities, publications, problems. *Social Psychology, 39*(3), 151–156. doi:10.1027/1864-9335.39.3.151

Weiss, K. M. (2009). Having a jolly good time—Together! Evolution by cooperative interaction. *Current Anthropology, 50*(2), 235–245.

Wever, E. G., & Bray, C. W. (1930). The nature of the acoustic response: A relation between sound frequency and frequency of impulses in the auditory nerve. *Journal of Experimental Psychology, 13*, 373–387.

Wheeler, M. A., Stuss, D. T., & Tulving, E. (1997). Toward a theory of episodic memory: The frontal lobes and autonoetic consciousness. *Psychological Bulletin, 121*, 331–354. doi: 10.1037/0033-2909.121.3.331

White, K. G. (2002). Psychophysics of remembering: The discrimination hypothesis. *Current Directions in Psychological Science, 11*, 141–145.

Whorf, B. L. (2012). Language, thought, and reality: selected writings of Benjamin Lee Whorf [2nd ed.]: introduction by John B. Carroll; foreword by Stephen C. Levinson. (J. B. Carroll, S. C. Levinson, & P. Lee, Eds.). Cambridge, MA: MIT Press.

Wigfield, A., Tonks, S., & Klauda, S. L. (2009). Expectancy-value theory. In K. R. Wenzel & A. Wigfield (Eds.), *Handbook of motivation at school* (pp. 55–75). New York: Routledge/Taylor & Francis Group.

Wilbur, C. J., & Campbell, L. (2010). What do women want? An interactionist account of women's mate preferences. *Personality and Individual Differences, 49*(7), 749–754.

Williams, T., & Williams, K. (2010). Self-efficacy and performance in mathematics: Reciprocal determinism in 33 nations. *Journal of Educational Psychology, 102*(2), 453–466.

Wineburg, S. S. (1987). The self-fulfillment of the self-fulfilling prophecy: A critical appraisal. *Educational Researcher, 16*(9), 28–37.

Wittchen, H. U. (2002). Generalized anxiety disorder: Prevalence, burden, and cost to society. *Depression and Anxiety, 16*(4), 162–171.

Wolfe, J. M., Kluender, K. R., Levi, D. M., Bartoshuk, L. M., Herz, R. S., Klatzky, R. L., Lederman, S. J., & Merfeld, D. M. (2012). *Sensation and perception* (3rd ed.). Sunderland, MA: Sinauer Associates.

Wolff, P. H. (1966). The causes, controls, and organization of behavior in the neonate. *Psychological Issues, 5*(1), 1–105.

Wolters, G., & Goudsmit, J. J. (2005). Flashbulb and event memory of September 11, 2001: Consistency, confidence and age effects. *Psychological Reports, 96*(3), 605–619.

Wood, J. M., Lilienfeld, S. O., Nezworski, M. T., Garb, H. N., Allen, K. H., & Wildermuth, J. L. (2010). Validity of Rorschach inkblot scores for discriminating psychopaths from nonpsychopaths in forensic populations: A meta-analysis. *Psychological Assessment, 22,* 336–349. doi:10.1037/a0018998

Woodiwiss, J. (2010). "Alternative memories" and the construction of a sexual abuse narrative. In J. Haaken & P. Reavey (Eds.), *Memory matters: Contexts for understanding sexual abuse recollections* (pp. 105–127). New York: Routledge/Taylor & Francis.

Woodman, T., Zourbanos, N., Hardy, L., Beattie, S., & McQuillan A. (2010). Do performance strategies moderate the relationship between personality and training behaviors? An exploratory study. *Journal of Applied Sport Psychology, 22*(2), 183–197. doi:10.1080/10413201003664673

Workman, L., Chilvers, L., Yeomans, H., & Taylor, S. (2006). Development of cerebral lateralisation for recognition of emotions in chimeric faces in children aged 5 to 11. *Laterality: Asymmetries of Body, Brain and Cognition, 11,* 493–507.

Worldometers: World statistics updated in real time. Retrieved August 21, 2010, from http://www.worldometers.info/weight-loss/

Wyman, A. J., & Vyse, S. (2008). Science versus the stars: A double-blind test of the validity of the NEO Five-Factor Inventory and computer-generated astrological natal charts. *Journal of General Psychology, 135*(3), 287–300. doi:10.3200/GENP.135.3.287-300

Xu, Y. (2010). Children's social play sequence: Parten's classic theory revisited. *Early Child Development and Care, 180*(4), 489–498.

Yamagata, S., Suzuki, A., Ando, J., Ono, Y., Kijima, N., Yoshimura, K., Ostendorf, F., Angleitner, A., Riemann, R., Spinath, F. M., Livesley, W. J., & Jang, K. L. (2006). Is the genetic structure of human personality universal? A cross-cultural twin study from North America, Europe, and Asia. *Journal of Personality and Social Psychology, 90*(6), 987–998.

Yamagishi, N. (2008). Investigation of attention mechanisms using brain imaging techniques. *Japanese Psychological Review, 51*(2), 347–355.

Yamaguchi, S. (1998). Basic properties of umami and its effects on food flavor. *Food Reviews International, 14*(2–3), 139–176.

Yates, F. (1966). *The art of memory.* Chicago: University of Chicago Press.

Yerkes, R. M., & Dodson, J. D. (1908). The relationship of strength of stimulus to rapidity of habit formation. *Journal of Comparative Neurological Psychology, 18,* 459–482.

Yu, C. (2008). A statistical associative account of vocabulary growth in early word learning. *Language Learning and Development, 4*(1), 32–62.

Zaragoza, M. S., Mitchell, K. J., Payment, K., & Drivdahl, S. (2011). False memories for suggestions: The impact of conceptual elaboration. *Journal of Memory and Language, 64*(1), 18–31.

Zatorre, R. J., Belin, P., & Penhune, V. B. (2002). Structure and function of auditory cortex: Music and speech. *Trends in Cognitive Sciences, 6,* 37–46. doi: 10.1016/S1364-6613(00)01816-7

Zeaman, D. (1949). Response latency as a function of amount of reinforcement. *Journal of Experimental Psychology, 39,* 466–483.

Zee, P. C. (2010). Shedding light on the effectiveness of melatonin for circadian rhythm sleep disorders. *Sleep, 33*(12), 1581–1582.

Zeki, S. (1993). *A vision of the brain.* New York, NY: Wiley

Zhang, L. J., Xiao, Y., Qi, X. L., Shan, K. R., Pei, J. J., Kuang, S. Z., Liu, F., & Guan, Z. Z. (2010). Cholinesterase activity and mRNA level of nicotinic acetylcholine receptors (alpha 4 and beta 2 subunits) in blood of elderly Chinese diagnosed as Alzheimer's disease. *Journal of Alzheimer's Disease, 19*(3), 849–858.

Zhu, Jing-Ning, & Wang, Jian-Jun. (2008). The cerebellum in feeding control: Possible function and mechanism. *Cellular and Molecular Neurobiology, 28*(4), 469–478.

Zimbardo, P. G. (2007). *The Lucifer effect: Understanding how good people turn evil.* New York: Random House.

Zinchenko, Y. P. (2009). Mass media as an effective tool for prevention of socio-psychological factors in the development of terrorism. *Psychology in Russia: State of the Art, 2,* 459–476.

Zubek, J. P. (1973). Behavioral and physiological effects of prolonged sensory and perceptual deprivation: A review. In J. E. Rasmussen (Ed.), *Man in isolation and confinement* (pp. 9–84). Chicago: Transaction Books.

INDEX

A

A-B-C theory of disturbance, 259
ablations, of brain, 38
Abrahams, O., 285
absent-mindedness, 118–119
absolute threshold, 55, 299
Abu Ghraib prison, 269
accommodation, 179, 299
acetylcholine, 33, 299
achievement motivation, 143–144
acquisition rate, 93
action potential, 29–30, 299
active deception, 19, 299
active strategies, 284
active vocabulary, 299
Adams, M. J., 118
adaptation, 299
    sensory, 56–57, 332
addictive disorders, 233, 244–247
ADHD. *See* attention-deficit/hyperactivity
    disorder
adolescents, 182, 250–251
adrenal glands, 37, 299
adrenaline (epinephrine), 36, 37, 299
afterimage, 299
aggression, 170, 273–278, 299, 314, 326
aggression-based impulse-control disorders,
    241–242
agonists, 31, 33, 39, 299
agoraphobia, 238–239, 299
agreeableness, 204–205, 300
Ainsworth, Mary, 184–186
alcohol, 34–35, 42, 175
alleles, 300
Allport, G. W., 201
Almas, E., 51
alpha waves, 46, 52, 300
altruistic behaviors, 282–283, 300
Alzheimer's disease, 33, 42

American Psychiatric Association, 226, 229
American Psychological Association (APA), 2–3,
    9, 18–20, 81
amnesia, 42, 114, 117, 248, 300
amplitude, 58, 62, 300
amygdala, 42, 157, 160, 300
anal characters, 213
analytical intelligence, 126
androgens, 166, 300
animals, 23–24
    insight and, 98–100
    instincts and, 135
    nervous system of, 27
    territoriality and, 274–275
    use in research, 20
animistic thinking, 300
anonymous research, 19, 300
anorexia nervosa, 164–165, 300
anosmia, 300
antagonists, 31, 33, 300
anterograde amnesia, 114, 117
Antheunis, M. L., 284
antidepressant drugs, 32–33, 256
antipsychotic medications, 236, 250, 256
antisocial behaviors, 273–278, 279–282, 314, 326
antisocial personality disorder, 253
anxiety disorders, 231, 237–241
    agoraphobia, 238–239, 299
    generalized anxiety disorder, 238, 315
    illness anxiety disorder, 252, 317
    OCD, 231, 239–240, 323
    panic attacks and panic disorder, 237–238,
        324, 325
    PTSD, 240–241, 327
    specific phobias, 239–240, 333, 334
APA. *See* American Psychological Association
APGAR scale, 173, 300
aphagia, 164, 300
applied behavior analysis, 236